THE HAND OF THE POET

POEMS AND PAPERS IN MANUSCRIPT

THE NEW YORK PUBLIC LIBRARY

HENRY W. AND ALBERT A. BERG COLLECTION OF

ENGLISH AND AMERICAN LITERATURE

verses, every line, every word.

d brittle pencils ever to try

blade's curve, or the throat of one bird

s to twig, ruffled against white sky.

and twilight mirrors ever to catch

one gl... ...sh of the splendor of

THE HAND OF THE POET

nter, Oh bullets of wax,

auty, the wild-swan wings, the storm of

d swan of a world is no hunter's game.

by Rodney Phillips,

Susan Benesch, Kenneth Benson, and Barbara Bergeron

lets than yours would the wh

rors than yours would crack in the flame

With essays by Dana Gioia

tter whether you hate your . . . self?

eyes that can see, your mind that can

sic, the thunder of the wings. Love th

RIZZOLI
NEW YORK

First published in the United States of America in 1997 by
Rizzoli International Publications, Inc.
300 Park Avenue South
New York, NY 10010

"The Magical Value of Manuscripts" appeared, in slightly different form,
in the *Hudson Review* 49, no. 1 (Spring 1996).

"The Prado of Poetry" appeared, in slightly different form,
in *The American Scholar* 66, no. 1 (Winter 1997).

The name "The New York Public Library" is a registered trademark
and the property of The New York Public Library, Astor, Lenox and
Tilden Foundations.

Permissions for the use of copyrighted material appear on pp. 332–349,
which constitute an extension of this page.

Library of Congress Cataloging-in-Publication Data
Berg Collection.
    The hand of the poet : poems and papers in manuscript : the New
    York Public Library Henry W. and Albert A. Berg Collection of
    English and American Literature / by Rodney Phillips . . . [et al.];
    with introduction and afterword by Dana Gioia.
        p.   cm.
    Includes bibliographical references and index.
    ISBN 0-8478-1958-2
    1. Manuscripts, English – New York (State) – New York – Catalogs.
2. Manuscripts, American – New York (State) – New York – Catalogs.
3. American poetry – Manuscripts – Catalogs. 4. English poetry –
Manuscripts – Catalogs. 5. Berg Collection – Catalogs.
I. Phillips, Rodney, 1946 –   . II. New York Public Library. III. Title.
Z2014.P7839   1997
[PR502]
821.008 – DC20   95-50472
                                                      CIP

Photography for this book by Peter Bittner of Spring Street Digital, Inc.
except for photographs on the following pages: 2 (Chris Felver); 22,
159, 160 (Earl Christian); 187, 252 (Harry Redl); 278 (Arthur Furst);
318 (Blackstone Studios)

Designed by Ann Antoshak

Printed in the United States of America

Contents

Foreword

THE NEW YORK Public Library owes its existence to the generosity in 1895 of John Jacob Astor, James Lenox, and Samuel J. Tilden, and throughout its first century the institution has been graced by many other generous gifts. But of all these benefactions, the Henry W. and Albert A. Berg Collection of English and American Literature remains one of the most extraordinary, the gift of one man as a memorial to his brother. Both medical men, the Drs. Berg shared a passion for books. Today the special collection bequeathed to the Library by Dr. Albert A. Berg is one of the world's primary sources for literary research, freely open to scholars and researchers.

And from the beginning, both Dr. Albert Berg and the Collection's first curator, John D. Gordan, strove to make its riches available to as wide a public as possible through a series of public exhibitions. The opening exhibition, in December 1941, was devoted exclusively to the work of Charles Dickens. Exhibitions over the following decades featured other writers represented in the collection, as well as selections from the Collection's newest acquisitions and thematic groupings of books and manuscripts. These exhibitions have been, for their visitors, a gift back from the Library to the city that Henry W. and Albert A. Berg loved so much.

As part of the Library's celebration of its Centennial in 1995–1996, Rodney Phillips, the present Curator of the Berg Collection, organized a two-part exhibition about the writing of poetry, featuring 100 English-language poets, that drew from the extraordinary literary and visual documents held by the Library, primarily in the Berg Collection, but also in the Carl H. Pforzheimer Collection of Shelley and His Circle, the Miriam and Ira D. Wallach Division of Art, Prints and Photographs, the Rare Books and Manuscripts Division, the Spencer Collection, and the General Research Division. *The Hand of the Poet: Original Manuscripts by 100 Masters* became the most extensive and best-attended exhibition in the Berg Collection's history. Through the exhibition and now this book, which has been adapted from it, the Library has been able to share these magnificent materials with the largest possible public. But as Mr. Phillips says, his intention was not just to display literary treasures, but to demonstrate "how really human poets are, how many drafts go into a poem – to surround the poet with context."

At a time of greatly expanding public interest in poetry, The New York Public Library is pleased to make available this exploration of the creative process. ∎

PAUL LeCLERC
President, The New York Public Library

Introduction

A CELEBRATION OF the writing of poetry, *The Hand of the Poet* comprises a wide variety of manuscripts and typescripts, from early drafts to the most polished of fair copies, by 100 English-language poets. Ranging from the 1625 Westmoreland Manuscript of John Donne's poems to 33 sonnets written by Julia Alvarez for her 33rd birthday in 1984, these pages demonstrate that writing is a process, and often very hard work, and that much of writing – as many of the chaotic, marvelously messy manuscripts pictured here prove – is rewriting. And then, rewriting again: as Marianne Moore (quoting Harry Levin) once assured a young and rather star-struck May Sarton, revision "is its own reward."

Multiple versions of a poem often only hint at the labor that attends poetic inspiration. Walt Whitman's "Out of the Cradle Endlessly Rocking," for example, was first published in a Brooklyn newspaper, in 1859, as "A Child's Reminiscence." Continually revised, this great poem appeared in all subsequent editions of *Leaves of Grass*, assuming its final form only in 1881. Dylan Thomas spent six years writing "On a Wedding Anniversary," going through at least a dozen drafts. The sheet included here contains the author's doodles, almost integral to the text but drawn, no doubt, to calm the poet and allow his imagination to range freely. Writing, it appears, can be entertainment too. But to an outside observer,

the process *can* look like torture: a single lyric by Jean Garrigue, for one, can have behind it scores and scores of drafts. Robert Lowell was a notorious reviser who often made changes even in the supposedly final setting copy of his poems. And some poems are in fact never finished: the "last" version was to Lowell sometimes just the latest draft. Sylvia Plath, however, apparently never abandoned a poem until she was satisfied with it, and most of her work, as her final typed drafts testify, is impressively polished. Like W. S. Merwin, she also used every scrap of paper available to her in her working drafts, handwritten or typed on the versos of drafts of other poems, or on the drafts of her novel, *The Bell Jar*. Amy Clampitt, too, followed her environmentalist instincts by writing on the backs of her husband's invitations to legal functions.

Scholars and other researchers consider themselves lucky when several working drafts of a poem have survived. But this is not always the case, and certain poems, or versions of poems, are known only in a single copy saved by a poet's friend, lover, or correspondent. Many of the poems of Lorine Niedecker, for instance, are known only from the versions of them embedded in the letters she sent to a friend, the poet-editor Cid Corman. And the beautiful Westmoreland Manuscript, which was written out by one of the poet's closest friends, represents the only extant manuscript source for three of Donne's Holy Sonnets.

The vast majority of these manuscripts are from The New York Public Library's Henry W. and Albert A. Berg Collection of English and American Literature, and thus this volume highlights the breadth of the collection's holdings, as well as the tastes of the curators and donors who have helped to form it. Some major English and American poets are missing (Shakespeare, Milton, Dryden, Poe, Hopkins, Crane, H.D., Roethke, Ashbery, for instance), but their archives are elsewhere, or nowhere. In presenting this particular group of writers and manuscripts, we hope to beguile the reader with *some* of the poetry of *some* of the best (or, at least, most intriguing) American and English poets.

This is also a book about the conversation of poets, with each other, and with their teachers, mentors, and heroes and heroines, about the life of poetry. Poets seem to seek the companionship of fellow poets, in person, on the page, and even across the centuries. This book catches some of these conversations on the wing, through quotations from poets on other poets, and through their tributes and comments to each other, both private and public, hostile and adulatory. After visiting Robert Burns's grave, Wordsworth was moved to write "To the Sons of Burns," a somber (and cautionary) tribute to the great Scottish bard. Elizabeth Bishop and Robert Lowell are represented by two of their greatest poems, which they dedicated to each other. In Sylvia Plath's copy of *Four Quartets*, the voluminous marginal notes of this most conscientious of undergraduates almost overwhelm Eliot's text. The joint translations of Paul Valéry by May Sarton and Louise Bogan, two independent souls grappling with the work of a French genius, are elegant examples of the art of collaboration. Donald Justice's variations on César Vallejo, W. S. Merwin's version of the 13th-century poet Rumi, James Merrill's of Constantine Cavafy, and Lowell's of Boris Pasternak: such "collisions" of greatly gifted writers attest to the increasingly international character of poetic conversation in our century.

And what did these people look like? With his faithful dog at his side, the ever-dashing Lord Byron plays the *grand seigneur* in silk robe and slippers (his misformed foot hidden by a stool). Elizabeth Barrett Browning's tiny slippers, carefully wrapped in the sheets of a Florentine newspaper by her husband more than a century ago, evoke the diminutive woman who created some of the most stirring love poems in the English language. An Edward Weston portrait of Robinson Jeffers bolsters the legend of the poet as a lone eagle. Thomas Hardy looks like a well-off pensioner; Whitman, a benevolent King Lear; and Kay Boyle, an elegant woman of the world. Edna St. Vincent Millay is ethereal; Charlotte Mew, grim; Anna Wickham, formidable. And a pencil actually crafted by Thoreau, and an image of the hands of Stanley Kunitz, remind us that tools other than the mind are used in writing, and that poetry is a craft, and has a physical side, a body that endures if not in the flesh, then on the written and printed page.

When they are not composing poetry, how do these imaginative individuals occupy themselves? Vladimir Nabokov hunts butterflies and composes his own chess problems (the latter represented in this volume by a manuscript page from *Poems and Problems*, the master's collection of both). Howard Moss gardens in Easthampton, and Burns carouses far into the night at the George Inn in Dumfries. May Sarton travels to Japan; Ai takes the bus to Kmart; and Frank O'Hara goes (it would seem) everywhere. Keats studies medicine, and William Carlos Williams practices it. Dana Gioia is a Vice President at Kraft General Foods, following in the footsteps of Wallace Stevens, for many years certainly the most unusual Vice President at Hartford Indemnity. Many of

the poets included here spent or spend time and energy in their relationships with others: Lewis Carroll with Alice; Philip Levine with his son Mark; Oscar Wilde with his genius; and Allen Ginsberg with his parents. And Randall Jarrell just might have been obsessed with his Black Persian cat, "Kitten," with whom he was photographed in 1942 and to whom he fed half his wartime Christmas veal roast two years later.

A charming photograph of Robert Lowell carrying his five-year-old daughter on his shoulder brings to mind the words of Dylan Thomas, who mused that one is "a poet for such a very tiny bit of his life; for the rest he is a human being, one of whose responsibilities is to know and feel, as much as he can, all that is moving around and within him." It is our hope that *The Hand of the Poet* will illuminate the lives and works of these wonderful writers, granting some sense of how the poet struggles to know and to feel. ∎

RODNEY PHILLIPS
Curator, the Henry W. and Albert A. Berg
Collection of English and American Literature,
The New York Public Library

BY DANA GIOIA

The Magical Value of Manuscripts

YOUNG ARTISTS ARE cruel, especially to their parents. Although my mother and father both worked six days a week, I did my best to keep Sunday from becoming their day of rest. Besotted by art books in the local public library, I was at 12 a voracious gallery-goer. Satisfying my aesthetic appetites, however, depended on nagging my parents to travel from industrial Hawthorne to the widely scattered cultural shrines of Southern California. And so one Sunday my exhausted father drove across Los Angeles to smoggy San Marino so I might visit the Henry E. Huntington Library and Museum. I was keen to take in the Gainsboroughs, Reynoldses, Constables, and Turners assembled by the late Robber Baron – the finest collection of Georgian painting outside London. I hardly knew there was a library on the hundred-acre estate, but since it also housed a small room of Renaissance madonnas, I decided to look it over.

The treasures of the Huntington Library are internationally known to scholars and bibliophiles, but to a working-class kid from Southwest L.A., they seemed more mysterious abstractions than objects of intrinsic interest. A nerdy autodidact, I was precociously well-informed on painting, but my literary taste ran to Edgar Rice Burroughs, Ray Bradbury, and H. P. Lovecraft. I shuffled dutifully from display case to display case in the manner of a 12-year-old boy – squinting, gawking, and gaping. I was indifferent to the Ellesmere Chaucer. The Gutenberg Bible impressed me only as a vague rarity. Shelley's notebooks and the manuscript of *Walden* got hardly a glance. But one exhibit held me spellbound. In a glass case in the main hall lay a fair copy of Edgar Allan Poe's "Annabel Lee," written in the author's small, meticulous hand.

I knew the poem well. Indeed, I knew most of it by heart. "Annabel Lee" was a favorite of my mother, who often recited it with obvious feeling. One purpose of poetry is to give us words to articulate our joys and sorrows without revealing them. Whenever my mother spoke Poe's words, I also heard between his lines the unspoken losses that had scarred her life.

For the moon never beams without bringing me dreams
    Of the beautiful Annabel Lee;
And the stars never rise but I see the bright eyes
    Of the beautiful Annabel Lee;
And so, all the night-tide, I lie down by the side
Of my darling, my darling, my life and my bride
    In her sepulchre there by the sea –
    In her tomb by the side of the sea.

But did I really know the poem? Staring at the manuscript, I found myself seeing it from a different perspective. I was overwhelmed by its sheer beauty – the elegant script in brown sepia with every letter perfectly formed, the way Poe had skillfully glued two pieces of paper together to make a single tall sheet so that the poem could be presented on one page. I knew also that Poe had intended for me to be overwhelmed. His wife dead, his career in tatters, sunk in debt, drinking heavily in the last year of his life, Poe had obviously labored

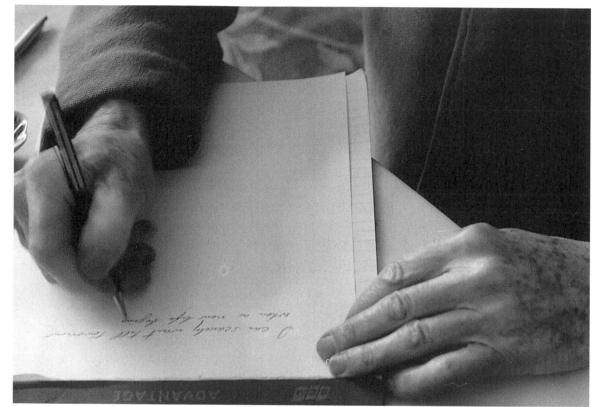

Among his friends, poet Stanley Kunitz has counted a number of the greatest painters of the 20th century, including Mark Rothko, Philip Guston, Willem De Kooning, and Robert Motherwell, and his home in Greenwich Village is filled with art, including paintings by his wife, Elise Asher. In a 1977 talk with his Provincetown neighbor Chris Busa (published as a Paris Review *interview in 1982, three years before Chris Felver made this photograph on the occasion of the poet's 80th birthday), Kunitz spoke a bit about painters and poetry: "I envy [painters] because there is so much physical satisfaction in the actual work of painting and sculpture. I'm a physical being and resent this sedentary business of sitting at one's desk and moving only one's wrist. I pace, I speak my poems, I get very kinetic when I'm working. . . . When I insist on poetry as a kind of action, I'm thinking very much in these terms – every achieved metaphor in a poem is a gesture of sorts, the equivalent of slashing of a stroke on canvas."*

to make this keepsake – probably given to some casual acquaintance – as beautiful an object as possible. For the first time in my life I had a sense of the complex, even contradictory human reality out of which art grows. I also saw how delicately the text of a poem balanced between two lives – those of the author and the reader. "Who touches this," Walt Whitman wrote of his own work, "touches a man." Looking at the manuscript through the glass, I wished I might someday make something so beautiful.

Since that afternoon I have been interested in literary manuscripts, especially autograph versions of poems. This interest has never been a consuming passion, and I have resisted the temptation to collect. (Any manuscript I could afford, I probably wouldn't want.) But in the intervening years I have rarely passed up the opportunity to attend a library exhibition, and in working on major critical projects, I examined whatever archival sources I could find, even if they did not bear directly on my topic. More recently I have spent considerable time studying many of the extraordinary manuscripts in the Berg Collection of The New York Public Library. In the process of this desultory research, I have come to wonder about the odd world of literary archives.

A great deal has been written about literary manuscripts, but nearly all of it has been bibliographic, textual, or commercial. Bibliographers assiduously catalogue and classify archival material. There are directories that list every known manuscript of Wordsworth, Coleridge, Shelley, and Yeats. Textual scholars customarily cross-reference manuscript variants in compiling definitive editions. Bookdealers and auctioneers publish lavish catalogues describing and often illustrating the literary manuscripts they hope to sell. The body of *descriptive* material about manuscripts is immense, but one finds virtually no critical or theoretical writing on the subject. There is little informed analysis or speculation, that is, on the problematic place of manuscripts in the broader literary culture; nor is much serious consideration given to their special status versus printed texts. If scholars have customarily discussed manuscripts in utilitarian terms, critics and theorists have ignored them altogether as a subject of independent inquiry.

In the absence of serious critical or theoretical interest, the terms for discussing manuscripts have mostly been set by the marketplace – the world of dealers, auction houses, and collectors. Although the private sector recognized the importance of manuscripts long before scholars and librarians made any systematic effort to retrieve and conserve them, the marketplace has done little to explore the real value of its material. It would not be altogether unfair to suggest that, like Oscar Wilde's cynic, the marketplace "knows the price of everything and the value of nothing." Of course, one might make the same complaint about the New York Stock Exchange. What the marketplace does is price things. Questions of value belong elsewhere.

The lack of speculative thinking and critical analysis, however, has not slowed the bustling world of literary manuscripts. Few areas of literary life are as full of purposeful and engaged activity. Thousands of librarians, curators, dealers, and scholars – as well as numerous private collectors – are currently building huge archives of primary materials. No other culture in history has even approached the level of collecting activity now routine in America. Our institutions spend vast sums to acquire and house manuscript material. Large crowds view public exhibitions of such material, while scholars fill reading rooms to study it in detail. Bibliographic journals, exhibition catalogues, and auction catalogues pour from the presses. Newspapers review major shows and cover significant auctions. Without fully articulating why, the culture has agreed that, even in an era of shrinking resources, collecting and preserving literary manuscripts is a priority. Two hundred years ago no one would have bothered to save the contents of most contemporary archives. Why have literary manuscripts become so widely valued? How did the change come about? And what do current assumptions about manuscripts reveal about modern literary culture?

"All literary manuscripts," Philip Larkin once observed, "have two kinds of value: what might be called the magical value and the meaningful value." No one today doubts the scholarly or "meaningful" importance of literary manuscripts. Auction houses and dealers sell them at ever-higher prices. Libraries announce the acquisition of a famous writer's papers with the same blare of publicity that accompanies a medical breakthrough. The public rationale for collecting manuscripts is that they provide information not usually found elsewhere. This scholarly argument is cogent if – as we shall see later – also incomplete. Manuscripts can solve factual problems, such as dating a poem or establishing an accurate text. It is not uncommon for a scholar studying the manuscripts of a literary work to discover that some obscure line in the standard printed text contains a mistranscription. Herman Melville's mysterious image in *White Jacket* of the "soiled fish of the sea" – much praised by F. O. Matthiessen – became, upon examination of Melville's original, the more literal "coiled fish of the sea." A famous critical puzzle turned out to be merely a misprint.

Manuscripts also illuminate the broader meanings of a literary work. Seeing what a poet cut out often helps clarify what was left in. Drafts can elucidate an author's intention in a particular piece. Diaries, letters, notebooks, and other documents add to the knowledge of a writer's life and milieu. Ezra Pound's compressed, cranky, and cryptic letters from Rapallo, Italy, prepare the reader for the allusive and increasingly idiosyncratic *Cantos* he wrote concurrently. The "meaningful value" of manuscripts often transcends their purely verbal contents. Sometimes even the physical materials used suggest certain insights about an author's life. Emily Dickinson's carefully composed and fastidiously recopied packets of poems, usually handbound in thread, not only reveal the poet's class position in the New England gentry, which could afford the materials and leisure to prepare such fascicles; the packets also show the essentially private medium that constituted Dickinson's "publication." Not even her family knew the extent of her literary output. After Emily died in 1886, her sister Lavinia was astonished to discover nearly 900 poems stashed away in a locked box.

Best of all, manuscripts often contain new work. Few authors publish everything they write. The *Nachlass* (to use the German term for an author's literary remains) almost inevitably reveals unknown material. The final version of John Keats's sonnet "Bright Star, Would I Were Steadfast as Thou Art" was found, inscribed in the author's hand, in a friend's copy of Shakespeare's poems. In extreme cases like those of Dickinson or Gerard Manley Hopkins, virtually all the work emerges posthumously from unpublished papers. Only a handful of Dickinson's 1,775 known poems appeared during her lifetime. Moreover, in the first editions of her work, her poems were rewritten by her editors into more conventional styles. Later editors returned to the manuscripts to restore her authentic versions. Hopkins published virtually nothing after joining the Society of Jesus – only three comic triolets and three Latin versions of English poems. His mature work did not appear until 1918,

nearly 30 years after his death. His literary executor, Poet Laureate Robert Bridges, carefully put together the first collection from four manuscripts he had assembled – like a classicist preparing an edition of Horace by collating and comparing the surviving manuscripts.

The manuscripts of a poem can be divided into three general categories – the working drafts, the final manuscript, and fair copies. Each type of manuscript affords certain insights into the author and the work. The working drafts (or worksheets) of a poem reveal the author's creative process. If all the worksheets survive, they track the poem's development from the author's initial impulse to the text's final form. Many authors, however, discard their drafts. Among the 7,000 items contained in the Huntington Library's Wallace Stevens archive, for example, one will find no worksheets. Working drafts also demonstrate the often significant differences in process between poets. Lord Byron seems to have written with remarkable swiftness and self-possession. His poems usually achieve some recognizable version of their ultimate shape in the first draft. The folio-size worksheets of *Don Juan* in the Berg Collection show whole passages being composed and decisively polished to their final form on the same sheet of paper. Elizabeth Bishop, however, could fret for years over a single poem. The surviving drafts of "The Moose" show that Bishop worked on the 168-line poem for more than 25 years before publishing it in

The New Yorker in 1972. (She then revised it again before putting it in a book.)

The final manuscript is in one sense merely the author's last draft of a poem or collection of poems. Although it represents the end of the private creative process, it also marks the beginning of the work's public life. The final manuscript leaves the writer's desk and enters the public realm of editors, publishers, lawyers, and censors. For earlier writers this final manuscript was written by hand. For modern authors it has usually been a typescript. (Even in the age of personal computers, most poets continue to send along a "hard copy" in addition to a digital disk.) The final manuscript is uniquely valuable because it is the version of the text the author submits for publication. In artistic terms, it stands as the work achieved; in scholarly terms, it often best reveals the authorial intention. Literary works are often cut, revised, repunctuated, and even censored before publication for reasons that have nothing to do with the author's wishes. The punctuation of *The Poetry of Robert Frost*, the standard complete edition of Frost's poems, for instance, differs – according to Donald Hall – in over 1,100 instances from the texts the poet himself put into print. By recasting Frost's poems into conventional punctuation, the book changes the rhythm and sometimes even the meaning of lines. If the best text of a poem is the one that represents the author's probable intentions, then the final manuscript provides a starting point for establishing that intention.

The comparison of the completed manuscript with the printed book can provide real revelations. E. E. Cummings's papers, for instance, show how the poet's language was sometimes censored because of the publisher's concerns about obscenity. "*No words changed*," he wrote Boni and Liveright, about the manuscript of his prose narrative, *The Enormous Room* (1922). He then specified that objectionable words should be deleted rather than replaced by euphemisms: "In cutting use dash ——— e.g. '——— it,' said etc. (not 'chuck it,' said etc.)." His publisher nonetheless substantially revised his book without his approval – dropping character sketches, changing punctuation, translating French phrases into English, and removing supposed indecencies. The author's true version did not appear until 1978. The manuscript of Robinson Jeffers's 1948 collection, *The Double Axe and Other Poems*, now at the Humanities Research Center in Austin, reveals how Random House asked the author to delete ten poems and change several others for political reasons. Publisher Bennett Cerf and editor Saxe Commins were offended by the poet's criticism of Franklin Roosevelt. Although Jeffers reluctantly agreed to the changes, Random House insultingly placed an unprecedented publisher's disclaimer at the beginning of the volume announcing the publisher's disagreement with the author's political opinions. While boasting of Random House's commitment to "the writer's freedom," the note makes no mention of the omitted poems and many emendations,

As longtime neighbors in the small town of Cummington, Massachusetts, poets Richard Wilbur and William Jay Smith amused themselves with public poetic jousting. Each Sunday the poet who arrived first to pick up his New York Times *at a local store would write a few teasing lines of rhyme on the other's newspaper. Here, Wilbur has left "I read me a poem by some Cajun" in the upper-left-hand corner of Smith's copy of the July 29, 1979, edition.*

which remained unknown until a scholar examined the author's manuscript decades later. Jeffers's original versions were not published until 1976 – 14 years after the poet's death.

Authors, of course, also make changes after their work has been accepted for publication. "When a man knows he is to be hanged in a fortnight," Samuel Johnson observed, "it concentrates his mind wonderfully." The prospect of imminent publication clarifies an author's intentions. "Final" manuscripts frequently reveal last-minute changes by the author. The Berg's typescript of Jeffers's *Solstice* (1935) shows small revisions in the poet's hand – changes made for artistic rather than political reasons. Robert Lowell's typescript for *Imitations* (1961) in the Berg contains massive reworking of many of the author's free translations. The proofing stage, which is the traditional point where a text moves from the author's handwriting or typing to mechanical reproduction (although the advent of word-processing and electronic

publishing has radically changed that process), also invites authorial changes. Seeing a text in the cold light of print changes an author's perspective. James Joyce repeatedly rewrote *Ulysses* in proof. Lowell's galleys of *Imitations* reveal his obsessive urge to revise. He once admitted that he could not see one of his own poems without feeling the need to change it.

A fair copy is an autograph version of a poem written out or typed by the author after its completion or publication. (A "fair" copy contains no revisions or disfiguring corrections, in contrast to a "foul" copy, which shows changes and emendations.) A fair copy, therefore, is often as much a keepsake as a literary artifact. Often intended as a gift or presentation piece, a fair copy usually displays the author's finest hand. Such manuscripts were immensely popular in the last century. Famous poets – and many poets truly ranked as celebrities then – were barraged with requests for autograph copies of their anthology pieces. The correspondence of 19th-century American poets reveals many such requests and replies. The Berg Collection, for instance, has a charming note from Henry Wadsworth Longfellow to Walt Whitman that accompanied a fair copy the Good Gray Poet had requested for two friends. The Collection also possesses no fewer than five fair copies of Oliver Wendell Holmes's patriotic mega-hit, "Old Ironsides."

To the confusion of archivists and scholars, worksheets, final manuscripts, and fair copies often end up in different locations. If worksheets are not discarded, they usually remain in the author's possession and are eventually placed with his or her papers. Working drafts, however, may also be sent to literary friends for comment and thereby end up in another writer's possession. Completed manuscripts almost inevitably remain in the files of editors or publishers. Fair copies are scattered among their recipients. It is a rare circumstance when an author's entire body of drafts and manuscripts – not to mention letters, journals, and diaries – ends up in one institution. Elizabeth Bishop's worksheets reside mainly at Vassar. Many of the final typescripts of her poems and collection remained in the files of *The New Yorker* and Farrar, Straus & Giroux, both of whose archives are now in The New York Public Library. Assorted other Bishop manuscripts are at Harvard, Washington University (St. Louis), and the University of Delaware, as well as in private hands.

Although the diaspora complicates certain types of research (and keeps biographers on the move), the much-lamented situation is not

without its advantages. An author's manuscripts are available to a broader constituency when they are dispersed; they are seen – in private research or public exhibition – by a more diverse audience. Centralization is not an absolute virtue in the arts. Having every Botticelli under one roof might simplify the work of art historians, but it would impoverish the experience and education of countless gallery-goers. The Stanford Library had modest special collections during my student years, but in 1975 James Healy donated a small but superb collection of modern Irish literature, including W. B. Yeats's own copies of all Cuala Press books with his unpublished annotations on each flyleaf. The directors of established Yeats archives may complain that such an important collection did not belong in California remote from most related material, but the Healy Collection was well cared for and much consulted. Its presence provided a tremendous boon to Stanford faculty and students.

"Fair is foul, and foul is fair," chant the prophetic witches in *Macbeth*, and indeed, literary archivists generally consider fair copies less significant than working drafts. Worksheets offer scholarly insights; fair copies often seem mere souvenirs. And yet fair copies sometimes contain variant readings of a text, which may reflect an author's second thoughts about a poem. The elegant copy of "Ulalume – A Ballad" that Poe gave to a teenaged girl he met a month before his death now stands as the definitive text of the poem. Fair copies also sometimes constitute the only surviving authorial manuscripts of a work, especially for pre-Romantic literature. What would textual scholars give for a copy – fair or foul – in Shakespeare's hand of *Hamlet*? The Westmoreland Manuscript, for example, represents an important authorial source for many of John Donne's English poems, and this exquisitely penned fair copy provides the only extant texts of three of the Holy Sonnets. Even when several sources exist, a copy of a poem carefully written out in the author's hand – or, as in the case of the Westmoreland Manuscript, that of an amanuensis – is a persuasive endorsement of the correctness of a particular reading. Worksheets may reveal the creative process, but a fair copy can help to establish an authoritative text of the finished poem.

But what is a finished poem? Is Paul Valéry correct in declaring that "a poem is never finished, only abandoned"? The study of literary manuscripts highlights a central issue of modern poetics – what constitutes a completed work of art? As Romantic philosophers shifted their attention from the analysis of a conventionally finished artwork to contemplation of the creative process, they initiated a shift in taste that continues today. Works that might have been considered incomplete and unsatisfying drafts a century earlier received enthusiastic approbation as fully achieved poems. In 1798, Samuel Taylor Coleridge, the central English Romantic theorist, published "Kubla Khan" with the subtitle "A Fragment." In 1820, John Keats allowed the text of his abandoned poem

"Hyperion," which ends in mid-sentence, to appear in a collection. Another of Keats's most famous "poems" is an incomplete, eight-line passage found in the margin of a manuscript. The lines may represent the first draft of a poem or a possible speech for a projected play. First printed in 1898, these lines seem to a modern sensibility perfectly self-sufficient.

This living hand, now warm and capable
Of earnest grasping, would, if it were cold
And in the icy silence of the tomb,
So haunt thy days and chill thy dreaming nights
That thou wouldst wish thine own heart dry of blood
So in my veins red life might stream again,
And thou be conscience-calmed – see here it is –
I hold it towards you.

If the Romantic period prized poetic fragments for revealing the artist's inner genius unfettered by the external constraints of classical form and propriety, the era also fostered an unprecedented reverence for literary manuscripts. Earlier ages had viewed a poet's holograph in purely functional terms. Once the text had been more decorously preserved in printed form, there was no special value seen in preserving the usually "foul" autograph copy. *Paradise Lost* was recognized on publication in 1667 as a masterpiece, but neither Milton nor his contemporaries took care to save the manuscript. Only one section of the huge original survived the curatorial indifference of immediate posterity. (This fragment, still bearing the ink smudges of the printer, now rests in the climate-controlled vaults of the Morgan Library.) The Romantic *Zeitgeist*, however, endowed a page written in a famous poet's hand with a talismanic power. Matthew Arnold may have erred in prophesying that poetry would replace religion in guiding mankind, but his prediction suggests how – at least among literati – poetic manuscripts became Victorian society's equivalent of holy relics. Indeed, the luxurious 19th-century leather bindings and satin-lined boxes that house many of the Berg's famous manuscripts are the bibliophile's versions of reliquaria.

This shift in sensibility could probably have occurred only in the 19th century at the height of print culture. This was the first age of mass literacy, inexpensive printing, and rapid communication. Successive waves of technological and commercial innovation – daily journalism, universal post, telegraph service, pulp paper, broad-scale advertising, dime novels – gradually changed the frame of reference for human knowledge and communication. For the first time in history, it seemed that most information was announced, disseminated, preserved, and codified on the printed page. Authors occupied a critical position in the new print-driven economy. To use a contemporary metaphor, writers created the programming that ran the information and entertainment networks of print culture. Before film, radio, television, recordings, telephones, and computers, the writer exercised a near monopoly on information. Since fame was a function of print, successful authors

could achieve vast celebrity; since ideas traveled most quickly and farthest in print, they could also exercise immense influence.

The poet commanded a unique and privileged position in 19th-century print culture. Embodying the still powerful link between the new age and earlier oral traditions, the poet practiced the most venerable literary art – rooted in spoken language but easily transmitted in print – and the typographic bard still played an almost priestly role. No one was shocked when a novelist or playwright went to the bad; those professions had at best dubious reputations. But a famously dissolute poet like Byron or the young Swinburne exercised the evil fascination of a fallen angel. Fiction now dominated commercial publishing, but successful poets like Tennyson or Longfellow outsold novelists. Coventry Patmore's *The Angel in the House* (1858), for example, sold over a quarter of a million copies. Children still memorized and recited famous poems as a central part of the curriculum. Newspapers printed or reprinted poems as a regular feature. Famous poets like Byron, Longfellow, or the Brownings enjoyed international celebrity. When Edison wanted to record the most famous voices in the English-speaking world, he approached Queen Victoria, Prime Minister Gladstone, and Tennyson. Meanwhile, Longfellow lived to see his birthday become a national holiday. Novelists commanded immense popularity, but only poets received such signal honors.

If technology had transformed the social identity of the poet, mass-production also changed the cultural status of his or her manuscripts. The uniformity of machine-printed books slowly imbued the handwritten page with a unique personal aura. As mechanical typography visually standardized written language, the reader was less likely to view an autograph copy of a poem purely as a piece of verbal communication; it now became a unique artifact that invited a different sort of attention. Impersonal communication was the function of print; the manuscript suggested a more individual and direct relation between reader and author – not through its text but its medium, which resembled a private communication. The omnipresence of mechanical print made the manuscript's medium its most important message.

The special value of a literary manuscript, therefore, does not come solely from the words it contains; the text can usually be found elsewhere in printed form. In purely functional terms – legibility, endurance, portability, and perhaps even accuracy – a book is usually more useful than an autograph. The manuscript's superior value originates, to use Walter Benjamin's term from "The Work of Art in an Age of Mechanical Reproduction," in its "aura" – "its presence in time and space, its unique existence at the place where it happens to be." A modern book is a standardized manufactured object; a copy in Chicago does not differ from those in Santa Rosa, Gainesville, or Johannesburg. A manuscript, however, not only exists as a unique entity whose total essence cannot be fully reproduced; it also survives as a historical artifact that can be

traced back to its creator. A modern edition of Byron's *Don Juan*, for instance, provides an authentic verbal and intellectual link between the past and present, but it does not possess the unreproducible and unsummarizable aura of total authenticity that the original manuscript does.

Benjamin had worried that the mass reproduction of art works led to their desacralization by destroying the aura of the original. His theory may or may not accurately pertain to the visual arts like painting where there is an identifiable original, but it proves problematic in literature. If someone asks a group of art historians where the original of Piero della Francesca's *The Flagellation* is located, they can confidently agree that it is to be found in the Galleria at Urbino. But if a group of literary scholars were asked where the original of *Hamlet* is found, they would not only be unable to say *where* it is, they would probably be unable to agree on *what* the original is – a modern scholarly text, a First Folio, a great performance, a lost acting version used by Shakespeare's company, a collective idea of *Hamlet* among all theatregoers? The mode of existence for literary works is a complex and perhaps insoluble problem. Mechanical reproduction, however, paradoxically provided an answer at least for the common reader. As developments of commercial printing in the 18th century turned books from luxury goods to commonplace objects, mass production may have indeed desacralized the book, but it did not destroy the magical aura of the literary work, only transferred it. The proliferation of printed books gradually created a new type of original – the author's manuscript, endowed with an aura of authenticity and authority by the hand of its creator.

The manuscript of a literary work became more than words; it represented a direct and unmediated physical link between viewer and author – a holy relic or shamanistic fetish. When Larkin, the most level-headed of poets, exclaims, "This is the paper he wrote on, these are the words as he wrote them, emerging for the first time in this particular miraculous combination," he reveals the long-term results of the new attitude – the *frisson* of devotional ecstasy, a sense of the sacred. This quality of untransferable authenticity explains why even the fragment of a great work (like the Morgan's fragment of *Paradise Lost*) possesses magical value far in excess of its scholarly contents. Philosophers may deride this subjective notion of communication with some justification; as an analytical method, it is overtly flawed. Yet who can deny that one learns something in such transactions – often something essential? Why else do scholars and biographers assiduously study manuscripts? Any reflective person recognizes how much learning happens outside the realm of analytical deduction. Most of what one knows comes from sensory, intuitive, and imaginative faculties. Reason may later examine and organize this learning, but one first assimilated it holistically.

The scholarly alibi of libraries that they acquire literary manuscripts for intellectual reasons, therefore, is inadequate at best. Those needs could be better served by microfilm or photocopies at a negligible fraction of the expense. Textual information can usually be found both more easily and completely in a variorum edition. Like the intricately rational web of theology woven around the irrational mysteries of faith, the sober explanations of institutions for hoarding literary relics seem like elegant *post-factum* justifications for what is essentially a sense of sacred awe. An institution of learning seeks significant manuscripts because they possess qualities that scholarship cannot entirely reproduce – an authentic, holistic connection with the great writers of the past. It is not the intellectual content of the manuscript that is important but its material presence – ink spots, tobacco stains, pinworm holes, and foxing included.

The magical nature of the author's hand can be seen perhaps most clearly in signed books – a special case in which handwriting and mechanical typography meet. An autographed and an unsigned copy of the same title have no significant difference in content except for a bit of ink across one page, but the autographed volume will usually sell at many times the price of the other copy. Bearing the mark that it once rested in the author's hands, the autographed volume is transformed from a mere book into a minor relic. Before the 19th century, owners signed their books mostly for two reasons – to prevent theft or to inscribe them as a gift. Alexander Pope's copy of Milton's *Poems* in the Berg, for example, bears its former owner's

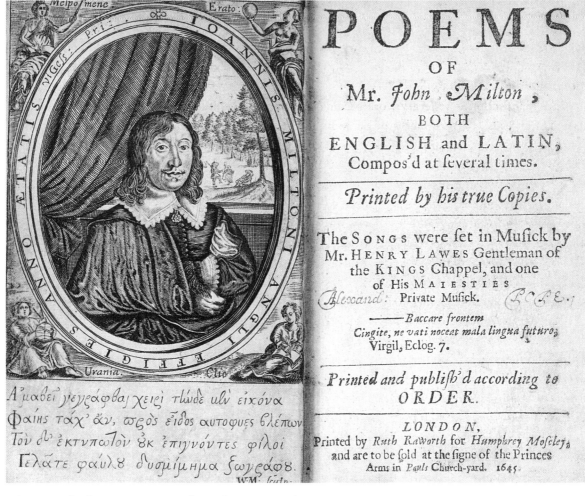

This copy of Milton's Poems *(1645) bears the signature of its owner,
Alexander Pope, on the title page. Pope further personalized the volume by
writing out, on a blank leaf at page 66, Milton's "At a Vacation Exercise
in the Colledge; Anno Ætatis, 19," in a beautiful hand, in imitation of
printing; and adding, at the end of the volume, in an elegant cursive hand,
Milton's "Latin Ode."*

signature, not Milton's, and the presentation copy of Pope's *The Rape of the Lock* (1714) was inscribed by the poet only because he gave it to a patroness. The notion of a stranger soliciting Pope to sign a copy of *The Rape of the Lock* would have seemed peculiar to the Augustan poet. Midway in the following century, however, it was so common for strangers to ask writers to autograph books that it proved a great nuisance to established poets. The autograph had become print culture's means of individuating mass-produced books by linking them with the author's person. Literary autograph collecting reached its peak at the turn of the century when Rudyard Kipling discovered that shopkeepers would rather keep a small check with his signature than cash it – true fame.

The autographed book exists as a midpoint between the anonymous nature of the manufactured book and the unique personal essence of the manuscript. If a book contains sufficient authorial additions, however, it gains the unique aura of the manuscript. The book has become a manuscript. In the Berg's copy of Tennyson's *The Princess* (1847), the poet has added several new short lyrics to his long didactic poem. These 1850 additions, which include "The Splendor Falls" and "Sweet and Low," now rank among his most popular poems. Sometimes one man's book became another man's manuscript. Coventry Patmore covered the margins of his copy of *The Princess* with a running commentary on Tennyson's poem – half praise, half criticism. Patmore's marginalia provides the modern

reader with a vivid sense of how the best Victorian poets read one another's work. Consulting with Siegfried Sassoon, poet Edmund Blunden covered his copy of Robert Graves's memoir, *Good-bye to All That* (1929), with their copious disagreements concerning the author's account of events; their commentary effectively recomposes the printed monologue into an argumentative dialogue in manuscript. Dissatisfied with Winifred Roy's translation of his novel *Despair*, Vladimir Nabokov reworked her version phrase by phrase, writing his more forceful and accurate English between the lines of the printed text. Now in the Berg, this book-*cum*-manuscript provides a vivid demonstration of Nabokov's practice both as novelist and translator. Perhaps the most extravagant case of "recomposition" on record appears in Andrew Motion's biography of Philip Larkin. The librarian-poet and his longtime girlfriend, Monica Sinclair, spent years "systematically defacing" and comically rewriting a copy of Iris Murdoch's 1956 novel, *The Flight from the Enchanter*, until they had transformed Murdoch's 300 pages, word by word, into a pornographic farce. Fate has a sense of humor: this singular literary artifact now rests in the special collections of the Brynmor Jones, Larkin's own library.

That the magic value of manuscripts surpasses their meaningful value can be further attested by the passion both private collectors and public institutions exercise in obtaining the personal effects of famous writers. In addition to Mrs. Browning's slippers, Dickens's desk, and Thackeray's pen, the Berg Collection possesses such modern relics as W. H. Auden's suitcase, Randall Jarrell's driver's license, E. E. Cummings's death mask, and Howard Moss's pencil sharpener. The auction prices for literary artifacts may be lower than for Marilyn Monroe or Elvis Presley memorabilia, but – the prestige of possession aside – the underlying motivations to acquire them are equally irrational and superstitious. The new owners hope mysteriously to gain some part of the original celebrity's power or allure.

Medieval towns once competed for the bodies of saints to protect their citizens from plagues and natural disasters. (One still sees the waxy cadavers of the blessed in the churches of southern Europe – displayed behind glass like rare manuscripts in a library exhibition.) If the physical remains of saints were unavailable, then their personal effects would suffice. Cloaks, missals, rosaries, belts, and shoe leather were all to be cherished for their talismanic power. While the Protestant North ridiculed this Southern Catholic custom, they did not escape its primal attraction; they merely translated it into secular terms. The remains of great poets were buried in Westminster Abbey; their personal effects and manuscripts were collected by libraries. Although there seems to be no commercial traffic in the bones of poets, Tennyson once claimed that dealers would have sold his toenail parings had they gotten hold of them. None of the esteemed laureate's clippings have been preserved for posterity, but locks

of his hair still exist. There are, in fact, many private and institutional collectors of literary hair. The Berg, for example, owns two locks of Whitman's famous gray mane.

Manuscripts also represent the imagination's passport; they allow the viewer to travel from the public and impersonal world of mechanical typography into the private, human world of the author – from literature as an institution to literature as friendship. A book is a public object collectively produced by many hands and designed for many readers; in contrast, even a typewritten draft seems intimate and individual. The manuscript – handwritten or typed – invites the viewer to step from the faceless crowd of readers and become an individual. It is tempting to portray manuscripts as objects of aesthetic contemplation, and the elegant fair copies of poets like Poe, Longfellow, or Keats reward such attention, but the intrinsic beauty of a charm is no measure of its magic. Reliquaria must be beautiful, not the relics. For this reason, foul copies often provide as much or more pleasure than fair copies; in the corrections, deletions, fragments, dead ends, and doodling, one discovers the author's humanity. Kipling and Cummings sometimes playfully illustrated their manuscripts and letters. Anne Sexton's triumphant "Sold to New Yorker" scrawled at the top of a typescript poem lets the viewer share the author's pride and pleasure. If the magnificence of the finished work excites our aesthetic imagination, the imperfections of the working drafts allow our participation.

On the back of his driver's license, Randall Jarrell pencilled a quotation – which he attributed to Samuel Johnson – that he then partially obscured with scribbled addresses and telephone numbers. It reads: "Nothing has more retarded the advancement of learning than the desperation of vulgar minds to ridicule and vilify what they cannot understand."

One suspects that Shakespeare's status has only been enhanced by the absence of manuscripts; he remains Olympian and behind his masterpieces. Among the well-documented moderns, Stevens has deepened the mystery surrounding his inner life by leaving no working drafts of mature poems. Perhaps the special appeal of final manuscripts and fair copies is that they provide the most direct comparisons between the private and public identities of the poet; they present more or less the same words one already knows from the printed page. If the words are identical between a manuscript and a printed text, then what one notices are the nonverbal aspects like the handwriting, paper, number of deletions or additions, even the stains – all the clues of the author's physical presence. Final manuscripts reveal the juncture between the secret realm of poetic inspiration and the external existence of the printed text.

The study of literary manuscripts also suggests the complex but vital connections between poetry and technology. In the visual arts, the impact of technical innovation like lost-wax casting, oil-based paints, color lithography, or daguerreotypy constitute an essential part of a medium's history. In literary studies, however, poetry is mostly seen as pure language generated by the writer's imagination in relation to the tradition. Scholars may study the economics and technology of publishing to understand the social identity of the poet, but the most intimate relation between technology and poetic composition remains largely unexplored, except by general theorists like Marshall McLuhan, Walter Ong, or Eric Havelock. Does anyone know, for example, the first significant poet to compose on a typewriter?

Only six years separate the composition of W. B. Yeats's 1917 volume, *The Wild Swans at Coole*, and William Carlos Williams's 1923 collection, *Spring and All*, which contains his famous "The Red Wheelbarrow," but the impact of technological change is already apparent. The Berg's copy of Yeats's manuscript exists only in the author's swift, strong hand. In 1917, Yeats still did not use a typewriter. His method of composition remained oral, aural, and manual – a scribal method not appreciably different from the procedures of Virgil, Dante, or Donne. Yeats never wrote a poem that did not rhyme. The forceful meter, symmetrical stanzas, and overt musicality of his verse demonstrate not only his mastery of traditional prosody but also his commitment to shaping poems in sonic terms. Perhaps Yeats's only technological advantage over Virgil is inexpensive paper, which allows him to take each poem through numerous drafts.

Six years after Yeats's book, however, what constitutes a poem in technical terms has broadened enormously. Williams's "The Red Wheelbarrow" exists primarily not as sounds moving through time but as words visually fixed in space. Like "The Wild Swans at Coole," Williams's typographic poem displays strict order and symmetry. There is no rhyme or meter, but each stanza contains an identical pattern of four words arranged in combinations of three and one.

so much depends
upon

a red wheel
barrow

glazed with rain
water

beside the white
chickens

Critics often celebrate Williams as the poet of natural American speech, but the visual technique of "The Red Wheelbarrow" deliberately subverts normal speech rhythms. By breaking the poem's single short sentence into eight shaped lines surrounded by the white space of a blank page, Williams forces the reader to slow down normal speech into the static visual rhythm of the poem. It is no coincidence that Williams kept a typewriter in his office to write between patients when a paper and pen would have been more convenient. Cummings also systematically explored visual features of typography that have no exact equivalents in speech – lower- and upper-case letters, visual symbols (like &, $, and %), arabic and roman numbers, punctuation, spacing, and abbreviation. For good reason, the Berg preserves his Royal typewriter along with his papers. The keyboard was integral to his creative process.

A literary manuscript allows the viewer to probe – however subjectively or inadequately – the mystery of artistic genius. If it is a great manuscript, it invites one to observe an author at a moment when he or she performed at the limits of human possibility. The printed text may allow one to view that performance from the stadium stand, but the manuscript puts one at the author's side. Here, as so often in the arts, there is a powerful element of voyeurism.

The urge to see the author face to face is not merely fandom; it is a deep-rooted, primitive human desire. The physical separation of the poet from the audience is a relatively recent phenomenon. For most of human history, the audience heard the poet's physical voice; a direct physical relationship was unavoidable in preliterate societies. Even after the introduction of the phonetic alphabet, which allowed writing to preserve the text of poems, the links with oral culture remained. In Roman times, a poet "published" his work by reading it aloud to an invited audience. Later, troubadours and Minnesingers sang or recited their poems. Handmade books were rare and expensive; the connection between poetry and oral presentation was an unbroken tradition from time immemorial. Only the introduction of printed books fully separated the living poet from his or her audience. The age of typography amounts to a small portion of total human existence – four or five centuries out of perhaps a million years.

The popularity of poetry readings is a reminder of the strong aural and tribal roots of poetry. Readings bring an audience into a direct physical relationship with the author – and momentarily form a tribe of like-minded listeners versus isolated readers. This longing for personal – and nonverbal – knowledge of the poet is also found in the now common practice of dust-jacket photos. Handwritten manuscripts satisfy the same desire in readers. The author's hand provides both a direct human link and a suggestive invitation to the viewer's imagination. Graphology may be only a pseudo-science, but it rests on a genuine insight: there is some essential connection between handwriting and character. Just because the connections cannot be standardized does not invalidate them. Different aspects of the writer's personality emerge in different hands, and the penmanship of the same person may shift noticeably according to mood. Biographer Edmund Morris has described handwriting's special ability to communicate the inner state of its author:

Script's primary power is to convey the cursive flow of human thought, from brain to hand to pen to ink to eye – every waver, every loop, every character trembling with expression. Type has no comparable warmth.

Examining the manuscripts of famous poets, one is often struck by how clearly some aspect of their character emerges in the handwriting. Poe's conspicuously beautiful hand reveals the same sensibility that articulated his dreamy aestheticism. Dickinson's eccentric script enlarges the letters so that a short poem sprawls across an entire page – one or two words stretching from margin to margin. "Don't mistake my short poem for a small poem," the handwriting shouts. Is anyone surprised that Longfellow has neater handwriting than Whitman? Or that Keats wrote with more deliberate care than Byron, whose quick, vertical hand dashes dramatically across the page?

The value our culture has placed on literary manuscripts reflects an admirable and ineradicable human impulse – the desire for a direct and authentic relation between art and its audience. Literature may be an institution, an imaginary library too vast and labyrinthine for any single reader to explore entirely, but the experience of studying great manuscripts reminds the viewer that each individual work is also a conversation, an imaginative and emotional transaction from one person to another, a bridge across time and place. Reading is never more intimate than with script. The hand of the poet reaches out to greet the reader. ∎

Note to the Reader
Where a printed text or excerpt accompanies a reproduction of a manuscript, that text reflects the poem as it first appeared in book form, in a poet's collected poems, or in a standard or scholarly edition; the differences between these texts and the manuscripts can sometimes provide insight into both the creative and the editorial processes.

William Wordsworth

1770–1850

Wordsworth was not pleased with Sir William Boxall's painting of him, and was equally chagrined when it was engraved ("I am much mortified about Boxall's print of me, for except my sister I cannot get anyone to look at it with pleasure."). This 1833 version by J. Cochran – one of at least five different engravings after the Boxall portrait published in the 1830s – circulated widely during Wordsworth's lifetime.

WILLIAM WORDSWORTH BEGAN his poetic career as a revolutionary who brought a new voice to English literature and ended it as a widely revered, orthodox-minded Poet Laureate. His family had intended him for the Church, but Wordsworth had no interest in such a career. After Cambridge, he traveled to France and became fired with enthusiasm for the French Revolution; but once back in England, his revolutionary ardor quickly cooled.

In 1795, Wordsworth settled with his beloved sister Dorothy at Racedown, in rural Dorsetshire, and began his close association with Samuel Taylor Coleridge. Three years later the two poets published (anonymously) their epoch-making *Lyrical Ballads.* Wordsworth was quickly established as the very embodiment of the psychologically acute poet whom he described in his famous preface to the *Lyrical Ballads* as one "endued with more lively sensibility, more enthusiasm and tenderness, who has a greater knowledge of human nature, and a more comprehensive soul."

In 1802, Wordsworth married Mary Hutchinson, a friend from childhood and, like the poet, a native of the Lake District. Around this time Wordsworth came under the patronage of a wealthy aristocrat whose generosity allowed him to publish his 1807 *Poems in Two Volumes*, which includes the poem that many consider his greatest achievement, "Ode: Intimations of Immortality from Recollections of Early Childhood." Wordsworth continued to write prolifically for the next four decades, but with a few exceptions, his works after 1807 display a falling off in quality and inspiration. Politically and religiously he grew more orthodox, evoking the scorn of the younger Romantics like Shelley and Byron.

Wordsworth's final years were for the most part serene. His later volumes were much praised, frequent comparisons to Shakespeare and Milton attesting to the august position Wordsworth had achieved by the end of his life. ∎

John Donne

1572–1631

This portrait of Donne in about 1620 – used as the frontispiece to Izaak Walton's The Lives of Dr. John Donne, Sir Henry Wotton, Mr. Richard Hooker, Mr. George Herbert – *is unusual in that it shows the poet draped in classical rather than ecclesiastical robes. Now most famous for* The Compleat Angler, *Walton, who numbered some of the most distinguished men of his age among his circle of friends, had first published his life of Donne in 1640. In 1670, a revised edition was published collectively with Walton's equally celebrated lives of Wotton, Hooker, and Herbert.*

He was the one English poet who was not afraid to acknowledge that he was composed of body, soul, and mind; and who faithfully recorded all the pitched battles, alarms, treaties, sieges, and fanfares of that extraordinary triangular warfare.

Rupert Brooke, "John Donne" in Poetry & Drama *(June 1913)*

JOHN DONNE WAS born in London to a venerable Roman Catholic family. In his 20s, having already written his worldly and witty *Elegies* and *Satyres*, Donne joined the Earl of Essex in celebrated naval expeditions to Cadiz and the Azores. The ambitious young Donne was appointed secretary to Sir Thomas Egerton, the Lord Keeper of England, in 1598; three years later, he secretly married Anne More, Lady Egerton's niece. The marriage was an egregious breach of convention and destroyed Donne's prospects for advancement through patronage. Anne's father secured his dismissal from Sir Thomas's service and even had him imprisoned for a few days.

Desperately trying to support his large family (he and Anne would have 12 children), Donne struggled at a series of careers before the increasing fame of his verses, which circulated widely in manuscript, brought him support from several aristocrats. Having abandoned his Catholicism during the 1590s, he gradually worked his way toward a restive Anglicanism, his mature religious poetry dramatically reflecting his spiritual struggles and hard-won faith. His anti-Catholic polemic *Pseudo-Martyr* (1610) attracted the attention of King James I, who, refusing Donne the state position he sought, insisted that the poet instead take Anglican orders. Ordained in the Church of England in 1615, Donne became a divine renowned for the eloquence and power of his sermons. In 1621, the poet, who as a young man had been famed for the wit and provocative sensuality of his verse, was made Dean of St. Paul's Cathedral in London.

Donne died several weeks after preaching his own funeral sermon, published later as *Deaths Duell*. He was interred in St. Paul's, his memory honored there by a startling effigy of the poet, dressed in his own shroud. ■

Perhaps the single most important manuscript source for Donne's poetry, the Westmoreland Manuscript was copied out around 1625 by Donne's close friend Rowland Woodward, probably as a gift for his patron, the first Earl of Westmoreland. Woodward may have worked from manuscripts in the poet's hand; this gives the Westmoreland Manuscript particular importance, since virtually no verse manuscripts in Donne's hand have survived. Opened here to four of the magnificent Holy Sonnets, this beautiful vellum-bound manuscript book contains many of Donne's earliest poems. For three of the Holy Sonnets, it is the sole manuscript source.

Holy Sonnet No. 8

At the round earths imagin'd corners, blow
Your trumpets, Angells, and arise, arise
From death, you numberlesse infinities
Of soules, and to your scattred bodies goe,
All whom the flood did, and fire shall o'erthrow,
All whom warre, dearth, age, agues, tyrannies,
Despaire, law, chance, hath slaine, and you whose eyes,
Shall behold God, and never tast deaths woe.
But let them sleepe, Lord, and mee mourne a space,
For, if above all these, my sinnes abound,
'Tis late to aske abundance of thy grace,
When we are there; here on this lowly ground,
Teach mee how to repent; for that's as good
As if thou'hadst seal'd my pardon, with thy blood.

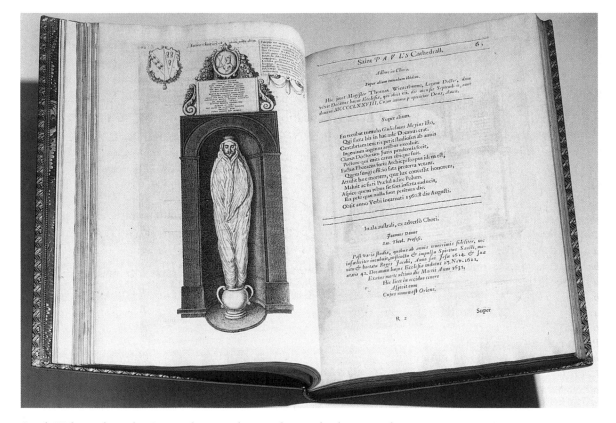

*Izaak Walton relates that Donne, knowing he was close to death, arranged
to have a final portrait of himself drawn, life-sized, on a large wooden
plank. Wrapped only in his burial shroud, he posed for this drawing
in his study, standing on the model of an urn. According to Walton, this
long-lost drawing provided the basis for the extraordinary effigy in St.
Paul's Cathedral produced by Nicholas Stone and his workshop, shown
here in an engraving from Sir William Dugdale's* History of St. Pauls
Cathedral in London *(1658). Although the story may be apocryphal, there
is something haunting, almost miraculous, about the statue: Stone's effigy
of Donne was one of the few monuments to survive the great fire that
devastated the Cathedral in 1666.*

Alexander Pope

1688–1744

This 1717 mezzotint is based on a portrait of Pope by the German-born Sir Godfrey Kneller, who was the most prominent portrait painter in England for more than 40 years. The poet and his portraitist became friends and, after Pope settled at Twickenham, close neighbors. The poet was fond of Kneller, though he appears to have considered him rather a buffoon. When Kneller was dying, Pope assured his friend that he would write his epitaph, and indeed Pope's verses appear on Kneller's monument in Westminster Abbey (the worst lines, Pope later claimed, that he had ever written).

A MASTER OF technique and the most glittering satirist in the English language, Alexander Pope took literary London by storm when, at the age of 23, he published *An Essay on Criticism*, a bold and bracing assault on the leading critics of his time. Pope's command of the heroic couplet, his dazzling and fluid versification, and his audacious wit are all evident in this early work. Pope's achievement is astonishing, especially considering the disadvantages of his baptism (Roman Catholic) and health (always precarious).

The eldest son of a retired linen merchant, Pope contracted tuberculosis of the spine at age 12, with terrible lifelong consequences (he was hunchbacked, tormented by headaches, and never grew taller than four foot six). Although illness plagued him and he was barred from public school and university because of his religion, Pope mastered Greek and Latin on his own and by the age of 16 had written his metrically sophisticated *Pastorals*.

In 1715, Pope published the first volume of his translation of the *Iliad*; its success established him as the dominant literary figure of his period. He also made a fortune, becoming the first English man of letters to support himself solely with his pen. Pope's popularity evoked resentment, of course; but Pope, a virtuoso of invective, always got the better of his critics: *The Dunciad*, its complex composition and publication extending from 1728 to 1743, is a masterpiece of literary revenge.

Pope's wealth brought him a country villa at Twickenham on the Thames outside of London, where he indulged his passion for gardening. The celebrated grotto he designed – a subterranean passageway stuccoed with seashells, precious ores, and pieces of looking-glass – was a favorite refuge for Pope, whom that other great satirist, Lord Byron, once aptly described as the "most *faultless* of Poets, and almost of men." ■

Pope asserted that he wrote "The First Satire of the Second Book of Horace Imitated" with great speed (in a letter to Jonathan Swift he said it was "writ in two mornings"). Writing during a bout of illness in December 1732–January 1733, he seems to have used whatever paper was at hand: part of the draft was dashed off on the back of a physician's prescription. The poem takes the form of a spirited dialogue with an old friend, William Fortescue, a lawyer whom Pope had met through the poet and playwright John Gay, and is a delightful example of Pope's wonderfully natural satiric genius at work. Maynard Mack has conjectured that at least portions of Pope's draft (this is the fourth of its eight pages) were written and revised by the poet as he lay in bed, recuperating at the London house of a noble admirer.

from **The First Satire of the Second Book of Horace Imitated**

I nod in company, I wake at night,
Fools rush into my head, and so I write.

. . .

Satire's my weapon, but I'm too discreet
To run a muck, and tilt at all I meet;
I only wear it in a land of Hectors,
Thieves, Supercargoes, Sharpers, and Directors.

Fronti Fides

MARTINI SCRIBLERI VERA EFFIGIES.

A Letter to the Publisher

He was, in modern parlance, a nérvosé. Abnormally sensitive to stimuli, his frail organization responded frantically to the slightest outward touch. If you looked at him he would spit poison, and he would wind himself into an endless mesh work of intrigues and suspicions if you did not. But it was not only in malignity and contortions that Pope's sensitiveness showed itself; throughout his life he gave proof of a tenderness which was something more than a merely selfish susceptibility, and of a power of affection as unmistakeable as his power of hate.

Lytton Strachey, in the Spectator, *November 20, 1909*

Newspaper and pamphlet attacks on Pope were frequent and often savage. One such publication, issued anonymously in response to the 1729 Variorum edition of The Dunciad, *was* Pope Alexander's Supremacy and Infallibility examin'd, *for which this engraving served as the frontispiece. Modeled (very loosely) on a 1722 portrait of Pope by Kneller, the simian caricature ridicules his misshapen form and at the same time plays on the way in which Pope's enemies frequently abbreviated his signature: "A. P——E." In other versions of this notorious lampoon, the great poet was topped off with the papal crown.*

William Blake

1757–1827

Blake's rapt, ethereal expression has helped to make this portrait famous. Allan Cunningham, Blake's unreliable contemporary biographer, explains that while Blake sat for the portrait, he was describing a visit he had received from the angel Gabriel. The original life-scale painting by Thomas Phillips, on which this engraving is based, is in the collection of the National Portrait Gallery in London.

WILLIAM BLAKE DISPLAYED his most famous traits – an almost hallucinatory imagination and a gift for rendering his visions on paper – very early. At age eight he is said to have told his mother that angels were roosting in a nearby tree.

He did not attend school, learning to read and write at home. When he was 10 he began to study drawing, and then went to work for James Basire, an engraver, who assigned his apprentice to draw the Gothic details of Westminster Abbey and its monuments. Enraptured, Blake slowly taught himself to draw by making portraits of statues in various churches. He so cherished this habit that at 21, when he began studying at the Royal Academy, he said he hated using live models. He earned his living as an engraver and simultaneously wrote poetry, including wicked epigrams to tease his artist friends.

In 1782, Blake married; the next year his first book, *Poetical Sketches,* was published by friends. Soon afterward Blake developed a method – cheaper than letterpress – for etching his poems and drawings onto copper plates, and used it to produce his first illuminated book, the *Songs of Innocence,* in 1789.

In Felpham, where the Blakes lived from 1800 to 1803 under the patronage of a rich dilettante poet, William Hayley, Blake was falsely accused of sedition by a soldier he had offended. He was acquitted, but the experience helped to develop his prophetic mythology, in which imagination would save mankind from repressive forces.

Little known during his lifetime as an artist and nearly unknown as a poet, Blake was "discovered" by the Pre-Raphaelites in the mid-19th century, but did not become famous for his rare double genius until nearly a century after his death. Now his poetry is read widely even separately from the illustrations in which he cradled his texts; his impact on later generations of poets has been profound. ■

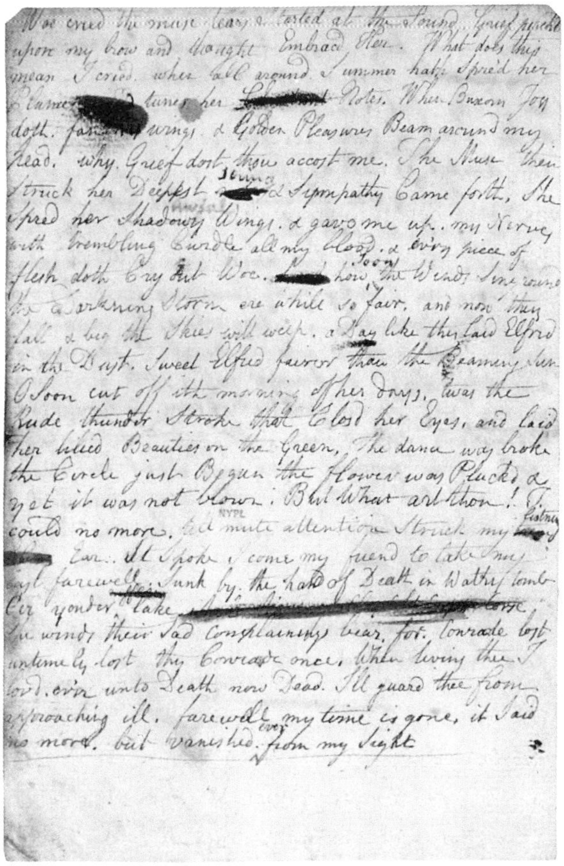

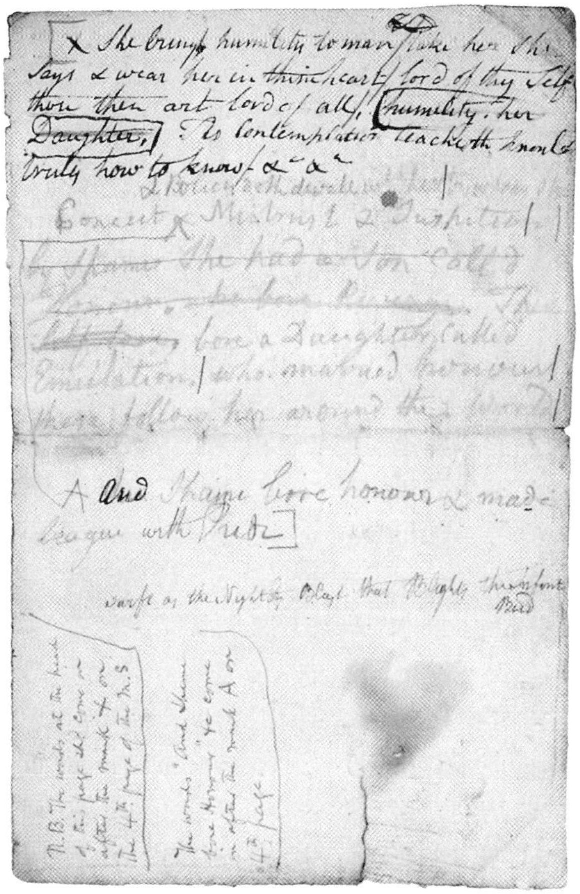

*These pages are from the earliest surviving Blake manuscript, ca. 1783,
which contains the texts for two poetic prose pieces. The first, beginning
"Then she bore Pale Desire," was published in 1903 by William Michael
Rossetti as "The Passions." The other, shown here, begins "Woe cried the
Muse"; it was first published in 1925 in* The Writings of William Blake,
*edited by Sir Geoffrey Keynes. This manuscript bears markings and notes
by Rossetti in red ink.*

from Woe, Cried the Muse

Woe, cried the muse, tears Started at the Sound. Grief percht upon my
brow and thought Embrac'd Her. "What does this mean," I cried, "when
all around Summer hath spred her Plumes and tunes her Notes, When
Buxom Joy doth fan his wings & Golden Pleasures Beam around my head?
Why, Grief, dost thou accost me?" . . . "O'er yonder lake the winds their
sad complainings bear for Comrade lost, untimely lost, thy Comrade once.
When living thee I lov'd ev'n unto Death; now Dead, I'll guard thee from
approaching ill; farewell my time is gone." It said no more, but vanished
ever from my Sight.

A continuation of the prophetic mode begun the previous year with America, *in its verse and magnificent illustrations* Europe – A Prophecy *(1794) recounts Blake's own complex mythological version of history: human misery would end, he predicted, with the unification of the goddess and god he called Enitharmon and Los, and the triumph of Orc, the rebellious, creative spirit with whom Blake identified. Only 12 copies of* Europe *are extant, and the Berg Collection's is perhaps the finest. Portions of some designs are color-printed, but all the plates are exquisitely painted, in watercolor and opaque pigment, by Blake himself.*

Robert Blair, a Scottish Presbyterian minister, published little verse, but his contemplative "The Grave" (1743) was immensely popular well into the 19th century. Blake was commissioned by entrepreneur R. H. Cromek to illustrate an 1813 edition of "The Grave," and produced drawings for it, but was infuriated when Cromek chose Luigi Schiavonetti, a more conventional artist, to make the etchings, using Blake's designs. Ironically, Blake's 12 illustrations for "The Grave" proved to be the poet's best-known work during his lifetime.

I was having these Blake visions [ca. 1949]. So. The thing I understood from Blake was that it was possible to transmit a message through time which could reach the enlightened, that poetry had a definite effect, it wasn't just pretty, or just beautiful, as I had understood pretty beauty before – it was something basic to human existence, or it reached something, it reached the bottom of human existence. But anyway the impression I got was that it was like a kind of time machine through which he could transmit, Blake could transmit, his basic consciousness and communicate it to somebody else after he was dead, in other words, build a time machine.

Allen Ginsberg in The Paris Review *(Spring 1966)*

William Upcott, a friend and patron of Blake's, kept an autograph album containing signatures, drawings, verses, and autobiographical notes by many prominent "authors, artists, foreigners & miscellaneous" (according to the album's hand-lettered title page). Samuel Taylor Coleridge, Charles Lamb, John Clare, Leigh Hunt, and many other distinguished men (and a few women) are represented. In the meticulously assembled index, Upcott lists Blake as "artist & author of designs for Blair's Grave &c." Beneath the left arm of his soaring angel, Blake himself has noted that he was "Born 28. Nov' 1757 in London / & has died several times since."

Robert Burns

1759–1796

This lithograph is based on a portrait by John Beugo, an Edinburgh engraver and close friend of Burns's; great admirers of each other's work, the two were neighbors in St. James's Square during the poet's second residence in the capital (winter 1787–88). Beugo's engraving, used as the frontispiece for the First Edinburgh Edition (April 1787) of Burns's poems, was considered by the poet and his family to be a superb likeness.

IT WAS, IN William Hazlitt's words, the very "real heart of flesh and blood beating in his bosom" that prompted Robert Burns to write poetry of almost unprecedented vitality and popularity. His first book – *Poems, Chiefly in the Scottish Dialect* – caused a sensation in 1786. Feted by the Edinburgh elite, the young poet was dubbed the "Heaven-taught plowman" by an early reviewer. Burns had certainly led a hardscrabble life, but this Scots-speaking poet was far more sophisticated than his aristocratic, English-speaking patrons realized.

Born into a family of impoverished tenant farmers, Burns received little formal education, but he read widely and attended school when he could be spared from the fields. Like his father, Burns failed as a farmer, seriously undermining his health in the process. Hard-drinking and lusty, he shocked many of his more righteous neighbors, for as one of his biographers noted: "It was not so much that he was conspicuously sinful as that he sinned conspicuously."

Discovering Robert Fergusson's Scots poems in 1782, Burns was inspired to write in the vernacular, going against the grain of the Scottish Enlightenment, which promoted the abandonment of Scots in favor of standard English. But in other respects, Burns was a true child of the Enlightenment. Anti-clerical, irreverent, and radical of temperament, he wrote brilliant satires of religious hypocrisy and was outspoken in his support of the American and French revolutions.

Burns spent the last years of his life working tirelessly on two important anthologies of Scottish traditional songs. Both collections were true labors-of-love for Burns: he worked – without credit and, despite severe financial strains, without pay – collecting, editing, and restoring ancient Scottish airs and songs, as well as writing verses of his own to accompany many of the traditional tunes. ∎

Bannockburn (Bruce to His Troops)

Scots, wha hae wi' WALLACE bled,
Scots, wham Bruce has aften led,
Welcome to your gory bed, –
    Or to glorious victorie. –

Now's the day & now's the hour;
See the front o' battle lour;
See approach proud EDWARD's power,
    Edward! Chains and Slaverie!

Wha will be a traitor-knave?
Wha can fill a coward's grave?
Wha sae base as be a slave?
    Traitor! Coward! Turn & flie!

Wha for SCOTLAND's king and law,
Freedom's sword will strongly draw,
FREE-MAN stand, or FREE-MAN fa',
    Caledonian! on wi' me!

By Oppression's woes and pains!
By your sons in servile chains!
We will drain our dearest veins,
    But they shall be – shall be free!

Lay the proud Usurpers low!
Tyrants fall in every foe!
LIBERTY's in every blow!
    Forward! Let us Do, or Die!!!

First published in 1794, "Bannockburn" celebrates the victory of the Scottish army (led by the Scots hero Robert Bruce) over the vastly larger English forces of Edward II on June 24, 1314. Burns was familiar with a folk tradition that Bruce's troops had marched into battle to the tune of an ancient air ("Hey tutti taitie"); "This thought," he later explained, "warmed me to a pitch of enthusiasm on the theme of Liberty & Independence, which I threw into a kind of Scots Ode, fitted to the Air, that one might suppose to be the gallant ROYAL SCOT's address to his heroic followers on that eventful morning." The Berg Collection's manuscript is an alternate version of the poem, for which Burns has rewritten the last line of each stanza to fit the tune of "Lewie Gordon." The printed text at right follows the punctuation and capitalization of the standard edition, but includes textual adjustments to reflect the variations in the Berg Collection's manuscript.

[John Allen] . . . has lent me a quantity of Burns's unpublished, and never-to-be-published, Letters. They are full of oaths and obscene songs. What an antithetical mind! – tenderness, roughness – delicacy, coarseness – sentiment, sensuality – soaring and grovelling, dirt and deity – all mixed up in that one compound of inspired clay!

Lord Byron, in his Journal, December 13, 1813

With characteristic disinterested generosity, Burns asked his friend Alexander Cunningham to intercede on the behalf of James Clarke, Master of the Moffat Grammar School, who in 1791 and early 1792 was in a heated row with the authorities and was convinced that he was about to lose his position. Here the poet writes (at "3 o'clock morn"), effusively, to thank Cunningham for his help with "poor Clarke" and to congratulate him on his recent engagement. After the poet's death, Cunningham took a leading part in promoting a subscription for the benefit of Burns's wife, Jean, and their children.

For honest Men delight will take
To shew you favour for his sake,
Will flatter You; and Fool & Rake
 Your steps pursue;
And of your Father's name will make
 A snare for you.

Let no mean hope your Souls enslave;
Be independent, generous, brave;
Your Father such example gave,
 And such revere!
But be admonished by his grave,
 And think, & fear.

Wm Wordsworth

ABOVE AND OPPOSITE

*During a tour of Scotland in August 1803, Wordsworth, his sister
Dorothy, and Coleridge visited the churchyard at Dumfries where
Robert Burns (a poet Wordsworth had admired since youth) was buried.
Several years later he composed his somber and admonitory "To the
Sons of Burns, after visiting their Father's grave, August 1803," and in the
summer of 1806 copied it out (above left) for Mrs. Eliza Fletcher, a recent
acquaintance. Mrs. Fletcher sent this copy to Gilbert Burns, one of the
poet's brothers, noting (in a letter now attached to the manuscript) that
Wordsworth "said you were the only person to whom he would give a
copy of it . . . he thought the subject of this was of too private and sacred
a nature for the publick eye." He apparently changed his mind. First
published in Wordsworth's* Poems *(1807), "To the Sons of Burns" was
also included in the first collected edition of his work, the two-volume
1815* Poems *(opposite).*

[Wordsworth] was of an opposite poetic type to Coleridge. Whether the bulk of his genuine poetic achievement is so much greater than Coleridge's as it appears, is uncertain. Whether his power and inspiration remained with him to the end is, alas, not even doubtful. But Wordsworth had no ghastly shadows at his back, no Eumenides to pursue him; or if he did, he gave no sign and took no notice; and he went droning on the still sad music of infirmity to the verge of the grave. His inspiration never having been of that sudden, fitful and terrifying kind that visited Coleridge, he was never, apparently, troubled by the consciousness of having lost it.

T. S. Eliot, "Wordsworth and Coleridge" in The Use of Poetry and the Use of Criticism *(London, 1933)*

106

VII.

ADDRESS

TO THE SONS OF BURNS

After visiting their Father's Grave.

(August 14th, 1803.)

Ye now are panting up life's hill!
'Tis twilight time of good and ill,
And more than common strength and skill
    Must ye display
If ye would give the better will
    Its lawful sway.

Strong-bodied if ye be to bear
Intemperance with less harm, beware!
But if your Father's wit ye share,
    Then, then indeed,
Ye Sons of Burns! for watchful care
    There will be need.

107

For honest men delight will take
To shew you favor for his sake,
Will flatter you; and Fool and Rake
    Your steps pursue:
And of your Father's name will make
    A snare for you.

Let no mean hope your souls enslave;
Be independent, generous, brave!
Your Father such example gave,
    And such revere!
But be admonish'd by his Grave,—
    And think, and fear!

Samuel Taylor Coleridge 1772–1834

This portrait, engraved by James Thomson after a painting by James Northcote, R.A., was published for the European Magazine, *1819.*

Coleridge the innumerable, the mutable, the atmospheric; Coleridge who is part of Wordsworth, Keats, and Shelley; of his age and of our own; Coleridge whose written words fill hundreds of pages and overflow innumerable margins; whose spoken words still reverberate, so that as we enter his radius he seems not a man, but a swarm, a cloud, a buzz of words, darting this way and that, clustering, quivering, and hanging suspended. So little of this can be caught in any reader's net.

Virginia Woolf, The Death of the Moth *(London, 1942)*

SAMUEL TAYLOR COLERIDGE was the almost preternaturally gifted youngest child of a Devonshire vicar, yet at Jesus College, Cambridge, he did not distinguish himself. Abandoning his studies, he fled his debtors and enlisted in the 15th Light Dragoons. Assuming the memorable alias of Silas Tomkyn Comberbache, Coleridge proved to be an inept soldier. In 1794, he met the then radical poet, and future Poet Laureate, Robert Southey. Together they planned a utopian "Pantisocracy" on the wild banks of the Susquehanna. The scheme collapsed, its only outcome Coleridge's marriage to Southey's sister-in-law, Sara Fricker – a most disastrous union.

In 1795, Coleridge met Wordsworth, and three years later the two of them published, anonymously, the first edition of the *Lyrical Ballads*. This revolutionary work, in its deliberate break with poetic tradition, helped inaugurate English Romanticism and set "modern" poetry on its course. After 1800, Coleridge struggled with a debilitating addiction to opium. He also fell hopelessly in love with Sara Hutchinson, Wordsworth's sister-in-law. His emotional and physical life progressively more miserable, he nevertheless developed a reputation as an unusually trenchant critic, brilliant lecturer, and dazzling conversationalist.

Coleridge, who virtually stopped producing verse after 1807, wrote in a great variety of poetic styles: colloquial and conversational ("This Lime-Tree Bower My Prison"); demonic and hallucinatory ("Kubla Khan"); grotesque and medievalizing ("Christabel"); profoundly introspective ("Dejection: An Ode"). He devoted the last decades of his life to the formulation of a grand synthesis of philosophy, theology, and poetry, but this ambitious project would remain incomplete. Perhaps, as Kathleen Raine has written, Coleridge was "hampered by the very vastness of his own mental process." ■

from **This Lime-Tree Bower My Prison [Addressed to Charles Lamb, of the India House, London]**

Well, they are gone, and here must I remain,
This lime-tree bower my prison! I have lost
Beauties and feelings, such as would have been
Most sweet to my remembrance even when age
Had dimm'd mine eyes to blindness! They, meanwhile,
Friends, whom I never more may meet again,
On springy heath along the hill-top edge,
Wander in gladness, and wind down, perchance,
To that still roaring dell, of which I told;
The roaring dell, o'erwooded, narrow, deep,
And only speckled by the mid-day sun;
Where its slim trunk the ash from rock to rock
Flings arching like a bridge; – that branchless ash,
Unsunn'd and damp, whose few poor yellow leaves
Ne'er tremble in the gale, yet tremble still,
Fann'd by the water-fall! and there my friends
Behold the dark green file of long lank weeks,
That all at once (a most fantastic sight!)
Still nod and drip beneath the dripping edge
Of the blue clay-stone . . .

One of Coleridge's most beautiful "conversation" poems, "This Lime-Tree Bower My Prison" is addressed to the essayist Charles Lamb, an intimate friend and lifelong admirer of the poet. In a July 1797 letter to Robert Southey, Coleridge explained the poem's genesis: "Charles Lamb has been with me for a week – he left me Friday morning. – The second day after Wordsworth came to me, dear Sara [Coleridge's wife] accidentally emptied a skillet of boiling milk on my foot, which confined me during the whole time of C. Lamb's stay & still prevents me from all walks longer than a furlong. – While Wordsworth, his Sister, & C. Lamb were out one evening; sitting in the arbour of T. Poole's garden, which communicates with mine, I wrote these lines. . . ."

Like his fabled conversation, Coleridge's notebook entries can dazzle and overwhelm. The entries in this handsome notebook are a testament to the scale of Coleridge's erudition and the breadth of his intellectual curiosity. There are many notes on literature (Dante, Spenser, Milton); philosophical, mathematical, and theological ruminations; sketches, outlines, and drafts for his 1818 course of lectures; and entries in Greek and Hebrew. There are also fascinating glimpses into Coleridge's personality and psychology. One cryptic note, headed "A Gnostic Whisper" (ca. May 1815), develops his then highly ambivalent attitude toward Wordsworth; and here, Coleridge ponders the position of the man of Genius in society.

from the Clasped Vellum Notebook (ca. May 1815)

Of the injurious Manner in which men of Genius are treated, not only as Authors, but even more when they are in social Company. – A is believed or talked of as a man of unusual Talent – People are anxious to meet him – if he says little or nothing, they wonder at the Report – never considering whether they themselves were fit either to excite or if self-excited to receive & comprehend him – But if with the simplicity of Genius he attributes more to them than they have . . . – & then they complain of him as not conversing but lecturing – he is quite intolerable – might as well be hearing a sermon – in short, in answer to some objection A replies, Sir! this rests on the distinction between an Idea & an Image, & likewise its difference from a perfect Conception. – Pray, Sir! explain! Because he can not do, & therefore does not, as if they were talking of a game of whist – Lord! how long he talks! . . . What is the practical Result? – That the man of Genius should live as much as possible with Beings that simply *love* him, from relationships or old associations – or with those that have the same feelings with himself, should he meet with them – but in all other company to cease to be the man of Genius – to make up his mind to appear dull or common place, as a Companion – to be the most silent, except upon the most trivial Subjects, of any in the company – to hum off questions with a joke or a pun, as not suiting a Wine table – & to trust only to his Writings.

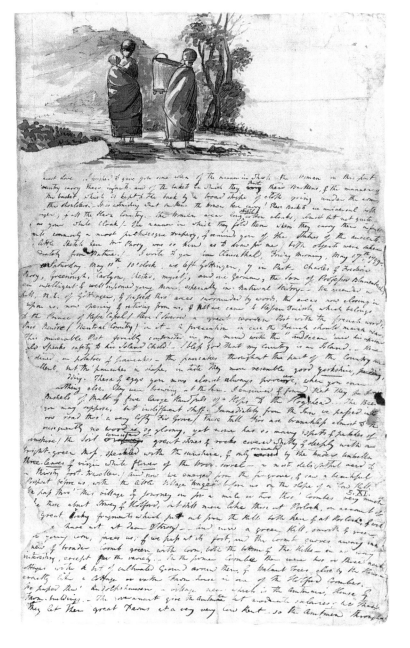

In September 1798, Coleridge
embarked for Germany
with William and Dorothy
Wordsworth. He had long
thought of visiting that country,
planning to "complete" his
education there. In this very long
(four densely written pages), very
large (9½" x 15½"), and richly
detailed letter from Clausethal,
the acutely observant and restless-
ly curious Coleridge writes to his
wife about his wanderings. The
pen-and-ink drawing at the head
of the letter (meant to illustrate
the "astonishing" manner in
which German women carry
their infants and "Burthens")
was drawn by Charles Parry,
a medical student whom
Coleridge had met at Göttingen
and with whom he traveled
in the Hartz Mountains.

Leigh Hunt

1784–1859

In this engraving, which appeared in Fraser's Magazine's *"Gallery of Illustrious Literary Characters" (December 1834), Hunt is portrayed as the rather dashing author of* Lord Byron and Some of His Contemporaries *(1828), a highly indiscreet memoir in which Hunt painted an unflattering portrait of his late friend, collaborator, and often exasperated patron. Hunt had good reason to be bitter: Byron had virtually abandoned Hunt and his family in Italy after the* Liberal *collapsed after only four issues; and it was only the advance for his book on Byron that allowed Hunt, his wife, and their numerous children to finally return to England. Hunt's comments on Byron in his later* Autobiography *(1850) were much more temperate.*

LEIGH HUNT WROTE voluminously during a long life that stretched from the height of English Romanticism well into the Victorian era. Although he wrote many fine essays and a superb autobiography, Hunt's most impressive gift was a generous and selfless ability to recognize – in others – genius and originality greater than his own. He introduced Keats to Shelley and, as a prescient and fearless editor, did much to promote the work of both poets. Closely associated with Byron, Hunt collaborated with him in Italy on the short-lived *Liberal* and later would encourage many other writers, including Browning, Tennyson, and Dickens. But it is for his connection to the "second generation" of great Romantic poets that he is best remembered.

Educated at Christ's Hospital school, Hunt was precocious, publishing his first volume of verse at 17. As editor (from 1808 to 1821) of the radical weekly the *Examiner*, Hunt and his circle (sarcastically dubbed the "Cockney School" by *Blackwood's*) were frequently attacked by the *Tory* press. Hunt was even imprisoned for two years, after the *Examiner* attacked the Prince Regent (the future King George IV) as a corpulent "Adonis" of 50 years – as Keats wrote, Hunt was prosecuted "for showing truth to flatter'd state."

Financial difficulties plagued Hunt for most of his life, but his later years were more settled: in 1844 he finally came into a legacy from Shelley, and three years later he received a Civil List Pension. Although he had to endure his friend Dickens's caricature of him – in *Bleak House* – as the genial sponger, Mr. Skimpole, Hunt was much beloved by his many friends and family. As Virginia Woolf wrote, in a tribute to Hunt: "These free, vigorous spirits advance the world; when one lights on them in the strange waste of the past, one says 'Ah, you're my sort.'" ∎

Abou Ben Adhem.

Abou Ben Adhem (may his tribe increase)
Awoke one night from a deep dream of peace,
And saw, within the moonlight in his room,
Making it rich, and like a lily in bloom,
An angel, writing in a book of gold.—
Exceeding peace had made Ben Adhem bold,
And to the presence in the room he said,
"What writest thou?" The vision rais'd its head,
And with a look made of all sweet-accord,
Answered "The names of those who love the Lord."
"And is mine one?" said Abou. "Nay, not so,"
Replied the angel.—Abou spoke more low,
But cheerly still; and said, "I pray thee then,
Write me as one, that loves his fellow men."

The angel wrote, and vanish'd.—The next night
It came again, with a great wakening light,
And shew'd the names whom love of God had bless'd,
And lo! Ben Adhem's name led all the rest.

Leigh Hunt.

He is a good man, with some poetical elements in his chaos; but spoilt by the Christ-Church Hospital and a Sunday newspaper, — to say nothing of the Surrey gaol, which conceited him into a martyr. But he is a good man. When I saw *Rimini* in MS., I told him that I deemed it good poetry at bottom, disfigured only by a strange style. His answer was, that his style was a system, or upon system, or some such cant; and, when a man talks of system, his case is hopeless.

Lord Byron, letter to Thomas Moore, June 1, 1818

Hunt wrote poetry throughout his life, but the 1830s produced two of his most popular and charming poems: "Jenny Kissed Me" and "Abou Ben Adhem" (both first published in 1838). The latter poem, a simple parable revealing that to love man is to love God, has been memorized by generations of schoolchildren. Well known for his boundless generosity and warmheartedness, Hunt surely approved of Abou Ben Adhem's instructions to the visiting angel to "Write me as one that loves his fellow men." Indeed, that line was used as Hunt's epitaph.

George Gordon Byron, Lord Byron 1788–1824

Ah, what a poet Byron would have been had he taken his meals properly, and allowed himself to grow fat – and not have physicked his intellect with wretched opium pills and acrid vinegar, that sent his principles to sleep, and turned his feelings sour! If that man had respected his dinner, he never would have written *Don Juan*.

William Makepeace Thackeray (writing as Michael Angelo Titmarsh), "Memorials of Gourmandizing" in Fraser's Magazine *(June 1841)*

THE SON OF a notoriously profligate father and an unstable mother, George Gordon Byron, Baron Byron found himself famous overnight when the first two cantos of *Childe Harold's Pilgrimage* were published in 1812. He then threw himself into radical politics while embarking on a series of love affairs that are chronicled in his marvelous letters and journals. In 1815, Byron married the brilliant but prim Annabella Milbanke. Their separation (one year and 13 days later), which Byron dissected tearfully in "Fare Thee Well," caused a scandal. "Mad – bad – and dangerous to know" in the opinion of Lady Caroline Lamb, one of his more ardent admirers, Byron left England in 1816, disgusted by the hypocrisies of the Regency society that had so recently lionized him. He never returned.

Frequently attacked as immoral, Byron's poetry enjoyed a tremendous vogue in England and throughout Europe. He died in Greece, where he had gone to assist the Greeks in their war of independence against their Ottoman oppressors – a rather Romantic demise that only enhanced Byron's great fame. Widely read but hardly *comme il faut*, even in death Byron aroused moral indignation. The Reverend John Styles of Kennington, England, memorialized Byron as a "denaturalised being who, having exhausted every species of sensual gratification and drained the cup of sin to its bitterest dregs, is resolved to show that he is no longer human, even in his frailties, but a cool, unconcerned fiend." The Victorians were especially disapproving, yet even that most exacting of critics, Matthew Arnold, expressed the sort of exasperated awe that Byron can inspire in even the firmest of natures:

When Byron's eyes were shut in death,
We bow'd our head and held our breath.
He taught us little; but our soul
Had felt him like the thunder roll. ∎

Byron was a master at dramatic self-presentation. His great good looks – which dazzled many a beholder – were beguiled by a subtly cultivated glamour to which many succumbed helplessly. Here he plays the grand seigneur, relaxing in what would appear to be a rather princely Italian palazzo, surrounded by both literary and military trappings – a combination that would have greatly pleased this most Byronic of poets. Elements of this engraving (the poet's head, posture, and all-important open shirt-collar) are based on Thomas Phillips's famous half-length oil portrait of Byron, which is now at Newstead Abbey.

from **Fare Thee Well**

Fare thee well! and if for ever –
  Still for ever, *fare thee well* –
Even though unforgiving, never
  'Gainst thee shall my heart rebel. –
Would that breast were bared before thee
  Where thy head so oft hath lain,
While that placid sleep came o'er thee
  Which thou ne'er can'st know again:
Would that breast by thee glanc'd over,
  Every inmost thought could show!
Then, thou wouldst at last discover
  'Twas not well to spurn it so –
Though the world for this commend thee –
  Though it smile upon the blow,
Even its praises must offend thee,
  Founded on another's woe –
Though my many faults defaced me,
  Could no other arm be found
Than the one which once embraced me,
  To inflict a cureless wound!
Yet – oh, yet – thyself deceive not –
  Love may sink by slow decay,
But by sudden wrench, believe not,
  Hearts can thus be torn away . . .

This is the earliest draft of one of Byron's most celebrated poems – a passionate cri de coeur *to his estranged wife, the former Annabella Milbanke. Theirs was an ill-starred match: Byron was soon exasperated by his wife's composure and propriety (he called her the "Princess of Parallelograms"); and poor Annabella soon enough could not tolerate her husband's outrageous behavior and inscrutable black moods (which she finally determined were* not *due to insanity). In the court of public opinion, Byron came off poorly; he was accused of all sorts of enormities and depravities in relation to Annabella. Legend has it that Byron wept as he composed "Fare Thee Well," but Lady Byron was not moved to throw herself back into her husband's arms, as Madame de Staël thought any woman would have done who had been addressed with such ardent verses. The manuscript's numerous stains and smears are, in fact, ink blottings.*

Percy Bysshe Shelley

1792–1822

The date on this drawing, 1798, is undoubtedly incorrect, as Shelley was only 6 years old in that year. The portrait clearly shows a youth of 15 or 16, the age at which Shelley, while studying at Eton, began to gain a certain reputation for his eccentric – if not iconoclastic – behavior and opinions.

PERCY BYSSHE SHELLEY drowned in Italy at age 29; a volume of Keats – doubled-back in a pocket – helped identify the body when it washed ashore. Cremation was quickly arranged, and with equal speed the Shelley legend was born. If one can credit the testimony of that colorfully dubious Romantic hanger-on, Edward John Trelawny, the angelic Shelley's heart was too pure to be consumed by fire – and, seeing this, Trelawny plucked it, unburnt, from the pyre. In England, Shelley was hardly mourned: one obituary triumphantly noted, "Shelley, the writer of some infidel poetry, has been drowned; *now* he knows whether there is a God or no."

Though born to the landed aristocracy, Shelley abandoned his family's conservative heritage at an early age, co-authoring an incendiary pamphlet, *The Necessity of Atheism*, during his first year at Oxford. He was promptly expelled, for – as a classmate later reasoned – how could society "keep such a rotten sheep in their fold?" A highly unconventional life followed. After the suicide of his first wife, Shelley married Mary Wollstonecraft Godwin, the daughter of prominent radical intellectuals and the future author of *Frankenstein*. Shelley and Mary settled in Italy, where Shelley – the center of the famous "Pisan Circle" – wrote his most beautiful works, leaving the grim masterpiece, "The Triumph of Life," unfinished at his death.

Shelley's poetry – intense, elaborately symbolic, dreamily abstract – was fired by a genuine, if unworldly, passion to reform the world. Critics have often been hostile; Lionel Trilling observed that Shelley "should not be read, but inhaled through a gas pipe." But in his greatest works – "Adonais," "Ode to the West Wind," *Prometheus Unbound* – Shelley is a powerful and moving poet, not the "beautiful and ineffectual angel" descried by Matthew Arnold "beating in the void his luminous wings in vain." ■

A Cat in distress
Nothing more or less
Good folks I must faithfully tell ye
As I am a sinner
It wants for some dinner
To stuff out its own little belly

2

You might'nt easily guess
All the modes of distress
Which torture the tenants of earth
And the various evils
Which like many devils
Attend the poor dogs from their birth

3

Some a living require
And others desire
An old fellow out of the way

Sonnets

To a balloon, laden with Knowledge

Bright ball of flame that thro' the gloom of east
Silently takest thine etherial way
And with surpassing glory dimmest each ray
Twinkling amid the dark blue Depths of heaven
Unlike the Fire thou bearest, soon shall thou
Fade like a meteor in surrounding gloom
Whilst that unquenchable is doomed to glow
A watch light by the patriots lonely tomb
A ray of courage to the opprest & poor,
A spark tho' gleaming on the hovels' hearth
Which thro' the tyrants' gilded domes shall roar
A beacon in the darkness of the earth
A Sun which o'er the renovated scene
Shall dart like truth where falshood yet has been

Sonnet

*On launching some bottles filled with Know-
ledge into the Bristol Channel.*

Vessels of heavenly medicine! may the breeze
Auspicious waft your dark green forms to shore
Safe may ye stem the wide surrounding roar
Of the wild whirlwinds & the raging seas;
And oh! if liberty e'er deigned to stoop
From yonder lowly throne her crownless brow
Sure she will breathe around your emerald group
The fairest breezes of her west that blow,
Yes! she will waft ye to some freeborn soul
Whose eye beam kindling as it meets your freight
Her heaven born flame in suffering earth will light
Until its radiance gleams from pole to pole
And tyrant=hearts with powerless envy burst
To see their night of ignorance dispersed.

OPPOSITE AND ABOVE

*Shelley's earliest poetic endeavor, composed around 1803–5, was "A
Cat in Distress," which he supposedly sent to his adoring sister, Elizabeth,
when she was away at school. She copied out the poem (opposite),
decorating her transcription with a pencil and watercolor sketch. Shelley's
heartfelt, if somewhat condescending, empathy for the poor and down-
trodden is expressed clearly; Elizabeth's transcription has preserved
what may be her brother's earliest quarrel with the established order. The
Esdaile Notebook (above) contains almost 60 early poems by Shelley,
most of them in his hand, as well as one or two poems by his first wife,
Harriet Westbrook Shelley. These two sonnets ("To a balloon, laden
with Knowledge" and "On launching some bottles filled with Knowledge
into the Bristol Channel") were inspired by some of Shelley's more
fanciful methods of distributing the political broadsides with which he
sought to remake the world.*

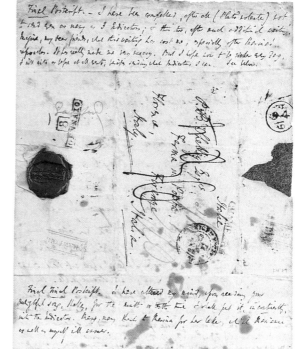

After completing three acts of his greatest achievement, Prometheus
Unbound, *Shelley immediately began work on another, this time histor-
ically based, drama,* The Cenci. *Shelley was sanguine that the new work
would prove to be both eminently stageable and popular, but he was
wrong on both counts: the play's exploration of incest and parricide,
as well as its allegedly blasphemous treatment of religion, placed it
beyond the pale for most Regency readers and critics.* The Cenci *was
dedicated to Leigh Hunt, who wrote Shelley on December 2, 1819
(above), to acknowlege "that true & cordial honour." Presumably,
the ink blots that add some drama to both sheets of Hunt's letter are
accidental embellishments.*

I received a copy of the *Cenci*. . . .
There is only one part of it I am
judge of — the poetry and dramatic
effect. . . . You, I am sure, will
forgive me for sincerely remarking
that you might curb your magna-
nimity, and be more of an artist,
and load every rift of your subject
with ore. The thought of such
discipline must fall like cold chains
upon you, who perhaps never
sat with your wings furled for six
months together. And is not this
extraordinary talk for the writer of
Endymion, whose mind was like
a pack of scattered cards?

*John Keats, letter to Percy Bysshe
Shelley, mid–late August 1820*

John Keats

1795–1821

The artist Joseph Severn sailed to Italy with Keats in September 1820 and attended him in his final illness. He wrote that Keats struck one immediately by "a peculiarly dauntless expression, such as may be seen in the face of some seamen" and that he was graced with "hazel eyes of a wild gipsy-maid in colour, set in the face of a young god." Almost all of Severn's numerous portraits of Keats (except the well-known 1819 miniature, on which this 1883 engraving is based, and the haunting sketch of Keats on his deathbed) are posthumous and are, undoubtedly, rather idealized representations of the poet.

JOHN KEATS – THE London-born son of a prosperous livery-stable manager – was a pugnacious, ardent, generous, and high-spirited youth who cared little for books, at least in his early schooldays. A classmate later reminisced that he was possessed of an absolute "*penchant*" for fighting, that thrashing friends, brothers – *anyone* – was "meat & drink" to him. But by age 14, Keats's passion was literature, which "he devoured rather than read." Orphaned in 1810 when his mother died, probably of tuberculosis, he was apprenticed to an apothecary. He later trained – halfheartedly – in surgery, often penning doggerel instead of taking proper notes during anatomy lectures. In December 1816, Keats finally abandoned medicine for poetry, flabbergasting his guardian, who called him a "Silly Boy."

Keats's second book, the woefully ambitious *Endymion* (1818), was savaged by the Tory press. *Blackwood's* sneered: "It is a better and wiser thing to be a starved apothecary than a starved poet; so back to the shop Mr John." Undeterred, Keats entered a period of rapid intellectual and poetic development, beautifully charted in his remarkable and moving letters. With astonishing speed, supreme confidence, and the greatest artistic mastery, Keats wrote virtually all his major poetry between January and September of 1819. This amazing creative flowering could not last.

On February 3, 1820, Keats coughed blood for the first time ("That drop of blood is my death warrant. I must die."). Here began the final phase of an excruciating *danse macabre* with the disease that had claimed not only his mother, but – little more than a year before – his beloved younger brother, Tom. He traveled to Italy in a desperate effort to regain his health, but died there on February 23, 1821, directing that the epitaph for his Roman grave be inscribed "Here lies one whose name was writ in water." ∎

A work of beautifully modulated despair and supremely controlled utterance, Keats's "Ode on Melancholy" explores the poet's painful sense that joy is inseparable from sorrow, that beauty is always transitory. This manuscript – a draft of the poem's third and final stanza – was originally attached to another sheet on which Keats had drafted the poem's first two stanzas. That sheet – brought to America by the poet's brother George in 1820, and later given by him to John Howard Payne, the actor, playwright, and lyricist of "Home Sweet Home" – eventually found its way to the Princeton University Library. The present manuscript was once owned by Charles Brown, a businessman with a toe-hold in London's literary circles, who was one of the poet's closest friends. His pencil sketch of Keats, which is now in the National Portrait Gallery in London, is perhaps the best portrait we have of the poet.

from **Ode on Melancholy**

She dwells with Beauty – Beauty that must die;
    And Joy, whose hand is ever at his lips
Bidding adieu; and aching Pleasure nigh,
    Turning to poison while the bee-mouth sips:
Ay, in the very temple of Delight
    Veil'd Melancholy has her sovran shrine,
        Though seen of none save him whose strenuous tongue
    Can burst Joy's grape against his palate fine;
His soul shall taste the sadness of her might,
        And be among her cloudy trophies hung.

from Keats's last letter to Fanny Brawne

To be happy with you seems such an impossibility! it requires a luckier Star than mine! it will never be. . . . Shakespeare always sums up matters in the most sovereign manner. Hamlet's heart was full of such Misery as mine is when he said to Ophelia "Go to a Nunnery, go, go!" Indeed I should like to give up the matter at once – I should like to die. I am sickened at the brute world which you are smiling with. I hate men and women more. I see nothing but thorns for the future. . . . I wish you could infuse a little confidence in human nature into my heart. I cannot muster any – the world is too brutal for me – I am glad there is such a thing as the grave – I am sure I shall never have any rest till I get there. . . . I wish I was either in your a[r]ms full of faith or that a Thunder bolt would strike me.

God bless you – J. K –

When Keats's love letters to Fanny Brawne were first published in 1878, not a few eminent Victorians were shocked. Matthew Arnold abhorred a great poet's "abandonment of all reticence and all dignity." And Swinburne, recoiling from the "piteous outcries" of Keats's "wailing and shrieking agony," asserted that the letters ought never to have been printed, adding for good measure that "it is no less certain that they ought never to have been written." Intense and extravagant they are, and perhaps none more so than this wrenching letter from August 1820, in which Keats, seriously ill, writes to Fanny, probably for the last time, with a wild and bitter alloy of helpless fury and equally helpless passion. This is the letter's third and last page.

... who but the supreme and perfect artist could have got from a mere colour a motive so full of marvel: and now I am half enamoured of the paper that touched his hand, and the ink that did his bidding, grown fond of the sweet comeliness of his charactery, for since my childhood I have loved none better than your marvellous kinsman, that godlike boy, the real Adonis of our age. . . . In my heaven he walks eternally with Shakespeare and the Greeks. . . .

Oscar Wilde, letter to Emma Speed (née Keats), the poet's niece, in March 1882, thanking her for the gift of the original manuscript of Keats's "Sonnet on Blue," after he lectured in her hometown of Louisville, Kentucky

Leigh Hunt Esqr with I. K's best greeting

ENDYMION:

A Poetic Romance.

BY JOHN KEATS.

" THE STRETCHED METRE OF AN ANTIQUE SONG."

LONDON:
PRINTED FOR TAYLOR AND HESSEY,
93, FLEET STREET.

1818.

Keats inscribed this copy of the first edition of Endymion *(1818) to that minor poet and generous soul, Leigh Hunt. He can fairly be said to have begun, as he himself wrote, as Hunt's "élève"; but Keats's estimation of his erstwhile mentor changed rapidly, and he could be scathing. Hunt was "certainly a pleasant fellow in the main when you are with him," Keats wrote his brother George in late 1818, but he "does one harm by making fine things petty and beautiful things hateful."*

Emily Brontë

1818–1848

Folded and stored away for many years on top of a wardrobe, and almost forgotten, this fragment of Branwell's painting of the four Brontë children was discovered by Mary Anne Nicholls (the second wife of Charlotte Brontë's husband) in 1914, some 80 years after it was painted. Believing that the only accurate likeness in Branwell's painting was that of Emily, Arthur Bell Nicholls had cut out her portrait and destroyed the remainder of the canvas. The fragment is now in the National Portrait Gallery, London.

AFTER THEIR MOTHER died in 1821, the Brontë children – Emily, Anne, Charlotte, and Branwell – were raised by their aunt, a crusty and affectionate soul, fond of a bit of snuff, who was much beloved by her charges. Their father – Irish-born and hard-driven – was the Anglican incumbent of Haworth, an isolated village surrounded by the Yorkshire moors. The children were each other's constant companions; from an early age their "highest stimulus . . . lay in attempts at literary composition." Except for a few brief intervals, Emily spent her entire life at Haworth, immersed in the quotidian patterns of the Parsonage and her beloved moors, and writing, with a sort of calm frenzy, some astounding poems and one of the greatest novels in the English language.

Probably around 1826, Emily and her sister Anne plunged headlong into the Pacific kingdoms of Gondal and Gaaldine. In elaborate prose narratives (now lost) and poems, the two sisters explored these imaginary islands with an intensity that made the unreal real. Here is Emily at 16, sitting at the kitchen table at Haworth Parsonage:

Taby [the cook] said just now come Anne pillopatate [peel a potato]. . . . The Gondals are discovering the interior of Gaaldine Sally mosley is washing in the back Kitchin . . . Anne and I have not Done our music exercise which consists of b majer Taby said on my putting a pen in her face Ya pitter pottering there instead of pilling a potate I answered O Dear, O Dear, O Dear I will derictly with that I get up, take a Knife and begin pilling. . . .

Of this incredible family, Emily Brontë was only the most incredible. Her poems, many of which were forged in the "Gondal Sagas," have the elemental force of the " 'large utterance' of a baby god"; they speak with a steely conviction that, as Virginia Woolf said of Brontë's achievement in *Wuthering Heights*, could "free life from a dependence on facts." ■

Her nature stood alone. . . . Alone in its negation of all that other mortals hold most dear; alone in its unwavering pity for frailty and error . . . not framed for bliss, and yet too strong for an eternity of groping torment, alien alike to spirits lost and blest. Rather, resolved into the elements she worshipped, she seems to find her immortality, transmuted, given back to earth again. Her spirit — one with the keen and searching airs that sweep wildly and sweetly over the wastes she loved — finds rest, and liberty, and wandering peace.

Charlotte Mew, "The Poems of Emily Brontë" in Temple Bar *(August 1904)*

Brontë's spiritual rapport with animals and the natural world was often considered eccentric; as Elizabeth Gaskell reported, one local maintained that she "never showed regard to any human creature; all her love was reserved for animals." In "And Like Myself Lone Wholly Lone," the poet expresses an almost mystical identification with a chained hawk and its "shining eyes." At least as early as 1841, the year the poem was written, Brontë had a pet hawk ("Nero"), which was kept in a cage after it was rescued from an abandoned nest on the moors. This manuscript, on the back of which are written eight lines of cursive Latin in Brontë's hand, is here reproduced just slightly larger than its actual size.

When Days of Beauty Deck
the Earth

When days of Beauty deck the earth
Or stormy nights descend
How well my spirit knows the path
On which it ought to wend

It seeks the consecrated spot
Beloved in childhood's years
The space between is all forgot
Its sufferings and its tears

This packed page of manuscript (which measures only 2¹/₄" x 3³/₄") contains three poems from November 1838: "When Days of Beauty Deck the Earth," "Still Beside That Dreary Water," and "There Swept Adown That Dreary Glen." An early draft of another poem ("The Starry Night Shall Tidings Bring") appears, crossed out, beneath the sketch of hills. On the verso, Brontë wrote out three more poems in the minute, cramped hand that so alarmed the Reverend Patrick Brontë. He was convinced that Emily and his other children – all of whom wrote their poems and stories in a tiny, almost indecipherable script – would ruin their eyesight (for Christmas in 1833, he gave Charlotte a manuscript notebook inscribed with this admonition: "All that is written in this book, must be in a good, plain and legible hand").

William Cullen Bryant

1794–1878

"Poetry is the worst mask in the world behind which folly and stupidity could attempt to hide their features," Bryant wrote in the first of four lectures on poetry that he delivered to the New York Athenaeum in April 1825, shortly after moving to the city. George Parker depicted the unmasked poet in this engraving after a painting by Henry Inman.

What estranges him from us is the tone of many of his poems — sonorous, grave, noble, edifying, oratorically ruminative. What we miss in him, a fair bit of the time, is what we find (to make an outrageous contrast) in John Donne. In Donne, we hear a complex man talking, whereas Bryant sometimes sounds like a statue.

Richard Wilbur, "A Word from Cummington" in Under Open Sky: Poets on William Cullen Bryant, *edited by Norbert Krapf (New York, 1986)*

WILLIAM CULLEN BRYANT repeatedly tried to give up poetry: "I said the poet's idle lore / Shall waste my prime of years no more, / For Poetry, though heavenly born, / consorts with poverty and scorn," he once wrote. He did not succeed. Although he became a powerful, liberal newspaper editor and New York City notable, history has obstinately enshrined him as a poet.

Bryant was born in Cummington, Massachusetts, where his mother's parents had been among the town's first settlers. His father was an overworked physician and occasional poet himself, who treated his sickly son Cullen with "hydropathy" – dunking him in the cold water of a nearby spring. Under his father's equally blunt tutelage, Bryant learned to write and rewrite poems before he was 10, when his first poem was published, in the *Northampton Hampshire Gazette*. Three years later, his political protest poem "The Embargo" was printed as a booklet. When Bryant's dreams of attending Yale were frustrated by his family's limited means, he began studying for the bar and practiced law reluctantly until 1825, when he moved to New York City to become editor of the *New York Review*.

In 1827, Bryant went to work for the New York *Evening Post*, launching his lifetime career. As editor-in-chief and part owner of the newspaper, he crusaded for the abolition of slavery, and helped to build both the Republican party and New York's Central Park. Meanwhile, he published four books of poetry, becoming the country's foremost poet and the first American poet to become well-known abroad. Bryant was 84 when, after giving a speech in Central Park, he suffered a fall which proved fatal. More than 60 years before, *The North American Review* had first published "Thanatopsis," Bryant's haunting poem on death, which attracted much attention to the young poet. In fact, throughout Bryant's long and richly productive life, "Thanatopsis" would remain his most acclaimed achievement. ■

Thanatopsis.

By William Cullen Bryant.

To him who, in the love of Nature, holds
Communion with her visible forms, she speaks
A various language; for his gayer hours
She has a voice of gladness and a smile
And eloquence of beauty, and she glides
Into his darker musings with a mild
And healing sympathy that steals away
Their sharpness ere he is aware. When thoughts
Of the last bitter hour come like a blight
Over thy spirit, and sad images
Of the stern agony and shroud and pall,
And breathless darkness and the narrow house,

"Thanatopsis" enjoys many distinctions: it is the most famous of Bryant's efforts, the earliest well-known work by an American poet, and a masterful example of blank verse. Repeatedly revised, it was composed over a six- to ten-year period, beginning, Bryant later said, when he was still a teenager. Before publishing the poem in his 1821 Poems, Bryant added a new beginning and ending. This fair copy was made in 1877, the year before the poet died. The title means "a view of or musing upon death."

Ralph Waldo Emerson 1803–1882

Walt Whitman said of his mentor, Emerson, "His usual manner carried with it something penetrating and sweet beyond mere description. There is in some men an indefinable something which flows out and over you like a flood of light – as if they possessed it illimitably – their whole being suffused with it. Being – in fact that is precisely the word. Emerson's whole attitude shed forth such an impression. . . . Never a face more gifted with power to express, fascinate, maintain."

NOW CELEBRATED AS an essayist, thinker, and poet, Ralph Waldo Emerson described his frustration with his own verse in acutely poetic prose: "though days go smoothly enough they do not bring me in their fine timely wallets the alms I incessantly beg of them. Where are the melodies, where the unattainable words?"

Born in Boston, Emerson was a clowning child and a middling student. At Harvard he was named class poet – after six others declined. Following college he taught school reluctantly, then studied theology, and became minister of a Boston church.

In 1829, he married Ellen Tucker, an aspiring poet. Her death from tuberculosis after only two years left him so desolate and bewildered that he opened her coffin 14 months later, on one of his daily visits to her tomb. Finally he resigned his ministry and sailed for Europe, staying ten months. On his return, he found his vocation, as a lecturer and essayist. With other members of the new Transcendental Club, he formed a philosophy that bestowed its hope and expectations on the individual soul.

Nature, his first and best-known book, begins with a paean to "The Poet," as prophet of creation's exquisite mysteries. Much of Emerson's own poetry is written in the stiff rhythm of iambic tetrameter, but his experiments inspired innumerable others, from Walt Whitman to Robert Frost.

In 1834 he remarried, but suffered again when Waldo, his first son, died at age five. His first book of poetry, published in 1847, includes *Threnody,* a long elegy to his son. By 1872, when Emerson listed favorite books during a speech in Washington, D.C., bookstores as far away as Boston promptly sold out of those titles. After gradually losing his formidable memory, he died quietly at 79. ∎

The earliest extant draft of "The Rhodora" is dated *1834, a year in which Emerson wrote several of the best poems of his life. This holograph is probably a fair copy written out later, since the text is the same as that of the version published in Emerson's* Poems *(1847), except in punctuation. The poem displays an idea that also became an anchor of Emerson's famous 1836 essay, "Nature," where he expresses it this way: "No reason can be asked or given why the soul seeks beauty. Beauty, in its largest and profoundest sense, is our expression for the universe."*

Emerson is so essentially a poet that whole pages of his are like so many litanies of alternating chants and recitations. His thoughts slip on and off their light rhythmic robes just as the mood takes him. . . .

Emerson is a citizen of the universe who has taken up his residence for a few days and nights in this travelling caravansary between the two inns that hang out the signs of Venus and Mars. This little planet could not provincialize such a man.

Oliver Wendell Holmes, Ralph Waldo Emerson *(Boston, 1892)*

from **The Rhodora**

Rhodora! if the sages ask thee why
This charm is wasted on the earth
    and sky,
Tell them, dear, that if eyes were
    made for seeing,
Then Beauty is its own excuse for being:
Why thou wert there, O rival of the rose!
I never thought to ask, I never knew:
But, in my simple ignorance, suppose
The self-same Power that brought me
    there brought you.

Henry David Thoreau

1817–1862

This wooden pencil was made by Henry David Thoreau, whose father, John, was a pencil manufacturer. When Henry returned to Concord after attending college, he developed better methods of preparing graphite until his family's pencils were, according to contemporary accounts, the best available in America. But Thoreau refused to devote himself to the family business, preferring to write and walk in the woods. Many of his Concord neighbors found this behavior puzzling.

AS A QUIET, iconoclastic young man, Henry David Thoreau burned most of his poems. His mentor, Ralph Waldo Emerson, had praised his poetry earlier as "the purest strain, and the loftiest, I think, that has yet pealed from this unpoetic American forest," but Emerson's enthusiasm quickly cooled. At his suggestion, Thoreau turned to journal-writing (he wrote little poetry thereafter) and spent two years, from 1845 to 1847, living quietly at the edge of a pond. This experience produced *Walden*, a book of nature-writing and philosophical commentary larded with some of the surviving early poems. Posthumously, *Walden* made him famous worldwide.

Born in Concord, Massachusetts, Thoreau rarely left his hometown except to attend Harvard, only 18 miles away. Long solitary walks were a lifelong habit, and supplied him with literary fodder. In a commencement speech at college, Thoreau startled the audience and foreshadowed his life by suggesting that man work only on the seventh day, and designate "the other six his Sabbath of the affections and the soul, – in which to range this widespread garden, and drink in the soft influences and sublime revelations of nature."

After Harvard, Thoreau taught briefly at the Concord grade school he had attended, but quit over his refusal to paddle the pupils. After operating his own school for three years, he went to live and write at Emerson's home in Concord. Thoreau never married, and his only known love was Ellen Sewall, the sister of one of his students, whose father forbade her to marry a man as odd as Thoreau.

In poetry as in life, Thoreau followed his own course: his poems owe more to the 17th-century metaphysical poets than to his contemporaries. After his death, the increasing fame of his prose won his poetry new, kinder appraisal, even from Emerson. In 1865, the first collection of Thoreau's poetry was published. ■

Thoreau wrote of this 1856 daguerreotype by Benjamin Maxham: "my friends think [it] is pretty good though better looking than I." His friend Horace Hosmer thought it the best likeness of Thoreau he had ever seen. It was made at the request of an admirer apparently unknown to Thoreau, who mailed him $5 in June 1856, with a request for two of his books and a daguerreotype of himself.

It was a pleasure and a privilege to walk with him. He knew the country like a fox or a bird, and passed through it as freely by paths of his own. He knew every track in the snow or on the ground, and what creature had taken this path before him. . . . Under his arm he carried an old music-book to press plants; in his pocket, his diary and pencil, a spy-glass for birds, microscope, jack-knife and twine. He wore a straw hat, stout shoes, strong gray trousers, to brave scrub-oaks and similax, and to climb a tree for a hawk's or squirrel's nest. He waded into the pool for the waterplants, and his strong legs were no insignificant part of his armor.

Ralph Waldo Emerson, in the Atlantic Monthly, *August 1862*

from **The Fall of the Leaf**

Far in the woods, these golden days,
  Some leaf obeys its Maker's call;
And through their hollow aisles it plays
  With delicate touch the prelude of the Fall.

Gently withdrawing from its stem,
  It lightly lays itself along
Where the same hand hath pillowed them,
  Resigned to sleep upon the old year's throng.

The loneliest birch is brown and sere,
  The furthest pool is strewn with leaves,
Which float upon their watery bier,
  Where is no eye that sees, no heart that grieves.

The jay screams through the chestnut wood;
  The crisped and yellow leaves around
Are hue and texture of my mood –
  And these rough burrs my heirlooms on the ground.

The threadbare trees, so poor and thin –
  They are no wealthier than I;
But with as brave a core within
  They rear their boughs to the October sky.

Poor knights they are which bravely wait
  The charge of Winter's cavalry,
Keeping a simple Roman state,
  Discumbered of their Persian luxury.

*The two extant manuscripts of "The Fall of the Leaf"
differ greatly, perhaps because the poem was part of a
series; in the longer of these versions (part of which is
shown here), Thoreau incorporated stanzas from three
of the other four poems in the series. To complicate
matters, the published text differs greatly from both the
drafts: Franklin Benjamin Sanborn, an acquaintance
and early biographer of Thoreau who edited some
of his poems, evidently decided that a poem entitled
"The Soul's Season" belonged with "The Fall of the
Leaf," and combined them into one in his 1895 Poems
of Nature.*

Dozens of specimens of leaves, grasses, and wildflowers were tucked into this journal kept by Sophia, John, and Henry David Thoreau, with the botanical names of each written by Thoreau on loose scraps of paper. The remarkably well-preserved specimens were gathered by Thoreau, and perhaps his brother and sister, in the course of long walks in the woods around Concord during the 1840s. Thoreau was especially fascinated by leaves. "In the veins and fibres of the leaf see the future tree," he wrote in an October 1843 journal entry. In Walden he developed the idea further, describing the leaf as a blueprint for all life: "The Maker of this earth but patented a leaf."

Henry Wadsworth Longfellow 1807–1882

Like Walt Whitman, Longfellow is usually pictured with a flowing beard. In fact he was clean-shaven until his 50s. In 1861, his face was burned when he attempted to help his second wife, Fanny, whose dress had caught fire as she sat sealing some locks of her daughters' hair into small packets in the library of their Cambridge, Massachusetts, home. She died a day later, to Longfellow's bitter grief.

Longfellow, reminiscent, polish'd, elegant, with the air of finest conventional library, picture-gallery or parlor, with ladies and gentlemen in them, and plush and rosewood, and ground-glass lamps, and mahogany and ebony furniture, and a silver inkstand and scented satin paper to write on.

Walt Whitman, quoted in Edgar Lee Masters, Whitman *(New York, 1937)*

NO ENGLISH-LANGUAGE poetry has been parodied more than Henry Wadsworth Longfellow's (Lewis Carroll's contribution is included in this book). That is a double-edged tribute to the vast popularity he enjoyed during his lifetime – he was by far the most famous American poet – and to his lack of cachet today. The same moral exhortations, exaggerated sing-song rhythms, and heart-rending narratives that were so satisfying to 19th-century readers sound fusty to the jaded modern ear.

Born in Portland in what is now the state of Maine, Longfellow attended Bowdoin College. His translation of one of Horace's odes prompted the college to offer the 18-year-old Longfellow its new professorship in modern languages, although he spoke none, other than English. Back at Bowdoin after three years of study in Europe, he overcame the dearth of textbooks by writing them himself. In 1835, he went on to Harvard, and thereafter rapidly produced *Voices of the Night* (1839), his first book of poems; *Ballads and Other Poems* (1841); and the prescient, earnest *Poems on Slavery* (1842). In 1845, he published *Poets and Poetry of Europe*, a massive anthology he had helped to translate from a dozen languages.

Soon afterward, especially after resigning from Harvard in 1854, Longfellow wrote the three long narrative poems for which he is most remembered, *Evangeline, A Tale of Acadie*, *The Song of Hiawatha*, and *The Courtship of Miles Standish*. The accidental death of his second wife in 1861 devastated him, but he continued to write and to receive visits and mail from fans. When he went to England in 1868, Queen Victoria received him. In 1884, two years after his death, a bust of Longfellow was reverently unveiled in Poets' Corner at Westminster Abbey. He is the only American poet represented there. ■

A Psalm of Life

What the heart of the young
man said to the psalmist

Tell me not, in mournful numbers,
Life is but an empty dream!
For the soul is dead that slumbers,
And things are not what they seem.

Life is real! Life is earnest!
And the grave is not its goal;
Dust thou art, to dust returnest,
Was not spoken of the soul.

Not enjoyment, and not sorrow,
Is our destined end or way;
But to act, that each to-morrow
Find us farther than to-day.

Art is long, and Time is fleeting,
And our hearts, though stout and brave,
Still, like muffled drums, are beating
Funeral marches to the grave.

In the world's broad field of battle,
In the bivouac of Life,
Be not like dumb, driven cattle!
Be a hero in the strife!

Trust no Future, howe'er pleasant!
Let the dead Past bury its dead!
Act, – act in the living Present!
Heart within, and God o'erhead!

Lives of great men all remind us
We can make our lives sublime,
And, departing, leave behind us
Footprints on the sands of time;

Footprints, that perhaps another,
Sailing o'er life's solemn main,
A forlorn and shipwrecked brother,
Seeing, shall take heart again.

Let us, then, be up and doing,
With a heart for any fate;
Still achieving, still pursuing,
Learn to labor and to wait.

Even before it was published in Voices of the Night, *Longfellow's first book of original poems, "A Psalm of Life" had been widely printed and admired – despite Longfellow's having "kept it some time in manuscript, unwilling to show it to any one, it being a voice from my inmost heart, at a time when I was rallying from depression." He was probably referring to his anguish over the death of his first wife, Mary, in 1835. Largely forgotten now, the poem has nonetheless left a scrap of itself in the English language, in the phrase "footprints on the sands of time," from stanza 7. This holograph copy was written out by Longfellow nearly 20 years after the book was printed, by which time the poet surely knew that he had left his own mark.*

The first of Longfellow's long narrative poems based on American history, Evangeline (1847) describes the separation of two young lovers, French Acadians expelled from Nova Scotia into New England during the French and Indian Wars. In the final version, Longfellow changed "Still stands the forest primeval," the opening of this fragment, to "This is the forest primeval." That is also the poem's famous first line. Samuel Longfellow, who wrote the note of authentication, was the poet's brother and reverent biographer.

Oliver Wendell Holmes 1809–1894

> You, more than anybody else, have the literary traditions of New England in your blood and brain. It was this special flavor that pleased my palate as I read. I recognize our surly limitations, but feel also the edging of poetry – northern, not tropical, but sincere and good of its kind.
>
> *James Russell Lowell, letter to Oliver Wendell Holmes, December 28, 1884*

MORE THAN ANY other American poet, Oliver Wendell Holmes had multiple callings: he was also a physician, professor, philosopher, and prose writer. Born in Cambridge, Massachusetts, where his father was a minister, he became known at Harvard for playful poems, one of which mournfully describes dancing with girls who were often taller than his own five feet.

In September 1830, while in law school, Holmes read a *Daily Advertiser* article reporting plans to scrap the rotting but historic Boston frigate *Constitution*. In response, he wrote a rousing protest poem; signed "H.," "Old Ironsides" was printed and reprinted around the nation. The following year, "The Last Leaf," a precocious, melancholy rumination on old age, won him more praise. Then, putting poetry aside and abandoning the law, he went to Paris to study medicine. (Holmes's son and namesake later studied law with alacrity, and went on to become one of the most famous justices in the history of the U.S. Supreme Court.) On his return to the United States in 1835, Holmes wrote several prize-winning medical papers, and published his first book of *Poems*.

Holmes oversaw the early toddling steps of both American literature and American medicine. When a group of Boston intellectuals founded a magazine, it was Holmes who named it *The Atlantic Monthly*. When the dentist W. T. G. Morton pioneered the use of ether as a painkiller, Holmes dubbed the technique "anesthesia." In 1846, he became a professor of medicine at Harvard. As a prose writer he was most famous for the "Breakfast-Table" series, a set of fictional dialogues among the residents of a boardinghouse, in which he humorously presented his liberal ideas. Just before he died at 85, Holmes called himself "the last leaf," referring to his own youthful poem. ∎

This photograph of Holmes by John S. Nutman, & Sons, Photographers, Boston, was found inserted into a copy of his book The Poet at the Breakfast-Table *(1872). In the warm and charming tone of all his "Breakfast-Table" books, Holmes recounts purported conversations around the table of a boardinghouse, with ample running commentary (the book is aptly subtitled "He Talks with His Fellow-Boarders and The Reader"). In this one, he indulges himself in a universal writer's fantasy: "I am going to take it for granted now and henceforth, in my report of what was said and what was to be seen at our table, that I have secured one good, faithful and loving reader, who never finds fault, who never gets sleepy over my pages, whom no critic can bully out of a liking for me, and to whom I am always safe in addressing myself." A few lines later, with an almost audible sigh, he adds, "A writer is so like a lover!"*

Old Ironsides.

Ay, tear her tattered ensign down!
  Long has it waved on high,
And many an eye has danced to see
  That banner in the sky, —
Beneath it rung the battle shout
  And burst the cannon's roar, —
The meteor of the ocean air
  Shall sweep the clouds no more!

Her deck, once red with heroes' blood,
  Where knelt the vanquished foe,
When winds were hurrying o'er the flood
  And waves were white below,
No more shall feel the victor's tread,
  Or know the conquered knee, —
The harpies of the shore shall pluck
  The eagle of the sea!

O better that her shattered hulk
  Should sink beneath the wave, —
Her thunders shook the mighty deep,
  And there should be her grave!
Nail to the mast her holy flag,
  Set every threadbare sail,
And give her to the god of storms,
  The lightning and the gale!

                Oliver Wendell Holmes.

By the time Holmes made this fair copy of "Old Ironsides," the unknown law student who wrote it had become a prominent physician and man of letters. "Old Ironsides" became Holmes's most popular poem, and it is still reprinted as a patriotic lyric. Holmes, who was known for his wit, would probably have been amused to see it taken so seriously.

James Russell Lowell

1819–1891

In 1843, Lowell was in New York, putting out the first (and only) three issues of his magazine, The Pioneer, *and being treated for eye trouble. He also spent a great deal of time in the studio of his painter friend William Page, whose familiar portrait of Lowell (shown here in an engraving by H. B. Hall) is, according to Ferris Greenslet, one of Lowell's early biographers, "a sad and shadowy likeness, much idealized . . . [that] hardly seems like the same man depicted in the daguerreotypes of the time. . . ."*

Lowell was not a grower – he was a builder. He *built* poems: he didn't put in the seed, and water the seed, and send down his sun – letting the rest take care of itself: he measured his poems – kept them within the formula.

Walt Whitman, quoted in Edgar Lee Masters, Whitman *(New York, 1937)*

LIKE HIS CONTEMPORARIES Emerson and Holmes, James Russell Lowell was the son of a minister and attended Harvard. There he studied lackadaisically, and wore a hat in chapel, so in his senior year he was "rusticated" to Concord, Massachusetts. Its people were "savages," he wrote with youthful scorn, and Emerson was "a poor little hawk stooping at flies." From Concord, Lowell wrote the Harvard Class Poem for 1838, a scathing attack on reformers, including the abolitionists he would later join.

Lowell graduated from Harvard Law School, but abandoned his law practice in 1842 to write full time. In 1843, he published his first book of poems. The next year he married Maria White, also a poet, and then went to work for two abolitionist newspapers.

During one year, 1848, Lowell wrote *A Fable for Critics*, a poem poking fun at most of his day's literary figures, including himself, and the first of *The Biglow Papers*. A masterpiece of political satire in verse, the *Papers* employ, to brilliant effect, the first-person vernacular of a fictional Yankee farmer, Hosea Biglow.

Gradually Lowell became associated with the "Fireside Poets," including Longfellow, Holmes, and Bryant. Using conventional prosody and familiar themes, they became famous; Lowell, who attempted more complex verse but faltered at it, was less well known.

In six years, from 1847 to 1853, Lowell suffered the deaths of three of his four children, and of his beloved wife. In the aftermath of these losses, he began lecturing on literature, succeeded Longfellow as a professor at Harvard, and became *The Atlantic Monthly*'s first editor. Toward the end of his life, the former abolitionist became an outspoken racist and fanatical anti-Semite – and a diplomat, representing his country in Spain and, in England, at the Court of St. James's. ■

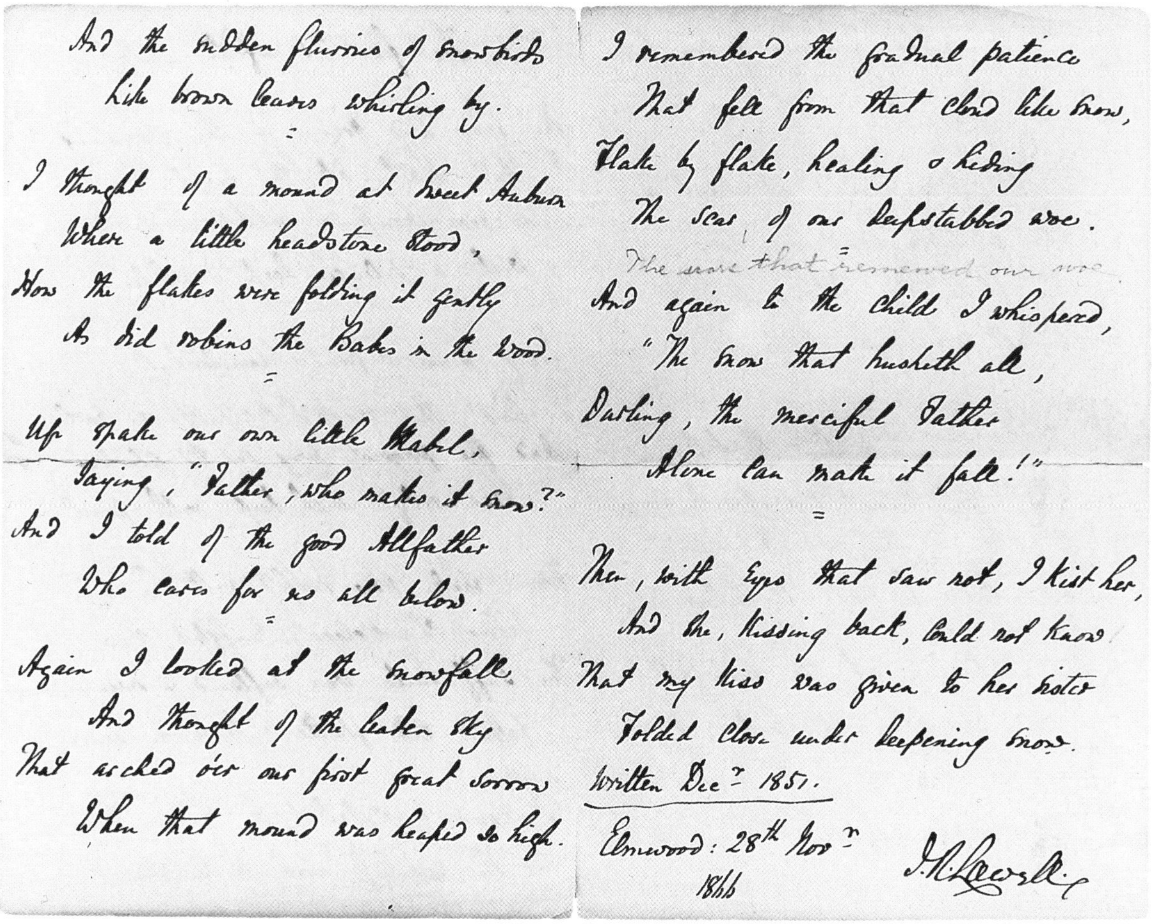

And the sudden flurries of snowbirds
Like brown leaves whirling by.

I thought of a mound at sweet Auburn
Where a little headstone stood,
How the flakes were folding it gently
As did robins the Babes in the wood.

Up spake our own little Mabel,
Saying, "Father, who makes it snow?"
And I told of the good Allfather
Who cares for us all below.

Again I looked at the snowfall
And thought of the leaden sky
That arched o'er our first great sorrow
When that mound was heaped so high.

I remembered the gradual patience
That fell from that cloud like snow,
Flake by flake, healing & hiding
The scar of our deep-stabbed woe.
The scar that renewed our woe.
And again to the child I whispered,
"The snow that husheth all,
Darling, the merciful Father
Alone can make it fall!"

Then, with eyes that saw not, I kist her,
And she, kissing back, could not know
That my kiss was given to her sister
Folded close under deepening snow.
Written Dec. 1851.

Elmwood: 28th Nov. 1866

J. R. Lowell

Blanche, the Lowells' first child, was born in December 1845; her parents were left in "deep-plunged woe" by her sudden death, in March 1847. Mabel, the second child referred to in "The First Snowfall," was born the following September. The poem was first published in the National Anti-Slavery Standard, *a New York–based abolitionist newspaper in which Lowell published poems and prose in the late 1840s and early 1850s, for a salary of $500 a year. Shown here are the second and third pages of a fair copy from 1866; the poem's first two stanzas are printed at the right.*

from The First Snowfall

The snow had begun in the gloaming,
　And busily all the night
Had been heaping field and highway
　With a silence deep and white.

I stood and watched by the window
　The noiseless work of the sky,
And the sudden flurries of snow-birds,
　Like brown leaves whirling by.

Walt Whitman

AFTER A LONG and colorful apprenticeship as newspaperman, schoolteacher, opera devotee, bohemian loafer, and author of a maudlin temperance novel (which he finished "with the help of a bottle of port or what not"), Walt Whitman published the first edition of *Leaves of Grass* in 1855. Virtually ignored by the press, *Leaves of Grass* was a response to Emerson's challenge: "I look in vain for the poet whom I describe . . . we have yet had no genius in America . . . [who] knew the value of our incomparable materials." The supremely self-assured Whitman (Long Island born, of "Mannahatta" the son) was ready to answer the call: "I was simmering, simmering, simmering; Emerson brought me to a boil."

The freely swinging, musical lines of *Leaves of Grass* heralded a new voice in American poetry – operatic, ardent, frankly sensual, brash, and democratic. Whitman continued to recast and expand *Leaves of Grass* throughout his life, and while critics were often scornful, he slowly began to attract many sympathetic, sometimes fervent, admirers. Although he would be the first American poet to win a truly international reputation, the epochal impact of Whitman's poetry – which D. H. Lawrence praised as the "perfect utterance of a concentrated, spontaneous soul" – did not become fully apparent until after World War I.

Whitman retired to Camden, New Jersey, in 1873, where he was paid homage by a stream of visitors, including, in 1882, Oscar Wilde. At the end of his long life, Whitman lovingly superintended the construction of an elaborate, extraordinarily expensive burial-vault for his remains and those of other Whitmans to follow (although only his name appears on the tomb). "Walt Whitman, a kosmos" died on March 26, 1892. ∎

252

The following, on this subject, is from an article entitled "Walt Whitman the Poet of Joy," by Standish O'Grady, in the "Gentleman's Magazine," London, December, 1875:

Of the new ideas which Whitman has cast as seed into the American brain, the importance which he attaches to friendship is the most remarkable. This appears to have been a subject over which he has brooded long and deeply. It is not possible that Whitman could have written as he has upon this and kindred subjects if he were merely a cultivated brain and nothing more. A thin-blooded, weak-spirited man may, doubtless, like Swedenborg, strike profound truths through sheer force of intellect, or may use violent and swelling language with little dilatation in his spirit ; but there is a genuineness and eloquence in Whitman's language concerning friendship which preclude the possibility of the suspicion that he uses strong words for weak feelings. It must not be forgotten that, though now latent, there is in human nature a capacity for friendship of a most absorbing and passionate character. The Greeks were well acquainted with that passion, a passion which in later days ran riot and assumed abnormal forms ; for the fruit grows ripe first, then over-ripe, and then rots. In the days of Homer friendship was an heroic passion. The friendship of Achilles and Patroclus was for many centuries the ideal after which the young Greeks fashioned their character. Nowadays friendship means generally mere consentaneity of opinions and tastes. With the Greeks it was a powerful physical feeling, having physical conditions. Beauty was one of those conditions, as it is now between the sexes. In the dialogues of Plato we see the extraordinary nature of the friendships formed by the young men of his time. The passionate absorbing nature of the relation, the craving for beauty in connection with it, and the approaching degeneracy and threatened degradation of the Athenian character thereby, which Plato vainly sought to stem both by his own exhortations and by holding up the powerful example of Socrates. There cannot be a doubt but that with highly developed races friendship is a passion, and like all passions more physical than intellectual in its sources and modes of expression.

· I will sing the song of companionship ;
I will show what alone must finally compact These ;
I believe These are to found their own ideal of manly
     love, indicating it in me ;
I will therefore let flame from me the burning fires that
     were threatening to consume me ;
I will lift what has too long kept down those smoulder-
     ing fires ;
I will give them complete abandonment ;
I will write the evangel-poem of comrades, and of love ;
For who but I should understand love, with all its sor-
     row and joy ?
And who but I should be the poet of comrades ?

This is strong language and doubtless genuine. Pride and love, I have said, Whitman considers the two hemispheres of the brain of humanity, and by love he means not alone benevolence and wide sympathy and the passion that embraces sexual relation, but that other passion which has existed before, and whose latent strength the American poet here indicates as a burning and repressed flame. Elsewhere he speaks of the sick, sick dread of unreturned friendship, of the comrade's kiss, the arm round the neck—but he speaks to sticks and stones ; the emotion does not exist in us, and the language of his evangel-poems appears simply disgusting.

Yes "disgusting" to fops and artificial scholars and prim gentlemen of the clubs but sane heroic full-blooded natural men will find in it the deepest God-implanted voice of their hearts.

A prominent Canadian psychiatrist, Dr. Richard Bucke spent years developing an idiosyncratic theory of the human mind, which he grandly christened "Cosmic Consciousness." His impassioned reading of Leaves of Grass *convinced him that Whitman was the precursor of a new type of human consciousness in which fear and hate would be displaced by a universalizing love of humanity. Bucke published* Walt Whitman, *his tribute to his master, in 1883, but nowhere in the text does he acknowledge Whitman's decisive hand in the volume: with a ruthlessness that must have wounded his friend's feelings, Whitman cut and rewrote large portions of the text, added important text of his own, and supplied extracts from articles by other writers. On this page from the galleys of Bucke's book, for example, Whitman pasted a clipping from an English magazine and then provided it with both an appropriate introduction and an indignant reply. All of Whitman's additions and revisions were incorporated by Bucke into the final published text.*

OPPOSITE

The painter Thomas Eakins, who lived in Philadelphia (a short ferry ride from Whitman's home in Camden), called on the poet on several occasions between 1887 and 1892, and took masterful portrait photographs of Whitman (those shown are from 1891–92). The earliest of Eakins's photographs were probably made in preparation for his luminous oil portrait of Whitman (1888), which, Whitman approvingly noted, made him look like "a poor old blind despised & dying king," although he thought that the artist erred "just a little – a little – in the direction of the flesh." The day after Whitman's death, Eakins and one of his young pupils made a death mask of the poet's face and shoulders.

A rapturously beautiful poem tracing the birth of the poetic impulse in a young boy stirred by the mournful aria of a mocking-bird on a Long Island beach, "A Child's Reminiscence" was first published in the Saturday Press, *as the magazine's "Christmas offering," on December 24, 1859. It was then included, with slight revisions, in the 1860 (third) edition of* Leaves of Grass. *With continued, and masterful, reshaping and tightening, it appeared in all subsequent editions of* Leaves of Grass, *assuming its final title – "Out of the Cradle Endlessly Rocking" – as part of the "Sea-Shores Memories" group in* Passage to India *(1871), and its final form in the 1881 edition of* Leaves of Grass. *This manuscript was used as printer's copy for the poem's publication in the* Saturday Press.

(follow copy, italics and all, line for line)   2

Rich A Child's Reminiscence

Pre = verse.

Out of the rocked cradle,
Out of the mocking = bird's throat, the musical shuttle,
Out of the boy's mother's womb, and from the nipples of her breasts,
Out of the Ninth = Month midnight,
Over the sterile · sea = sands, and the fields beyond, where the child leaving his bed, wandered alone, bare = headed, bare = foot,
Down from the showered halo and the moonbeams,
up from the mystic play of shadows twining and twisting as if they were alive,
Out from the patches of briars and blackberries,
From the memories of the bird that chanted to me
From your memories, sad brother — from the fitful risings and fallings I heard,

*under notice—under editorial head
Saturday Press Dec 24*

Elliott

Walt Whitman's Poem.

Our readers may, if they choose, consider as our Christmas or New Year's present to them, the curious warble by Walt Whitman of "A Child's Reminiscence" on this our first page — Like the "Leaves of Grass," the purport of this wild and plaintive song, well = enveloped and eluding definition, is positive and unquestionable, like the effect of music. The piece will bear reading many times — perhaps indeed only comes forth, as from recesses, by many repetitions.—

A much admired and widely imitated master of self-definition, Whitman was also a master of self-promotion. His relentless maneuvering for publicity has at times given pause to even his most zealous admirers. Whitman unabashedly proclaimed himself (in an anonymous, Whitman-penned review of the first edition of Leaves of Grass) as "the begetter of a new offspring out of literature." In this editorial notice, published anonymously in the Saturday Press, he recommends "A Child's Reminiscence" to the magazine's readers, helpfully pointing out that Walt Whitman's latest "curious warble" will "bear reading many times – perhaps indeed only comes forth, as from recesses, by many repetitions."

They might have put on his tombstone WALT WHITMAN: HE HAD HIS NERVE. He is the rashest, the most inexplicable and unlikely — the most impossible, one wants to say — of poets. He somehow is in a class by himself. . . . Who would think of comparing him with Tennyson or Browning or Arnold or Baudelaire? – it is Homer, or the sagas, or something far away and long ago, that comes to one's mind only to be dismissed. . . . We can surely say about him, "He was a man, take him for all in all. I shall not look upon his like again" – and wish that people had seen this and not tried to be his like: one Whitman is miracle enough, and when he comes again it will be the end of the world.

Randall Jarrell, "Some Lines from Whitman" in Poetry and the Age (New York, 1953)

Emily Dickinson

1830–1886

At the highest summit of her art, she resembles no one. She begins to cast forward toward the future: to produce poems in which we recognize, as one French critic has said, both the *voyant* faculty of Rimbaud and Mallarmé's feeling for the mystery and the sacredness of the word. . . . [S]he can describe with clinical precision the actual emotional event, the supreme moment of anguish, and even her own death itself. And she finds symbols which fit the event – terrible symbols.

Louise Bogan, "A Mystical Poet" (an address delivered in 1959 at the bicentennial celebration of the town of Amherst, Massachusetts)

EMILY DICKINSON RARELY wandered from her home, a large and imposing presence on Main Street in Amherst, Massachusetts. Thomas Wentworth Higginson – a prominent writer and reformer who with amazed incomprehension had become a friend and important correspondent with Dickinson – saw the Homestead as a "more saintly & elevated 'House of Usher.'" Her father bought her many books, but begged her not to read them, because "they joggle the Mind." She went away to school, but could not accept the "depth and fulness" of religious orthodoxy, and so was unhappy. It is said that she renounced, that she withdrew from the world; but her poems – almost 1,800 that we know of – are held fast in the double-sway of an immediacy of perception and a charged transcendence that joggle the mind as few books can. Few poets have been so alive to the beautiful and evanescent strangeness of the creatures and *things* of this world:

How still the Bells in Steeples stand
Till swollen with the Sky
They leap upon their silver Feet
In frantic melody!

Dickinson's letters – marvelous, obscure, and in an English that is hers alone – place her firmly in a rich world of beloved friends and family. Her power was glimpsed (if with baffled awe) by some few who surrounded her, but Dickinson's fame was posthumous. Her eyes surveyed a kingdom uncharted until our century, when, at last, the world caught up with the "Least Figure – on the road" whose fierce and fearless genius "went out upon Circumference" and struck a Heaven that cannot be reached. ∎

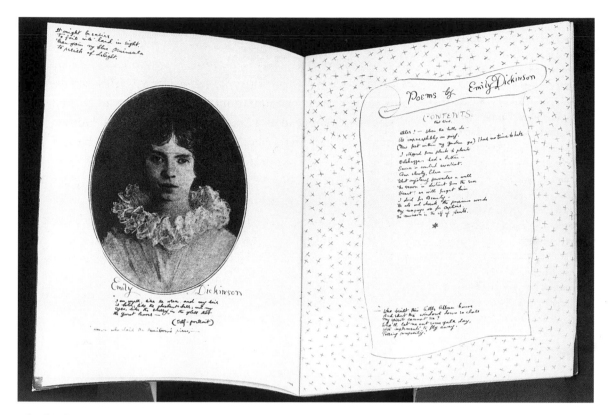

This lovely notebook – inscribed on its front cover in pen-and-ink "for Siegfried / from Emily & Stephen" – was made by Stephen Tennant as a gift for the poet Siegfried Sassoon in 1929, at the height of their rather tumultuous affair. A poet, artist, and aesthete, Tennant had been blessed, according to his biographer, with a mother who delighted in wandering about her villa on the Riviera "putting sprigs of peach blossom in the bird cages and talking about Emily Dickinson." It is therefore not surprising that her son adored Dickinson; he quoted her frequently, and during a sojourn in Bavaria in 1929, he whiled away the hours reading her poems while Sassoon worked on his new book, Memoirs of an Infantry Officer.

Though the Great Waters Sleep

Though the great Waters sleep,
That they are still the Deep,
We cannot doubt –
No vacillating God
Ignited this Abode
To put it out –

*During her lifetime, only a hand-
ful of Emily Dickinson's poems
were published, but she often
sent copies of her poems in letters
to friends. This manuscript of
"Though the Great Waters Sleep"
was sent to Benjamin Kimball
in 1885 as a tribute to his cousin,
Judge Otis P. Lord, one of
Dickinson's dearest friends, who
had died two years earlier. After
Dickinson's death in 1886, her
sister Lavinia discovered a locked
box containing almost 900
poems, and thereafter worked
tirelessly to see that her sister's
poems should be published. The
first two volumes of selections,
prepared in 1890 and 1891 by
Mabel Loomis Todd and Thomas
Wentworth Higginson, finally
brought Dickinson the public she
had never had during her lifetime,
but both seriously misrepresented
her art, for Higginson had altered
Dickinson's texts in an effort
to tame what he considered to be
unorthodoxies of rhyme, meter,
and even language. The printed
text above is taken from Thomas
H. Johnson's* The Poems of Emily
Dickinson, *which is the standard
edition of the poet's work.*

Elizabeth Barrett Browning 1806–1861

As a teenager, Elizabeth Barrett wrote in one of her notebooks, "My mind is naturally independent and spurns that subserviency of opinion which is generally considered necessary to feminine softness." This pencil portrait of her as a girl is thought to be by one of her two sisters, Henrietta or Arabella.

A music that is at once . . . passionate and . . . profound, a creative energy that is born of the spirit, a winged rapture that is born of the soul, a force and fervour of mere utterance that has all the wonder of the prophet, and not a little of the consecration of the priest.

Oscar Wilde, "English Poetesses" in Queen, *December 8, 1888*

ELIZABETH BARRETT BEGAN writing poems at age 4, sitting on the floor of her green-draped bedroom, high among the domes and minarets of her family's mock-Ottoman castle in Herefordshire. She began studying Greek, Latin, and Hebrew soon afterward. Injured at 15 by a fall from a pony, she kept filling tiny leatherbound notebooks with poems in her spindly hand.

Barrett's father doted on her; she was equally fond of him, but the bond later proved stifling when he forbade her to marry. Further isolated by her ill health, which she may have exaggerated, Barrett spent nearly all of her 20s and 30s confined to her father's London townhouse, even as her poems made her famous. In "Lady Geraldine's Courtship," she paid tribute to another poet, Robert Browning, and on January 10, 1845, he wrote her a fervent thank-you beginning, "I love your verses with all my heart, my dear Miss Barrett. . . ." Many more letters followed until, on May 20, Mr. Barrett finally permitted a visit. After 91 visits (carefully counted by Browning), they married secretly on September 12, 1846, and eloped to Italy. Her father never spoke to her again, refusing to answer or even open her pleading letters.

The Brownings settled in a Florence townhouse called Casa Guidi. One morning during the summer of 1849, a few months after the birth of their son Wiedemann, Elizabeth slipped a sheaf of papers into her husband's pocket as he stood gazing out a window. Today the somber yet ardent *Sonnets from the Portuguese* (one of Browning's nicknames for his wife) are among the most famous love poems in English.

In 1861, after living with delicate health and a morphine addiction for all of her adult life, Elizabeth Barrett Browning developed a severe cough and died in her husband's arms. ■

The Berg Collection owns four leatherbound holograph notebooks, each of which easily fits in the palm of a hand, in which Elizabeth Barrett Browning composed drafts of various poems, apparently from the mid-1830s to the mid-1840s. The notebooks contain drafts of many of her published poems, including, in addition to "Grief" and "Tears" (above), "To Flush, My Dog," "The Romaunt of the Page," "The Name," "A Vision of Poets," and "Rhyme of the Duchess May." "Grief" and "Tears" were published in 1844 in her Poems (opposite).

In August 1844, Barrett Browning "with a great gasp of courage" sent this copy of her newly published Poems, *inscribed, to William Wordsworth (then Poet Laureate), whom she had met only once, on May 28, 1836, at a dinner party given by a distant cousin, John Kenyon. Afterward she wrote breathlessly that she had "trembled in my soul and my body" as she sat down next to Wordsworth, but also noted that she would not have "singled him out from the multitude" as a great man.*

128   SONNETS.

TEARS.

THANK God, bless God, all ye who suffer not
More grief than ye can weep for. That is well—
That is light grieving ! lighter, none befel,
Since Adam forfeited the primal lot.
Tears ! what are tears ? The babe weeps in its cot,
The mother singing : at her marriage-bell,
The bride weeps : and before the oracle
Of high-faned hills, the poet hath forgot
That moisture on his cheeks. Commend the grace,
Mourners, who weep ! Albeit, as some have done,
Ye grope tear-blinded, in a desert place,
And touch but tombs,—look up ! Those tears will run
Soon, in long rivers, down the lifted face,
And leave the vision clear for stars and sun.

SONNETS.   129

GRIEF.

I TELL you, hopeless grief is passionless—
That only men incredulous of despair,
Half-taught in anguish, through the midnight air,
Beat upward to God's throne in loud access
Of shrieking and reproach. Full desertness
In souls, as countries, lieth silent-bare
Under the blenching, vertical eye-glare
Of the absolute Heavens. Deep-hearted man, express
Grief for thy Dead in silence like to death ;
Most like a monumental statue set
In everlasting watch and moveless woe,
Till itself crumble to the dust beneath !
Touch it ! the marble eyelids are not wet—
If it could weep, it could arise and go.

These tiny slippers and other items were wrapped in this front page of the July 4, 1861, edition of the Florentine newspaper La Nazione, *inscribed, probably by Robert Browning, "Relics, unknown of whom, Ba's own, July '61." Barrett Browning had died only five days before the newspaper was printed, on June 29. "Ba" was another of Browning's names for his wife.*

Alfred Lord Tennyson

1809–1892

After observing Tennyson at the Art Treasures Exhibition in Manchester on July 30, 1857, Nathaniel Hawthorne wrote in his notebook: "Tennyson is the most picturesque figure, without affectation, that I ever saw; of middle size, rather slouching, dressed entirely in black, and with nothing white about him except the collar of his shirt, which methought might have been clean the day before. He had on a black wide-awake hat . . . beneath which came down his long black hair, looking terribly tangled; he had a long pointed beard, too, a little browner than the hair, and not so abundant as to incumber any of the expression of his face . . . [which] was very dark, and not exactly a smooth face, but worn, and expressing great sensitiveness. . . . [I]n his whole presence I was indescribably sensible of a morbid painfulness in him, a something not to be meddled with."

IN 1824, ALFRED Tennyson – the young son of a learned, unstable, and often violently drunken rector – rushed wildly outside to carve "Byron is dead" in sandstone upon learning of the poet's death. Melancholia and eccentricity seem to have draped Somersby Rectory like suffocating ivy, and Alfred's morbidity and extreme sensitivity could only have been exacerbated by his fondness for prostrating himself among the headstones of the churchyard at moments of acute emotional distress. In his odd way, Dr. Tennyson was sanguine that his handsome, bookish, and extremely nearsighted son (fourth-born of an alarmingly strange brood of 12 children) had an illustrious future: "If Alfred should die," he once noted calmly, "England will have lost a great poet."

Even before he entered Trinity College, Cambridge, Tennyson had published a volume of precocious verse over which the author of *Don Juan* cast his long, and at this period almost inevitable, shadow. His third volume of verse, *Poems* (1833), was expertly and scathingly skewered in the *Quarterly Review* (by the very J. W. Croker who had savaged Keats's *Endymion* in 1818); in the same year, Arthur Hallam, Tennyson's most intimate friend from Cambridge, died suddenly in Vienna. Tennyson was grief-stricken, but out of this loss he began to fashion his supreme achievement, *In Memoriam*, a noble and moving sequence of 131 elegies that, when finally published in 1850, established his fame. He succeeded Wordsworth as Poet Laureate (1850), accepted a peerage (1884), and was brashly hailed from the other side of the Atlantic by Walt Whitman, as "The Boss." Critical reverence then turned to scorn (Auden, while granting Tennyson the "finest ear, perhaps, of any English poet," described him as the "stupidest" of the lot), but recent assessments have restored luster to the reputation of the poet whom Longfellow warmly extolled as the "sweet historian of the heart." ∎

RIGHT AND OPPOSITE
Tennyson's manuscript notebook from 1845–47 contains early drafts and fragments of The Princess, *a curious poem that argues, in a fanciful and convoluted manner, for women's rights. Although it was taken quite seriously by the public of its day (and sold very well), critics and many of those closest to Tennyson were dismayed by the work. Tennyson lived long enough to see it wittily satirized by Gilbert and Sullivan in* Princess Ida *(1884). The notebook is filled with the author's pen-and-ink sketches (mostly heads in profile – see opposite); its text differs radically from that of the work's first edition (1847). Shown at right is an early draft of "Now Sleeps the Crimson Petal."*

Now droops the breeze among the lemon bowers
Nor waves the pale cypress in the palace walk
Nor winks the gold fin in the porphyry font
The firefly wakes & waken thou with me.
Now lies the Earth all Danaë to the stars
And all thy heart lies open unto me
Now slides the silent shining meteor on & leaves
A pale shining furrow as thy thoughts in me.
Now folds the lily all her sweetness up
And slips into the bosom of the lake
So fold thyself my dearest thou & slip
Into my bosom & be lost in me.

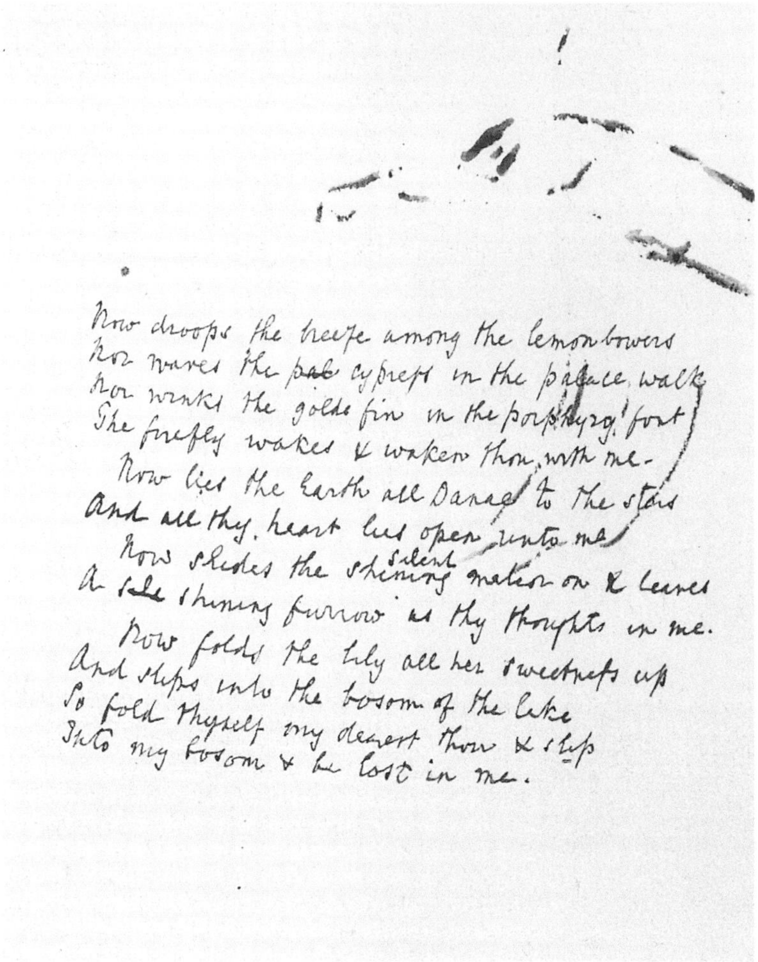

To me, Tennyson shows more than any poet I know (perhaps has been a warning to me) how much there is in finest verbalism. There is such a latent charm in mere words, cunning collocations, and in the voice ringing them, which he has caught and brought out, beyond all others. . . . Yes, Alfred Tennyson's is a superb character, and will help give illustriousness . . . to our Nineteenth Century. . . . His very faults, doubts, swervings, doublings upon himself, have been typical of our age.

Walt Whitman, "A Word About Tennyson" in The Critic *(New York) (January 1, 1887)*

Now Sleeps the Crimson Petal

Now sleeps the crimson petal, now the white;
Nor waves the cypress in the palace walk;
Nor winks the gold fin in the porphyry font.
The fire-fly wakens; waken thou with me.

Now droops the milk-white peacock like a ghost,
And like a ghost she glimmers on to me.

Now lies the Earth all Danaë to the stars,
And all thy heart lies open unto me.

Now slides the silent meteor on, and leaves
A shining furrow, as thy thoughts in me.

Now folds the lily all her sweetness up,
And slips into the bosom of the lake.
So fold thyself, my dearest, thou, and slip
Into my bosom and be lost in me.

I

I was the prince & heir of Alibey:
My father thought a king a king & held
His scepter, as a Pedant holds his wand
To-lash offence, & with long arms & hands
Reach'd out & pickt offenders from the mass
In judgement. Now it chanced that I had been,
While life was yet within the blade, betrothed
To one, a neighbouring Princess. She to me
Was proxy-wedded with a bootless calf
At eight Julies of age. From time to time,
Like odour circling round a hidden flower,
Came murmurs of her beauty from the West.
And still I wore her portrait at my heart.
But when the days drew nigh that I should wed,
My father sent ambassadors with gems
And spices, gifts, to bring fetch her. These brought back
A present, a great labour of the loom,
But therewithal an answer vague as wind.
They saw the king: he took the gifts: he said
There was an old-world compact, that was true:
But then she had a will: was he to blame
And she had fancies, loved to live alone
Among her women: certain, would not wed.
    That morning in the presence room I stood
With Cyril & with Florian, my two friends:
The first a gentleman of broken means
His father's fault: the last my other heart.

William Makepeace Thackeray 1811–1863

Thackeray made thousands of caricatures and drawings, and illustrated his own serialized novels. Little sketches like this one, a pencil portrait of himself caricatured as a jester with mask and bells, identified him to readers of his early published work, since he used aliases such as "Michael Angelo Titmarsh" (like Thackeray, Michelangelo had a broken nose). Through his writings and his drawings, Thackeray became one of the greatest jesters of his time, mimicking and teasing to provoke, he said, compassion as well as laughter.

WILLIAM MAKEPEACE THACKERAY's earliest recorded line of poetry – "Cabbages, bright green cabbages" – is a satire of a sentimental poem about "violets, dark blue violets." He wrote it to lighten the indignities of one of the boarding schools to which he was sent at age five and a half after the death of his father, a British East India Company official in Calcutta. For the rest of his life Thackeray kept writing and sketching parodies.

He spent 16 months at Trinity College, Cambridge, writing for student magazines like the *Snob*, and gambling so much that he had accumulated debts of £1,500 by the time he departed (without a degree) in 1830. Next he went to Germany for eight months and enjoyed "days of youth most kindly and delightful," impaired only by reproachful letters from his mother, and his own Victorian conscience. After unsuccessful stints at the law, painting, and newspaper work, Thackeray became a freelance writer and illustrator in 1837. His 1836 marriage to Isabella Shawe was briefly happy; after the death of their second child in 1839, and the birth of a third in 1840, Isabella suffered a severe depression and was permanently committed to a mental hospital in 1842.

Thackeray used pseudonyms until 1843, when he signed the dedication in *The Irish Sketch Book*. After monthly installments of *Vanity Fair* began appearing in January 1847, the tall, elegant Thackeray was suddenly feted by the same high society that he had skewered in the novel. His poems, like his drawings, run the gamut from incidental doodles to exquisitely apt renderings of scenes and emotions, tinged with his characteristic melancholy. "Thackeray was always trifling, and yet always serious," wrote his friend Anthony Trollope. In prematurely declining health, Thackeray died, aged 52, of a cerebral hemorrhage in the elegant London house he had built for himself. ■

Seventeen young rosebuds in a ring
With clustering sister flowers beset
Twined in a blooming coronet
With Lucy's servants this day bring.
Be this the birth-day wreath she wears
All fresh and bright, and symbolling
The number of her budding years
The ~~modest~~ maiden blushes of her Spring.

~~Fair types~~ Emblems of Love & Youth & Hope
True hearts and friends your Mistress greet.
Continue to be pure and sweet
And grow the lovelier as you ope.
Delicate nursling!
~~Rose that fond Care~~ hath fenced about
By fondest care, and ~~And nursing parents~~ cherished so
You scarce have heard of Storms without
Of thorns that bite or winds that blow.

Thackeray wrote this poem – "Lucy's Birthday" – for the 17th birthday of Lucy Baxter, the youngest child in a New York family who befriended Thackeray as soon as he met them, on his first visit to the United States, in the fall of 1852. He often dropped into their house on Second Avenue for dinner, or to rest in a particular yellow armchair. Thackeray was fond of Lucy, who was about the same age as one of his own two daughters, and he became genially infatuated with her sister Sally, three years older. The poem exists in several manuscript versions, of which this is apparently the first. Although the general sense of the poem varies little from draft to draft, many of the words changed. "Virgin," "pure," "budding," and "maiden" were deleted or replaced by the milder "sweet," "fair," and "young." The poem was published in his first book of poetry, Ballads, in 1855.

Dear Miss Gassiot. I cannot find my fine pens, or I could have made a much finer crown and 3. But I think you beat me, and that your little hand is more legible than that of your most respectful humble Servant

W M Thackeray

Thackeray was proud of his knack for tiny writing, and jokingly said he would earn a living at it if he gave up novels. Here, in an 1861 note to Harriet Gassiot, he has written "The Lord's Prayer" in a circle approximately the size of a dime (with enlargement above).

. . . much pleased with what I saw of him – his manner is simple and unaffected: he shows no anxiety to shine in conversation though full of fun and anecdote when drawn out.

Charles Lutwidge Dodgson (Lewis Carroll), after a meeting with Thackeray on May 9, 1857, quoted in Derek Hudson, Lewis Carroll *(London, 1954)*

Lewis Carroll

1832–1898

Carroll enclosed this 1877 photograph of himself with a note to one of his child-friends, the 12-year-old Florence May Balfour Foster, known as Birdie. "My dear Birdie," he wrote, "I send you one carte and ten kisses. The carte you may keep as long as you like, but I hope you will give me one or two of the kisses back when next we meet. Your loving friend, Lewis Carroll."

Nobody indeed would have been more shocked than Mr. Dodgson at being classed with the anarchical artists who talked about *l'art pour l'art*. But, in spite of himself, he was a much more original artist than they.

G. K. Chesterton, "Lewis Carroll" in The New York Times, *January 24, 1932; reprinted in his* Handful of Authors: Essays on Books & Writers, *edited by Dorothy Collins (London, 1953)*

FOR NEARLY ALL of the 19th century's latter half, a pale, rigid man with a stutter, who wore black ecclesiastical robes, a black top hat, and black and gray cotton gloves, lived at Christ Church college in Oxford. He was Charles Lutwidge Dodgson, a mathematics lecturer and Church of England deacon, so punctilious that he kept records of what food he served each of his dinner guests and where they sat at his table, and a cross-referenced register of every letter he wrote and received, with 98,721 entries.

Under the pen name Lewis Carroll, that man also wrote some of the most madcap verse and prose in English or any other language (his works have been translated into scores of them). Dodgson wrote his first masterpiece, *Alice's Adventures in Wonderland* (1865), for Alice Liddell, a daughter of the dean of Christ Church, after she asked him to transcribe the tales he had told during a long summer day they spent boating on the Isis River, near Oxford, in 1862. In the written version he included verses not unlike those he had composed as a child, serving as poet, puppeteer, and master of ceremonies for his seven sisters and three brothers. He continued writing light verse all his life and, with "Jabberwocky," he lodged deliciously ominous nonsense in the minds of millions of readers.

Never married, Carroll systematically sought the friendship of small girls. He was at ease, it seems, only in their company. Also an avid photographer, he specialized in making portraits of his "child-friends." As *Alice* and its sequel, *Through the Looking-Glass*, became wildly successful, their author rigorously avoided fame. The year before he died, of bronchitis, he began returning mail addressed to Lewis Carroll, marking it "not known." Given the oddity and paradoxes of his nature, that is probably still true. ■

Finally my Hiawatha
Took a saturate solution,
Which was made of hypo-sulphite,
Which again was made of soda—
(Very difficult the word is
For a metre like the present)
This completed every picture.

   First in order came the father:
He would have a crimson curtain
Looped about a marble pillar,
With the corner of a table,
Of a rose-wood dining-table.
He would hold a scroll of something,
Hold it firmly in his left-hand:
He would keep his right-hand buried
(Like Napoleon) in his waistcoat:
He would gaze into the distance,
Like a man who sees a vision,
At 12..30 in the morning,
While the servants bring in luncheon—
And the picture failed completely.

   Next in order came the mother:
She came dressed beyond description,
Dressed in jems and silks and satins
Far too gorgeous for a duchess.
In her hand she held a nosegay
Rather larger than a cabbage.

All the time that she was taken,
Still the lady chattered, chattered,
Like a monkey in the forest.
"Is my head enough in focus?
Would it do a little sideways?
Shall I hold the nosegay higher?
Will it come into the picture?"
And the picture failed completely.

   Next, the eldest son was taken:
He discoursed on lines of beauty,
Lines that curved about the picture,
Centering in the golden breast-pin—
(He had got it out of Ruskin,
Author of "The Stones of Venice,"
"Seven Lamps of Architecture,"
"Modern Painters," & some others:
But he had not altogether
Taken in the writer's meaning)
And the picture failed completely.

   Then the eldest daughter followed:
She suggested very little—
Only begged she might be taken
With her look of "passive beauty."
Her idea of passive beauty
Was a squinting of the right-eye,
Was a drooping of the left-eye,

Scholars claim to have counted more than 1,000 parodies of Henry Wadsworth Longfellow's poem Hiawatha, *and indeed Carroll introduced a printed version of his "Hiawatha's Photographing" (shown here in manuscript) with the note, "In these days of imitation, I can claim no sort of merit for this slight attempt at doing what is known to be so easy." Instead, he drew attention to his poem's subject, photography, which was not at all an easy discipline when he took it up in the 1850s: the chemical process was slow, painstaking, and expensive, and the sitters sometimes became equally troublesome, as Carroll describes in this amusing poem. First published by Edmund Yates in his magazine* The Train *in December 1857, "Hiawatha's Photographing" was reprinted, considerably altered, in Carroll's verse collection* Rhyme? and Reason? *(1883).*

Carroll was a brilliant portrait photographer, especially, of course, of children. Alice Liddell and her sisters, Lorine and Edith, often sat for him in the late 1850s and early 1860s, until, in 1864, Alice's mother forbade any further outings with Carroll. The next year, when he saw Alice, aged 12, he wrote, "Alice seems changed a good deal, and hardly for the better – probably going through that awkward stage of transition." He made one last photograph of her when she was 18, looking prim and distant. But like Carroll's other child-friends, Alice recalled him fondly. In a 1932 memoir, she wrote, "We used to go to his rooms . . . escorted by our nurse. When we got there, we used to sit on the big sofa on each side of him, while he told us stories, illustrating them by pencil or ink drawings as he went along. When we were thoroughly happy and amused at his stories, he used to pose us, and expose the plates before the right mood had passed." This photograph of Alice (seated) and one of her sisters was made around 1860.

Robert Louis Stevenson 1850–1894

Lloyd Osbourne, who made this pen-and-ink portrait of Stevenson, was Fanny's son by her first husband and Stevenson's constant companion from the time of his marriage to the end of his life in Samoa. Osbourne claimed that he had painted the watercolor map that ignited Stevenson's imagination one day in the summer of 1881, and resulted in Treasure Island. *"Had it not been for me, and my childish box of paints, there would have been no such book as* Treasure Island," *Osbourne wrote. Stevenson, however, recalled that it was he who had made the map.*

ROBERT LOUIS STEVENSON made himself unforgettable by settling in 1890 in Samoa with his aging Scottish mother (in a prim white Victorian widow's cap), his American wife, Fanny, her two children, and many bare-chested Polynesian servants. Many readers unaware of the legend still know Stevenson's name, since his book *A Child's Garden of Verses* is in the bedrooms of millions of English-speaking children. The best-known of Stevenson's poetry, he wrote most of the poems in this magical collection in bed when he felt too ill to write prose.

Stevenson was born in Edinburgh, into a deeply religious family. He was sickly as a child and throughout his life. His father, two uncles, and grandfather were lighthouse engineers, so it went without saying that "Smout" (his childhood nickname) would follow suit. Although he won a silver medal for a paper, "On a New Form of Intermittent Light for Lighthouses," at 21, he already knew that he wanted to write.

One of his first publications, an article on Robert Burns in *The Cornhill Magazine*, had earlier been rejected by the *Encyclopedia Britannica* for criticizing the Scottish poetical icon. In 1878, Stevenson published his first book, describing a river-trip in France, and followed it with other travel books. In 1876, in France, he met Fanny Osbourne, whom he married four years later after an arduous, near-fatal trip to California in pursuit of her. As Stevenson made his name as a prose writer with *Treasure Island*, *Kidnapped*, and *The Strange Case of Dr Jekyll and Mr Hyde*, he also wrote poetry. *Underwoods* (1887) includes many occasional verses, and a section of poems in Scots. Some of his *Ballads* (1890) tell tales of the South Seas, where he had been traveling.

Stevenson died suddenly at his home on the island of Upolu, aged only 44. ∎

To Mrs. E. F. Strickland

The freedom and the joy of days
When health was with us still,
The pleasure of green woods and ways
And of the breathing hill:
These that so dear a value set
Upon the times of yore,
We may remember, may forget –
We must enjoy no more.
As in strange lands, when exiles meet
And dream of long ago,
They with a nearer kindness greet
The sharers of their woe:
So, all unknown, from far away,
I, lady, turn to you –
Your fellow exile from the day,
The breezes and the dew.

This manuscript was found inserted into a copy of Stevenson's New Poems and Variant Readings *(1918), and was used as the text for the poem's first publication, long after Stevenson's death, in* Robert Louis Stevenson: Collected Poems *(1950). When Stevenson wrote this poem, he and Fanny were living in a yellow brick, ivy-covered house that his parents had bought for them in Bournemouth, and he was just finishing* Kidnapped, *one of his most famous books. This is the only extant manuscript of Stevenson's gallant salute to Mrs. Strickland, whose identity remains a mystery.*

Mr Stevenson delights in a style, and his own had nothing accidental or diffident; it is eminently conscious of its responsibilities and meets them with a kind of gallantry – as if language were a pretty woman and a person who proposes to handle it had, of necessity, to be something of a Don Juan.

Henry James, "Robert Louis Stevenson" in Century Magazine *(April 1888)*

Rudyard Kipling

1865–1936

Kipling (seen here in a portrait from the late 1880s, probably shortly before he left India for England) began as a reporter, an acute and amazingly retentive observer who, as he wrote, didn't take notes: "If a thing didn't stay in my memory I argued it was hardly worth writing about."

BORN IN BOMBAY to talented and artistic English parents, Rudyard Kipling was educated in England at a distinctly unprestigious public school in the North Devon seaside resort of Westward Ho! Poor eyesight barred him from athletics, but he developed a reputation as the school's *littérateur*, and soon became secretary of its literary society. Returning to India in 1882, he worked as a journalist in Lahore, employing his keenly observant eye and often empathetic intelligence to gain insight into virtually every aspect and level of the Anglo-Indian culture of his day. From these experiences, Kipling fashioned a body of work that portrays – colorfully, and with great vibrancy and skill – the frequently overlapping worlds of rank-and-file soldiers, civil servants, engineers, and even animals on the highly charged, teeming canvas of late 19th-century colonial India. Returning to England in 1889, he settled in the London of the Decadents (Oscar Wilde mischievously welcomed him as the "genius who drops his aspirates"), tacked a notice to his door ("To Publishers, A Classic while you wait"), and ambitiously set out to conquer the capital of the Empire. He quickly achieved international literary celebrity.

Literary modernists – offended by Kipling's jingoistic and imperialistic biases; by the facile journalistic vulgarity they saw in much of his work; and, undoubtedly, by his accessibility and vast fame – often viewed "Rudyard the dud yard" (Pound) with contempt. Though he was probably the first English author to own an automobile (and the first to win the Nobel Prize), Kipling was most emphatically not a man of the 20th century. Amazingly prolific, he wrote many works that continue to enchant (foremost among them *Kim*, his enchanting and poetic novel of India), but even during his lifetime his critical reputation plummeted drastically. And yet T. S. Eliot, in 1919, prophetically christened Kipling "a laureate without laurels." ■

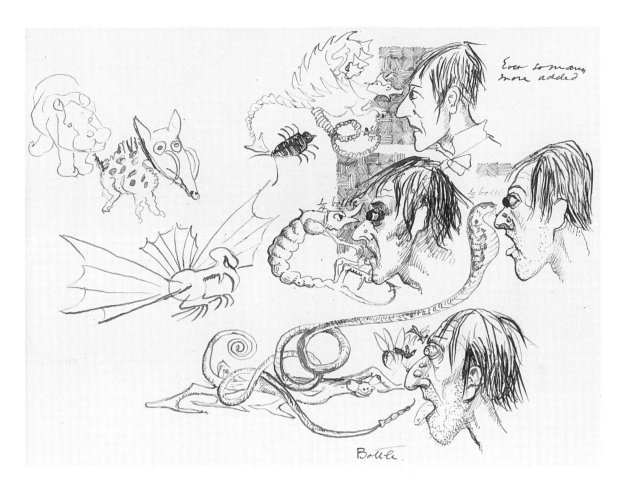

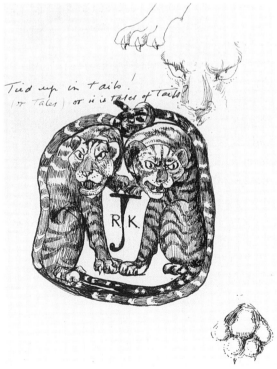

ABOVE

This sketch, entitled "Absinth," begins on its recto with three portraits – captioned "Just one liqueur," "Another," and "Another, and another" – of an initially well-groomed man who quickly deteriorates under the insidious influence of absinthe, a particularly potent and dangerous liqueur that was widely imbibed in the 19th century. The finale of Kipling's virtuoso sketch (on the verso of the sheet, shown here) is a hallucinogenic vision of the sorry man's final incarnation after "Ever so many more added."

LEFT

That Kipling was one of those rare writers who was also a gifted artist, witty caricaturist, and entertaining doodler should perhaps not come as a surprise: his father was an illustrator, craftsman, and professor of architectural sculpture at a Bombay art school; and two maternal uncles were prominent Victorian artists (one of them was the painter and designer Edward Burne-Jones). This pen-and-ink sketch is Kipling's design for his own bookplate.

If I had to pick one writer to invent a conversation between an animal, a god, and a machine, it would be Kipling. To discover what, if they ever said, the dumb would say — this takes real imagination; and this imagination of what isn't is the extension of a real knowledge of what is, the knowledge of a consummate observer who took no notes. . . . Knowing what the peoples, animals, plants, weathers of the world looked like, sound like, smell like, was Kipling's *métier*, and so was knowing the words that could make someone else know. You can argue about the judgment he makes of something, but the thing is there. . . .

Randall Jarrell, "On Preparing to Read Kipling" in A Sad Heart at the Supermarket *(New York, 1962)*

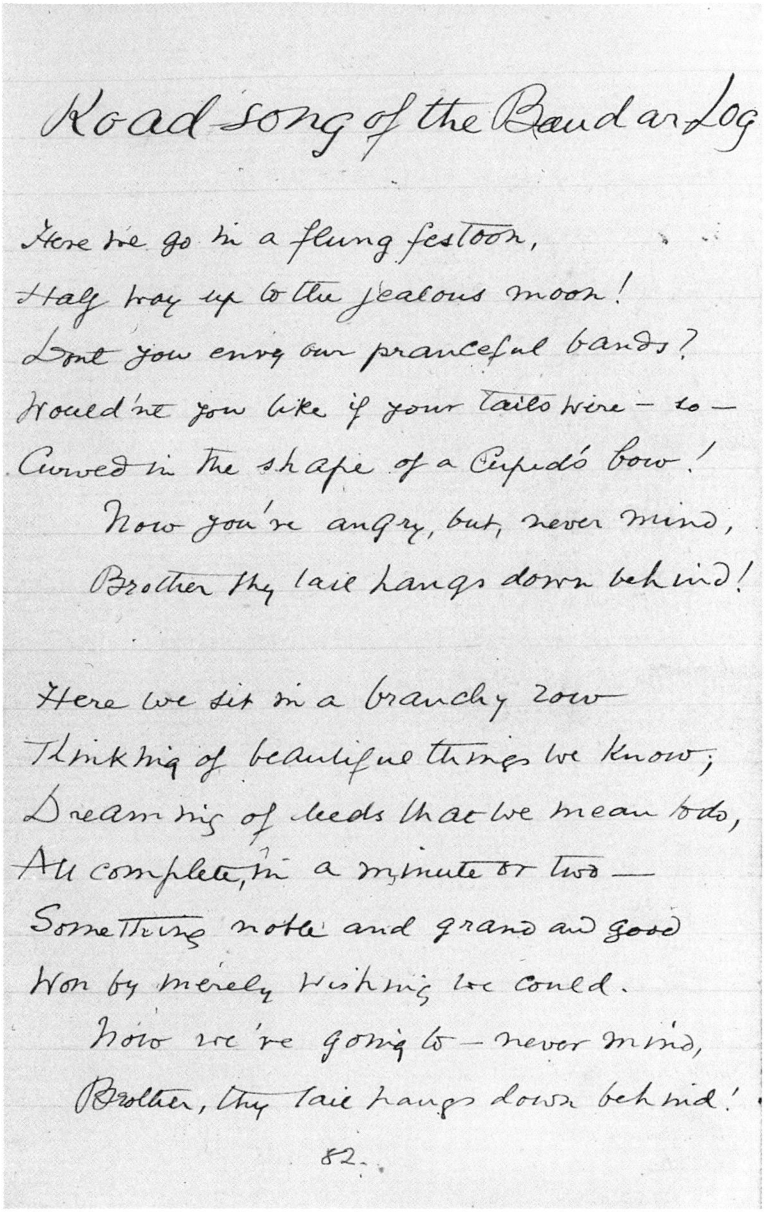

Road-Song of the Bandar-Log

Here we go in a flung festoon,
Half way up to the jealous moon!
Don't you envy our pranceful bands?
Would'nt you like if your tails were — so —
Curved in the shape of a Cupid's bow!
  Now you're angry, but, never mind,
  Brother thy tail hangs down behind!

Here we sit in a branchy row
Thinking of beautiful things we know;
Dreaming of deeds that we mean to do,
All complete, in a minute or two —
Something noble and grand and good
Won by merely wishing we could.
  Now we're going to — never mind,
  Brother, thy tail hangs down behind!

82.

Shown here are the first two stanzas of "Road-Song of the Bandar-Log" – first published as part of "Kaa's Hunting" in The Jungle Book – the swaying, silly song of the heedless and benighted Bandar-Log monkeys, for whom Kipling arranges a particularly gruesome fate. This fair copy was written by Kipling in a marvelous notebook – illustrated throughout with his fluid, inventive, and often witty drawings and decorated titles – given by him to Florence Garrard, one of the great (and hopeless) loves of his life.

Thomas Hardy

1840–1928

When Hardy was buried at Westminster Abbey, his ashes were placed in Poet's Corner before a distinguished assemblage including George Bernard Shaw, Rudyard Kipling, and Prime Minister Stanley Baldwin, while throngs of people paid their respects in a frigid rain outside. Meanwhile, at Stinsford, in the remote Dorset countryside where Hardy was born, another large crowd stood in the sunshine. Hardy's literary friends and his family had been unable to agree on where to bury him until they hit on a compromise: they summoned a surgeon, who removed Hardy's heart, wrapped it in a towel, and put it in a biscuit tin. The tin was buried at Stinsford. This photograph of Hardy in 1924 is part of an album assembled by Sir Sydney Carlyle Cockerell, one of Hardy's literary executors.

IN HIS POETIC prime at age 77, Thomas Hardy was irked that critics seemed to think poets "must all be impractical in the conduct of their affairs; nay, they must almost, like Shelley or Marlowe, be drowned or done to death, or like Keats, die of consumption." Hardy had a point, since his own long life was an indispensable ingredient in his poetry.

Hardy was born in the village of Higher Bockhampton, in Dorset, folkloric countryside that provided the landscape for most of his writing. His father was the latest in a long line of master builders. A frail child, Hardy did not attend school until he was 8, and at 16 he began a five-year apprenticeship to an architect. He went on to work in that trade in London, meanwhile keeping a vow to read only poetry – no prose except newspaper writing – for nearly two years, and writing dozens of poems. Unable to get them published, Hardy moved back to Higher Bockhampton in 1867, and began writing novels. From 1871 to 1874, he published a novel a year, culminating in *Far from the Madding Crowd*. By 1896, he had produced 15 novels, including *Tess of the d'Urbervilles* and *Jude the Obscure*, and 50 short stories.

Wealthy and well-known in the late 1890s, he quit novel-writing and returned to poetry, publishing his first collection, an odd mixture of old and new work called *Wessex Poems*, when he was 58. His third book of poetry, *Time's Laughingstocks* (1909), was the first to sell well, and in it Hardy reached his full stride, with powerful narratives and deft prosody. For many years Hardy's first marriage gradually worked its way to painful disaster, but his wife's death in 1912 abruptly rekindled his love, with the cruel, irreparable irony typical of a Hardy poem. He poured his regret into verses that still stand among his most beautiful, though he wrote nearly 500 more before his own death 16 years later. ■

The Man He Killed

'Had he and I but met
By some old ancient inn,
We should have sat us down to wet
Right many a nipperkin!

'But ranged as infantry,
And staring face to face,
I shot at him as he at me,
And killed him in his place.

'I shot him dead because –
Because he was my foe,
Just so: my foe of course he was;
That's clear enough; although

'He thought he'd 'list, perhaps,
Off-hand like – just as I –
Was out of work – had sold his traps –
No other reason why.

'Yes; quaint and curious war is!
You shoot a fellow down
You'd treat if met where any bar is,
Or help to half-a-crown.'

The Man he Killed.

Scene: The settle of "The Fox" Inn, Stagfoot Lane.
Characters: The speaker (a returned soldier), & his friends, natives of the hamlet.

I.

"Had he & I but met
By some old ancient inn,
We should have sat us down to wet
Right many a nipperkin.

II.

"But ranged as infantry,
And staring face to face,
I shot at him, as he at me,
And killed him in his place.

III.

"I shot him dead, because —
Because he was my foe,
You see; my foe of course he was;
That's clear enough; although

IV.

"He thought he'd 'list, perhaps,
Off-hand like — just as I —
Was out of work — had sold his traps —
No other reason why.

V.

"Yes; quaint and curious war is!
— You shoot a fellow down
That you would treat where any bar is,
Or help to half-a-crown."

Thomas Hardy.

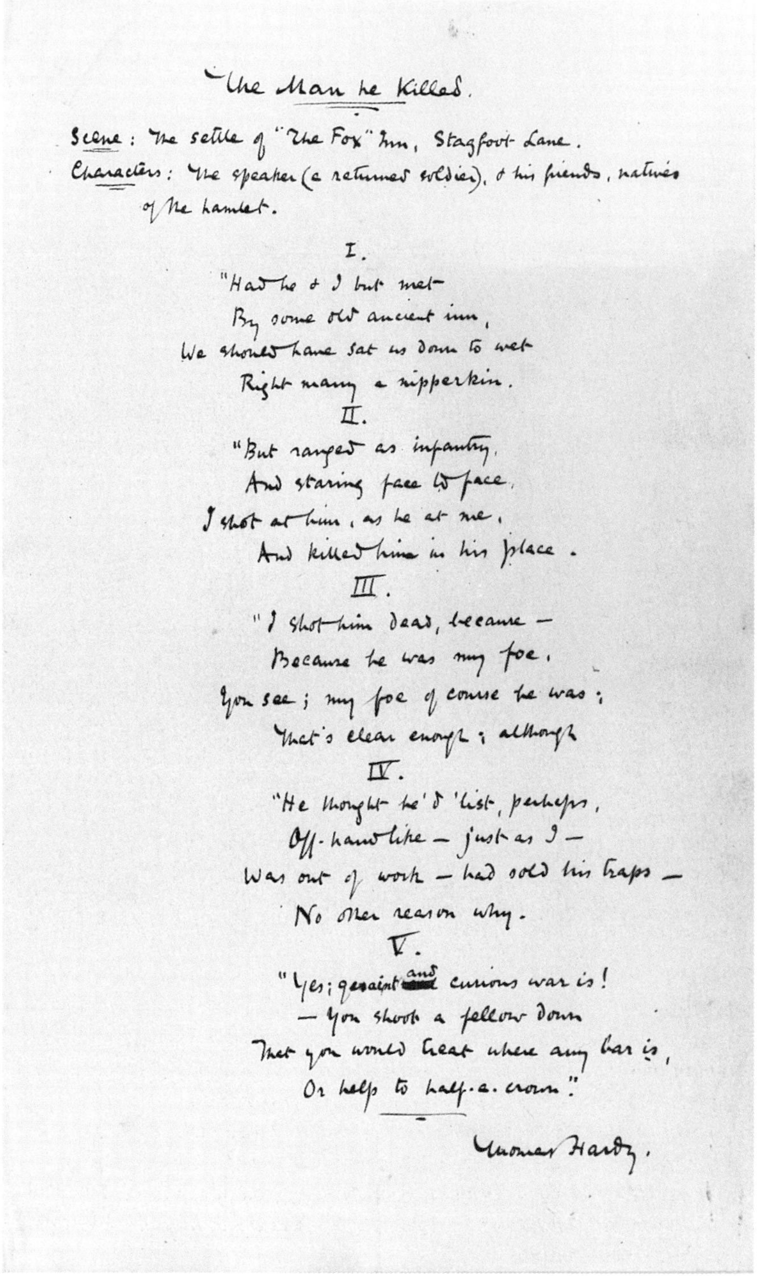

First published in 1902, "The Man He Killed" is a reaction to the Boer War, which ended in May of that year, and an illustration of one of Hardy's favorite themes: the casual cruelty of fate. "Stagfoot Lane," the setting of this poem, was named after Hartfoot Lane, near the Puddletown of Hardy's childhood.

Emma Lavinia Gifford (whose portrait photograph is preserved, with a lock of her hair, in this leather locket) met Hardy in 1870 at the North Cornwall parish of St. Juliot's when the young assistant architect arrived to plan the restoration of the church; the two were married in September 1874. In a notebook memoir, Emma painted a rosy account of their courtship and early life together, along with bitter sequels recounting the deterioration of their marriage. Hardy's discovery of Emma's notebook after her death in 1912 brought on an attack of painful remorse. The matching memorial tablets he designed for Emma and himself were put up in St. Juliot Church.

My first Master was Thomas Hardy, and I think I was very lucky in my choice . . . he was modern without being too modern. His world and sensibility were close enough to mine . . . so that, in imitating him, I was being led towards not away from myself, but they were not so close as to obliterate my identity. If I looked through his spectacles, at least I was conscious of a certain eyestrain.

W. H. Auden, "Making, Knowing and Judging" in The Dyer's Hand, and Other Essays *(New York, 1962)*

Charlotte Mew

1869–1928

The novelist May Sinclair described Mew as a "poet whose heart beats like a dynamo beneath an iron-grey tailor-made suit." Shown here around 1921, she was once asked in a bookshop, "Are you Charlotte Mew?" and her characteristically wry reply was: "I am sorry to say I am."

She has no tricks or graces. She is completely mistress of her instrument, but she does not use it for any but the most austere purpose. . . . All that she wrote had its quality of depth and stillness. No English poet had less pretensions, and few as genuine a claim to be in touch with the source of poetry.

Humbert Wolfe, in a review of Mew's The Rambling Sailor, *in the* Observer, *September 5, 1929*

IN AN IMPASSIONED essay on Emily Brontë, Charlotte Mew wrote that Brontë's "nature stood alone. That was the awful fact – the tragedy of her life." Mew also, hauntingly, stands apart. Her life – plagued by family tragedy, the specter of insanity, and the crushing despair of unrequited love – was appallingly difficult. "Wild as storm" (as she said of Brontë), but fiercely controlled, she poured her turbulence and torment into poems that bristle with highly idiosyncratic rhythms and syntax, and ache with an oddly veiled passion.

Of her siblings, three died before the age of five, and two spent their entire adult lives in mental institutions. Only her beloved and devoted sister Anne remained, and the two shared a life together in Bloomsbury for almost 50 years, struggling to maintain a household that included their childish and demanding mother and Mew's cherished parrot, Wek. Charlotte began to write poetry and prose at an early age, and, after the mid-1890s, published stories and essays regularly in prominent literary journals. Her first book of poems, *The Farmer's Bride* (1916), attracted sympathetic and influential admirers – most prominently Thomas Hardy, whom she revered.

The mid-1920s were fairly serene: a Civil List Pension brought some financial stability, and her reputation was growing. But Anne's death in June of 1927 devastated Mew: she was inconsolable, and tormented herself with the idea that Anne had been buried alive. On March 24, 1928, in a shabby nursing home, Mew poisoned herself by swallowing a glass of disinfectant. When a doctor tried to revive her, she begged: "Don't keep me, let me go." A local London paper recorded the death of "Charlotte New, said to be a writer." Mew would probably have found the blunder grimly amusing. ■

Love Love Today

Love, Love to-day, my dear,
Love is not always here;
Wise maids know how soon grows sere
The greenest leaf of Spring;
But no man knoweth
Whither it goeth
When the wind bloweth
So frail a thing.

Love, Love, my dear, to-day,
If the ship's in the bay,
If the bird has come your way
That sings on summer trees;
When his song faileth
And the ship saileth
No voice availeth
To call back these.

Sir Sydney Cockerell, the Director of the Fitzwilliam Museum, was so impressed with The Farmer's Bride *that he sent copies to many of his literary friends, including Thomas Hardy, who would be moved to describe Mew as "far and away the best living woman poet," one whose work "will be read when others are forgotten." Mew sent this fair copy of "Love Love Today" to Cockerell in a letter of August 28, 1919, noting that it was "written for music, & [is] not quite 20th century!" She went on: "It is not published & perhaps I shall one day put an air to it...." According to a friend, Mew had "a delicate touch on the piano," but whether she set this melancholy lyric to music is not known.*

Hilaire Belloc

1870–1953

Poor Mr. Belloc looked as though the grave were the only place for him. He has grown a splendid white beard and in his cloak, which with his hat he wore indoors and always, he seemed an archimandrite. He lost and stole and whatever went into his pockets, toast, cigarettes, books never appeared, like the reverse of a conjuror's hat. He talked incessantly, proclaiming with great clarity the grievances of 40 years ago. . . . At times he was coaxed by the women to sing and then with face alight with simple joy and many lapses of memory, he quavered out old French marching songs and snatches from the music halls of his youth. He is conscious of being decrepit and forgetful, but not of being a bore.

Evelyn Waugh, in his Diary, May 1, 1945

MASSIVE, OFTEN BELLIGERENT, and always controversial, Hilaire Belloc was a combative, barnstorming, and incredibly prolific man-of-letters who achieved great fame (and notoriety) during his long life. Radically pro-Catholic, hostile to both capitalism and socialism, a sort of truculent literary revolutionary with – paradoxically – a tendency to revere the past, Belloc wrote in many genres, employing his pen (his "free lance") with great skill and effect as he explicated and defended his fiercely held religious and social beliefs.

Born near Paris, the son of a French barrister and his British wife (who was a leader in the suffragist movement), Joseph Hilaire Pierre René Belloc was educated at Oxford, where he quickly gained a reputation as a brilliant debater. In 1896, he married a Californian, Elodie Agnes Hogan; she was a powerful influence in Belloc's life, and her death in 1914 was a severe blow. He donned black broadcloth, the uniform (and trademark) with which he took on the world for the remainder of his life.

With his combination of wit, sentiment, clarity, and vivid rhetoric, Belloc was considered a dangerous and formidable adversary. He was a commanding presence, and his barbed pen brought him a wide audience, and many enemies. H. G. Wells, once friendly with Belloc, came under fierce attack after publishing *The Outline of History* (1925), a book Belloc felt attacked the Faith ("Europe is the Faith, and the Faith is Europe" was his credo). Belloc's *The Jews* (1922), an outspoken essay on what he called the "Jewish problem," was, he believed, an evenhanded analysis of the inevitable confrontation between a majority and a minority; it was, and remains, controversial. Belloc's close association with G. K. Chesterton (another prominent pro-Catholic polemicist and his greatest ally) led George Bernard Shaw to identify a marvelous new literary beast, which he christened the "Chesterbelloc." Ironically, it is for Belloc's light verse – exuberant drinking songs and wonderfully funny and gruesome rhymes for children – that the back half of Shaw's once terrifying quadruped is best remembered today. ■

To make 8 pp
2 Much

2

ABOUT JOHN, WHO LOST A FORTUNE BY THROWING STONES.

By H. Belloc

Indent 6 em

JOHN VAVASSOUR de Quentin Jones
Was very fond of throwing stones
At Horses, People, Passing Trains,
But 'specially at Window-Panes.
Like many of the Upper Class   *①
He liked the Sound of Broken Glass
It bucked him up and made him gay:
It was his favourite form of Play.
But the Amusement cost him dear,
My children, as you now shall hear.

John Vavassour de Quentin had
An Uncle, who adored the lad,
And often chuckled: "Wait until
You see what's left you in my will!"
Nor were the words without import,
Because this uncle did a sort
Of something in the City which
Had made him fabulously rich.
Although his brother, John's Papa,
Was poor, as many father's are.

He had a lot of stocks and shares *②
And half a street in Buenos Ayres
A bank in Rio, and a line
Of Steamers to the Argentine.
And options more than I can tell,
And bits of Canada as well;
He even had a mortgage on
The House inhabited by John.
     His will, the cause of all the fuss,
Was carefully edited thus:-
               in

1.
     A line I stole with subtle daring,
     From Wing-Commander Maurice Baring.
2. But this pronunciation varies:
     Some people call it Bu-enos Ayr-es."

One of Belloc's collections, Cautionary Tales for Children *(1907), describes with unwholesome zeal the awful outcomes of wayward children, among them "Rebecca, Who Slammed Doors for Fun and Perished Miserably." With his* New Cautionary Tales *(1930), Belloc introduced some new incorrigibles, such as the young and foolish John Vavassour de Quentin Jones of "About John, Who Lost a Fortune by Throwing Stones." One of John's missiles catches his dozing uncle "smartly in the eye," and with great speed Uncle William, who had formerly doted on John, changes his "Famous Will," leaving everything to Miss Charming, his accommodating nurse.*

Oscar Wilde

1854–1900

At Trinity College, Dublin, where he studied before Oxford, Wilde began a lifelong infatuation with ancient Greek culture and literature. His reverence was not overly pedantic, however, and Wilde elucidated some important distinctions: "To be really mediaeval one should have no body. To be really modern one should have no soul. To be really Greek one should have no clothes."

[Wilde] lived with no self-mockery at all an imaginary life; perpetually performed a play which was in all things the opposite of all that he had known in childhood and early youth; never put off completely his wonder at opening his eyes every morning on his own beautiful house, and in remembering that he had dined yesterday with a duchess, and that he delighted in Flaubert and Pater, read Homer in the original and not as a schoolmaster reads him for the grammar.

William Butler Yeats,
Autobiographies *(London, 1926)*

THE EPITOME OF *fin-de-siècle* Aestheticism and the greatest wit and conversationalist of his generation, Oscar Fingal O'Flahertie Wills Wilde excelled at Oxford, where his rooms were noted for their exotic splendor. Notorious for his provocative witticisms and foppish attire, Wilde was regally convinced of his genius. Still, he had momentary insecurities: "I hope," he exclaimed at Oxford, "I shall be able to live up to my blue china."

After a wildly successful lecture tour of America in 1882, Wilde returned to England and, armed with pen and *bons mots*, set out to conquer the fashionable and aristocratic circles of late Victorian London. His macabre and ambiguous moral fable, *The Picture of Dorian Gray*, appeared in 1891, the same year that he met Lord Alfred Douglas, the great, and fatally ill-starred, romance of his life. In 1892, Wilde began, with *Lady Windermere's Fan,* his rapid ascent to the absolute summit of the English theater. Shortly after the triumphant opening of *The Importance of Being Earnest* in February 1895, Wilde instituted an ill-advised suit for slander against Lord Alfred's father, the Marquess of Queensberry. The action miscarried disastrously, and Wilde soon found himself in the docket, prosecuted for homosexual offenses. He was found guilty, and sentenced to two years' hard labor; even before his conviction, *Earnest –* Wilde's most perfect achievement – was withdrawn by the management of the St. James's Theatre, and replaced with Henry Arthur Jones's *The Triumph of the Philistines.*

Released from prison in May 1897, Wilde moved to France, where he lived under an assumed name. He died in the rather shabby Hôtel d'Alsace in Paris, on November 30, 1900. Contemplating, shortly before his death, the great cost of his projected medical treatment, Wilde sighed, "Ah, well, then, I suppose that I shall have to die beyond my means." ∎

Impression du voyage.

The sea was sapphire coloured, and the sky
Burned like a heated opal through the air
We hoisted sail; the wind was blowing fair
For the blue *islands* lands that to the Eastward lie.
From the steep prow I marked with quickening eye
Zakynthos every olive grove and *creek*
Ithaca's cliff, Lycaon's snowy peak,
And all the flower-strewn hills of Arcady.
The flapping of the sail against the mast,
The ripple of the water on the side,
The ripple of girls' laughter at the stern,
The only sounds: — when 'gan the West to burn
And a red sun upon the seas to ride,
I stood upon the soil of Greece at last.

*Like several other lyrics in Wilde's first collection (Poems, 1881),
"Impression du Voyage" shows Wilde's affinity for French culture as
well as the influence of Whistlerian impressionism. The book's success
brought the flamboyant young poet (who would soon land in New York
announcing that he had "nothing to declare but his genius") and the
credo of Aestheticism ever more prominently before the startled, often
disapproving gaze of the Victorian literary establishment.*

Ernest Dowson

1867–1900

The artist Sir William Rothenstein was a friend of Oscar Wilde's and a prominent figure in the social, literary, and artistic circles of fin-de-siècle *London. He is said to have lured Dowson, who was reluctant to be drawn, to sit for his portrait (seen here in an engraving by Emery Walker) in exchange for a night's lodging in his studio on one of many occasions when the young poet had missed the last train to his father's house at Limehouse.*

ADELAIDE FOLTINOWICZ, THE daughter of Polish immigrants and a waitress in her father's Soho (London) restaurant, was only 12 when her "curving white neck" first entranced the languid gaze of Ernest Dowson, the Pater- and Verlaine-intoxicated son of a well-to-do dock owner. Perhaps he was somewhat befuddled by "chablis and soda" (a favored combination) when he first met the young girl who would leave him "idolatrous for the rest of [his] days." Dowson's passion bewildered those who were not bewitched by Adelaide's crooked nose and red hands, but as he wrote a friend: "I seem to have seen the mysteries and if I fail to be explicit, it is because my eyes are dazzled." Adelaide may or may not have inspired Dowson's most famous poem ("Non sum qualis eram bonae sub regno Cynarae"), but her poor, hapless, yet eternally sacred spirit haunted Dowson's life. His crushing, almost predestined despair over his inevitable loss of her similarly haunts his small but exquisite body of verse.

In the 90s, Dowson dove headlong into the literary and social *danse macabre* of *fin-de-siècle* London. He recited his verses in his "pleasing pathetic tenor voice" to Yeats, Lionel Johnson, and other members of the Rhymers' Club who gathered nightly at the Cheshire Cheese in Fleet Street and, inflamed by black coffee, tobacco smoke, and Aestheticism, labored mightily to "purify poetry of all that is not poetry." After a series of shattering blows – his father died (probably a suicide) in 1894; his mother hanged herself six months later; and he learned that Adelaide was to marry a waiter in her father's restaurant – Dowson drifted restlessly between France and London, worked fitfully on translations from the French, and, with an almost fevered concentration, abandoned himself to absinthe and other vices. His death in England in 1900 shocked Wilde, who saw in Dowson a "tragic reproduction of all tragic poetry." ∎

"Non sum qualis eram bonae
Sub regno Cynarae".

Last night, ah yesternight, betwixt her lips and mine,
There fell thy shadow, Cynara, thy breath was shed
Upon my soul, between the kisses and the wine;
And I was desolate and sick of an old passion,
    Yea, I grew desolate and bowed my head:
I have been faithful to thee, Cynara, in my fashion.

All night, upon my breast, I felt her warm heart beat,
Night long within mine arms, in love and sleep she lay;
Surely the kisses of her bought, red mouth were sweet.
    But I was desolate and sick of an old passion,
    When I awoke and found the dawn was gray:
I have been faithful to thee, Cynara, in my fashion.

I have forgot much, Cynara, gone with the wind,
Flung roses, roses, riotously, with the throng,
Dancing to put thy pale, lost lilies out of mind,
    But I was desolate and sick of an old passion,
    Yea, desolate, because the dance was long:
I have been faithful to thee, Cynara, in my fashion.

[The Decadents] sit pale and listless, because they have seen the face of Death between the roses.... Of poets who have written in this way the greatest and perhaps most typical is Ernest Dowson ... a genius broken by the world, with a body ruined by sin and intemperance, and the soul of a poet. His poems gave almost no sign of his more ignoble life.... Each is a lyric of beauty and pathos, the expression of some one mood or passing emotion, a sigh or a tear, and as near to faint music as speech can come. "You have created a new shudder," Victor Hugo wrote of Baudelaire in a memorable phrase. One might say of Dowson that he had created a new sigh.

Rupert Brooke, in a lecture at Rugby School when he was 18, quoted in The Prose of Rupert Brooke *(London, 1956)*

On February 7, 1891, Dowson wrote to his friend Arthur Moore, begging him to "criticize the-on-the-other-side-appended versicles" (above) that he had composed the day before. The versicles were those of the once notorious poem "Non sum qualis eram bonae sub regno Cynarae," in which the speaker invokes, in the ripest 90s manner, the two very different women – one chaste and pale, the other opulent and bought – who haunt him. This celebrated poem, with its equally celebrated refrain ("I have been faithful to thee, Cynara! in my fashion.") is as droll as it is steamy. The title, taken from an ode of Horace (as the index of any edition of his poems will demonstrate, Dowson was blessed with the soul of a Latinist), can be translated as: "I am not as I was under the sway of the good Cynara."

William Butler Yeats

1865–1939

Yeats and Ezra Pound spent the winters of 1914–17 at Stone Cottage, a four-room house in Sussex; this portrait by Arnold Genthe, made on one of Yeats's visits to New York, dates from the beginning of that period. During those winters, Pound served as the older poet's secretary, began his famous Cantos, *and tried to teach Yeats fencing. Yeats tried to indoctrinate Pound in occult practices. More important, they shared their divergent ideas about poetry and became warm friends. When they met in 1908, Pound had already carefully studied Yeats's works, but he later said that he spent the first six years of their friendship "learning how Yeats did it."*

OFTEN CALLED THE greatest English-language poet of the century, William Butler Yeats at first alarmed his parents because he was so slow to learn to read. As a teenager he began writing poems, with the encouragement of his father, an Anglo-Irish lawyer turned portrait painter. Instead of university, "Willie" attended art school in his native Dublin.

At the same time, Yeats began his lifelong study of mysticism, which he called "the revolt of the soul against the intellect." During his first seance he began twitching and banging on a table, and by 1893 he had attained the esoteric fifth rank of magical expertise, as a member of the Hermetic Order of the Golden Dawn. Like Blake, whom he studied intensely, Yeats developed a mythological sense of history that informs and animates many of his poems. But his great, lyrical work breathes with familiar, entirely human longings: for youth, beauty, and requited love.

Six feet and one inch tall, with long fingers and a lock of hair that fell over his forehead, Yeats wore a large gold ring and preferred flowing cravats to ties, the better to cultivate an artistic image. When his first mature poem, "The Wanderings of Oisin," was published in 1889, it brought him a visit from a beautiful reader, Maud Gonne, who said the work had made her weep. Yeats remained hopelessly in love with her until he died. Gonne was a radical Irish nationalist; Yeats preferred to try to reconcile Catholic and Anglo-Irish politics and sensibilities, and to elevate Irish culture by means of a National Literary Society. This largely failed, but in 1898 Yeats launched the Irish Literary Theatre, which eventually became the famous Abbey Theatre.

Yeats was awarded the Nobel Prize in 1923. In a lecture delivered to the Friends of the Irish Academy at the Abbey Theatre one year after the poet's death, T. S. Eliot placed Yeats in the company of those few poets "whose history is the history of their own time, who are a part of the consciousness of an age which cannot be understood without them." ∎

"Who dreamed that beauty passes like a dream?" That line fairly weeps defiance to the un-ideal, if you will understand what I mean by that. The Rose of the World, The Fiddler of Dooney, The Lake Isle of Innisfree, Down by the Sally Gardens, The Song of the Wandering Aengus, the Song of the Sad Shepherd – those are all poems. One is sure of them. They make the sense of beauty ache.

Robert Frost, letter to Sidney Cox, ca. September 15, 1913, in Selected Letters of Robert Frost, *edited by Lawrance Thompson (London, 1965)*

The Wild Swans at Coole, *published by The Macmillan Company in 1919, is a revision of a book of the same title hand-printed in 1917 at Yeats's sisters' Cuala Press. The earlier book included 29 poems and the play* At the Hawk's Well. *For the 1919 volume, Yeats deleted the play and added 17 poems. Yeats sold the entire book manuscript, along with several others, to his friend John Quinn, an Irish-American lawyer and literary collector, in exchange for Quinn's paying off some debts of the poet's father, John Butler Yeats, who was then living in New York.*

[handwritten manuscript pages of the poem]

The Wild Swans at Coole

The trees are in their autumn beauty,
The woodland paths are dry,
Under the October twilight the water
Mirrors a still sky;
Upon the brimming water among the stones
Are nine-and-fifty swans.

The nineteenth autumn has come upon me
Since I first made my count;
I saw, before I had well finished,
All suddenly mount
And scatter wheeling in great broken rings
Upon their clamorous wings.

I have looked upon those brilliant creatures,
And now my heart is sore.
All's changed since I, hearing at twilight,
The first time on this shore,
The bell-beat of their wings above my head,
Trod with a lighter tread.

Unwearied still, lover by lover,
They paddle in the cold
Companionable streams or climb the air;
Their hearts have not grown old;
Passion or conquest, wander where they will,
Attend upon them still.

But now they drift on the still water,
Mysterious, beautiful;
Among what rushes will they build,
By what lake's edge or pool
Delight men's eyes when I awake some day
To find they have flown away?

This pencil and watercolor sketch was made by the poet's brother, Jack
Butler Yeats, around 1900.

OPPOSITE

*"The Wild Swans at Coole," written in October 1916, is a pensive, lyrical
meditation on the passing of time, and its sad effects on the poet. Yeats
was 51 when he wrote it at Coole Park, the County Galway estate
of his patron and friend, Lady Augusta Gregory, the distinguished Irish
playwright and poet. He had just unsuccessfully proposed marriage to
Maud Gonne, 19 years after his first proposal to her. Feeling that finally
his heart – unlike those of the swans – had "grown old," Yeats gave up
hope. The next year he married Georgina Hyde-Lees.*

James Stephens

1882–1950

JAMES STEPHENS

In his book Vale, *novelist George Moore describes the discovery of Stephens by his mentor, the artist and poet A.E. [George W. Russell], who made this crayon portrait of Stephens in 1920: "And every Thursday evening the columns of Sinn Fein were searched, and every lilt considered, and every accent noted; but the days and the weeks went by without a new 'peep-o-peep, sweet, sweet,' until the day that James Stephens began to trill; and recognizing at once a strange songster, AE put on his hat and went away with his [bird]cage, discovering him in a lawyer's office. A great head and two soft brown eyes looked at him over a type-writer, an alert and intelligent voice asked him whom he wanted to see. AE said that he was looking for James Stephens, a poet, and the typist answered: 'I am He.'"*

FEARING THAT HE might not be able to finish his great last novel, *Finnegans Wake*, due to failing eyesight or nerve, James Joyce decided that the Irish poet and novelist James Stephens might be capable of finishing it for him. In 1929, Joyce spent an entire week explaining the plan of *Finnegans Wake* to Stephens, and on another occasion translated his poem "Stephen's Green" into French, German, Latin, Norwegian, and Italian. Joyce believed that he and Stephens had been born in the same city (Dublin), at the same hour, on the same day, month, and year. His quick wit, good humor, and intelligence made Stephens a favorite literary friend not only of Joyce, but of other writers and artists of the time.

There is no verifiable record of Stephens for the first 14 years of his life, and although he told Joyce he was born on February 2, 1882, he may indeed have been born on February 9, 1880, as some records indicate. As he came to be a fantasy in the inner life of James Joyce, Stephens had his own fantasy version of his life. Although he lived in London the last 20 years of his life, and maintained a flat in Paris, Stephens was an Irish nationalist intensely interested in Irish folklore, myth, and history. He produced an excellent journalistic account of the Easter Uprising of 1916; a superior book of adaptations of Gaelic poetry, *Reincarnations* (1918); and three works of fiction based on Irish myth. Stephens's poetry varies widely, from the simple and straightforward to the abstract and abstruse. At its best, it is a beautiful mystic poetry of visionary love. He is, however, much better known for his prose works. Stephens made nine speaking tours to the United States in the 1920s, and during the 1940s made almost 100 broadcasts over the BBC. He died the day after Christmas, St. Stephen's day, in 1950. ∎

note: Print variation 13 (page 24) in this form: 6 verses of 3 lines each & one of one line

All comes & goes,
The rose
Blossoms and fades away!

Grey leaps to gold,
And gold
Sleeps into grey!

And all that leaped
From clay
Is sleeped in clay!

— But He,
The Self
The watcher of the Race,

The One,
The Witness,
Knower of the Plot,

Who bears life
As a mask
Upon a face

He goeth not!

This form will probably take 2 pages, and alter the pagination

Stephens

note.

XIII
XII

All comes and goes: the rose
Blossoms and fades away!

Grey leaps to gold: and gold
Sleeps into grey:

And all that leaped from clay
Is steeped in clay—

But He, the Self,
The Watcher of the Race:

The One, the Witness,
Knower of the Plot,

Who bears life as a mask
Upon a face

He goeth not.

See note on front page giving the form, 6 verses of 3 lines each, in which the above is to be printed

24

Stephens's long poem, or poetic sequence, Theme and Variations *was composed throughout the 1920s, and stanzas were sometimes published separately. Stephens continued to revise the poem even during the publication process, and sometimes after. Here, on page proof for the 1930 publication by the Fountain Press, he changes the length of the lines of one of the sequence's lyrical variations. There are 16 variations in this sequence as published in 1930, and 23 as published in Stephens's* Collected Poems *in 1954.* "All Comes and Goes" *began as variation 12, was changed to 13, and ended up as variation 20.*

Well, I was astonished. I was admired at last. Joyce admired me. I was beloved at last; Joyce loved me. Or did he? Or did he only love his birthday, and was I merely coincident to that? When I spoke about my verse, which was every waking minute of my time, Joyce listened heartily and said "ah." He approved of it as second of February verse. . . .

James Stephens on James Joyce on James Stephens, "The James Joyce I Knew" in *The* Listener, *October 24, 1940*

Robert Frost

1874–1963

Collected Poems *(1930), for which this photograph served as the frontispiece, won Frost the second of his four Pulitzer Prizes, but some critics accused him of burying his head in the sand, in lines like "One luminary clock against the sky / Proclaimed the time was neither wrong nor right" (from "Acquainted with the Night"). The time was clearly "wrong," they said, amid the political and economic convulsions of 1930. Frost shot back in an essay published in the student newspaper at Amherst College, where he had taught since 1916: "it is not possible to get outside the age you are in to judge it exactly. . . . Witness the many who in the attempt have suffered a dilation from which the tissues and the muscles of the mind have never been able to recover natural shape. . . . They can write huge shapeless novels, huge gobs of raw sincerity bellowing with pain and that's all they can write."*

IT IS USUALLY quiet, cold, and dark in a Robert Frost poem, and the speaker is alone, keeping his stark Yankee thoughts to himself. Frost gave a new poetic sound to that kind of solitude.

New England's patron poet was born in San Francisco. He, his sister, and their Scottish-born mother moved to Massachusetts after the death of Frost's father, a brilliant, alcoholic journalist, in 1885. Frost enrolled at Dartmouth, but, lonely and impatient with college life, lasted less than one semester. He published his first poetry while trying to persuade his high school sweetheart, Elinor White, to marry him. After she did, in 1895, Frost worked as a journalist and taught school, spent 18 months studying at Harvard, and then settled in New Hampshire as a part-time teacher and incompetent chicken farmer. He was, however, developing his own form of blank verse, constructing poetic order from the calm iambic rhythm of narrative conversation. He burned with ambition, but managed to publish only in small journals until he was nearly 40.

In 1912, the Frosts abruptly moved with their four small children to England. Frost's first book, *A Boy's Will*, was published there almost immediately, and he met Ezra Pound and the Welsh writer Edward Thomas, who quickly became one of his few close friends. Returning to the United States in 1915, Frost found he had turned into a star poet (Pound's favorable review of *A Boy's Will* in Harriet Monroe's *Poetry* magazine helped to create a name for the then-unknown Frost, and Pound made acidic note of the fact that Frost, a particularly American poet, had been discovered in England). For the rest of his long life, he wrote, taught, and cultivated his steadily growing reputation. In letters and lectures, he pioneered theory, including the idea that whole sentences have sounds of their own. In public, he became a de facto poet laureate, with an appearance at John F. Kennedy's inauguration, birthday greetings from the U.S. Senate, and a namesake mountain in Vermont. ■

The Freedom of the Moon

I've tried the new moon tilted in the air
Above a hazy tree-and-farmhouse cluster
As one might try a jewel in the hair.
I've tried it fine with little breadth of lustre,
Alone, or with a star almost as shining
Both far gone west and visibly declining.

I put it shining anywhere I please.
By walking slowly on some evening later,
I've pulled it from a crate of crooked trees
And brought it over glossy water greater,
And dropped it in and seen the image wallow,
The color run, all sorts of wonder follow.

Robert Frost
For Gilbert H Montague

August 1926

Mr. Frost has, in fact, gone back, as Whitman and as Wordsworth went back, through the paraphernalia of poetry into poetry again. With a confidence like genius, he has trusted his conviction that a man will not easily write better than he speaks when some matter has touched him deeply, and he has turned it over until he has no doubt what it means to him, when he has no purpose to serve beyond expressing it, when he has no audience to be bullied or flattered, when he is free, and speech takes one form and no other.

Edward Thomas, "A language not to be betrayed" [review of Frost's North of Boston] *in* New Weekly, *August 8, 1914*

In the early winter of 1926, Frost read "The Freedom of the Moon" in a chapel at Wesleyan University. A sophomore named Lawrance Thompson arrived late, just in time to be enraptured by the second stanza and to become "a Frost addict," by his own account. Frost eventually chose Thompson to write his authorized biography. It took most of Thompson's life, and in the end, the massive, three-volume work was so critical that it led Howard Moss, poetry editor of The New Yorker, *to describe Frost as "a mean-spirited megalomaniac." Frost's reputation is still distended by two extremes, of his and Thompson's making: twinkly-eyed, homespun, firewood-splitting Yankee; and conniving, depressive, insecure literary blackguard.*

Edward Thomas

1878–1917

This portrait, after a photograph by Frederick H. Evans, was used as the frontispiece for Thomas's Collected Poems *(1921). Based in London, Evans was a bookseller and publisher as well as a gifted photographer.*

He was so imperturbably the poet through everything to the end. If there is any merit in self-possession, I can say I never saw anyone less put off himself by unaccustomed danger, less put off his game. His concern to the last was what it had always been: to touch earthly things and come as near to them in words as words would come.

Robert Frost, quoted in Lawrance Thompson, Robert Frost: The Years of Triumph *(New York, 1970)*

IT WAS NOT until December 3, 1914, that the first of Edward Thomas's poems "began to run," as he put it. He was 36. Between that day and the following June he poured out half of his lifetime *oeuvre* of poetry and then, in July, enlisted to fight in World War I. After a stint as a map-reading instructor, he became an artilleryman and sailed for France in January 1917. In April, seven months before the end of the war, Thomas was killed by a shell. He had seen only eight of his poems in print, but posthumously he has become known as one of the century's most original poets.

Born to Welsh parents in south London, Thomas spent his holidays at the rural homes of his relatives. By age 15 he had discovered a love of the countryside and a desire to write, and satisfied both appetites with nature essays. In 1899, when he was 20 and still an undergraduate at Oxford, he married Helen Noble. The next year, their first child, Merfyn, was born and Thomas began eking out a living as a critic and essayist, while suffering intermittent bouts of depression. For the next 15 years, he turned out scores of reviews, journalism, and books like *Beautiful Wales*.

Then, in 1913, Thomas met and immediately liked Robert Frost, who had moved to London the previous year. It was Frost who suggested that Thomas write poems, and who wrote later, "Edward Thomas was the only brother I ever had." They discussed the depression from which both suffered, and exchanged ideas about poetry. Both sought to make verses from simple, conversational language, and both were enamored of nature. But Thomas, as Frost later said, was an original type of war poet. There is hardly a bullet or a trench in his poems. Instead, he gently mourns the world that, as he realized presciently, World War I would help to destroy. ■

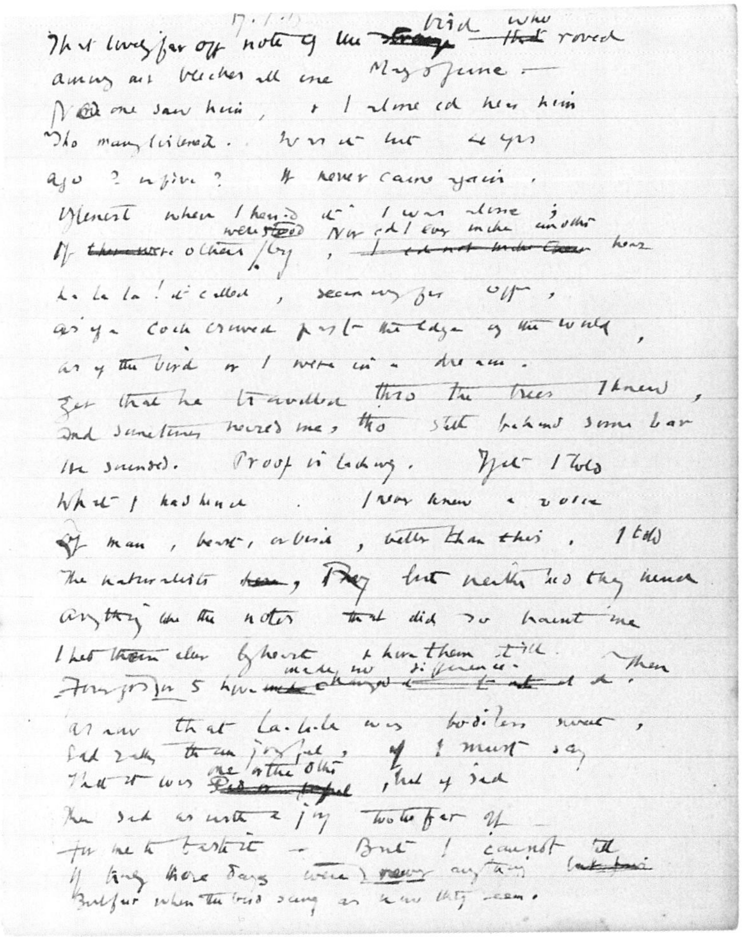

On January 17, 1915, about six weeks after he began composing poems, and when he was considering whether to enlist in the British Army, Thomas wrote out two versions of "The Unknown Bird," which would become one of his best-known poems, in an exercise book from the Bedales School, where the poet's wife taught. The versions (one of which is shown here) differ greatly from each other and from the final poem.

from **The Unknown Bird**

VERSION 1:
That lovely far-off note of the bird who roved
Among our beeches all one May and June

VERSION 2:
That bird that whistled 3 soft and lovely notes
Down in the beech woods all one May & June

PUBLISHED TEXT:
Three lovely notes he whistled, too soft to be heard
If others sang; but others never sang
In the great beech-wood all that May and June.

From boyhood, Thomas loved long walks and was an amateur naturalist. He knew the names of innumerable wildflowers and sometimes pressed them into his notebooks like Thoreau, whom he admired. This notebook is open to the entries for October 9 and 10, 1896, when Thomas was 18 years old. Years later, he discovered that his new friend Robert Frost shared his love of what Frost called "botanizing" – walking in the woods and collecting samples – and the two often went out together. After such walks, Thomas would agonize over not having chosen a different route, where they might have found better flowers. Tongue in cheek, Frost wrote what was to become the final stanza of "The Road Not Taken," one of his most famous poems, and sent a fair copy of it to Thomas, with no comment.

Siegfried Sassoon

1886–1967

This photograph of Sassoon was inscribed on the back from Stephen Tennant to Sir Edward Howard Marsh, probably in the spring of 1929, when Tennant and Sassoon were enjoying a bucolic holiday together in Bavaria. Sassoon was most likely homosexual, and during the period following World War I carried on relationships with a series of younger men, the one with Tennant being the most serious and the most tumultuous. A talented artist, particularly with watercolors, Tennant designed the covers for some of Sassoon's books. Suffering from tuberculosis, he put an end to the relationship in May 1933, and Sassoon married Hester Gatty on December 18 of that year.

AMONG TOO MANY others, the poets Rupert Brooke, Charles Hamilton Sorley, Isaac Rosenberg, Edward Thomas, and Wilfred Owen died in World War I. Robert Graves and Siegfried Sassoon were, along with Edmund Blunden, the surviving poets of their generation. Sassoon's major poetry, written during and immediately after the war, is original, careful, and affecting, graphically portraying the horrors and irrationality of trench warfare in the first books of modern antiwar poetry: *The Old Huntsman* (1917), *Counter-Attack* (1918), and *Picture Show* (1919). Recognized as the fullest representation of the Soldier Poet and as a major pacifist poet, Sassoon suffered brutal flashbacks throughout his life.

Sassoon was born into a privileged upper-middle-class family; his father was descended from an important Jewish family, and his mother was the daughter and sister of important sculptors and painters of the day. After being privately tutored, he entered the educational system late, spending a few years at Marlborough College and Clare College, Cambridge, where he failed to take a degree. Sassoon was a dedicated and ferocious soldier for most of the war, but in 1917 turned pacifist and protester. After convalescing in a hospital for a near nervous breakdown, he returned to the front; then, having been mistakenly shot in the head by one of his own men, he was sent home in July 1918. Despite several passionate homosexual relationships of some length and an early correspondence with the homophile writer Edward Carpenter, Sassoon married in 1933, at the age of 47. Although he separated from his wife, he continued a lifelong relationship with her and his son, George.

In the 1930s and after, Sassoon's poetry – now on philosophical and religious themes – became lyrical, withdrawn, and fragile; his six prose volumes, three of them "fictionalized" autobiography, are classics of English literature. Until his death, in 1967, Sassoon lived a simple, meditative, almost ascetic country life, converting to Catholicism in 1957. ∎

Reprinted in Counter-Attack (1918), "The Rear-Guard" first appeared in September 1917 in an issue of The Hydra; Journal of the Craiglockhart War Hospital, which also included Wilfred Owen's anonymously published "Extract from ye Chronicles of Wilfred de Salope, Knight." Sassoon and Owen met in the hospital and developed a close friendship, with Sassoon encouraging Owen, whom many consider to have been the most promising of the English Soldier Poets. Owen died a week before the war ended in 1918. Sassoon, a much-decorated soldier, had been wounded several times, once by a bullet through the neck. In the summer of 1917, with Bertrand Russell's help, he composed a statement of protest against the conduct of the war in Europe; it was printed as a leaflet, but its distribution was cut short by the military police. Sassoon was ordered to report to Craiglockhart as a result of an army medical board's pronouncement on the fragility of his mental health; he had, it appears, been saved from prison through the intervention of his friends Robert Graves and Edward Howard Marsh. This incident is the source of two fascinating novels by Pat Barker, Regeneration (1991) and The Eye in the Door (1993). Sassoon's marginal notes on this manuscript are probably addressed to Marsh.

Here's a story from Hindenburg's Trench (× *underground trench which goes for miles*)

The Rear-Guard.

Groping along the tunnel × step by step
He winked his prying torch with patching glare
From side to side, and sniffed the unwholesome air.

Tins, bottles, boxes, shapes too vague to know —
A mirror smashed, the mattress from a bed;
And he, exploring, — fifty feet below
The rosy gloom of battle overhead.

Tripping, he grabbed the wall; saw someone lie
Humped & asleep, half-hidden by a rug;
And stooped to give the sleeper's arm a tug —
"I'm looking for Head-Quarters."   No reply. —
"God blast your neck," (for days he'd had no sleep);
"Get up and guide me through this stinking place."
Then, with a savage kick at the silent heap,
He flashed his beam across a livid face
Horribly glaring up; and the eyes yet wore
Agony dying hard ten days before;
And twisted fingers clutched a blackening wound.

Alone, he staggered on until he found
Dawn's ghost, that filtered down a shafted stair
To the dazed, muttering creatures underground
Who hear the boom of shells in muffled sound.
Then, with the sweat of horror in his hair,
He climbed through darkness to the twilight air,
Unloading hell behind him, step by step.

S. April. 23rd.

(3 hours in 6 days!)

We were trying to take Fontaine - lez - Croisilles, (failed again yesterday, apparently).

> *incapable of doing what I have undertaken to do tomorrow, — which is to go to Wellington College & give a reading of my works to 250 boys & a formidable phalanx of their instructors! However they offered me £20, which seemed absurd to refuse, & I am 'killing two birds' etc, by combining it with a visit to my paralysed friend Dr. H. Head, who now lives a few miles from Reading. "Dear dear dear, what a life, what a life," as Nellie Wallace says —*
>
> *Everyone suddenly burst out singing ..." etc*
>
> *(Famous poet reading poems at Wellington.)*
>
> *yrs ever.*

Sassoon wrote this characteristi-cally gentle and self-effacing letter to Tennant's sister Anne in November 1929, just before he and Stephen left on a trip to Italy in order to rest and enjoy the therapeutic effects of the warm weather (Tennant's tuberculosis had been much aggravated by the death of his mother and his devoted "nannie" earlier that year). Sassoon ends the letter with some humor at his own expense concerning a reading he is to give at Wellington College the next day, including this caricature of himself, the "Famous poet reading poems at Wellington," intoning his 1919 poem "Everyone Sang," which concerns the Armistice.

. . . regardless of fault or fashion, every book of Sassoon's poetry has had a serious claim on the world's attention. . . . It was not just that in *Counter-Attack* he had published some important poems which were still direct and exciting; it was not his instinctive or temperamental principles; it was nothing to do with a rusticated lyrical tradition. It was directness, an evocative honesty of the eyes, and a harshly sweet resonance reminiscent of a violoncello.

Peter Levi, "Sassoon at Eighty" in Poetry Review *(Autumn 1966)*

Rupert Brooke

1887–1915

In 1901–2, when this photograph was taken, the teenaged Rupert Brooke was a student at Rugby School.

The death of Rupert Brooke fills me more and more . . . with the sense of the fatuity of it all. He was slain by bright Phoebus' shaft – it was in keeping with his general sunniness – it was the real climax of his pose. I first heard of him as a Greek God under a Japanese sunshade, reading poetry in his pyjamas at Grantchester, at Grantchester, upon the lawns where the river goes. Bright Phoebus smote him down. It is all in the saga.

O God, Oh God, it is all too much of a piece: it is like madness.

D. H. Lawrence, letter to Lady Ottoline Morrell, April 30, 1915

RUPERT BROOKE WAS the perfect Englishman, intelligent, well-educated, handsome, articulate, and socially adept. He attended Rugby School, where his father was a tutor, and then Kings College, Cambridge. His friends included Henry James, Virginia Woolf, James Strachey, and Sir Edward Howard Marsh, all immensely powerful in the literary world of prewar London. His knowledge of the history and tradition of English poetry was, by all accounts, astonishing.

A first collection of his poems was brought out by a major publisher when he was 23. Four years later, Rupert Brooke died (of blood poisoning) in the Aegean the day before his battalion landed for the bloody battle at Gallipoli. Brooke was buried on the Greek isle of Skyros. Only 11 of the 14 officers in his battalion survived through 1914.

A second volume of Brooke's poems was published posthumously in 1915, and by 1926 sales of his work had earned over £300,000 for his estate. His reputation was closely guarded by his trustees (his mother and a friend, the eminent surgeon and bibliographer Sir Geoffrey Keynes). Plaques and memorials were dedicated to him, and schoolchildren imitated his verse. A collected poems was published in 1918 and another was issued in 1946, a bibliography of his work was published in 1954, and an edition of collected prose appeared in 1956.

In reaction to Brooke's great popularity, his poetry has been dismissed by some critics as patriotic gush or as romantically and deludedly idealistic. A measured understanding of the man or the poet has, not surprisingly, been submerged beneath various images and myths, including that of the Golden Apollo, the soldier-poet, and the nature poet. His sexuality and sexual preferences have been the subject of intense critical-literary scrutiny. Nevertheless, Brooke's best poems still display a complex irony, youthful wit, control, and authority. They seem surprisingly fresh, sometimes funny, playful, and attractively odd. ■

Heaven

Fish (fly-replete, in depth of June,
Dawdling away their wat'ry noon)
Ponder deep wisdom, dark or clear,
Each secret fishy hope or fear.
Fish say, they have their Stream and Pond;
But is there anything Beyond?
This life cannot be All, they swear,
For how unpleasant, if it were!
One may not doubt that, somehow, Good
Shall come of Water and of Mud;
And, sure, the reverent eye must see
A Purpose in Liquidity.
We darkly know, by Faith we cry,
The future is not Wholly Dry.
Mud unto mud! – Death eddies near –
Not here the appointed End, not here!
But somewhere, beyond Space and Time.
Is wetter water, slimier slime!
And there (they trust) there swimmeth One
Who swam ere rivers were begun,
Immense, of fishy form and mind,
Squamous, omnipotent, and kind;
And under that Almighty Fin,
The littlest fish may enter in.
Oh! never fly conceals a hook,
Fish say, in the Eternal Brook,
But more than mundane weeds are there,
And mud, celestially fair;
Fat caterpillars drift around,
And Paradisal grubs are found;
Unfading moths, immortal flies,
And the worm that never dies.
And in that Heaven of all their wish,
There shall be no more land, say fish.

This manuscript of "Heaven" was sent from Honolulu, where the poem was composed, to Brooke's close friend Sir Edward Howard Marsh, littérateur, philanthropist, and editor of the influential Georgian Poetry *anthologies. The poem appeared in the second volume of Brooke's poems,* 1914 and Other Poems, *which was published posthumously by Marsh, and in the second* Georgian Poetry *volume of 1915.*

Isaac Rosenberg

1890–1918

His experiments were a strenuous effort for impassioned expression; his imagination had a sinewy and muscular aliveness; often he saw things in terms of sculpture, but he did not carve or chisel; he *modelled* words with fierce energy and aspiration, finding ecstacy in form, dreaming in grandeurs of superb light and deep shadow; his poetic visions are mostly in sombre colours and looming sculptural masses, molten and amply wrought.

Siegfried Sassoon, foreword to The Collected Poems of Isaac Rosenberg *(New York, 1949)*

IN 1886, THE likelihood of conscription into the Russian Army led Dovber Rosenberg to flee Siberia and immigrate to England. Twenty-nine years later, to his horror, his slight, awkward son, Isaac, enlisted into a "bantam" batallion in the British Army's 40th division. It wasn't that Isaac wanted to fight: trying to support himself as an artist had proved so hard that he was tempted by the soldier's wage of one shilling per day.

Rosenberg was born in Bristol, the first city where his father earned a scant living as a peddler, and for most of his childhood he shared one room with seven family members at the back of a rag and bone shop in London's Jewish quarter. Like William Blake, Rosenberg had a double talent for painting and poetry that surfaced early. He wrote poems before he was ten, and sketched passersby on the sidewalk. Later, he studied art at the University of London's Slade School with the help of three women patrons, and produced some memorable portraits before settling on poetry. When he self-published his first book of poems, *Night and Day*, in 1912, one of his friends tried hawking it in the street, but sold none of the 50-odd copies.

Among the well-known war poets, Rosenberg was the only non-officer. Although his unit had been granted a rest after fighting off a German advance, he volunteered to return to the front, where he was killed in combat on April 1, 1918, at the age of 27. Spottily educated, Rosenberg never fully developed his talent, but many critics have been struck by the raw originality of his phrasing. "I will ride the dizzy beast of the world," reads an exuberant but, for him, mistaken line in his long verse-drama *Moses*. ∎

This drawing of Isaac Rosenberg was made by H.C. Hammond at Bolt Court Art School in 1914.

This pen-and-ink portrait of Rosenberg was made by H. C. Hammond (the undated photograph pasted onto the sheet shows the poet in military uniform). Hammond was an acquaintance of Rosenberg's from the London County Council School of Photo-engraving and Lithography, also called the Bolt Court Art School, where Rosenberg studied in 1909 and 1910. On the day Hammond made this drawing in 1914, Rosenberg had dropped by for a visit.

Break of day in the trenches.
==============================

The darkness crumbles away.

It is the same old Druid Time as ever,

Only a live thing leaps my hand,

A queer sardonic rat,

As I pull the parapets poppy

To stick behind my ear.

Droll rat, they would shoot you if they knew

Your cosmopolitan sympathies,

(And God knows what antipathies).

Now you have touched this English hand

You will do the same to a German

Soon, no doubt, if it be your pleasure

To cross the sleeping green between.

It seems odd thing, you grin as you pass

Strong eyes, fine limbs, haughty athletes,

Less chanced than you for life,

Bonds to the whims of Murder,

Sprawled in the bowels of the aarth

The torn fields of France.

What do you see in our eyes

At the boom, the hiss, the swiftness,

The irrevocable earth--buffet?....

What rootless popies dropping--

But mine in my ear is safe---

Just a little white with the dust.

"*Break of Day in the Trenches*" *is the most famous of Rosenberg's war poems, many of which were indeed written in the trenches of the Western Front in France. In the late summer and autumn of 1916, Rosenberg mailed several evolving, differing versions of this poem to his friend and patron Sir Edward Howard Marsh, then private secretary to Winston Churchill; to Sonia Cohen, with whom he was in love; and to the American editor Harriet Monroe, who published it in the December 1916 issue of* Poetry *magazine. The Berg Collection's manuscript is one that Rosenberg sent to Marsh.*

Humbert Wolfe

1885–1940

OTHER men have written worse
than the author of this verse,
but at least they had the wit
not to go, and publish it.

*Humbert Wolfe, lampooning
himself, in* Lampoons
(London, 1927)

*In addition to his devotion to the
cause of poetry, Wolfe was a tire-
less, imaginative, and responsible
civil servant, a worker among
workers. In recognition of his ser-
vice, he was made a Commander
of the British Empire in 1918.*

POET, TRANSLATOR, LAMPOONIST, playwright, literary critic,
and highly decorated civil servant, Umberto Wolff was born
in Milan in 1885; that same year, Wolfe later reminisced, he
"lost no time in crossing to Bradford in the West Riding of
Yorkshire . . . and remained there till he left it for Oxford some
18 years later." Wolfe (who did not change his name until
1918) entered Wadham College as a scholar, having successfully
tackled the entrance exams with a combination of "freshness"
and "inspired cheek." He seems to have enjoyed himself
tremendously; he did brilliant work that showed up the
boys from Harrow and Eton, met James Elroy Flecker, and –
"disturbed by metaphysics" – poured his heart into poetry.

After World War I, Wolfe began his bureaucratic advance
(by day) as a highly regarded, but "uncivil Civil Servant";
meanwhile, he devoted himself (by night) to poetry and criti-
cism. His reviews appeared regularly in the *Observer* and
other papers, and his poems – graceful, deceptively modern,
and often pitched low, in the voice of a sophisticated but distant
observer – began to be noticed. As he later wryly noted, the
continuance of his steadily flourishing literary career was
"not wholly prevented" when he authored, for the Carnegie
Foundation, one of his less immediately appealing prose
works, *Labor Supply and Regulation* (1923). *London Sonnets*,
his first volume of verse, appeared in 1920, and for the next
two decades he published prolifically: translations (Heine,
Ronsard, the *Greek Anthology*); studies of Shelley, Tennyson,
and Herrick; memoirs; and a "poetic ballet" that was produced
at the Mercury Theatre in 1936. Virginia Woolf thought
him a "theatrical looking glib man"; and Wolfe once wrote of
himself, perhaps revealingly, that "His only merit is that of
a hard worker." But he was a gifted satirist, and his poetry –
tart, fanciful, sardonic, and often bracingly strange – can still
startle and enchant. ■

Wolfe was a superb student at Wadham College, Oxford, where he was awarded a second in classics in 1905, and a first in humanistic literature in 1907. In this photograph of the Canning Club, the handsome young Wolfe appears in the top row, fourth from the left.

London Sonnets *(1920), Wolfe's first book of poetry, is a curious mix of satire and delicate description, but it is also clearly the work of a promising poet, versatile in his use of a variety of formal techniques. "The Deserted Lover at the Restaurant," entitled "Grey Eyes at the Restaurant" in this undated version, was part of an early manuscript of* London Sonnets, *but does not appear in the printed volume.*

The Deserted Lover at the Restaurant [Grey Eyes at the Restaurant]

The black-coat waiters hover with the plates
  or from the ice-filled buckets pour the wine
  not guessing that on each of those who dine
another Waiter in the darkness Waits . . . .
The grey-eyed ghost who leans behind her chair
  hears through her laughter, deep as in a well
  the far-fetched echoes muttering in Hell.
And one cold hand clutches the splendid hair.
The pale slim devil with the boyish lips
  behind her lover, as he meets her eyes
  (grey as a dream of dawn in Paradise)
curves hungry fingers crimson to the tips.
  I clear. I only see that silent crew
  myself long dead and damned because of you.

Anna Wickham

1884–1947

Recovering in Paris from the death of her four-year-old son, Richard, in 1922, Wickham met the woman of letters and lesbian writer Natalie Barney, with whom she fell in love. In 1926, on one of her frequent visits to Paris, she was photographed by Berenice Abbott, who was then the student of Man Ray, and part of the circle of intellectuals and artists around Barney's salon in the rue Jacob. Among other frequenters were Gertrude Stein, Rilke, Valéry, Colette, and Proust.

BORN IN ENGLAND, Edith Alice Mary Harper spent most of her childhood in Australia. Her mother was a "sensationalist" and psychic much drawn to death. Her father – well-read, proud, handsome, but "eternally an amateur" – was convinced of his daughter's genius. He presented her early verses to Queensland's most notable poet, who solemnly pronounced that the girl would be a poet "if she has enough pain." For her hapless father this amounted nearly to a "form of self-belief," and he made her swear at the age of ten that she would be a poet. This "curious and very emotional pact" was sealed on Wickham Terrace in Brisbane; Edith Alice Mary Harper was duly discarded, and in 1904, Anna Wickham sailed for Europe.

Wickham trained in Paris with Jean de Reszke (one of the great singers of the age), but she abandoned her musical ambitions to marry Patrick Hepburn, a lawyer and astronomer. They were happy for a time, and had four sons; but Hepburn violently objected to Wickham's writing, and she was committed to an asylum for six weeks. Uncowed, she wrote compulsively. She was published by Harold Monro and Alida Klementaski (of the Poetry Bookshop), and in America, Louis Untermeyer was an influential admirer. Iconoclastic and uncompromising, Wickham wrote of the divided, tortured self: her children meant the world to her, but she was possessed of a creative daemon that spoke fearlessly with the "incompetence of pain." Although she wrote hundreds of poems, only a small percentage have been published. She asked that the following lines be used to preface all her books: "Here is no sacrificial I, / Here are more I's than yet were in one human, / Here I reveal our common mystery: / I give you woman." A German firebomb destroyed many of her manuscripts and much of her correspondence in 1943; four years later, having seen her beloved sons through the nightmare of World War II, she hanged herself.

Once, loudly voicing her scorn at an art show, Wickham was threatened with eviction; unflustered, she turned on the luckless gallery owner: "You'd better retract, my good man. I may be a minor poet, but I'm a major woman!" ∎

Poems by Anna Wickham

Bridegroom

Man I shall beget tomorrow
Where is he?
Life a load, the load a sorrow,
Better not to be.
Man I shall beget tomorrow
Non-existent – where is he?

He is spread in fields of wheat,
Low in grass that cows shall eat.
There are fragments of himself
High upon some warehouse shelf.
Any atom he may be
Any atom may be he.

She the focus will control,
The new body; but the Soul?
That is free.
The husk is made of any meat,
Any grass or any wheat.
But man alone has personality,
He alone is _he_;
The man is, I get tomorrow,
Whole in destiny
Can I then be free?

I was helped into the world with forceps . . . and I was actually put by on the chest of drawers for the dead. I yelled, and so was set out on my difficult way. . . . My father . . . despaired of my ever having any brains as the forceps had left so many bruises on my head. In time, however, I healed and my capable mother made a creditable baby out of me. . . . One evening when I was three months old . . . Father was reading, his feet on the mantlepiece. Struck by a passage in his book, he brought down his feet upsetting a boiling kettle over me. . . . For sometime after, I lived in oiled cotton wool. For the second time I escaped death. I take it that God used these means to sensitise a nervous system to his uses. . . .

Anna Wickham, "Fragment of an Autobiography: Prelude to a Spring Clean" (1935) in The Writings of Anna Wickham (London, 1984)

Wickham met and became friendly with Frieda and D. H. Lawrence in 1914 and spent time with the novelist wandering the Hampstead Heath, deep in discussions of philosophy, religion, and poetry. In her essay "The Spirit of the Lawrence Women," Wickham remembered: "Lawrence's insistence that Frieda should be a house-mother and only a house-mother, made him a sort of cartoon manhood, and raised an atmosphere of burlesque. The necromancer had not enough magic to compel the tiger to become a shrewmouse. But continuously he made his attempts. . . . It is to be remembered well of him that he had the grace to trim Frieda's hats." Lawrence copied out "Bridegroom" – published under the title "Outline" in the pseudonymous Songs of John Oland *(1911) and in* The Man with a Hammer *(1916) – and several other of Wickham's poems and sent them to Sir Edward Howard Marsh, for possible inclusion in one of his* Georgian Poetry *anthologies.*

D. H. Lawrence

1885–1930

Edward Weston took several photographs of Lawrence in Mexico City on November 4, 1924. This print was made from the only surviving negative from that sitting.

The young English poets who trod hard on Lawrence's heel learned some of their most valuable lessons from [his later work]. Lawrence taught them to be sensitive, to be at ease, to be good-natured, to be sane. He taught them that no subject is closed to the poet who is himself truthful and free. . . .

Louise Bogan, "Verse" in The New Yorker, *March 20, 1948*

D. H. LAWRENCE was a legendary and visionary figure, veiled by mysticism and mythology. One of the greatest of 20th-century novelists, he also wrote more than a thousand poems, many on the great subjects of love, sex, and death. His writing is a dialogue with himself, in which he sorts out beliefs and feelings, in an especially delicate and personal response to life. Despite the controversies surrounding his sexual, artistic, and political beliefs, and the notoriety attending the publication of *The Rainbow* (1915) and *Lady Chatterley's Lover* (1928), Lawrence's work displays a chaste, pure, passionate nature. Like Robert Burns before him, he is distinguished by the naturalness of his writing and the authenticity of his struggle. His is the poetry of whispers in the air on late summer nights.

The son of a coal miner and a would-be schoolteacher, David Herbert Lawrence was dramatically affected by the roughness of his father, whom he resented, and the intellectual pretensions of his mother, whom he adored. He left home in 1903 for a job teaching school in Croydon, near London, and began publishing his poetry in the major literary journals and anthologies of the day. In London, he was unhappy, seeming to run afoul of both the legal authorities and the arrogance of the literary coteries of the time.

Lawrence's life as both a man and a writer began anew when he met Frieda von Richthofen Weekley, who was later to become his wife. Her influence set the poet free both from his past and from the confines of England, which he had called "a long gray ashy coffin." They remained constant companions in a marriage – as much battlefield and struggle as pleasureable idyll – that lasted 18 years, until Lawrence's death of tuberculosis on March 2, 1930. In those years, Lawrence composed the best of his work, traveling in pilgrimage from one sun-drenched, bright field of light to another, searching. ■

Lawrence sent this manuscript of "Erotic," an early poem written around 1911, to his friend Edward Garnett; it was among the poems Garnett passed on to his son David, a writer and the husband of Virginia Woolf's niece Angelica Bell. Like Sir Edward Howard Marsh, Edward Garnett served as a literary advisor and agent for Lawrence, attempting to place his poems for publication. "Erotic" remained unpublished until its inclusion, with 15 other poems now in the Berg/Garnett collection, in an appendix to the 1964 edition of Lawrence's Complete Poems.

Erotic

And when I see the heavy red fleece
Of the creeper on the breast of the house opposite
Lift and ruffle in the wind,
I feel as if feathers were lifted and shook
On the breast of a robin that is fluttered with pain,
And my own breast opens in quick response
And its beat of pain is distributed on the wind.

And when I see the trees sway close,
Lean together and lift wild arms to embracc,
I lift my breast and lean forward,
Holding down my leaping arms.

And when black leaves stream out in a trail
  down the wind,
I raise my face so it shall wreathe me
Like a tress of black hair,
And I open my lips to take a strand of keen hair.

And when I see the thick white body of
  train-smoke break
And fly fast away,
I stifle a cry of despair.

Frieda's gracious reply to a con-
dolence message from Edward
Garnett following Lawrence's
death deals with the possible
editorship for a collection of
Lawrence's letters, which were
ultimately edited by Aldous
Huxley and published in 1932.
She included with the letter
copies of Lawrence's wood
engravings of his symbolic
phoenix, originally designed to
serve as a badge for Lawrence's
ever more elusive utopian
dream colony, Ranamin. In
response to his offer of money
for the letters (presumably an
advance), Frieda ends the letter,
"It's good of you to offer me
so much money, but you know,
there may be quite a lot, it
seems strange after our poverty –
but how rich we really were."

Lawrence drew him.

Vence
Monday

Dear Edward,
                    I was so glad to get
your letter, we neither of us forgot
ever, what you meant to us in our
first being together & what you meant
to Lawrence as the midwife of his
genius! I cant say anything yet
about your doing the letters, The
will is'nt proved yet, so I have
no right, Then I must ask Aldous,
as he is doing it. But do send me
copies of the letters, I should love to see them.
About my own, I have my doubts,

Robert Graves

1895–1985

I agree with you more and more about Graves. He is a mischievous soul, but few poets have more dash and charm, and he makes almost any poet seem repetitious and conventional.

Robert Lowell, unpublished letter to Randall Jarrell, October 24, 1957

In the "Red Branch Songbook," the poet's mother wrote out her verses about Robert and his siblings. This notebook also records, in his hand, some of the future poet's first works, such as the poem "Who did that?" Estranged from his parents from the time of his relationship with Laura Riding on, Graves did not attend the funerals of either of them.

A MODERN PROSPERO, throughout most of his life on the beautifully romantic island of Mallorca, Robert Graves cultivated a colorful and dramatic sense of grandeur and integrity. Best known now for the historical novels *I, Claudius* and *Claudius the God and His Wife Messalina*; the autobiographical memoir of World War I, *Good-bye to All That*; and the elegant restatements of *The Greek Myths* and *The White Goddess*, Graves published more than 50 volumes of poetry during his life. He has been intensely popular and widely admired, as the words of Stanley Kunitz suggest:

Some people have the impression that Robert Graves is not a man but a syndicate. How else explain the prodigality and variety of his production? Even if we ignore his novels, stories, memoirs, essays, criticism, polemics, translations, mythologies, exegeses, lectures, and miscellaneous what-nots, we are left with a formidable body of work in verse, all of it stamped with the characteristic quality of a style that Graves himself once described as "hand-made, individual craftsmanship."

Graves was born in 1895 of upper-class parents and participated dramatically in World War I, after which poetry became his life and his religion. From 1926 to 1940, he lived a notoriously volatile and complicated life with the poet Laura Riding. For the final 20 years of his life, he and his last wife, Beryl, enjoyed a time of relative serenity in the by-now-famous villa in Deya, Mallorca. In the 1960s, a series of lecture tours brought the poet a measure of fame, particularly in the United States, and in the 1970s, *I, Claudius* became a huge success on television. But the last years of his life were both tortured and empty. In December of 1985, Robert Graves died after an amazing long journey of a life at the edge of a very wide ocean. ■

*These candid snapshots of Robert Graves were probably taken in
England in the early 1950s.*

This apparently unpublished poem shows Graves at his simplest and most delightfully imaginative and natural. This manuscript was part of the holograph and typescript manuscript of Graves's 1959 Collected Poems, but the poem was dropped from that volume before publication. Like Moore and Auden, Graves continuously revised his poetry, even after it was published. The Berg Collection holds several other holograph and typescript drafts of "The Chaos Song," including one typescript where it is entitled "Six in Chaos" and a clean typescript from which the text below was transcribed.

The Chaos Song

'I had one, but the wheel came off.'
'I had one, but it cried.'
'I had one, but every screw was loose in it.'
'I had one, but I wasted all the juice of it.'
'I had one, but I never found a use for it.'
'I had one, but it died.'

'I had one, but the wheel came off.'
'I had one, without a view.'
'I had one, but forgot to put a chain on it.'
'I had one, but the cherries left a stain on it.'
'I had one, but we never ate a grain of it.'
'I had a nice one too.'

'I had one, but the wheel came off.'
'I had one that couldn't crawl.'
'I had one, but I don't know what's become of it.'
'I had one and I wish I still had some of it.'
'I had one, but the children made a drum of it.'
'I had the worst of all.'

Elinor Wylie

1885–1928

Elinor Wylie was much admired for her beauty, and perhaps not surprisingly, many who knew her felt free to comment on her vanity and unhappiness. Louis Untermeyer called her "one of the most beautiful women I have ever known and the vainest," while Kathleen Norris noted, "Three men – one might say men of distinction – had married her – and many others had indicated their admiration in unmistakable terms, but 'dissatisfied' was the word that inevitably was fitted to her, and everyone who knew her wondered what on earth she wanted." This portrait was probably made in the 1920s.

A STRIKING AND glamorous woman, Elinor Wylie aroused passion, admiration, and hostility: Virginia Woolf labeled her "hatchet minded" and "cadaverous," but Edmund Wilson praised her as a "master of a divine language" and a "free spirit as few bohemians are." A former editor of *Vanity Fair* who rubbed shoulders with the literary giants of her day, Wylie shunned the expectations and conventions of society. Her struggle to define herself as a wife and a poet informed her poetry and prose, which pointedly dealt with themes of entrapment and isolation.

Born into a prominent family with social, political, and financial connections in Philadelphia and Washington, D.C., Wylie married Philip Hichborn, the well-connected, dashing, and unstable son of an admiral, in 1905. When she abandoned her husband and young son in late December 1910, and vanished with lawyer Horace Wylie, whose wife would not grant him a divorce, the press had a field day. In England, the new couple lived as "Mr. and Mrs. Waring." After the "Warings" returned to the States in late spring 1915 (they were finally able to marry in 1916), Wylie began to write in earnest. Praise from a *Poetry* editor for "Sea Lullaby" (1919) encouraged her further, and two years later she published her second collection, *Nets to Catch the Wind* (her first, *Incidental Numbers*, had been privately printed in England, at her mother's expense, in a limited edition of 60 copies).

Increasingly frail and high-strung after several miscarriages, Wylie divorced her husband in 1923 to marry William Rose Benét, an intimate friend of her brother Henry and an ardent admirer of her poetry. Although their relationship had deteriorated and they had begun to live apart, Wylie was with Benét in the study of their New York apartment at 36 West 9th Street when she died of a stroke on December 16, 1928, a copy of Donne's *Sermons* tumbling from her hands before she collapsed to the floor. ■

Sonnet

I am the new Penelope who weaves
A tapestry of singing; -- See, the crossed
And subtle filiments are all embossed
With scarlet flowers and with silver leaves,
Twined in a pattern where the sense perceives
A tongue of flame, a tracery of frost,
A tortuous loveliness foredoomed and lost;
My hand destroys it, ere my hand achieves.

Still in despair I ravel out the web
I wrought in pride; -- imperfect is the plan
Of my presumptuous toil; -- I see afar
The true design -- the tides' increase and ebb,
The loom, entangling proud Aldeberan,
The shuttle, threaded to a falling star.

Elinor Wylie
Bar Harbor - Mt. Desert
Maine

*This sonnet, characteristic of Wylie's best work, is apparently unpublished;
many of her manuscripts were lost in a fire, and this typescript was pre-
sumably unknown to William Rose Benét when he compiled her* Collected
Poems *in 1932 and the* Last Poems *(actually the previously uncollected
poems) in 1943. This typescript and those for several other unpublished
poems were given to the Berg Collection by Wylie's sister, Nancy Hoyt.*

Aestheticism (à la Wilde, Dowson, and Whistler) perfumes this coolly macabre poem, with its pale images of white and silver reflecting the poet's obsession with those colors (Wylie cultivated an austere beauty, and often wore dresses of white or silver, some designed by the Parisian master of haute couture, *Paul Poiret). On the back of this manuscript, which is written in the poet's juvenile hand, are the poem's final three stanzas, which go on to record the choking, beating, and strangling of a "strong little boy" at the hand of the sea. Years later, Wylie added a note, addressed probably to her sister, just below the final stanza: "For your consolation, I may say that the child is now supposed to have run away (from a* very *cruel mother) & besides he is 15 years old, which I didn't know." Wylie revised the final stanza before including "Sea Lullaby" in* Nets to Catch the Wind *(1921).*

Sea Lullaby

The old moon is tarnished
With smoke of the flood,
The dead leaves are varnished
~~varnished~~
With color like blood.

A treacherous smiler
With teeth white as milk,
A savage beguiler
In sheathings of silk.

The sea creeps to pillage,
She leaps on her prey;
A child of the village
Was murdered today.

Oh, she was beautiful in every part! —
The auburn hair that bound the subtle brain;
The lovely mouth cut clear by wit and pain,
Uttering oaths and nonsense, uttering art
In casual speech and curving at the smart
On startled ears of excellence too plain
For early morning! — *Obit*. Death from strain;
The soaring mind oustripped the tethered heart.

*Edna St. Vincent Millay, from "To Elinor Wylie"
(in answer to a question about her)*

Edna St. Vincent Millay 1892–1950

She is like nothing at all but herself . . . when she and this generation are gone, the die which stamped her style will be broken.

Elinor Wylie, quoted in Jean Gould, The Poet and Her Book: A Biography of Edna St. Vincent Millay *(New York, 1969)*

IN 1912, CORA Millay urged "Vincent," one of the three daughters she raised alone in rural Maine, to enter a national poetry contest. "Renascence," a long meditation on nearly drowning as a child, won acclaim and a prize for "E. Vincent Millay, Esq.," to whom the first congratulatory letter was addressed. In fact, the poet was an ethereal, low-voiced, 20-year-old woman with ribbons in her flowing red hair. When she recited "Renascence" in public a few months later, an astounded stranger offered her a scholarship to college. The poem had changed the course of her life.

After Vassar College, Millay moved to New York City's Greenwich Village, where she spent five flamboyant, unmarried years that have cemented her name to just one of her lines of verse: "My candle burns at both ends . . ." She went to Europe as a correspondent for *Vanity Fair* and wrote poems prolifically, especially the love sonnets for which she is now best known. Millay became famous writing formal verse in an unapologetically modern voice. She won the Pulitzer Prize in 1923, campaigned against the execution of Sacco and Vanzetti in 1927, and during World War II wrote propaganda poems to cheer on the U.S. Army.

Many of Millay's proud, pained sonnets were written for Arthur Davison Ficke, a poet, lawyer, and Army officer who was married. He also wrote many sonnets for her, eventually divorced, and was married again, but not to Millay. In 1923, after a three-month courtship, Millay married Eugen Jan Boissevain, a tall, athletic Dutch coffee importer.

Two years later they moved to Steepletop, an old, remote farmhouse in Austerlitz, New York, with a piano but no telephone. Millay lived in relative isolation there until she died of a heart attack on the landing of the stairs, after having sat up all night smoking and reading a translation of the *Aeneid*. ∎

This portrait by Arnold Genthe of Millay at about age 21 is one of the best-known photographs of the poet, and captures the delicate beauty that pleased so many admirers. Unfortunately, some of them have paid more attention to the poet than to her poetry. Observing this, the critic Sandra Gilbert wrote that Millay "might be said to have stood for another phenomenon: the rise of a group of women poets whose fame was as theatrical as it was literary." Louise Bogan once shrewdly remarked, "It is a dangerous lot, that of the charming, romantic public poet, especially if it falls to a woman."

OPPOSITE

The October 1918 issue of The Sonnet published Millay's "Possession," which, as this typescript indicates, was originally titled "To a Rejected Love." Kept in an envelope from The Sonnet addressed to Edna Millay and later marked by the poet "unpublished Verse," this typescript bears a note from Millay to her sister Kathleen which reads "These sonnets are not quite as I want them yet, but I shan't change them very much." (The other sonnet in question was "To Another Poet," which begins: "Into the golden vessel of great song.") 139 Waverly Place was the address of the frigid one-and-a-half-room apartment in Greenwich Village where Millay lived with her sister Norma in the winter of 1918. At the time, Millay was working as an actress, playing Annabelle, a foolish young woman, in The Angel Intrudes, a one-act play written by Floyd Dell, who was one of her numerous lovers and suitors.

TO A REJECTED LOVE

I know I said, "I am weary of you,----go;"

   Too many patient days had there held place,

   Neglected, in my sunless window-space,

A silly plant that would not cease to grow,

And troubled me with blooming, till to throw,

   Broken, upon the ashes, in the face

   Of all the world, this constancy, and grace

With rarer growth my room, seemed good,----I know;

Today there is a difference. Today,

   Courted, esteemed, the unconsidered thing

   Sits in my neighbor's window blossoming,

   Richer in color, marvellously grown;

I watch till the drawn shade shuts it away;

   I want you back. I want you for my own.

These sonnets are not quite as I want them yet, but I shan't change them very much.

                ----Edna St. Vincent Millay,
                  139 Waverly Place,
                  New York City.

Robinson Jeffers

1887–1962

Edward Weston photographed Jeffers in several sessions during the last two weeks of May 1929, making over 50 Graflex negatives. On May 18 he wrote: "I photographed Jeffers out on the rocks, his face oceanward. Almost everyone would become heroic in such surroundings – certainly Jeffers. . . . I now realize, knowing him better, that Jeffers is more himself on grey days. He belongs to stormy skies and heavy seas. Without knowing his work one would feel in his presence, greatness. His build is heroic. . . . His profile is like the eagle he writes of."

"IT WOULD NOT have been written at all," Robinson Jeffers said of his poetry, "except for certain accidents that changed and directed my life." The first was his birth, to an erudite Presbyterian minister who taught him Greek and Latin before he was 12, and then took him to Switzerland for more rigorous schooling. Returning to the United States at age 15, Jeffers finished college in two years. He began graduate work in philosophy and comparative literature and then switched to medical school; he did well, but quit to study forestry. After giving up forestry, Jeffers languished by the beach until he joined Una Call, the second major "accident" of his life.

Una and Jeffers had met during his first year of college at the University of Southern California, where they took Miss M. G. Borthwick's Advanced German and read *Faust* together. Una was at the time the beautiful, unconventional wife of a Los Angeles lawyer; seven painful years later, she divorced her husband to marry Jeffers.

The couple became enchanted by Carmel, California, and decided to build their home at the edge of its jagged coastline. Carmel also provided the austere, wild landscape and raw tone of many of Jeffers's poems, such as the narrative "Tamar," which abruptly made him famous after he self-published it in 1924. But fame intruded on the isolation of Robinson, Una, and their twin sons, so they shunned it. Gradually critics shunned Jeffers too: in 1932 he was on the cover of *Time*, but by 1938 *The Selected Poetry of Robinson Jeffers* was coldly dismissed by the same magazine. In 1948, Random House added a highly unusual note to his antiwar collection, *The Double Axe*, expressing "disagreement over some of the political views" expressed in the volume.

After the death of his cherished Una in 1950, Jeffers was "left waiting for death, like a leafless tree"; he died in 1962. ∎

(118)

```
                LOVE THE WILD SWAN

"I hate my verses, every line, every word.
Oh pale and brittle pencils ever to try
One grass-blade's curve, or the throat of one bird
That clings to twig, ruffled against white sky.
Oh cracked and twilight mirrors ever to catch
One color, one glinting flash, of the splendor of things.
Unlucky hunter, Oh bullets of wax,
The lion beauty, the wild-swan wings, the storm of the wings."
---This wild swan of a world is no hunter's game.
                                    miss
Better bullets than yours would never-break the white breast,
Better mirrors than yours would crack in the flame.
Does it matter whether you hate your . . . self? At least
Love your eyes that can see, your mind that can
Hear the music, the thunder of the wings.  Love the wild swan.
```

Jeffers' nightmare world, in which reality is squeezed and beaten into the shape of a brutal adolescent's dream, is, however, more relevant to our present situation than it was when it burst upon us, twenty years or so ago. If Jeffers now pitches his tone so high that it becomes a shriek of hysteria, he is only screwing up to their utmost the tensions of our scene.

Louise Bogan, in A Poet's Alphabet: Reflections on the Literary Art and Vocation *by Louise Bogan, edited by Robert Phelps and Ruth Limmer (New York, 1970)*

"Love the Wild Swan" begins as a poet's lament that his verses cannot adequately reproduce "one color, one glinting flash, of the splendor of things." But in the last six lines, Jeffers answers himself with an exhortation to set aside his artistic longings and adore natural splendor directly, even if it cannot be captured. In this poem, Jeffers also tips his hat to Yeats, by mentioning wild swans. Yeats's "The Wild Swans at Coole" describes "their clamorous wings" and "the bell-beat of their wings"; here, Jeffers writes of "the storm of the wings" and "the thunder of the wings."

William Faulkner

1897–1962

Faulkner, seen here in a 1954 portrait photograph by Carl Van Vechten, often referred to himself as a "failed poet." From his teens well into his 20s, he wrote hundreds of poems, laboriously reworking many of them. But by 1933, when he published A Green Bough, *his second and last volume of verse, he had already produced two of his prose masterworks,* The Sound and the Fury *(1929) and* As I Lay Dying *(1930).*

ON AUGUST 6, 1919, *The New Republic* published a poem by a young ex-bank clerk and former RAF-Canada cadet from Oxford, Mississippi. The magazine paid $15 for "L'après-midi d'un faune" (title from Mallarmé) – and William Faulkner made his first appearance in print. As slaphappy as "the lucky country boy at his first crap game," he sent in additional poems, but they were rejected without explanation. With the wonderful impertinence of youth, he then typed up Coleridge's "Kubla Khan" and submitted it to *The New Republic*. This time Faulkner received some feedback from the editor: "We like your poem, Mr. Coleridge, but we don't think it gets anywhere much."

In his 20s, Faulkner also didn't seem to be going anywhere much, attending to schooling and career in a notably desultory fashion. His passion for Swinburne and his disinclination to work were viewed dubiously around Oxford (one town wag dubbed him Count No 'Count). He attended Ole Miss sporadically, wrote a lot of poetry, adopted a British accent, and bragged skillfully about his (purely imaginary) military exploits (in the 1940s, *Twentieth Century Authors* solemnly reported that he "had two planes shot down under him" in France). With *Sartoris* (1929), the first novel in his complex and brilliant Yoknapatawpha saga, he finally found his voice; with a technique adapted from Joyce and a refinement of the extremely ripe language with which he had been experimenting in his verse, Faulkner began a richly imagined exploration of "that little patch up there in Mississippi" where he had started from. By turns violent, heartbreaking, macabre, and comic, his great series of novels dazzle with a Balzacian historical sweep that lends great specificity to an imaginative landscape that takes on mythic proportions. As Robert Lowell wrote, Faulkner's bypath – Mississippi – "was no bypath but a universe." ■

Where I am dead the clover ~~xxxx~~ loved of bees
Sings in the greening grass, that it be more green,
The wind combs leaves of sunlight in the trees
And golden leaves are where no leaves have been.

skying poplars ~~seem~~ dream
Where I am dead two ~~poplars skyward swirl~~
In ultimate green rush the river by:---
bowed mange of the stream
Two arrows sped the ~~green bow of the world~~,
And to his wake pin the enwinged sky
The water peircing, pinning down the sky.

Where I am dead the yawning sunset grieves
Lazily, that night should be so soon,
And all the sun-drunk ~~xxxxx~~ trees cup windless leaves
To catch the thin white liquor of the moon.

Where I am dead the aimless wind that strays
The greening corridors where all springs dwell
"How are you? are you faint, or sad?" it says.
answer:
And where I'm dead I ~~say:~~ "O I'm well."

William Faulkner
New Orleans
9 February 1925

Born male and single at early age in Mississippi. Quit school after five years in seventh grade. Got job in Grandfather's bank and learned medicinal value of his liquor. Grandfather thought janitor did it. Hard on janitor. War came. Liked British uniform. Got commission R.F.C. pilot. . . . Crashed. Cost British gov't £2000. Quit. Cost British gov't $84.30. King said, "Well done." Returned to Mississippi. Family got job: postmaster. Resigned by mutual agreement on part of two inspectors. . . . Had $700. Went to Europe. Met man named Sherwood Anderson. Said, "Why not write novels? Maybe won't have to work." Did. . . . Now flying again. Age 32. Own and operate own typewriter.

William Faulkner, letter to the editor of Forum *magazine, published in same (April 30, 1930) with Faulkner's "A Rose for Emily"*

In early 1925, Faulkner left Oxford for New Orleans, intending to sail for Europe; but the Vieux Carré entranced him, and he delayed his departure until early July. He traded yarns and drank well into the night with the celebrated writer Sherwood Anderson, finished the first draft of his first novel (Soldier's Pay), *and hung around the Quarter's cheap restaurants, cafés, and speakeasies. During his stay in the city, Faulkner wrote impressionistic sketches of New Orleans (which were immediately accepted by the* Times-Picayune) *and worked on his poetry, including "Where I Am Dead the Clover Loved of Bees" (which he never published).*

Wallace Stevens

1879–1955

William Cole, head of publicity at Alfred A. Knopf, Stevens's publisher, organized a National Book Awards committee on which Stevens served in 1952, the year Rollie McKenna took this photograph. Cole later recalled: "I think Virginia Woolf said about T. S. Eliot, he was a man who wore a four-piece suit, and that's the impression I got of Stevens. He was very austere; in fact, frightening. He was a very large man, with a great belly and a head like a melon. And a difficult fellow." This portrait belonged to Howard Moss, a poet and poetry editor of The New Yorker *magazine, where it was pinned to the wall of his office for many years.*

BECAUSE WALLACE STEVENS said that life *is* poetry, many readers cannot fathom his own life as a portly, sedentary insurance lawyer in Hartford, Connecticut. But as the critic Frank Kermode realized, "no poet ever wrote so fixedly from within the human head as Stevens." Stevens's spectacular, pinwheeling imagination, and his longing to show that poetry could fill the modern void created by the absence of God, were often hidden under what Robert Frost disdainfully called a "porky-pie" hat, and he wore indistinguishable dark-gray suits all his life. He brewed tea in the afternoons on a gas ring at his office, where his secretary typed both his memos and his poems.

Born and raised in Reading, Pennsylvania, where his father was a lawyer and his mother a schoolteacher, Stevens attended Harvard. He then worked briefly as a journalist in New York, before attending law school. He worked at six different firms in New York from 1904 until 1916, when he lost his job and moved to Hartford with his wife, Elsie. In 1932, the Stevenses bought the Hartford house where they lived for the rest of their lives, firmly avoiding literary society despite Stevens's increasing fame. In 1934, he became a vice-president of the Hartford Accident and Indemnity Company, where he worked for the rest of his life.

A late-blooming poet, Stevens was considered intellectual even though he kept his distance from universities, and cosmopolitan even though he never set foot in Europe. He began writing vigorously in 1914 and *Harmonium*, his first book, was published when he was 44. As he became more prolific, he continued to examine his favorite early themes, especially poetry itself, in longer poems and more formal prosody. "The Man with the Blue Guitar," a famous example, is a wistful inquiry into the imagination and its role in the tangible world. ■

There are no bears among the roses,
Only a negress who supposes
Things false and wrong

About the lantern of the beauty
Who walks, there, as a farewell duty,
Walks long and long.

The pity that her pious egress
Should fill the vigil of a negress
With heat so strong!

The Virgin Carrying a Lantern
— W. Stevens: Harmonium

The Virgin Carrying a Lantern

There are no bears among the roses
Only a negress who supposes
Things false and wrong

About the lantern of the beauty
Who walks there, as a farewell duty,
Walks long and long.

The pity that her pious egress
Should fill the vigil of a negress
With heat so strong!

The riot of gorgeousness in which Mr. Stevens' imagination takes refuge, recalls Balzac's reputed attitude to money, to which he was indifferent unless he could have it "in heaps or by the ton."

Marianne Moore, "Well Moused, Lion" [review of Harmonium] *in* The Dial *(January 1924)*

This copy of Stevens's "The Virgin Carrying a Lantern" was made by one poet, Louise Bogan, and mailed to another, May Sarton, in June 1955. There are no drafts of Stevens's mature poetry in his own hand, since he apparently destroyed them after they had been typed out by a secretary at his business office. Stevens and his wife were also unusually private about their lives: several of Stevens's acquaintances and colleagues found it odd that they had never seen the inside of his house.

William Carlos Williams 1883–1963

This photograph was taken in the early to mid-1950s by Marion Morehouse at Patchin Place in New York's Greenwich Village, where Morehouse lived with her husband, poet E. E. Cummings. In "Life with Father," a memoir in the William Carlos Williams Newsletter, *William Eric Williams described his father: "His eyes were dark brown, always searching, looking not only at you but into you; not impolitely, but in an interested kind of way. . . . His dominating facial feature of course was his nose, which he recognized and early on glorified in his own poem 'Smell.' . . ."*

Williams is a writer to whom writing is a grinding of the glass, the polishing of a lens by means of which he hopes to be able to see clearly. His delineations are trials. They are rubbings of reality.

Wallace Stevens, "Rubbings of Reality" in Briarcliff Quarterly *(October 1946)*

WILLIAM CARLOS WILLIAMS was an obstetric and pediatric physician for over 40 years in Rutherford and Passaic, New Jersey. Working long hours, he cared for his patients, often tough working mothers, with tenderness and respect. But above all, he loved poetry. He was devoted to the craft, delivering into the world not quite as many poems as babies (nearly 2,000). Perhaps because he was both poet and practical man of medicine, Williams's poetry is often the most accessible and straightforward of all high modernist literature.

Williams's poetics (his concept of the poem as a "field," his privileging of the line as the primary unit, and his use of the rhythm of spoken English) have been highly influential with American poets of the latter half of this century: Louis Zukofsky, George Oppen, Charles Olson, Robert Duncan, Denise Levertov, Allen Ginsberg, and Robert Creeley all acknowledge Williams as a major influence. His poems often organize words in much the same way that his artist and photographer friends – among them Marsden Hartley, Charles Demuth, Charles Sheeler, Alfred Stieglitz, and Marcel Duchamp – organized visual images.

Born in Rutherford, New Jersey, Williams attended Horace Mann High School in New York City and the University of Pennsylvania, where he studied medicine and met Ezra Pound, H.D., and Demuth. At the end of 1912, after studies in Europe, he married Florence Herman; the following year, they moved to 9 Ridge Road in Rutherford, where they lived, constant companions, for the next 50 years. From this one place, the American original William Carlos Williams transported the usual things of everyday life into the formal world of the poem. Flowers, wheelbarrows, chickens, garbage and broken glass, hearts on sleeves – these are the stuff of his work. ■

THE RED WHEELBARROW

so much depends
upon

a red wheel
barrow

glazed with rain
water

beside the white
chickens

William Carlos Williams

(January 29, 1963)

Williams died on March 4, 1963, just a little more than a month after he signed this typescript of "The Red Wheelbarrow," his most famous poem (originally published in Spring and All, *1923).*

Ezra Pound

1885–1972

Pound's ideal reader is a person who has experienced real discomfort at being shut up, in a railway train, lecture hall, or concert room, with well-modulated voices expressing careful, well-bred opinions on the subject of the arts. Such a reader will remember his own impulse to break into argot and obscenity. . . .

Louise Bogan, "Make It New" in Selected Criticism *(New York, 1955)*

MAJOR CHANGES in the writing of literature, if not in the thinking of thought, occurred in the early part of this century. These changes, and the writing that came after, are known collectively as modernism. Ezra Pound is thought by many to be the architect of these changes, at least in the English-speaking world, because of his enthusiastic support of modern writing and his active encouragement of a variety of other writers. The great poets of the 20th century, including Yeats, Frost, Joyce, Eliot, Marianne Moore, William Carlos Williams, and H.D. (Hilda Doolittle), were among his literary comrades in this effort.

Pound was born in Hailey, Idaho, on October 30, 1885; attended Hamilton College and the University of Pennsylvania; taught at Wabash College in Crawfordsville, Indiana; and in 1908, at the age of 23, left the United States for self-imposed exile in London. In 1924, he began his life in Italy, where he died in 1972.

As an editor and translator, Pound was a veritable juggernaut, helping to found the magazine *Poetry* in 1912, and publishing his ground-breaking translations from the Chinese in 1915 as *Cathay*. Issued over a number of years, *The Cantos* is among the most ambitious poetic projects of this or any century. Its fragmented, associational compositional method has been highly influential among 20th-century poets.

But there is no denying Pound's controversiality and the ambivalence he arouses even among those who acknowledge his place in the history of modernist literature. In 1949, he was arrested for treason in connection with his propaganda broadcasts from Italy for the Axis forces during World War II. Judged to be insane, he was incarcerated for 12 years in St. Elizabeth's Hospital in Washington, D.C. (during which time the award to him in 1949 of the prestigious Bollingen Prize created an unprecedented literary furor). The poet Louis Zukofsky summed up the situation in a few words: "He may be condemned or forgiven. Biographers of the future may find his character as charming a subject as that of Aaron Burr. It will matter very little against his life's work overshadowed in his lifetime by the hell of Belsen which he overlooked." ■

Hotel Italia , Rapallo , 28 ,5 . '59
Activities of M.M. often of interest . C.P
however VERY deficient in detail , re/
where and what . Extremely difficult to get A
ANY of my contemporary colleagues to touch
on ANY topic of primary interest or
importance.

Notable effort on part of
most institutions to
divert attention to
minor serendipity.

Do you or she note
the more
active writers of
your generation.
as distinct fromthe********   pests ?

*Pound was a notably energetic correspondent, and after his return to
Italy in the late 1950s, he printed his own cards with his passport photo,
which came in handy for shorter notes, such as this one written from
Rapallo in 1959 to Chester Page, a classical pianist, collector, and friend
of Marianne Moore. Pound's longer letters are usually written as a series
of fragments, quotations, and citations, mirroring the style of* The Cantos,
his great poetic sequence.

And Thus in Nineveh

"Aye! I am a poet and upon my tomb
Shall maidens scatter rose leaves
And men myrtles, ere the night
Slays day with her dark sword.

"Lo! this thing is not mine
Nor thine to hinder,
For the custom is full old,
And here in Nineveh have I beheld
Many a singer pass and take his place
In those dim halls where no man troubleth
His sleep or song.
And many a one hath sung his songs
More craftily, more subtle-souled than I;
And many a one now doth surpass
My wave-worn beauty with his wind of flowers,
Yet am I poet, and upon my tomb
Shall all men scatter rose leaves
Ere the night slay light
With her blue sword.

"It is not, Raana, that my song rings highest
Or more sweet in tone than any, but that I
Am here a Poet, that doth drink of life
As lesser men drink wine."

*This manuscript of Pound's "And Thus in Nineveh"
was purchased from the archive of the publisher
Elkin Mathews, and may have been the setting copy
for the poem's first appearance in print, in Pound's
1909 collection* Personae, *Pound's first regularly
published volume (*A Lume Spento *had been privately
printed in Venice a year earlier). The poem is
characteristic early Pound in its intensity and passion,
as well as in the sharpness of its images and its
exoticism, embodied in the persona of a singer
of the Babylonian Empire.*

T. S. Eliot

1888–1965

Frank Morley – an American author, editor, and old friend of Eliot's, affectionately nicknamed "Whale" (to Eliot's "Possum") – helped bring the poet into Faber & Gwyer (later Faber & Faber), of which Morley was a founding director. Although Eliot generally presented himself to the world with great gravity and sobriety, in fact he had a wicked streak: at Faber & Faber he enlivened board meetings with firecrackers on the Fourth of July. Eliot used this 1926 photograph of himself in front of the company's London offices as a postcard to Morley (postmarked January 31, 1941, from Cambridge, Massachusetts).

T. S. ELIOT'S INTENSELY concentrated and allusive poetry radically altered literary taste on both sides of the Atlantic, particularly between the two world wars. He had perhaps an even greater impact as a literary and cultural critic – his essays and lectures substantially transformed the ways in which readers and critics responded to literature.

An embodiment of the purest English traditionalism, Thomas Stearns Eliot was actually born to a well-to-do Missouri family. He studied at Harvard and then at Oxford, where Bertrand Russell noted that Eliot's manners were "of the finest Etonian type." By 1928, the expatriate American had declared himself "classical in literature, royalist in politics, and Anglo-Catholic in religion."

Ezra Pound – that grand, impossible head-usher of literary modernism – met Eliot in 1914 and was astounded by his early poems, writing Harriet Monroe that Eliot had "modernized himself *on his own*." He spoke with a distinct new voice: ironic, cool, immediate. In the aftermath of an emotional crisis, Eliot wrote *The Waste Land*; after Pound's radical editing, it was published in 1922 (the original manuscript of the poem, with Pound's corrections, is one of the greatest treasures of the Berg Collection). Hallucinatory, fragmented, and disturbing, *The Waste Land* is a vision of Eliot's own psychic turbulence as well as his despairing response to the cultural disintegration of postwar Europe. Many readers were baffled by the poem (nothing but "so much waste-paper," intoned the *Manchester Guardian*), but Eliot quickly became a central figure of the literary avant-garde.

Eliot's poetry and criticism were a lifelong waltz with literary tradition, which he saw as a vital force modifying and enriching the present (*The Waste Land* is soaked in the literatures and cultures of the past). Seeking to illumine the present with a rigorous assessment of the past, Eliot himself became an inescapable "classic." ■

A Game of Chess.

~~IN THE CAGE.~~

The Chair she sat in, like a burnished throne
Glowed on the marble, where the swinging glass
Held up by standards wrought with golden vines
From which one tender Cupidon peeped out
(Another hid his eyes behind his wing)
Doubled the flames of seven-branched candelabra
Reflecting light upon the table ~~where~~ as
The glitter of her jewels róse to meet ~~its~~ it,
From satin cases poured in rich profusion;
In vials of ivory and coloured glass
Unstoppered, lurked her strange synthetic perfumes
Unguent, powdered, or liquid- troubled, confused
And drowned the sense in odours; stirred by the air
That freshened from the window, these ascended,
Fattening the candle flames, which were prolonged,
And flung their smoke into the laquenaria,
Stirring the pattern on the coffered ceiling.
Upon the hearth huge sea-wood fed with copper
Burned green and orange, framed by the coloured stone,
In which sad light a carved dolphin swam;
Above the antique mantel was displayed
In pigment, but so lively, you had thought,
A window gave upon the sylvan scene,
The change of Philomel, by the barbarous king
So rudely forced, yet ~~xxxxx~~ there the nightingale
Filled all the desert with inviolable voice,
And still she cried (and still the world pursues)
Jug Jug, into ~~the~~ dirty ear ~~of death. lost.~~
~~And other Tales, from the~~ old stumps and bloody ends of time
Were told upon the walls, ~~where~~ staring forms
Leaned out, ~~and~~ hushed the room ~~and~~ closed it ~~in.~~
~~There~~ were footsteps on the stair,
Under the firelight, under the brush, her hair
Spread out in ~~little~~ fiery points ~~of will~~
Glowed into words, then would be savagely still.

"My nerves are bad tonight. Yes, bad. Stay with me.
"Speak to me. Why do you never speak. Speak.
"What are you thinking of? What thinking? ~~Thinxx~~ What?
"I never know what you are thinking. Think".

I think we met first in rats' alley,
Where the dead men lost their bones.

"What is that noise?"

The wind under the door.

"What is that noise now? What is the wind doing?"

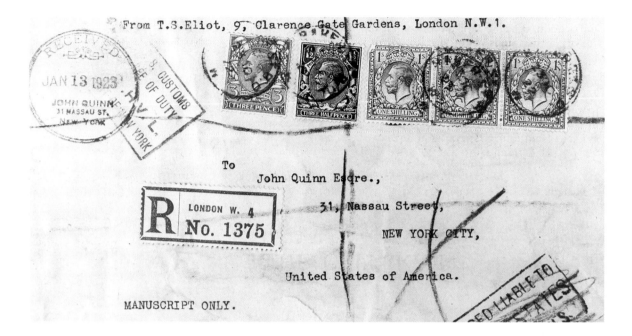

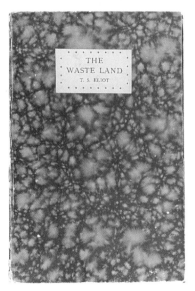

THIS PAGE AND OPPOSITE

First published in the October 1922 issue of The Criterion, The Waste
Land *has inspired mountains of elucidation and rumination, and Eliot even
provided his own footnotes (the beginning of a typescript draft of Part II,
"A Game of Chess," with Ezra Pound's boldly scrawled criticisms, is at
left). Virginia Woolf thought it a "d—d good poem," and in 1923, she and
her husband, Leonard Woolf, brought out the first English edition (right)
at their Hogarth Press. The Woolfs had first met Eliot in November 1918
when he came to dinner at Hogarth House. In her postmortem on the
evening, Virginia wrote to Roger Fry of a "strange young man" whose
"sentences take such an enormous time to spread themselves out that we
didn't get very far." Three years and seven months later, Eliot read to
her from a new work: "He sang it & chanted it rhythmed it. It has great
beauty & force of phrase: symmetry; & tensity. What connects it together,
I'm not so sure. . . . One was left, however, with some strong emotion.
The Waste Land, it is called. . . ." In 1922, Eliot presented a large cache
of his manuscripts to John Quinn, a wealthy American lawyer, prominent
collector, and patron of the arts who had acted skillfully as the young
poet's unpaid literary agent in America.* The Waste Land *typescript was
sent in the envelope above.*

Fourth Caprice in Montparnasse

We turn the corner of the street
And again
Here is a landscape grey with rain
On black umbrellas, waterproofs,
And dashing from the slated roofs
Into a mass of mud and sand.
Behind a row of blackened trees
The dripping plastered houses stand
Like mendicants without regrets
For unpaid debts
Hand in pocket, undecided,
Indifferent if derided.

Among such scattered thoughts as these
We turn the corner of the street;
But why are we so hard to please?

COMPLETE POEMS OF
T. S. Eliot.

FOR
JEAN VERDENAL
1889-1915,
MORT AUX DARDANELLES.

...TU SEI OMBRA ED OMBRA VEDI.
...PUOI, LA QUANTITATE
COMPRENDER DEL AMOR CH'A TE MI
SCALD.
QUANDO DISMENTO NOSTRA VANITATE
TRATTANDO L'OMBRE COME COSA SALDA.
PURG. XXI.

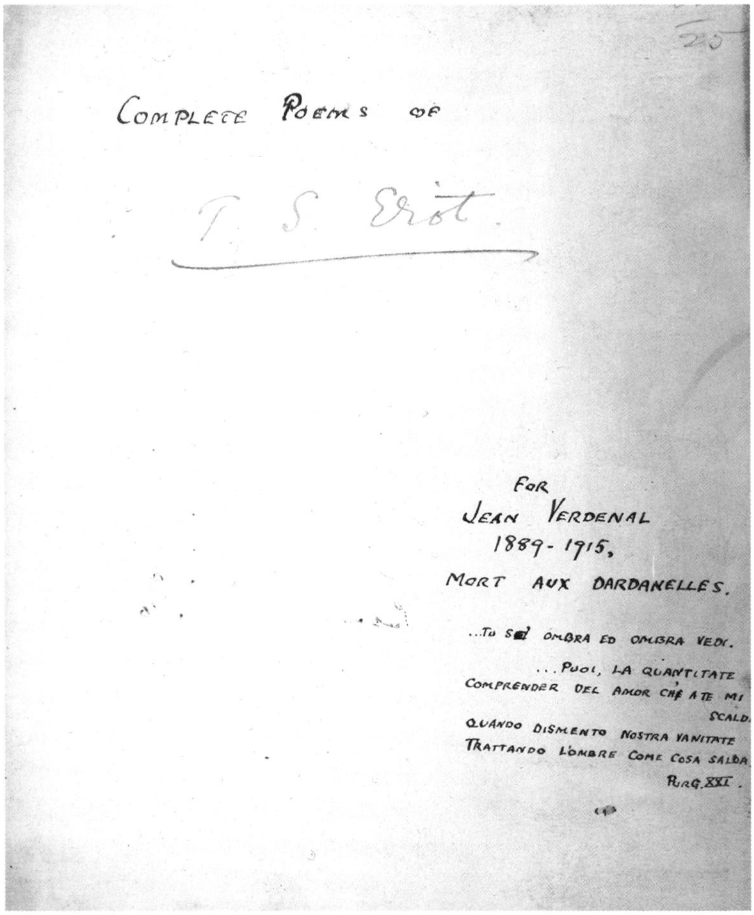

Among the manuscripts Eliot gave to John Quinn were many loose sheets of holograph and typescript poems, and a notebook of early poems (whose title page is shown above). The notebook is filled with autograph copies of Eliot's earliest poems, many of which were subsequently published in Prufrock and Other Observations *(1917) and* Poems *(1920); it is dedicated, as is* Prufrock, *to Jean Verdenal, a French medical student with whom Eliot struck up an intense friendship during his "romantic year" in Paris (1910–11). In 1996, Faber and Faber published an annotated edition of the poems found in the notebook and the accompanying sheets (*Inventions of the March Hare: Poems 1909–1917*), splendidly edited by Christopher Ricks. Many – including "Fourth Caprice in Montparnasse" (written in December 1910) – had never before been published.*

Marianne Moore

1887–1972

Moore's first book of poems, published in 1921 by her friends H.D. (Hilda Doolittle), Bryher (Winifred Ellerman), and Robert McAlmon at the Egoist Press, contains the first and longest – 12 lines – version of her famous poem "Poetry" (as originally published in the magazine Others *in 1919). The poem was eventually revised to 3 lines for the* Collected Poems *of 1967.*

MARIANNE MOORE HAS been called a reserved Salome, who uncovers the truth slowly, languorously, veil by veil. Though her poems are often descriptions of animals, they are not merely about moose and mice, but about philosophy and belief. Her poetry is both clear and opaque, transcendent and immanent, scholarly and frolicking.

Born in Kirkwood, Missouri, Moore grew up in Carlisle, Pennsylvania. In 1918, she moved with her mother to New York City, where she stayed until her death. From 1921 to 1925, Moore worked as an assistant at the Hudson Park Branch of The New York Public Library; this experience shows in her love of detail, her enchantment with learning and erudition, and her faith in tools and methods – all primary characteristics of a good librarian. Later, she was assistant editor of the influential literary magazine *The Dial* for three years.

Moore's home at 260 Cumberland Street in Brooklyn, and later her apartment at 35 West 9th Street, became shrines for literary pilgrims. The most eloquent of them, the poet Donald Hall, described his visits to Moore in his 1992 book, *Their Ancient Glittering Eyes*. In the 1950s and 60s, Marianne Moore became for some the ideal personification of a poet, and was even commissioned by Ford Motor Company to think up a name for its new, "modern" automobile (it was later christened the Edsel, not one of Moore's suggestions, which had included Mongoose Civique and Utopian Turtletop). Her fondness for sports and sportsmen (baseball players in particular) resulted in many opportunities for the white-haired Moore to pose for photographs with a variety of athletes, among them Joe DiMaggio and the University of Texas baseball team. ∎

This portrait photograph by George Platt Lynes was inscribed by Moore in October 1943 to her friends Hildegarde and James Sibley Watson, the latter of whom with Scofield Thayer had purchased The Dial *magazine in 1919 and refashioned it into a major modernist journal of art and literature. Moore's second book,* Observations *(1924), was published by the Dial Press and won the Dial Award. Becoming an editor of* The Dial *in May 1925, Moore subsequently published the work of Ezra Pound, William Carlos Williams, Louis Zukofsky, George Oppen, and other great modernist writers. Moore's own remarkable reviews and "Comments" in* The Dial *are almost poems in themselves (she did not publish any of her own poetry in* The Dial *or anywhere else from 1926 to 1931).* The Dial *ceased publication in July 1929.*

Moore frequently revised her own work, removing lines, changing line lengths or the number of stanzas, deleting stanzas altogether, and excising poems from her collected editions with enthusiasm. But this poem, first published in Sequoia *(Autumn 1957) as "Oh to Be a Dragon," was by its 1959 publication in* O to Be a Dragon *only slightly revised, and that in its title, with the "Oh" compressed to "O." One of the notes to this poem, at the back of the 1959 volume, states that Solomon's wish was for "an understanding heart." The source is I Kings 3:9.*

O to Be a Dragon

  If I, like Solomon, . . .
  could have my wish –

my wish . . . O to be a dragon,
a symbol of the power of Heaven – of silkworm
size or immense; at times invisible.
  Felicitous phenomenon!

During the latter part of her life, Moore attained something of the status of a celebrity, which emphasized the poet's interest in sports (particularly baseball). Though a lifelong fan of the Brooklyn Dodgers, Moore was photographed in 1965 at Shea Stadium with New York Mets manager Casey Stengel and the team's owner, Joan Payson. Looking the perfect older woman, she was at other times photographed in such "unpoetic" places as the Belmont Park racetrack and the New York City nightclub Toots Shor. A subject for more than her share of the time's most important photographers, including Cecil Beaton, George Platt Lynes (see p. 160), and Henri Cartier-Bresson, Moore also posed with, among others, boxer Muhammad Ali, artist Alexander Calder, dancer-choreographer Martha Graham, and the University of Texas baseball team.

E. E. Cummings

1894–1962

I think of cummings as Robinson Crusoe at the moment when he first saw the print of a naked human foot in the sand. That, too, implied a new language – and a readjustment of conscience. . . . I don't think he should be held too closely to account for some of his doodles, his fiddling with the paraphernalia of the writing game. He has been for a good part of the last twenty years like the prisoner in solitary confinement who retained his sanity by tossing a pin over his shoulder in the dark and spending long hours searching for it again.

William Carlos Williams, "Lower Case Cummings" in The Harvard Wake *(Cummings Number – Spring 1946)*

Elephants took on totemic significance for Cummings, who frequently embellished his letters, notes, and inscriptions with vivacious drawings of his beloved pachyderms – as in this charming thank-you note to one of his closest friends, Hildegarde Lasell Watson.

On June 24, 1915, the boldest speaker at Harvard's commencement ceremonies mounted a high-spirited defense of "The New Art." Edward Estlin Cummings commended Cubism and Futurism; he extolled Arnold Schönberg (surely a rare occurrence at an American university in those days); and he caused President Lowell to go brick-red by reciting, with great enthusiasm, some poetry by Lowell's scandalously *moderne* sister, Amy ("Why do the lilies goggle their tongues at me"). In closing, the Cambridge-bred iconoclast regaled his audience with excerpts from Gertrude Stein's *Tender Buttons* (". . . please butter all the beef-steak with regular feel faces . . ."). Writing to Ezra Pound 30 years later about this, the first of his many successful public performances, Cummings recalled that the Stein really "laid 'them' in the aisles."

After Harvard, Cummings worked in the mail-order division of a publishing house in New York for as long as he could take it (two months); volunteered for a Red Cross ambulance unit in France during World War I; traveled extensively in Europe; and married both unhappily (twice) and happily (this last to Marion Morehouse, a fashion model who dazzled Edward Steichen and many others, and who later became a distinguished photographer). Fiercely individualistic, anti-authoritarian, and deeply suspicious of intellection ("feeling is first"), Cummings issued dire bulletins about the "prurient philosophers" who "pinched / and / poked" the "sweet spontaneous / earth." His many beautiful lyrics are almost entirely dependent on the rapt and intensely emotional acuity with which he observed himself and the beauties (and inanities) of the everyday. He remains – despite a difficult style that cannot mask his arch-Romanticism – one of America's most enduringly popular poets, an ironic fate for a poet who really had very little use for "mostpeople." ∎

suspecting children.

what is
a
voyage

?

up
upup:go
ing

downdowndown

com;ing won
der
ful sun

moon stars the all,& a

(big
ger than
big

gest could even

begin to be)dream
of;a thing:of
a creature who's

O

cean
(everywhere
nothing

but light and dark;but

never forever
& when)un
til one strict

here of amazing most

now,with what
thousands of(hundreds
of)millions of

CriesWhichAreWings

A committed pacifist ("no artist surely is a mankiller"), Cummings "avoided the American army" when the United States entered World War I by volunteering in June 1917 for the Norton-Harjes Ambulance Service, a unit serving in France. His subsequent misadventures – he was imprisoned by the French under mistaken charges of disloyalty – are the basis of his vivid and hilarious memoir, The Enormous Room. Released from La Ferté-Macé detention camp in December 1917, he returned to New York only to find himself, to his inexpressible dismay, drafted into the U.S. Army in July of the next year. Cummings was horribly bored in the Army and (according to his testimony) the "most un-at-home" man in the service. This 1918 photograph was taken by his father while he was on leave from Camp Devens in Massachusetts.

OPPOSITE

An enchanting evocation of voyage and discovery, this late lyric ("what is") is charged with the characteristic metrical, syntactical, and typographical irregularities of the poet whom Randall Jarrell once described as a "magical bootlegger or moonshiner of language." Cummings – who at 16 had been enraged when the Cambridge Review dropped a word from his sonnet homage to a retiring headmaster – was highly distrustful of typesetters and always scrutinized proofs meticulously. On this galley proof for the poem's publication in Fresco in 1960, Cummings (always very concerned with the look of the poem on the page) has requested "plenty of (blank) space" at both the top and bottom of the page.

Vladimir Nabokov

1899–1977

Probably about the time Nabokov sat for this portrait, he fell intensely in love with Valentina Evgenievna Shulgin, or "Lyussya," the 15-year-old sister of a friend. He was 16 and the poems, many written for her, poured out in a torrent (and were then scrupulously copied into an album by his mother). After one was accepted by the journal Vestnik Evropy *("Herald of Europe"), Nabokov published* Stikhi *("Poems," 1916), a collection of 68 poems, in an edition of 500 copies; all the reviews were negative, except for one by a journalist who was trying to curry favor with the young poet's father. By the time* Stikhi *was published, the love affair had cooled.*

BEST KNOWN TO American readers for his apt descriptions of Midwestern motel rooms and rented Chevrolets, Vladimir Nabokov was born a Russian aristocrat whose mother wrapped herself in seal furs and a bearskin to go shopping by sleigh, attended by a footman in a cockaded hat. As a child, Nabokov studied English and French with tutors, but that hardly accounts for the cultural and linguistic leaps he made after his family fled the Russian Revolution in 1919. He also had a photographic memory and a passion for detail, which he put to extraordinary use in his studies of the English language, the United States, chess, butterflies, and poetry.

Nabokov wrote his first poems at Vyra, his family's beloved country estate, an adolescent "rolling the words on [his] tongue with the glazed-eyed solemnity of a tea-taster." The writing of poetry continued apace; on just one day, New Year's, 1919, Nabokov wrote three poems, marking them "10–11 A.M.," "4–5 P.M.," and "9:30–11 P.M." By the time he graduated from Cambridge in 1922, he was awaiting the publication of his third and fourth books of poetry. Then, for 18 years, Nabokov lived in Germany and France; after World War II began, he went into exile a second time, moving to the United States with his wife, Véra, and son, Dmitri.

For years he struggled: writing and teaching, trying to earn a living – and hunting butterflies. A self-taught lepidopterist, Nabokov published prolifically on the intricate wing markings, genitalia, and classification of the butterfly. In 1948, he became a professor at Cornell University, where he soon began work on his translation of Pushkin's masterpiece *Eugene Onegin* (a seven-year project), and continued to write novels. When Nabokov was 59, *Lolita* (first published in Paris in 1955 because American publishers had been afraid to touch it) abruptly made him rich again. In 1961, the lifelong exile chose to move to a suite in a luxury hotel in Switzerland, where he died 16 years later, one of the world's most celebrated writers. ■

12  122

00134

ON TRANSLATING «EUGENE ONEGIN»

1

What is translation? On a platter
A poet's pale and glaring head,
A parrot's screech, a monkey's chatter,
And profanation of the dead.
The parasites you were so hard on
Are pardoned if I have your pardon,
O, Pushkin, for my stratagem:
I travelled down your secret stem,
And reached the root, and fed upon it;
Then, in a language newly learned,
I grew another stalk and turned
Your stanza patterned on a sonnet,
Into my honest roadside prose —
All thorn, but cousin to your rose.

2

Reflected words can only shiver
Like elongated lights that twist
In the black mirror of a river
Between the city and the mist.
Elusive Pushkin! Persevering,
I still pick up Tatiana's earring,
Still travel with your sullen rake.
I find another man's mistake,
I analyze alliterations
That grace your feasts and haunt the great
Fourth stanza of your Canto Eight.
This is my task — a poet's patience
And scholiastic passion blent:
~~The shadow of your monument.~~
Dove-droppings on your monument.
~~January 8, 1955~~

1955

"On Translating 'Eugene Onegin,'" first published in The New Yorker
*in 1955, describes Nabokov's frustrations with Pushkin and his great
poem, and defends his famous decision to translate that monument of
Russian literature into free verse, jettisoning Pushkin's rhyme and meter
to give his literal meaning instead. Ironically, of course, this poem is
written in iambic tetrameter. This sheet, used as setting copy for* Poems
and Problems, *shows Nabokov's handwritten revision of the last line,
15 years after the poem's first appearance. The sheet is pasted together
from a page cut out of* Poesie (1962), *an edition of Nabokov's poetry
in English with Italian translations.*

I suppose that someone like Nabokov, if he put poetry first, would be capable of writing an extremely fine and witty poetry in more than one language. Perhaps more than two. But he's exceptional, isn't he? I doubt that there are many people who could do it, because in poetry, especially, you write out of such intimate and, in some degree, unexamined feelings about words. You know the words of your own language as you know your brothers and sisters and your wife and your children – which is to say very deeply, and yet not altogether clearly.

Richard Wilbur, quoted in "An Interview with Richard Wilbur" by Irv Broughton, Mill Mountain Review 2, no. 2 (1975)

Mate in two moves

A self-interference freak not for the conservative solver. It was composed in Montreux, on October 3, 1968 (in the afterglow of completed Ada) and published ~~I believe, around Christmas~~ in the *Evening News*, London, *December 24, 1968*

Nabokov practiced both chess and poetry all his life, and linked them together very early: in the autumn of 1918, he wrote poems and chess problems into the same notebook and called it, in Russian, "Poems and Schemas." This typescript shows one of the 18 chess problems that Nabokov published late in life in his book Poems and Problems *(1970). "I refuse to apologize for its inclusion," Nabokov wrote of the chess. "Chess problems demand from the composer the same virtues that characterize all worthwhile art: originality, invention, conciseness, harmony, complexity, and splendid insincerity."*

W. H. Auden

1907–1973

Among the mutual American acquaintances of Auden and Isherwood was the painter Paul Cadmus. In 1943, Cadmus made pen-and-ink sketches of both men (Auden is at the right) on the half-title page of a copy of the published version of The Ascent of F6 *(1937), a play Auden and Isherwood wrote together during a month in Portugal in 1936. The two writers began their friendship when Auden was 11 and Isherwood, 13. Isherwood later wrote fondly, "I remember him chiefly for his naughtiness, his insolence, his smirking tantalizing air of knowing disreputable and exciting secrets." As for Auden's appearance, he recalled, "I see him frowning as he sits opposite me in the choir, surpliced, in an enormous Eton collar, above which his great red flaps of ears stand out on either side of his narrow scowling pudding-white face."*

ON AN AFTERNOON walk in March 1922, Wystan Hugh Auden, a brilliant schoolboy planning to become a mining engineer, was startled when another boy asked if he had written any poetry. Three years later at Oxford, asked again, Auden removed his large pipe to give a recital of his own verse in a calm and brazen voice.

Auden was the cherished third son of a physician and nurse in York, England. Tall, rumpled, pale, and tireless, he became famous in his 20s as a left-wing poet, but was disenchanted by a trip to Spain during the Spanish Civil War. Back in England, he felt stifled by his political reputation and by the insular world of British letters, so in January 1939, Auden left for the United States with his friend and co-author Christopher Isherwood. Many British intellectuals saw this as a desertion: he seemed to be sloughing off politics and the looming war. "Poetry makes nothing happen," Auden retorted enigmatically in his elegy to Yeats, written just after his arrival in New York City. He settled there, sticking to a sacred daily writing schedule even as he fell in love with Chester Kallman, took gymnastics classes, embraced Christianity, and shared a series of cluttered apartments with other writers. Auden also taught and lectured widely. Just before his death in 1973, he became a restless poet-in-residence at his old Oxford college, Christ Church.

Struggling with private sorrows and the bewilderments of the 20th century as they deepened during his lifetime, Auden wrote essays, plays, and opera libretti as well as a large body of poems, which, he believed, should be spoken aloud. The music of his lines is often irresistible, his odd imagery haunting, and he is known for verse that uses the rhythms and phrases of colloquial speech without sacrificing grace. His poems are much beloved by readers, many of whom also fondly recall his face – young and impudent, or wrinkled and alcoholic near the end of his life – as if they had known it. ■

He wrote . . . some of the strongest, strangest and most original poetry that anyone has written in this century; when old men, dying in their beds, mumble something unintelligible to the nurse, it is some of those lines that they will be repeating.

Randall Jarrell, in Kipling, Auden & Co.: Essays and Reviews, 1935–1964 *(New York, 1980)*

from **Stop All the Clocks,**
as published in The Ascent of F6

Hold up your umbrellas to
    keep off the rain
From Doctor Williams while he
    opens a vein;
Life, he pronounces, it is finally
    extinct.
Sergeant, arrest that man who
    said he winked!

Shawcross will say a few words
    sad and kind
To the weeping crowds about
    the Master-Mind,
While Lamp with a powerful
    microscope
Searches their faces for a sign
    of hope.

And Gunn, of course, will drive
    the motor-hearse:
None could drive it better, most
    would drive it worse.
He'll open up the throttle to its
    fullest power
And drive him to the grave at
    ninety miles an hour.

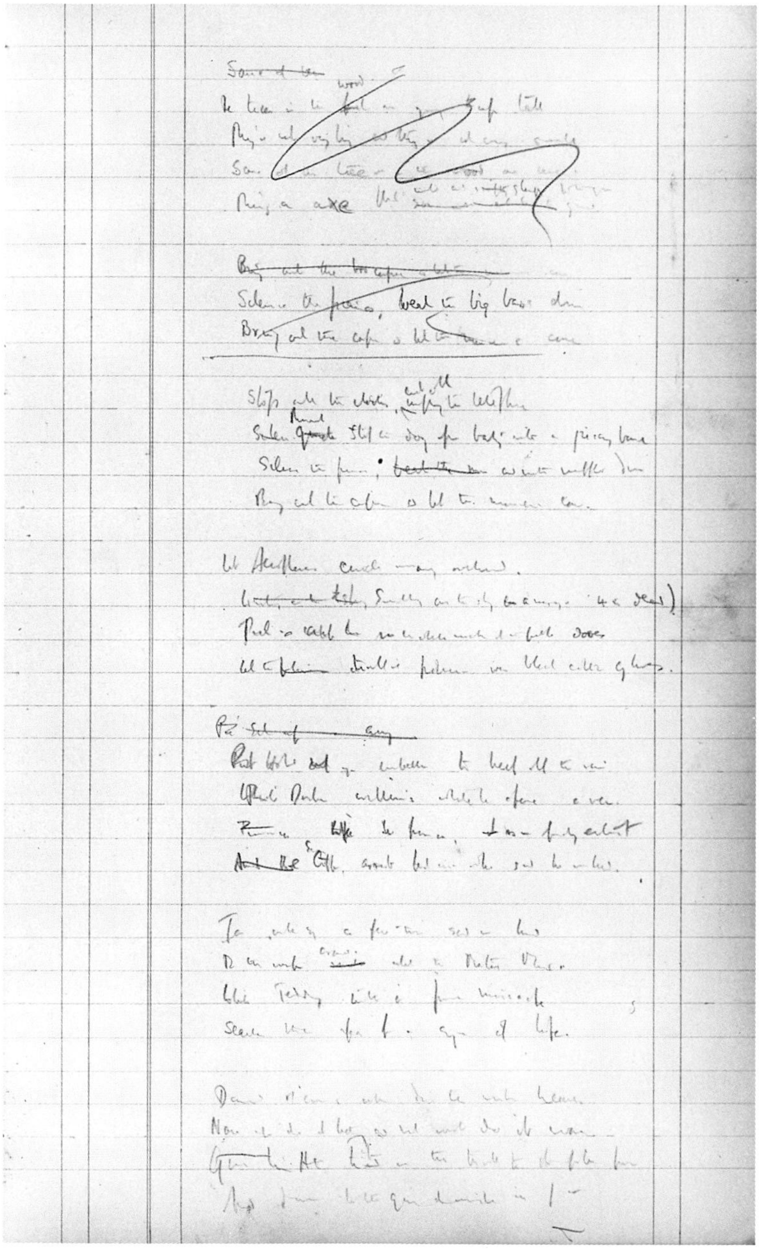

When it comes, will it come without warning
    Just as I'm picking my nose,
Will it knock on my door in the morning
    Or tread in the bus on my toes,
Will it come like a change in the weather,
    Will its greeting be courteous or bluff,
Will it alter my life altogether?
    O tell me the truth about love.

S.S. Aramis
Jan 1938

3

Funeral Blues
Stop all the clocks, cut off the telephone,
Prevent the dog from barking with a juicy bone,
Silence the pianos and with muffled drum
Bring out the coffin, let the mourners come.

Let aeroplanes circle moaning overhead
Scribbling on the sky the message He Is Dead,
Put crêpe bows round the white necks of the public doves,
Let the traffic policemen wear black cotton gloves.

He was my North, my South, my East and West,
My working week and my Sunday rest,
My noon, my midnight, my talk, my song;
I thought that love would last for ever: I was wrong.

The stars are not wanted now; put out every one,
Pack up the moon and dismantle the sun,
Pour away the ocean and sweep up the woods;
For nothing now can ever come to any good.

Colwell July 1937

4

Calypso
Driver, drive faster and make a good run
Down the Springfield Line under the shining sun.

78

LEFT AND OPPOSITE
*"Stop All the Clocks" (also known
as "Funeral Blues") changed
dramatically between published
versions. The poem began as part
of Auden and Isherwood's play*
The Ascent of F6, *where it formed
a sarcastic commentary on the
death of a pompous official;
the verses that Auden scribbled
into one of his composition note-
books (opposite) correspond to
the printed text of the play. But
when Auden rewrote the poem
for publication in* Another Time:
Poems *(1940; left), he replaced
the last three stanzas with eight
new lines, leaving the rest of
the poem untouched. In so doing,
he transformed the arch tone
of the original poem into one of
candid, private desolation. English
composer Benjamin Britten,
whom Auden had met in 1935,
created a spectacular blues setting
for the poem in* The Ascent of F6,
*but the song was cut after the
play's first performance. Britten's
version was published in 1980,
in a collection of cabaret songs.
The poem gained renewed celebri-
ty when the 1940 revision was
featured in the 1994 film* Four
Weddings and a Funeral.

This striking photograph of Auden was taken by George Platt Lynes sometime in the mid-1940s; its minimalist composition provides a good foil for Auden's attire. The poet called himself "one of those persons who generally look like an unmade bed," and he was proud of it, according to biographer Humphrey Carpenter. As for his home, it was "usually in a chaos which looks as though a mythical beast had gotten drunk and wandered through shitting books and soiled shirts," Chester Kallman wrote. But nothing was more punctilious and ordered than the daily work schedule Auden set for himself, often beginning with a three-hour stint of writing from 6 to 9 a.m. "To achieve anything today," he said, "an artist has to develop a conscious strictness in respect of time which in former ages might have seemed neurotic and selfish, for he must never forget that he is living in a state of siege."

Louise Bogan

1897–1970

Louise Bogan's art is compactness compacted. . . . She uses a kind of forged rhetoric that nevertheless seems inevitable. . . . Anodynes are intolerable to her. She refuses to be deceived or self-deceived. . . . We need not be told that life is never going to be free from trouble and that there are no substitutes for the dead; but it is a fact as well as a mystery that weakness is power, the handicap a proficiency, that the scar is a credential, that indignation is no adversary for gratitude, or heroism for joy. There are medicines.

Marianne Moore, "Compactness Compacted" [review of Bogan's Poems and New Poems*], first published in* The Nation *in 1941; reprinted in* Predilections *(New York, 1955)*

LOUISE BOGAN SPENT her childhood in a series of New England mill towns, subject to the "passionate dissimilarity" of her constantly battling parents. She began writing as a "life-saving process" while a student at the Girls' Latin School in Boston, and at age 22 moved to New York, publishing her first volume of poetry, the superbly assured *Body of This Death*, four years later. For Bogan, the best poems were those – as she told May Sarton – in which the "technique takes up the burden of feeling *instantly*." Darkly impassioned and relentlessly self-critical, Bogan achieved in her highly polished lyrics that rare thing for which she praised Emily Dickinson: the fearless, and clinically precise, description of the "actual emotional event."

In a 1951 essay on Ivy Compton-Burnett, Bogan placed that wicked novelist in the select company of artists who – as she put it – "with the aid of the comic spirit, are able to enlarge life by imposing inexorable patterns on it." That Bogan admired Compton-Burnett should not surprise: both were masters of form, in sovereign control of their materials; and both were possessed of the sort of mordant gaze that dissects the human animal and its entanglements with beautiful, devastating restraint. While Bogan's formally rigorous poetry – written, as Theodore Roethke noted, out of the "severest lyrical tradition in English" – often flashes with the wit of the Metaphysical poets (to whom she was often compared), her comic spirit is most lustrously served forth in her brilliant letters and in splendid literary criticism that is a model of clarity, acuity, and fair-mindedness, nicely seasoned with a few well-aimed dagger thrusts. There are many ways to enlarge life. There are – as Marianne Moore knew – medicines. ■

Elizabeth Mayer – at left with Louise Bogan in a 1948 photograph – was a cultivated German émigré who had settled with her family in New York in 1936. A remarkable woman who had known D. H. Lawrence and Rilke in Europe, and to whom W. H. Auden dedicated his New Year Letter *in 1940, Mayer collaborated with Bogan on several translations from the German, including a classic version of Goethe's* Sorrows of Young Werther. *Bogan developed a warm friendship with her "collaboratrix," whose "intelligent curiosity and intellectual fire" she greatly admired. She was convinced, as she wrote May Sarton in 1954, that Mayer had "lived about five or six lives."*

OPPOSITE

A record of a recurring subconscious experience that had troubled Bogan for years, "The Meeting" is a taut and nightmarish exploration of the bleak landscape at "the deepest bottom of the dream" where silence and a "shifting of the eyes" are mercilessly – and inevitably – succeeded by betrayal. Bogan wrote that she had been haunted by the "materials" of this somber poem for many years when, in May 1956, the first lines hit her and the poem "came out practically whole." After the poem was published in The New Yorker *on February 9, 1957, Bogan wrote Glenway Wescott that its faithless "dream-creature" had first come to her in the guise of her second husband, the novelist Raymond Holden, from whom she was divorced in 1937.*

Louise Bogan
709 West 169th Street
New York City

THE MEETING

For years I thought I knew, at the bottom of the dream,
Who spoke but to say farewell,
Whose smile dissolved, after his first words,
Gentle and plausible.

Each time I found him, it was always the same:
Recognition and surprise,
And then a silence, after the first words,
And a shifting of the eyes.

Then the moment when he had nothing to say
But only smiled again,
But this time toward a place beyond me, where I could not stay—
No word 3 men ⊙
~~And woke again.~~

But now I am not sure. Who are you? Who have you been?
Why do our paths cross?
At the deepest bottom of the dream you are let in,
A symbol of loss.

Eye to eye we look, and we greet each other
Like friends from the same land.
Bitter compliance! Like a faithless brother
You take and drop my hand.

In 1940, the young poet May Sarton wrote for the first time to Louise Bogan, who, like Sarton, was concerned about the indifference, even hostility, shown to lyric poetry in their age. In response, Bogan urged Sarton to "do what one can, and not sell out." Although the two writers did not meet face to face for 13 years, an important literary friendship was begun with that initial exchange. In 1956, they collaboratively translated a number of poems by the French Symbolist poet Paul Valéry. The translations – including that of "Vue," shown here in a preliminary typescript version by Sarton (who was fluent in French) extensively revised in Bogan's hand – were commissioned by the Bollingen Foundation, which decided in the end to publish literal prose translations by someone else. Several of the Bogan-Sarton translations were, however, ultimately published in The Hudson Review *and* Poetry.

~~Seen~~

If the beach leans, if the shadow

On the eye breaks down and weeps,

If the ~~azure~~ sky is tears, ~~just so~~ so

(Pure, flush with the {salt of / salty} teeth)

The ~~virgin~~ fresh smoke ~~or the air~~ aerial,

Rocked in herself, then ~~breathed~~ exhaled

Toward the ~~standing ocean~~ vertical there

~~Drowsing within its empire~~

She, without hearing them said,

~~If the wind trembles her lip~~

Plays at allowing to fade

A thousand vain words, to reshape

Under the damp flash of teeth

The so soft fire beneath.

This is really impossible, but I expect that with a fusing of our views we may reach something--at least better than this. I am not sure what "se muer" means in this context. It seems to mean according to the dictionary moulting- "to shed its skin" to "break" (of a voice at puberty) and this is a bit confusing. The syntax has me completely buffaloed! I have thought that possible a dash after "just so" and another after "empire" might frame this sequence as an interpolation, but is this the sense? Whew!

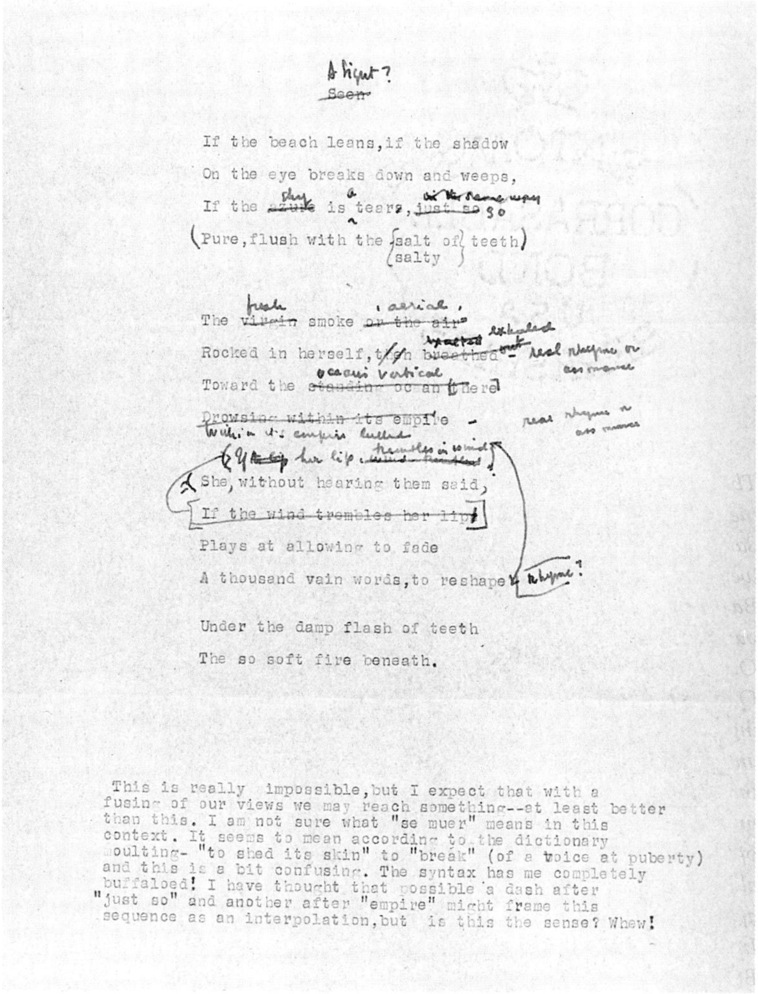

Kay Boyle

The folksinger Joan Baez first
met Kay Boyle in California's
Santa Rita Prison, where they
were both jailed – along with
Baez's mother and sister – after
participating in a sit-in at the
Oakland Induction Center in
October 1967. Thus began a last-
ing friendship between the Baezes
and the woman who reclined
on her prison cot, as the singer's
mother recalled, with the "dignity
of a queen." Indeed, they were
all arrested again later that year
after another blockade of the
Induction Center. In 1979, after
Boyle had endured two hours of
surgery for an impacted wisdom
tooth, Joan Baez sent her this
affectionate get-well note, with
its humorous caricature of a
patched-up Kay Boyle – white
earrings in place and glass in
hand – announcing imperiously:
"DR. SAYS I CAN HAVE DUBONNET
ON FRIDAY. GOD DAMMIT ISN'T
IT FRIDAY??"

KAY BOYLE WAS primed for the 20th century by an extraordi-
nary mother. A sort of modernist *naïf*, Katherine Evans Boyle
regaled union organizers in Cincinnati with *Ulysses* (convinced
that contemporary labor could only be inspired by contempo-
rary literature), and read Gertrude Stein's *Tender Buttons* to
her dinner guests in Bryn Mawr (on one memorable evening,
the Stein so convulsed one gentleman with laughter that he had
to be helped from the table and put to bed). And in New York,
she marched her enraptured 11-year-old daughter through the
scandalous 1913 Armory Show, where Marcel Duchamp (future
godfather to the youngest of Kay Boyle's six children), Brancusi,
and other modernist renegades had begun to haul the 20th
century into the 20th century. It follows, then, that Kay Boyle –
after fleeing Cincinnati (that "nest of reactionary stagnation"),
and stopping for a brief layover in Greenwich Village – should
land smack in the middle of the 1920s avant-garde in France,
where cries of "down with Henry James, down with Edith
Wharton, down with the sterility of *The Waste Land*" were
taken quite seriously.

Based primarily in Europe for 30 years, Boyle believed
deeply that "the writer must recognize and must accept his
commitment to his times." In a long and often tumultuous
career, she bore eloquent witness – in short stories, novels,
poems, and essays – to the horrors that gripped her century.
With a commitment to social justice bred in the bone, Boyle
helped feed the families of conscientious objectors during
World War I, and – in her seventh decade – was twice impris-
oned after demonstrating against the Vietnam War. A striking
woman immortalized in glamorous portraits by George Platt
Lynes, Louise Dahl-Wolfe, and other master photographers,
Boyle joked late in life that she saw herself "as a dangerous
'radical' cleverly disguised as a perfect lady." ■

After an apprenticeship with Man Ray, Ohio-born Berenice Abbott established her own studio at 44, rue du Bac in Paris, and began producing beautiful portraits that capture – as Muriel Rukeyser has written – the "magnetic strangeness" of the human face. In New York in 1946, she photographed an old acquaintance from her days in Paris, Kay Boyle, uncharacteristically somber in this compelling portrait, but, as ever, effortlessly soigné in a pin-striped suit and her trademark white bone earrings. Boyle reminisced in 1989 that she began to wear white earrings in 1939, when she was living in France, on the eve of World War II. As the political situation worsened, a French friend hastened to buy all the white earrings she could find because, she told Boyle, "white earrings are a sign of courage." Hearing this, Boyle immediately "went out and bought some too."

Do not speak of yourself (for God's sake) even when asked.
Do not dwell on other times as different from the time
Whose air we breathe; or recall books with broken spines
Whose titles died with the old dreams. Do not resort to
An alphabet of gnarled pain, but speak of the lark's wing
Unbroken, still fluent as the tongue. Call out the names of stars
Until their metal clangs in the enormous dark. Yodel your way
Through fields where the dew weeps, but not you, not you.
Have no communion with despair; and, at the end,
Take the old fury in your empty arms, sever its veins,
And bear it fiercely, fiercely to the wild beast's lair.

Kay Boyle, "Advice to the Old (Including Myself)"

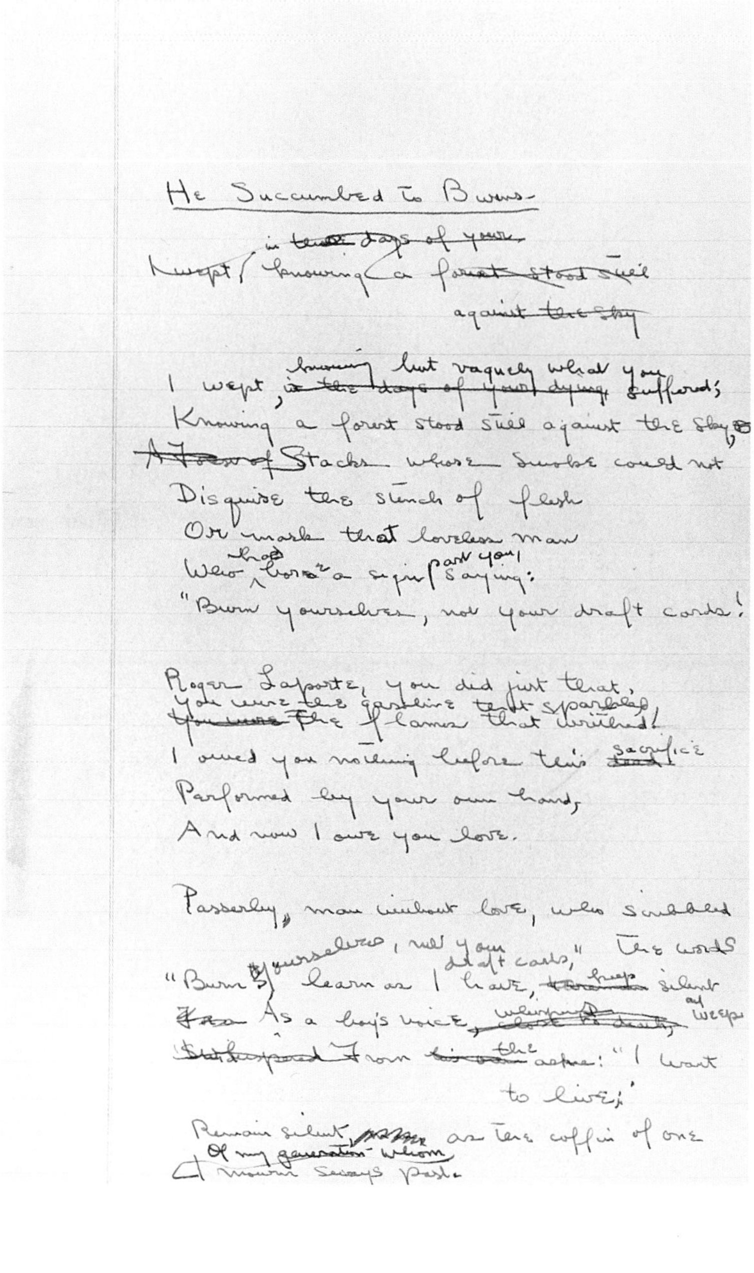

He Succumbed To Burns

[handwritten draft manuscript]

"He Succumbed to Burns" is a
moving elegy for Roger LaPorte,
a 21-year-old ex-seminarian who
immolated himself in front of
the United Nations in New York
on November 9, 1965. In an
essay written two years earlier,
Boyle had urged writers to speak
"briefly and clearly of the dignity
and integrity of the individual
man." And here she celebrates the
memory of a now-forgotten young
pacifist who, as The New York
Times noted, had "looked nothing
like the stereotype of the long-
haired 'Vietnik' or peace demon-
strator." The poem is a telling
example of the sort of transforma-
tion a gifted writer can effect on
rather unpromising materials: the
earliest version of this poem was
actually written, in late 1965, by
Boyle's youngest daughter, Faith
Gude, whose heartfelt but awk-
ward and sentimentalized tribute
to LaPorte is preserved in a
typescript in the Berg Collection.
Boyle, who was frequently, and
not without some justification,
accused of high-handedness by her
children, rewrote her daughter's
poem with ruthless and unerring
skill, and then, Faith Gude recent-
ly recalled, sent it back with
"comments."

Lorine Niedecker

1903–1970

Jonathan Williams, a friend and fellow poet, published two elegant collections of Niedecker's poetry, T&G: The Collected Poems (1936–1966) (1969) *and the posthumous collected edition,* From This Condensary (1985). *Williams also edited and published* Epitaphs for Lorine (1973), *a small booklet including 30 tributes in the form of poems, by A. R. Ammons, Cid Corman, Guy Davenport, Allen Ginsberg, Denise Levertov, George Oppen, Carl Rakosi, Charles Reznikoff, Gilbert Sorrentino, and others. In February 1967, Williams (also an accomplished photographer) visited Niedecker and her husband at their home on South 6th Street in Milwaukee, where he took this photograph on February 8 or 9.*

FROM FEBRUARY 1957 until November 1963, the poet Lorine Faith Niedecker worked as a cleaning woman in the Fort Atkinson, Wisconsin, Memorial Hospital. "I should draw a picture of myself," she wrote to her mentor and lifelong friend, Louis Zukofsky, "covered with dust mops, pails, kitchen cleanser, cloths, brooms, etc. wondering where I am down those long halls past all those doors." She had previously worked as a proofreader for a trade paper, *Hoard's Dairyman*, from 1944 to 1950. Accustomed to hard work and poverty throughout her life, Niedecker developed a careful and simple experimental aesthetic to frame her observations on natural themes, populist politics, love, and friendship.

A shy woman with thick glasses and unruly waved blonde hair, whose favorite drink was a grasshopper, Niedecker lived her whole life in Wisconsin, most of it on Black Hawk Island, at the mouth of the Rock River, and most of it in one of two small cabins. Having written poems while in high school, she was inspired to a life of poetry by the discovery of the "Objectivist issue" (October 1931) of *Poetry* magazine edited by Zukofsky, who would be her poetic life-companion. Her own poems – authentic and playful works of art – began appearing in national literary magazines with the February 1933 issue of *Poetry*.

Intensely private, Niedecker strove to live the life of the mind far from the centers of literary culture with which it is usually associated. On her instructions, her husband destroyed her journals and other papers after her death. She herself had already destroyed the first ten years of her correspondence with Zukofsky and censored many of her later letters, tearing out sections she believed were too personal. She lived a radical life, loyal to fact and feeling, a poet who "chose to be rich by making her wants few." ∎

March 15

Dear Cid:
          Snowing.   Well here they are -   I never let a poem out
without some trepidation tho all the alternatives seem to have been
whirled thru the air and shoveled away.

My life   to wild green   of the soft
  by water -   arts and letters   and serious -
    Hear   Rabbits   Water

spring's   raided
  first frog   my lettuce
    or board   One boat

out on the cold   two -
  ground   pointed toward
    giving   my shore

Muskrats   thru birdstart
  gnawing   wingdrip
    doors   weed-drift

(Above to have been spoken to tape the day JW was here but then
gave up the idea - I've never read aloud.)

                    "Shelter"
                                                 (i.e. folded)

          Hold damp
          cellar-black beyond
          the main atrocities
          my sense of property's
          adrift

          Not burned we sweat -
          we sink to water Death
          (your hand! -
            this was land)
          disowns

                    ——

Rx xxxxx
xxxxxxxxxxxxxxxxxx
xxxxxxxxxxxxxxxx
xxxxxxxxxxxxxxxxxx

xxxxxxxxxxxxxxxxx   You see here
xxxxxxxxx   the influence
                            of inference
xxxxxxxxxxxxx
xxxxxx   Moon on rippled
                            stream and hear

          ——   'Except as
                            and unless'

                                ——

*Niedecker corresponded with
the poet and editor Cid Corman
for over 20 years, and many of
her poems survive only through
her letters to him. In this 1967
letter, Niedecker included five
poems, all of which were pub-
lished in Corman's groundbreak-
ing literary periodical* Origin, *in
the October 1967 issue, under
the collective title "Hear & See."
Three poems are shown here;
the other two were written
on the flaps of the aerogramme.
In 1976, Corman's Elizabeth
Press published Niedecker's*
Blue Chicory.

someone crossed this field last night:

day reveals

a perspective of lavender caves

across the snow.   someone

entered the dark woods.

*Denise Levertov, "The Footprints"
in* Epitaphs for Lorine, *edited
by Jonathan Williams (Penland,
N.C., 1973)*

Where does the boat go, Cid asked.

It goes to the mouth of the river or stops just before at a restaurant-tavern. (This is about a mile from our house.)

When I was 18 I bought a Wordsworth and took the book, with me down here toward evening. I didn't quite know, yet I think I was vaguely aware that the poetry/current (1921) was beginning to change.

Niedecker was intensely attached to her home and to Black Hawk Island, an area of summer homes and fishing cabins. But although geographically isolated, she created her own poetic community through her correspondence with other poets. She sent this watercolor sketch and note to Cid Corman in December 1964.

Louis Zukofsky

1904–1978

A collection of short poems written between 1944 and 1956, Some Time *was published – beautifully – by the poet Jonathan Williams as* Jargon 15, *and was underwritten by Edward Dahlberg, Robert Duncan, James Laughlin, and Lorine Niedecker, among others. The cover poem, "Little Wrists," was set to music by the poet's wife, Celia Thaew.*

BORN IN BROOKLYN and reared on Manhattan's Lower East Side, Louis Zukofsky was introduced to language and literature at an early age. As he recounted in his *Autobiography* (1970):

My first exposure to letters at the age of four was thru the Yiddish theaters, most memorably the Thalia on the Bowery. By the age of nine I had seen a good deal of Shakespeare, Ibsen, Strindberg and Tolstoy performed – all in Yiddish. Even Longfellow's "Hiawatha" was to begin with read by me in Yiddish, as was Aeschylus' *Prometheus Bound*. My first exposure to English was, to be exact, P.S. 7 on Chrystie and Hester Streets. By eleven I was writing poetry in English, as yet not "American English," though I found Keats rather difficult as compared with Shelley's "Men of England" and Burns' "Scots, wha hae."

With a Master's degree from Columbia at age 18, Zukofsky worked at Nedicks as a counter boy for a while. He taught at the University of Wisconsin for a year, worked in various WPA arts projects, was a substitute teacher in the New York City public schools for eight months, and taught at Queens College and the Brooklyn Polytechnic Institute (1947–66).

Zukofsky wrote scores of poems collected under the title *All* (1966); *Prepositions* (1981), a collected essays; *Bottom: On Shakespeare* (1986), a hermetic critical work; and an astonishingly strange translation of the Roman poet Catullus. His 803-page poem *"A"* was composed on the same general model as *The Cantos* of Ezra Pound, with whom Zukofsky had an intense, troubled relationship. Zukofsky was repelled by Pound's politics, as Pound was frustrated over Zukofsky's refusal to endorse his "economic" theories (Zukofsky later declined to discuss politics at all). Still, Zukofsky struggled to remain devoted to his early mentor and sponsor. Although the two maintained a voluminous correspondence, they met only three times; their final meeting was at St. Elizabeth's Hospital.

A gentle iconoclast, Zukofsky was idolized by certain poets who came of age in the 1960s. Masters of literary modernism, too, paid homage: both Pound's *Guide to Kulchur* (1938) and William Carlos Williams's *The Wedge* (1944) were dedicated to him. ■

Master photographer Ralph Eugene Meatyard here captures the enigmatic
aura that surrounded Zukofsky, who in this 1967 photograph moves
against the background of a mysterious keyboard. Everything, including
the poet – one eye in the dark and one dark eyebrow visible below a wave
of silver hair – is blurred, everything in his world seems to be moving in
and out of focus. Is he smiling, or whispering – just a little?

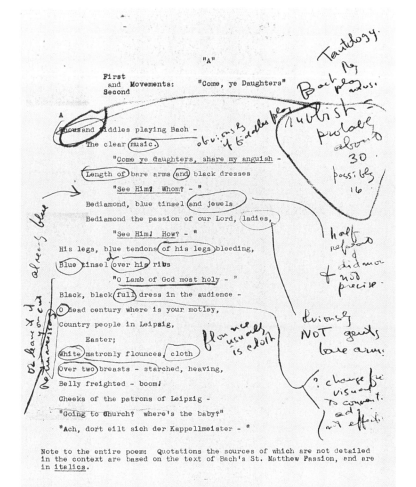

His wife, Celia, said of him that he loved reading Spinoza as other men might love bread, and there is a deep kinship with Wittgenstein as with Aristotle, in that the world is to think, whether of or in or with.

Robert Creeley, *Foreword to Zukofsky's* Complete Short Poetry *(Baltimore, 1991)*

Like many modernists, Zukofsky was influenced by Ezra Pound: through Pound's influence he was asked to edit the landmark "Objectivist issue" of Poetry *magazine in 1931; and his long poem "A," written from 1928 until 1974, was partly composed, like Pound's* Cantos, *by the appropriation, translation, or transliteration of other texts. The first section, shown here in an early draft annotated by Pound, refers to a concert of Bach's* St. Matthew Passion *at Carnegie Hall; the "perfection" of Bach's music becomes a condition to which poetry can aspire. Other sections of "A" are more enigmatic, and include meanings known only to the poet. And yet throughout, Zukofsky struggles to bring everyday things and actions into the texture of his poem, often in a pure and serene, childlike way. Zukofsky appears to have incorporated most of Pound's suggestions into the final version of this first movement.*

Charles Olson

This portrait of the artist as a young boy hardly suggests the man and poet Guy Davenport would eulogize in 1976 in Parnassus, Poetry in Review: *"His poetry is inarticulate. His lectures achieved depths of incoherence. His long poem* Maximus *was left unfinished, like most of his sentences. He put food in his pockets at dinner parties. . . . He was like Coleridge a passionate talker for whom whole days and nights were too brief a time to exhaust a subject. . . . He was taller than doors and had the physique of a bear. . . . He was interested in everything. . . . You couldn't step twice into the same Olson lecture. . . . He is a prophet crying bad weather ahead and has the instruments to prove it."*

WITH HIS BEARLIKE personality, Charles Olson, an iconoclastic and mesmerizing teacher and writer, valued self-discovery, writing as process (or the process of writing), directness, precision, and "objectivity" above all else. His influence – disseminated at first through a devoted nonacademic network of writers centered around the *Black Mountain Review* and *Origin* magazine and later through his famous essay "Projective Verse" (published in 1950), his great lyrical poem "The Kingfishers," and his *magnum opus*, *The Maximus Poems* – helped to shape a generation of poets who would bring a new consciousness – collagist, independent, antiformalist, visionary – to postwar American poetry.

His concepts (developed from the thoughts of Pound and Williams) of "composition by field" and "the line as measured by the breath" played a significant role, emotionally if not technically, in the development of poetries of open form and in the "liberation" of countless numbers of poets. Many of his students, whether at the now-legendary Black Mountain College in the Blue Ridge Mountains of North Carolina, that notoriously progressive hotbed of radical art and politics, or elsewhere (he taught at the State University of New York at Buffalo and the University of Connecticut in the 1960s), acknowledge that contribution. One of them, novelist and essayist Francine du Plessix Gray, who attended Black Mountain College at the age of 20, gives some sense of the enormous, if underestimated, impact Olson has had on writers and writing in the second half of the 20th century:

His legacy went beyond published texts. I do not adulate Olson or Black Mountain the way most of its members have, feeling ambivalent about the sham and the magnificence of the man, the dangers and the vision of the place. But I thank him every week of my life for his prophetic emphasis on the valor of subjectivity and candor, of disobedience against form and state; and also for that fatherly rigor which eventually enabled me to write at all. ■

Olson aimed "to cut this new instant open." How? By declaring war on iambics and rhyme ("the dross of verse"); by striving for an open organic form ("no line must sleep"); by producing a live look on the page, with benefit of typography; by insisting, sometimes in Latin, that the idiom must be colloquial; by professing inside information about history and women; by attacking fools and enemies and false ancestors; by sounding direct and walking crosswise. . . .

Stanley Kunitz, "Charles Olson & Co." in A Kind of Order, A Kind of Folly *(Boston, 1975)*

In February 1957, the Vienna-born photographer Harry Redl photographed Olson at the photographer's apartment at the corner of Haight and Ashbury in San Francisco, just after the dissolution of Black Mountain College, where Olson had been rector from 1951 to 1956. Jonathan Williams would later recall his first meeting with Olson at Black Mountain, where Williams was the pupil and Olson very much the teacher, particularly in his writing workshops: "when he stood up to display his amplitude (6' 9", 245 lbs) and his courtliness of manner, the first things to strike me were the literal charm of the man and the intensity with which he peered at the human subjects in front of those big, thick glasses of his. The 'high energy transfer' he asked of poems was what was already built into his nervous system and physiognomy."

In 1956, after the closing of Black Mountain College, Olson moved back to his much loved Gloucester, Massachusetts, a seaport and vacation town north of Boston, where he had spent summers as a child. Gloucester is the site and the context for his Maximus Poems, *a poetic sequence he began in 1950 and worked on until his death. "Maximus, from Dogtown – I" was written after Olson and fellow poets Michael McClure and LeRoi Jones (Imamu Amiri Baraka), and Donald Allen, editor of the influential* New American Poetry *anthology (1960), visited the Dogtown Meadows in 1959. On this, the first page of a five-page manuscript, Olson weaves together several strands: translations of Hesiod and Heraclitus (from* The Portable Greek Reader, *edited by W. H. Auden), a folktale of sailor James Merry and a bull, a geological description of Gloucester Rock, and an allusion to Melville's* Billy Budd. *Despite its awkwardnesses and occasional incoherencies,* Maximus *is a powerful and affecting work of art.*

```
MAXIMUS,FROM DOGTOWN -I

   proem

The sea was born of the earth without sweet union of love
                  Hesiod says
But that then she lay for heaven and she bare the thing
                  which encloses
every thing, Okeanos,the one which all things are and
                  by which nothing
is anything but itself, measured so
screwing earth, in whom love lies which unnerves the
                  limbs and by its
heat floods the mind and all gods and men into further
                  nature


                  Vast earth rejoices,

deep-swirling Okeanos steers all things through all
                  things,
everything issues from the one, the soul is led from
                  drunkenness
to dryness, the sleeper lights up from the dead,
the man awake lights up from the sleeping


     WATERED ROCK
of pasture meadow orchard road where Merry
died in pieces tossed by the bull he raised himself, to
                  fight
in front of people, to show off his
                  Handsome Sailor ism

died as torso head & limbs
in a Saturday night's darkness
drunk trying
to get the young bull down
to see if Sunday morning again he might
before the people show off
once more
his prowess - braggart man to die
among Dogtown meadow rocks


                       "under" the dish
                       of the earth
                       Okeanos under
                       Dogtown
                       through which (inside of which)
                              the sun passes
                       at night -
                              she passes the sun back to
                       the east through her body
                       the Geb (of heaven) at night

     Nut is water
     above & below, vault.
```

Stanley Kunitz

1905–

This drawing by Leonard Baskin appeared on the title page of The Coat Without a Seam: Sixty Poems 1930–1972 *(1974), a handsome limited edition published by Baskin's Gehenna Press.*

READING HIS POETRY, Stanley Kunitz stands at the podium like a flamingo, on one leg with one hand tucked into his pocket like a wing. And his words soar. The effect is inspirational. Writing for over 70 years, he has created a personal and interior poetry, characterized by a richness of psychological detail. Tender affection and nobility of purpose underlie the psychic journey and search for community that his poetry traces; and Kunitz has, in fact, created communities for poetry in Provincetown and New York. Although he has received almost every honor and prize the poetry world offers, he remains a dedicated, generous promoter of the work of others. Having lost his own father before he was born, Kunitz has been a spiritual father to innumerable poets through his editorship of the Yale Series of Younger Poets and as a teacher in Columbia University's Writing Program and elsewhere. But "teacher" seems almost too ordinary a word to describe his impact on the writing of poetry in America.

A friend of painters as well as of poets, Kunitz is married to the painter Elise Asher, with whom he spends half the year in New York City's Greenwich Village and half the year in Provincetown, Massachusetts. In Provincetown, his enthusiasm for horticulture is evident in his legendary garden, which beautifully combines the power of an abstract work of art with the basic materials of everyday life: flowers, leaves, bushes, trees. This is also the strategy he follows in his poetry, putting into words his own spiritual exercises in the arenas of love: "It was the disturbance of the heart that really concerned me and that insisted on a language." His poetry, as Robert Lowell said of the early poem "Father and Son," is "full of natural and impossible things." ■

Born in Worcester, Massachusetts, Kunitz received his Bachelor's and Master's degrees from Harvard in 1926–27, after which he began a varied career as poet, editor, essayist, translator, gardener, and mentor of young poets. His first book of poems, Intellectual Things, *appeared in 1930, when he was 25. At the H. W. Wilson Company in New York, he conceived and developed its famous biographical reference series of world authors past and present. His teaching career did not begin until 1946, on his return from military service in World War II, when he succeeded his friend Theodore Roethke at Bennington College. The poet Marie Howe, who studied with him later at Columbia, reminisced in 1989: "He taught us to love our own stories, what we had hidden, what we had been ashamed of. He taught us to turn into those obsessions that haunted us and hurt us, to turn into their deeper dark. And we looked at his own work and saw that he had done so, and that he had made of those turnings, poetry. And we took courage and tried."*

S. is standing in a small room, reading to himself.
It is a privilege to see S.
alone, in this serene environment.
Only his hand moves, thoughtfully turning the pages.
Then, from under the closed door, a single hazelnut
rolls into the room, coming to rest, at length,
at S.'s foot. With a sigh, S. closes the heavy volume
and stares down wearily at the round nut. "Well," he says,
"what do you want now, Stevens?"

Louise Glück, from "Four Dreams Concerning the Master"

*"The Thing That Eats the Heart"
(which is included in Kunitz's
1958 Pulitzer Prize–winning
Selected Poems) has the density,
fierceness, and internal dialectic –
"the quarrel with the self," in
Yeats's phrase – characteristic of
his early and middle poetry. In his
later work, a shimmering body of
lyrics written over the last three
decades, Kunitz has stripped away
the formal prosody and highly
figured language, and moved to a
style that is spare, lean, natural,
and affecting.*

The Thing That Eats the Heart

The thing that eats the heart comes wild with years.
It died last night, or was it wounds before,
But somehow crawls around, inflamed with need,
Jingling its medals at the fang-scratched door.

We were not unprepared: with lamp and book
We sought the wisdom of another age
Until we heard the action of the bolt.
A little wind investigates the page.

No use pretending to the pitch of sleep;
By turnings we are known, our times and dates
Examined in the courts of either/or
While armless griefs mount lewd and headless doubts.

It pounces in the dark, all pity-ripe,
An enemy as soft as tears or cancer,
In whose embrace we fall, as to a sickness
Whose toxins in our cells cry sin and danger.

Hero of crossroads, how shall we defend
This creature-lump whose charity is art
When its own self turns Christian-cannibal?
The thing that eats the heart is mostly heart.

Jean Garrigue

1912–1972

Jean and I were in Paris and one day we were walking down in the bird market. Here were thousands of birds being exhibited for sale, and Jean was absolutely enchanted. It was pure heaven to be among ten thousand birds. So, the next thing I knew I was on board the Cunard liner *Caronia* with thirty-eight birds. The worst crossing in thirty years. . . . They all got sea-sickness, and the thirty-eight birds fell to the bottom of the cage. They put their legs up in the air, and I called the ship's doctor and we fed them brandy, and they all suddenly jumped up and began to sing. It was Jean's influence.

Stanley Kunitz, from "Jean Garrigue . . . A Symposium" in Twentieth Century Literature *(Spring 1983)*

SHE WAS FOUND at three o'clock in the morning, wandering blissfully among the tombstones in a moonlit cemetery some miles from the little bungalow in which she had been born. "It's so beautiful here," she calmly explained to an undoubtedly startled search party; and with that, three-year-old Gertrude Louise Garrigus was picked up from her moon-drenched landscape and transported back home to Madison Street in Evansville, Indiana. Eleven years after that nocturnal ramble, Gertrude Louise discovered Keats, Shelley, and – above all – H.D. (who "made daring to write poetry seem possible"). She was soon enveloped in a cloud of cigarette smoke in her third-floor bedroom, where she pored over a much-prized first edition of Edna St. Vincent Millay and wrote into the night, quite unconcerned that she had been expelled from school for repeatedly (and intentionally) going up the down staircase.

Never at home in the "flat land" of her birth, the young poet felt herself "delivered and as it were in possession of a tongue" when she came to New York City in 1940. Rechristening herself Jean Garrigue, she quickly gained attention for glittering and complex verse that – as she said of Emily Dickinson's – is driven by "velocities of intuition." A restless romantic in search of an absolute language capable of illuminating the "intangible wild essence" of *things* (cats and fountains, a broken grasshopper, the "straw of snatched-up sunlight" in the beak of a Bleecker Street pigeon), Garrigue wrote ardently of the terrible beauties that so stagger the heart.

In 1971, while poet-in-residence at the University of California at Riverside, Garrigue was diagnosed with Hodgkin's disease, and returned east to begin treatment. Three days before her death, in late December 1972, she played poker in bed and listened to Bach's B minor Mass, knowing that her seventh volume of verse would be published posthumously, and that a note on a draft for her late, great poem – "Studies for an Actress" – read simply: "I lived for certain grandeurs that fade fast – me, JG." ■

ABOVE

Virginia Herrmann – a musician who began her long and close association with Garrigue in Indianapolis (where both attended high school) – managed to pin down her mercurial and chameleon-like friend in the hollow of a tree in Frenchtown, New Jersey, one day in August 1966. The portrait of Garrigue that resulted was, according to the photographer, composed with the utmost care, for she placed Garrigue strategically between "the good poison ivy on the left and the bad poison ivy on the right."

LEFT

Garrigue's mother was musical, and her beloved elder sister, a concert pianist, made "by her playing a very paradise of sound"; and indeed, music was woven into the fabric of Garrigue's own life and art. And the innate musicality of her long lines could be catching: in this 1944 exercise for Paul Hindemith's composition class at Yale, Virginia Herrmann took as her inspiration Garrigue's oddly sinister, but somehow bracing, encomium to a fat, talented, but now dead laboratory rat who "gives clues the coarse human, fattened / By his consolations, cannot."

On one of the Last Trains to White River Junction, XXXXXXX N.H.

It interferes very little
As it lays down its way.
When it needs to it follows a river
But does not prevent the roots fromtheir water
Nor by the smut-faced boulder
A small stream from joining a larger one.
Nor smashes up hills nor splits them like a loaf,
Roots and the intricate indwellings thereof
Exposed, and the mud like molten wax
Oozing and bleeding away.
Nor savages nuances of meadow   Nor removes ledges of sunlight
Nor rips away mosses   Cliffed paralels of rock
Nor gouges out fxxxxxxxxxxxx brake in a hollow
Nor requires that woods stand like scorched matchsticks   sawn woods stand like
Nor musters out ranks of cornstalks   so many mathsticks
Nor engorges great swatches of dingle
Of ostrich fern, in the swamp the blue heron

You travel with it and the stones by the river
By the tussocked damp meadows
with ponds set glittering like an eye in the head
In the fine lashwork of twigs and boughs in a tangle
Continually sweetened so near their mother the water   by the long run of sweet
Is not mathematically severe   ater
Nor of the convenience of martial order
The scrolls, the cartouche of mists, wisps,
breathings in crooks and bends
Fume out from a hill undismayed by the disarrays of so much unfolding
discontinuous flowing
Is content to let be,

Let be the green maze of mole hills, of ridges
In pastures the serene flanks of white horses
In a smolder of very green   Under light that dazes and deifies
That dazes and deifies
Cows winding in eskers   Cows winding in among eskers

And up the l af-panneled hill riding west to al that sky
Illumination wtihout fire
That Dazingand deifieng   *   Light
Cows winding in among the eskers

And up the leaf-panneled hill riding west
Light oxxxxxx dazing and deifying
Cows winding in among the eskers

Poems. I wish to write poems. My plan of work and project.

In 1944 Thirty-Six Poems and a Few Songs appeared in the volume known as Five Young American Poets, published by New Directions.

In 1947 a book of poems, The Ego and the Centaur, was published by the same house.

In this spring of 1953 another book, to be entitled, The Monument Rose, is appearing with the Noonday Press.

I am also at work on a further collection of poems to be published by the Oxford Press in late '53 or early '54. This collection will represent further extensions and dimensions--longer poems, and simply those poems that I have not yet had the time to perfect.

Poems are conceived in time, and work is a slow crystallization, and any work in process and progress depends upon the happy accident of insights and fores ghts and upon the deepest plumbing of the theme that "base" metals may be transmuted into "noble" ones.   I have been teaching for the last two years, as has been indicated elsewhere. But speaking and writing, or elucidation and exploration do not serve the same god, and I happen to find that rational emphasis of the one gives little light to that dark in which the yearning for the expressing of beautiful relationships in form, musttunnel and work. One wants time off to know and find out/before the fires of time burn out. The poems is what is snatched,fxom amongst other things, from the fires of time.

Poetry was born from magic; it grew up with religion; it survived the age of reason; how is it to continue to be heard in the pandemonium of slogans, loud speakers, madhouse slanders, high explosive fears that seem to diffuse man in complexities of environment outrunning his capacity to grasp? The poet's magical interpretation of the universe is confronted by the vast impersonal rationalization of science, and once more, it is the poet, as I think Goethe says somewhere, who must take the risks. A poem is far more than a self expression. It is a strange compromise between the demands of self, the world, and Poetry. Rilke in his "Archaic Torso of Apollo" ends by saying 'You must change your life' and this, we know from many experiences, is what art does. It challenges the surface platitudes of existence. When complexities become dense, the poet may be said to snatch from memory, from sensation, the very seed of the future,, by giving perce tions that might otherwise never be known.

A sort of artistic credo, this succinct and eloquent autobiographical statement was typed out by Garrigue in the spring of 1953, probably for a grant application. Invoking Goethe and Rilke, she takes the "grander route to Parnassus" (the same highway on which she saw Marianne Moore speeding along); for it is, she writes, the poet who "may be said to snatch from memory, from sensation, the very seed of the future, by giving perceptions that might otherwise never be known."

OPPOSITE

A fearless and unabashed poet of ecstasy and fire, Garrigue had – as she said of Marianne Moore – the "total courage to realize all of her uniqueness." Her poetic voice is exalted, difficult, rhetorical, and elaborate, and yet, as Robert Lowell noted, her poems are graced with a kind of "Book of Hours simplicity," a quality beautifully evident in this late poem, "On Going by Train to White River Junction, Vt." First published in The New Yorker *on November 20, 1971 (in a final version that differs significantly from this early, and differently titled, typescript draft – one of the dozens that exist for this poem), this lovely poem is a serene and richly detailed journey into the metaphysical heart of memory and landscape.*

May Sarton

1912–1995

Sarton first met Sir Julian Huxley (from whose papers this photograph is drawn) in 1936, during one of her many extended sojourns in Europe. He was a distinguished biologist, writer, and secretary of the Royal Zoological Society; his wife, Juliette, was one of Sarton's most important muses, for whom she wrote a beautiful sonnet sequence, "These Images Remain" (included in The Land of Silence, *1953). At the end of 1936, Sarton wrote Juliette from New York: "I fell in love with you both at first sight – Julian in a storm in Cornwall and you in a little white jacket in a green room when I was so frightened by being early that I would have read you the whole of 'Testament of Beauty' [a long philosophical poem by Robert Bridges] rather than have to talk."*

ON A JUNE evening in 1937, a young American poet watched with enchantment as Virginia Woolf – looking "like a seahorse, delicate and fabulous" – stepped into Elizabeth Bowen's "cool underwatery drawing room" in London. It was, for May Sarton, the beginning of a most "*Waves*-ian" evening, at the end of which she sat at the feet of the writer who – as she wrote Louise Bogan many years later – stated with the highest artistry "what women's lives are." The essence of Sarton's own prodigiously varied body of work, and its power and enduring appeal, lie in what she so admired in Woolf: one woman's "real, unblinking coming to terms" with complex, mysterious, gorgeous "ordinary life."

Born in Belgium, Eléanore Marie Sarton was brought to America at the outbreak of World War I (her remarkable mother carrying with her a copy of *Leaves of Grass*). At school, Sarton shocked the authorities when she defended Ibsen; at age 17, she dismayed her parents when she chucked Vassar for a theatrical apprenticeship in New York. After 1936, Sarton devoted herself to writing, and supported herself by teaching and lecturing – with great success – across America. Her wide-ranging literary correspondence and extremely popular journals chronicle the life and art of an idealistic, ardent, and deeply compassionate writer who strove mightily to keep herself "perfectly open and transparent" to experience so that whatever came her way would be met "with an innocent eye." In many genres, but above all, in poetry ("the true work of the soul"), Sarton found a place – built on "the quicksand of despair" – where her strong sense of personal honesty and the innate inner lyricism of her voice created a warm and welcoming "house where every man may take his ease." ∎

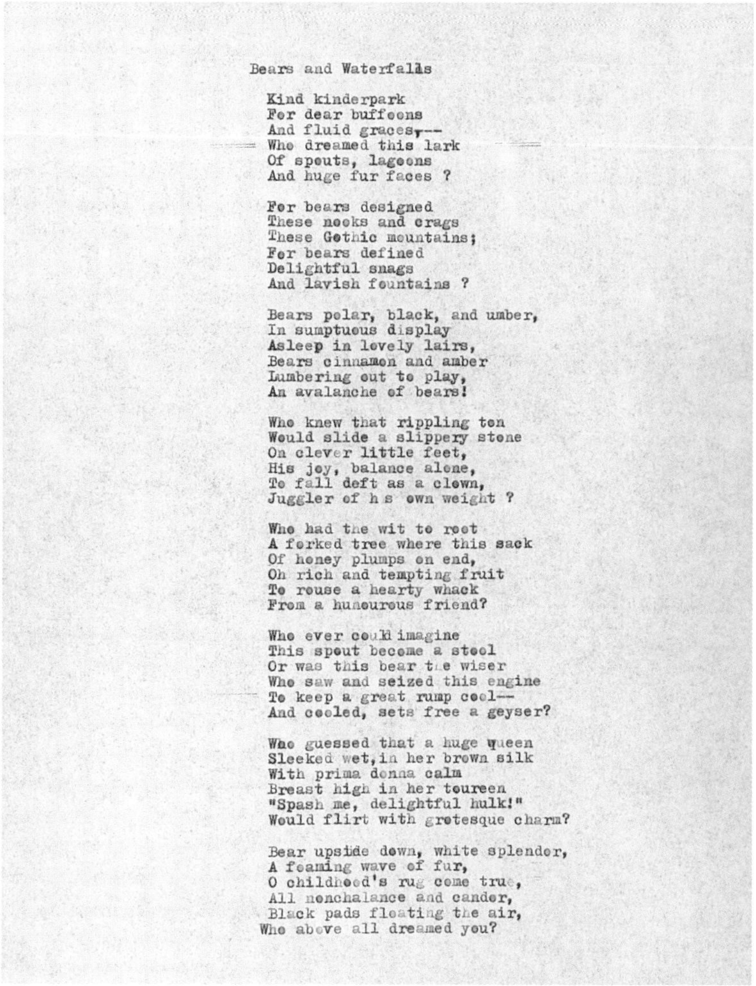

```
Bears and Waterfalls

Kind kinderpark
For dear buffoons
And fluid graces,--
Who dreamed this lark
Of spouts, lagoons
And huge fur faces ?

For bears designed
These nooks and crags
These Gothic mountains;
For bears defined
Delightful snags
And lavish fountains ?

Bears polar, black, and umber,
In sumptuous display
Asleep in lovely lairs,
Bears cinnamon and amber
Lumbering out to play,
An avalanche of bears!

Who knew that rippling ton
Would slide a slippery stone
On clever little feet,
His joy, balance alone,
To fall deft as a clown,
Juggler of h s own weight ?

Who had the wit to root
A forked tree where this sack
Of honey plumps on end,
Oh rich and tempting fruit
To rouse a hearty whack
From a humourous friend?

Who ever could imagine
This spout become a stool
Or was this bear the wiser
Who saw and seized this engine
To keep a great rump cool--
And cooled, sets free a geyser?

Who guessed that a huge queen
Sleeked wet, in her brown silk
With prima donna calm
Breast high in her tureen
"Spash me, delightful hulk!"
Would flirt with grotesque charm?

Bear upside down, white splender,
A foaming wave of fur,
O childhood's rug come true,
All nonchalance and candor,
Black pads floating the air,
Who above all dreamed you?
```

from **Bears and Waterfalls**

When natural and formal
Are seen to mate so well,
Where bears and fountains play,
Who would return to normal?
Go back to human Hell?
Not I. I mean to stay,

To hold this happy chance
Forever in the mind,
To be where waters fall
And archetypes still dance,
As they were once designed
In Eden for us all.

Throughout her life, Sarton wrote eloquently of the landscapes that embraced her. Like her mother, she cultivated gardens with an almost religious fervor, but animals held perhaps the highest place of all in her imagination and life. In the delightful "Bears and Waterfalls," Sarton wrote with deep feeling of the "creaturely" creatures, convinced that they, in their amazing way, can "help us be more fully human." She often wrote in what she called a "white heat," going through 60 or even a hundred drafts of a poem, and indeed, the final version of this poem differs significantly from the draft shown here, particularly in the addition of the poem's last two – and crucial – stanzas (see above, right).

This book of verse is as strange as it should be. The landscapes inner to this author are nigh as numerous as the poems in her book. The author is in love with discrepancies, for she adores love itself, and as equally loves that polar purity called snow. . . . Miss Sarton is able to do a thing hitherto impossible – she can warm snow, and regard it and love with a passion that makes them equally lovely. . . . Miss Sarton is strange also in that she is passionately thoughtful. Indeed, whatever she does is done at the stress of its and her own being.

James Stephens, reviewing Sarton's Inner Landscape *(1939) in* The Sunday Times *(London), April 16, 1939*

In 1962, Sarton undertook a round-the-world journey to mark her 50th birthday, and she was the perfect Ulysses for such an odyssey. Facing the marvelous worlds of Japan, India, and Greece, this "weightless traveler" experienced a sort of spiritual/poetic outward-turning and reawakening, which she distilled into some of her most luminous and most surprising poems (collected in 1966 in A Private Mythology). This notebook – filled with early versions of some of the poems of Japan collected in that volume – also contains drafts of several unpublished poems.

Muriel Rukeyser

1913–1980

Rukeyser enclosed this "out-of-focus" snapshot of herself holding her "very in-focus" five-week-old son, William (Laurie), in a letter from California (written in late October or early November 1947) to May Sarton, to whom she observed: "This is all learning and delights – the[y] sleep better than they tell me – everything better than everyone had warned."

BROUGHT UP IN an affluent New York family in which there was no idea of "a girl growing up to write poems," Muriel Rukeyser broke away early, declining to "grow up and become a golfer." She studied at Vassar, but left without a degree when her father's real estate and Wall Street investments failed at the beginning of the Depression. Striking out on her own after two years in Poughkeepsie, she returned to New York to "write poems, have a job." Her first book of poetry – *Theory of Flight* (1935) – announced a voice at once audacious and authoritative.

For more than 40 years, Rukeyser built a lifework distinguished by generosity of spirit, breadth of subject matter, and a soaring lyricism: poetry, biographies, translations (Octavio Paz, Gunnar Ekelöf), screenplays, and essays (her autobiographical/critical meditation, *The Life of Poetry*, is a particularly fine example of her evocative prose). Her life itself was rich in political engagement: at 19, she was arrested while covering the Scottsboro trial in Alabama (she contracted typhoid fever in jail); and late in life, in poor health, she bore witness before the gates of a prison in South Korea to protest the death sentence of a prominent dissident poet. "Large of body and larger of spirit" (as Alice Walker fondly recalled), Rukeyser wrote in passionate counterpoint to her age, and she always argued compellingly for an expansive vision of life ("Pay attention to what they tell you to forget").

Critics often sneered (Randall Jarrell felt "about most of her poems almost as one feels about the girl on last year's calendar"), but Rukeyser never wavered in her task: to celebrate and honor the lives of men and women who are "unpraised and vivid and indicative." ■

FOR MY SON

You come from poets, kings, bankrupts, preachers, attempted bankrupts,
        builders of cities, salesmen,
the great rabbis, the kings of Ireland, failed drygoods storekeepers,
        beautiful women of the songs,
great horsemen, tyrannical fathers at the shore of ocean, the western
        mothers looking west beyond from their windows,
the families escaping over the sea hurriedly and by night —
the roundtowers of the Celtic violet sunset,

the diseased,
the radiant,

                    fliers,   men thrown out of town, the man bribed by his
        cousins to stay out of town, teachers, the cantor on Friday
        evening, Hearstmen, *the lurid newspapers,*
strong women gracefully holding relationship, the Jewish girl going to
        parochial school, the boys racing/their iceboats on the Lakes,
like all men,   *went out and refused of wars,*
you come from singers, the ghettoes, the famines, men who built villages
that grew to our solar cities, students, revolutionists, the pouring of
        buildings, the ~~Wall Street Journal,~~ *market newspapers,*
a poor tailor in a darkening room,
a wilderness man, the hero of mines, the astronomer, a white-faced
        woman hour on hour teaching piano and her crippled wrist,
like all men,
you have not seen your father's face
but he is known to you forever in song, the coast of the skies, in
        dream,
and in your self made whole, whole with yourself and whole with others,
the stars your ancestors.

father among our light, among our darkness,

The woman stood before the diamond in the velvet
window, saying "Wonder of nature."

Rukeyser brought a female consciousness to American poetry, writing
frankly "from the body, a female body." In "Nine Poems for the Unborn
Child" (1948), she traced her own difficult pregnancy: unmarried in
California and abandoned by the child's father, her family aghast at her
condition, she journeyed, in this remarkable and pathbreaking sequence,
from "the childless years alone without a home" to the space where in
the daylight the poet waits for the grace of the world: "To live, to write,
to see my human child." Fifteen years later, Rukeyser wrote "For My
Son," a tumbling, incantatory, exuberant chronicle of her fatherless
son's illustrious predecessors, revealing to him that she has followed his
splendid line back to "the stars your ancestors."

THE AESTHETIC WEASEL

A weasel
Rode an orange easel
With an outboard diesel.

What's
Cooking?

Old Mole, not looking,
Took one of his shots,
Spoke in the stilly time:

It's subt-
le, but
He did it for the rhyme.

after Christian Morgenstern
Tr. by M. Rukeyser

Going to the barber.
The bells are riding
on the blue water.
The boats are riding
into the light.

Rukeyser, who translated Bertolt Brecht's Uncle Eddie's Moustache, *also wrote (and in some cases illustrated) her own children's books, in which she is at her most direct and delightful. In this sketchbook for* I Go Out, *Rukeyser's text floats serenely in the midst of her fluid watercolor paintings, but when the book was published in 1961, the illustrations were by Leonard Kessler.*

In her translations of nonsense poetry by Christian Morgenstern (1871–1914), Rukeyser seems thoroughly at home in that poet's sublimely silly but somehow so sensible imaginary world. "The Aesthetic Weasel" was one of eight translations from the German master of metaphysical word-play originally intended for the "Games" section of The Speed of Darkness. *But in the end, they, and the charming illustrations by Rukeyser that accompanied them, were dropped from the book.*

I still keep "The Speed of Darkness" on my desk. It glistens here like the first washed flowers in spring when you sent it to me. Section one goes whammy! Then flows out like an infusion of blood into the body. I just want to tell you again, beautiful Muriel, mother of everyone, how I cherish your words as much as the memory of your good face.

Anne Sexton, letter to Muriel Rukeyser, November 1, 1967

Adrienne Rich has called Rukeyser "our twentieth-century Coleridge, our Neruda, and more." Few poets in our time have so beautifully balanced lyricism with a passion for social and political transformation. In "Käthe Kollwitz," one of the most powerful poems from The Speed of Darkness, *Rukeyser asks a question and then – famously – answers it: "What would happen if one woman told the truth about her life? / The world would split open . . ." An outspoken and lifelong opponent of racism and war, Rukeyser knew all about the horrors of her nightmare century. But her voice was affirmative, never cynical. In a fond tribute, Denise Levertov once described Rukeyser as a "tall, leonine woman, a genuinely sybilline presence." This 1952 portrait by Rollie McKenna captures the poet who is always there to remind us that "if we lived in full response to the earth, to each other, and to ourselves, we would not breathe a supernatural climate; we would be more human."*

Delmore Schwartz

1913–1966

I remember his electrical insight as
the young man,
his wit & passion, gift, the whole
young man
alive with surplus love.

John Berryman, Dream Song 155:
"I can't get him out of my mind"

There's a memorial today at N.Y.U.,
your last appearance, old heroic
friend.
I hope the girls are pretty
and the remarks radish-crisp
befitting you
to allay the horror of your lonely
end,
appease, a little, sorrow & pity.

John Berryman, Dream Song
152: "I bid you then a raggeder
farewell"

NAMED, HE VARIOUSLY claimed, for a delicatessen, an actor, or an apartment building on New York City's Riverside Drive, Delmore Schwartz said he hoped posterity might assign him an adjective: "Delmorean." It has not, but Schwartz's poetry has endured well beyond the short span of his tortured life.

He was born in Brooklyn in 1913, to a father who had emigrated from Romania and made a million in real estate. Schwartz's mother, Rose, became so lonely when her husband left her in 1923 that she accompanied her two sons to summer camp. After Harry Schwartz died in 1930, his family learned that he had lost almost his entire fortune in the stock market crash a few months earlier, and Delmore Schwartz thus was fated to become an impecunious poet instead of an heir.

After studying at the University of Wisconsin, New York University, and Harvard, Schwartz began publishing poetry and essays in literary journals. In 1938, almost to the day of his 25th birthday, his *In Dreams Begin Responsibilities* appeared. Poems combined with a play and a short story, it was "the only genuine innovation," Allen Tate wrote, since Ezra Pound and T. S. Eliot. This wonderful book includes Schwartz's best-known poems, bearing his characteristic feel for language, his slow rhythm, and his fearful interest in fate and the passage of time. In his 30s and 40s, Schwartz taught literature and was poetry editor of *Partisan Review* and *The New Republic.* When he won the Bollingen Prize in 1960, he was the youngest poet ever to have been so honored.

But Schwartz had trouble sustaining himself and his work after his early success. Two marriages fell apart and he began drinking, using barbiturates, tearing telephones from walls, and wildly accusing his friends of betrayal. He died on a landing of the Columbia Hotel in Manhattan, from a heart attack suffered while taking out the garbage; his body lay in the morgue unclaimed for three days. ∎

In 1938, Polly Forbes-Johnson,
a photography student in her
20s, was sent by James Laughlin,
the founding editor of New
Directions, to Delmore Schwartz's
apartment to make this portrait.
The place was "a dump," she
has recalled. Twenty years later,
the writer Alfred Kazin visited
Schwartz in another of his New
York abodes, "the kind of room,"
Kazin wrote, "that could have
been chosen only by someone
with an extraordinary knowledge
of all the murderously bad rooms
put aside and carefully preserved
by the heartless state for poets
to die in." The scar visible on
Schwartz's forehead was from
a childhood accident.

Poem

Now, in the naked bed, in Plato's cave,
Reflected headlights slowly slid the wall,
Carpenters hammered below the shaded window,
Wind troubled the window curtains all night long.
A fleet of trucks strained uphill, grinding,
Their freights, as usual, hooded by tarpaulin.
The ceiling lightened again, the slanting diagram
Slid slowly off. I heard the milkman's chop,
His striving up the stair, the bottle's chink,
Rose from bed and lit a cigarette,
Walked to the window. The stony street extended
The stillness in which buildings stand about
The street-lamp's vigil and the horse's patience.
The winter sky, its points still breaking needles,
Turned me back to bed with exhausted eyes.

Strangeness grew in the motionless air. The loose
Dim film greyed. Shaking wagons, hoove's waterfalls
Sounded faroff, increasing, louder and nearer.
A car coughed, starting up. Morning, softly
Melting the air, lifted the half-covered chair
From underseas, kindled the mirror on
The wall. The bird chirped tentatively, whistled,
Chirped and whistled, so! Perplexed, still wet
With sleep, affectionate, hungry and cold. So, so,
O son of man, the ignorant night, the rumors
Of building and movement, the travail
Of early morning, the mystery of beginning
Again and again,
               while History is unforgiven.

---

*"In the Naked Bed, in Plato's Cave" was written when Schwartz was 23
and already suffering from insomnia, his longtime scourge and the
poem's subject. "Plato's cave" refers to an allegory from Plato's Republic,
in which people permanently confined to a cave confuse the outside
world with the shadows it casts on the walls of the cave – something
like an insomniac watching headlights from the street traveling along
the bedroom wall.*

Dylan Thomas

1914–1953

The photographer Marion Morehouse and her husband, E. E. Cummings, invited Thomas for a Saturday afternoon visit to their home in Greenwich Village soon after he arrived in the United States; he had asked to meet them. The two poets admired and enjoyed each other, trading "the curiously double-edged iconoclasm that marks the work and character of each of them," as John Malcolm Brinnin, who organized Thomas's trips to America, put it. This photograph by Morehouse was used as the frontispiece for Thomas's Collected Poems, *published in New York just after his death.*

DYLAN THOMAS IS difficult to wrest from the legend that he helped foster by breakfasting on ale, giving money to strangers, stealing shirts from the closets of friends and relatives, and reading poems in a voice that wound itself majestically around the shapes of his beloved words.

Only 30 years before he died, Thomas was a grubby boy in the coastal Welsh city of Swansea, pelting cats with snowballs, according to his unforgettable memoir, "A Child's Christmas in Wales." At 15, mesmerized by the sounds of words, Thomas began writing poems into exercise books. At the same time, he was failing his exams at the Swansea Grammar School, so he left at 16 and went to work for the South Wales *Evening Post*, reading copy aloud for proofreaders. Since he was "inclined to dramatise everything," according to one exasperated colleague, Thomas read too slowly; he switched to reporting until he lost the job altogether just over a year later. Meanwhile he wrote, giving the chanting, comforting authority of a psalm to the unearthly images in "And Death Shall Have No Dominion." Published by the *New English Weekly* when he was 18, this became one of Thomas's most famous poems.

In 1934, he moved to London. When his first book of poetry, *18 Poems*, appeared barely a month later, one reviewer called it "an unconducted tour of bedlam," but others noted "unusual promise" and a preponderance of "secretory or glandular" images. In 1937, Thomas married the wild and beautiful Caitlin Macnamara. During World War II, he wrote screenplays for documentary and propaganda films, and became well known as both a poet and a pub-crawler. In 1950, he made the first of his four reading tours around the United States, where his unchecked "poetic" drunkenness fascinated audiences but eventually killed him, on November 9, 1953. ∎

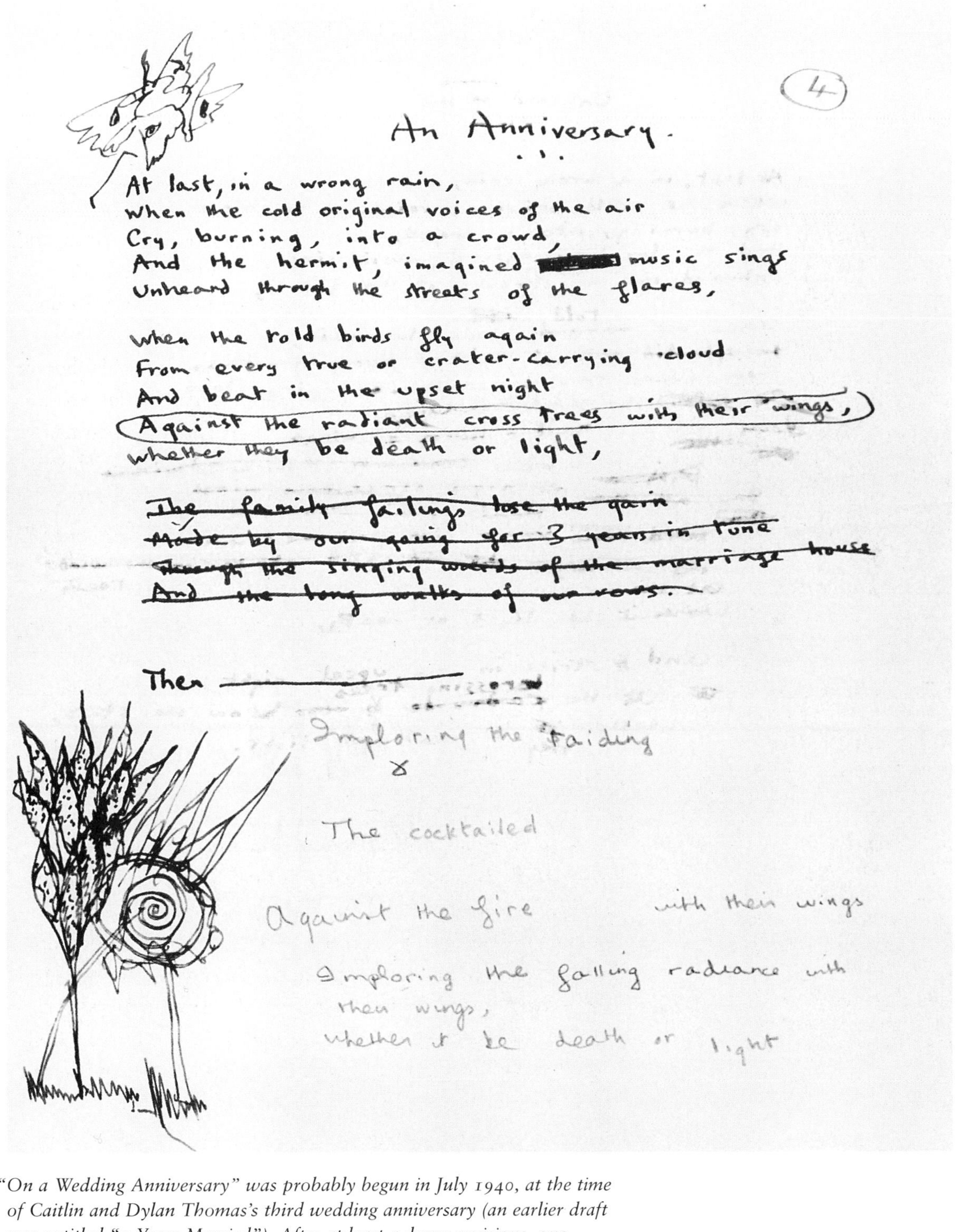

④

An Anniversary.

At last, in a wrong rain,
When the cold original voices of the air
Cry, burning, into a crowd,
And the hermit, imagined ████ music sings
Unheard through the streets of the flares,

When the cold birds fly again
From every true or crater-carrying cloud
And beat in the upset night
Against the radiant cross trees with their wings,
Whether they be death or light,

~~The family failings lose the gain~~
~~Made by our going for 3 years in tune~~
~~through the singing words of the marriage house~~
~~And the long walks of our vows.~~

Then ─────────────

Imploring the faiding
x

The cocktailed

Against the fire   with their wings

Imploring the falling radiance with
their wings,
whether it be death or light

"On a Wedding Anniversary" was probably begun in July 1940, at the time
of Caitlin and Dylan Thomas's third wedding anniversary (an earlier draft
was entitled "3 Years Married"). After at least a dozen revisions, one
of which is shown here, the poem was published in the British magazine
Poetry in January 1941, and Thomas shortened and greatly changed it
again for his book Deaths and Entrances (1946). For example, in the
poem's second line, "the cold original voices of the air" began as a modest
phrase, "the few, still voices." Thomas was especially horrified by the
bombing of London, and he incorporated many wartime images here.

DYLAN THOMAS

In April 1950, during the six-week marathon of readings and far-flung visits that constituted his first visit to the United States, Thomas stayed at the home of Ruth Witt-Diamant in San Francisco. Witt-Diamant, who taught at San Francisco State College and founded the Poetry Center there, provided a welcome change after what Thomas described as "the great general glutinous handshake of a clutch of enveloping hostesses"; she even sent presents to the Thomases' three children. In 1951, planning his second American trip, Thomas wrote this letter to ask Witt-Diamant to arrange another stay in San Francisco. She did, and he and Caitlin visited together.

The Boat House,
Laugharne,
Carmarthenshire,
Wales.
10 October, 1951

Darling Ruth,
By this long time you will have, if not forgotten me —— who could forget that lordly, austere grace and grave demeanour, the soberly matured wisdom, dedicate, reverend, chaste and aloof, that incorruptible ascetic, that Santyana of Wales? —— at least have come most justly to loathe the very hiccup of my name. (Of Tram's opinion of me, I daren't think. I found, this week, a long, fond letter to him in a pile of socks and poems, unposted since last Christmas. I am writing to him on bent knees, wagging my bum like a spaniel, but expect no answer. Give him my love. I very often think of him and Bill, of Gavin, and, of course, of you who made my ranting holiday ridiculously happy, who showed me the exhibitionest floodlit seals and the pansied Pacific baths and the starry city and Millers mountain, and gave me polar bear and artichokes, and laughed with me and at me till I felt more at home than at home where it's only at, and made me want more than anything to lurch back to the beautiful West where men are sometimes men and the bars are always exultantly open and the wind and sea and people are right and raffish and twis of fruit juice breed in the ice box.)

He was not afraid to ask for what he wanted. When he was bored with literature and wanted life, he asked for that, too. And it was from the exercise of simple rights that Thomas started to become a legend. For who among us dares to ask for what he wants, dares to say what he means, dares to live a life that is interesting to him rather than to a thousand other people?

Howard Moss, in an interview broadcast over radio station WBAI-FM, New York, November 1958, quoted in A Casebook on Dylan Thomas, *edited by John Malcolm Brinnin (New York, 1960)*

Soon after Thomas arrived in New York in 1950, an English acquaintance introduced him to the White Horse Tavern on Hudson Street, where he was photographed by Bunny Adler in 1953. This Greenwich Village landmark became his favorite bar in the city, and it was there that Thomas drank his last two beers, on November 4, 1953. Shortly afterwards, he was admitted to the emergency room at St. Vincent's Hospital and lapsed into an alcoholic coma. He died five days later.

Randall Jarrell

1914–1965

Jarrell was born in Nashville, but soon after his birth his parents moved to California, where Jarrell's father, Owen, worked as an assistant to a photographer. In 1925, Jarrell's parents divorced and Jarrell's mother took him back to Nashville, but he returned to California for part of 1926, living with his paternal grandparents. Jarrell fondly recalled this stay nearly 40 years later in his masterly three-part poem "The Lost World." He is shown here in an engaging portrait taken by his father in Los Angeles when Randall was about age three.

BY WRITING SO many memorable, scorching lines of prose, Randall Jarrell risked overshadowing his poetry. He must have known that he would be remembered as a critic when he wrote, for example, that another poet's verse seemed to have been written "*on* a typewriter, *by* a typewriter." Even as an undergraduate at Vanderbilt University, Jarrell was so outspoken that one of his teachers, Robert Penn Warren, gently asked him to stop "terrorizing" the other students. Yet Jarrell went on to become a lifelong, much-admired teacher himself.

In 1942, just after he published *Blood for a Stranger*, his first book of poetry, Jarrell left his job at the University of Texas, where he had taught since September 1939, to enlist in the Army. He hoped to become a pilot, but instead spent the war at bases in Texas, Illinois, and Arizona, sorting mail, training navigators – and writing poetry. Jarrell became one of the best-known World War II poets; his "The Death of the Ball Turret Gunner" represents him and the war in innumerable anthologies. After a brief stint in New York as literary editor of *The Nation*, Jarrell moved to North Carolina in 1947 to become a professor at Woman's College (later the University of North Carolina at Greensboro). In addition to dozens of essays crackling with his rage and delight, Jarrell published seven books of poetry. Supermarkets and Sears, Roebuck catalogs found their way into his verse as easily as B-24 bombers once had.

In 1952, Jarrell divorced his first wife and married Mary von Schrader, with whom he had what she later described as a "round-the-clock inseparability." They shared his love of football, auto racing, and fine cars (an awestruck student remembered him driving a Mercedes convertible in the rain with the top down). Near age 50, his joy was suddenly muffled by depression. Two years later, while out for an evening walk, Jarrell was struck by a car and killed instantly. ∎

90 North

At home, in my flannel gown, like a bear to its floe,
I clambered to bed; up the globe's impossible sides
I sailed all night—till at last, with my black beard,
My furs and my dogs, I stood at the northern pole.

There in the childish night my companions lay frozen,
The stiff furs knocked at my starveling throat,
And I gave my great sigh—the flakes came huddling,
Were they really my end? In the darkness I turned to
    my rest.

Here, the flag snaps in the glare and silence
Of the unbroken ice. I stand here,
The dogs bark, my beard is black, and I stare
At the North Pole. And now what? Why, go back.

Turn as I please, my step is to the south.
The world—my world spins on this final point
Of cold and wretchedness: all lines, all winds
End in this whirlpool I at last discover.

And it is meaningless. In the child's bed
After the night's voyage, in that warm world
Where people work and suffer till the and
That crowns the pain—in that Cloud-Cuckoo-Land

I reached my North and it had meaning.
Here at the actual pole of my existence,
Where all that I have done is meaningless,
Where I die or live by accident alone—

6

Where, living or dying, I am still alone;
Here where North, the night, the berg of death
Crowd to me out of the ignorant darkness,
I see at last that all the knowledge

I wrung from the darkness—that the darkness flung me—
Is worthless as ignorance: nothing comes from nothing,
The darkness from the darkness. Pain comes from the
    darkness
And we call it wisdom. It is pain.

7

"90 North" is one of Jarrell's earliest, and best, poems. It was published in Jarrell's first book, Blood for a Stranger; Jarrell reworked the poem in his personal copy of the volume, which is filled throughout with his extensive revisions. Since the North Pole is an idea defined by its relationship to other places, not a visible landmark, an explorer trying to reach it would find only "the glare and silence / Of the unbroken ice." The same thing would happen, Jarrell implies, to someone who made life into a search for a single, simple destination. W. H. Auden, who greatly influenced Jarrell, also made metaphors of polar exploration and mountaineering, notably in The Ascent of F6.

*Jarrell was so passionately fond of Kitten, the cat pictured with him here
in 1942, that after he left Austin to enlist in the Army that same year,
he wrote to his wife, "I miss you more than anything – more than Kitten,
even." During the war he gave his meat rations to Kitten, and in January
1945, he wrote to a literary acquaintance, "We always give our cat
herring roe for Christmas, but there wasn't any, so we gave him half our
veal roast."*

His mind, unearthly in its quickness, was a little boyish, disembodied, and
brittle. His body was a little ghostly in its immunity to soil, entanglements,
and rebellion. As one sat with him in oblivious absorption at the campus bar,
sucking a fifteen-cent chocolate milk shake and talking eternal things, one
felt, beside him, too corrupt and companionable. He had the harsh luminosity
of Shelley – like Shelley, every inch a poet, and like Shelley, imperiled perhaps
by an arid, abstracting precocity. Not really! Somewhere inside him, a breezy,
untouchable spirit had made even then its youthful and sightless promise
to accept – to accept and never to accept the bulk, confusion, and defeat of
mortal flesh. . . .

Robert Lowell, in Randall Jarrell; 1914–1965, *edited by Robert Lowell,
Peter Taylor, and Robert Penn Warren (New York, 1967)*

John Berryman

1914–1972

In 1965, Berryman won both the Pulitzer Prize (for 77 Dream Songs*) and a Guggenheim Fellowship; thanks to the latter, he sailed in late August 1966 for Ireland. The next spring he was photographed along the coast outside of Dublin by Terence Spencer for a rollicking feature in* Life *magazine ("Whisky & Ink, Whisky & Ink," July 21, 1967). Dublin delighted him: he could stalk the ghosts of Yeats and Joyce, and – better yet – carouse with living Dubliners, a loquacious and lyrical lot "blazing with self-respect" who quite outshone, for Berryman, those dreary New Yorkers who sit in their bars and "stare with glazed eyes at television sets."*

IN 1914, JOHN Allyn Smith, Jr. was born to a small-town banker and a schoolteacher who had met in an Oklahoma boardinghouse and had wed – in the event, most unhappily – because "they were the only people who could read and write for hundreds of miles around." In a Florida dawn less than 12 years later, John Allyn Smith, Sr. – alienated from his wife, Martha, and tormented by insomnia – walked behind the family's apartment building in Tampa and shot himself through the heart. His widow quickly remarried. The new family moved north, and Martha ("Jill Angel") Berryman's fiercely loved son – having taken his stepfather's name – entered P.S. 69 in Jackson Heights, Queens, as John Berryman, Jr. It was, however, a "dreadful banker's grave" that schooled the future poet's heart.

At Columbia, Berryman "walked with verse as in a trance" and dazzled his professors. After two years in England – where he did brilliant work at Cambridge, failed to drink Dylan Thomas under the table, and had high tea with Yeats ("Immortality is mine!") – Berryman returned to New York richly appointed in tweeds and British accent. His first major work, *Homage to Mistress Bradstreet* (1953) – a long poem in which he daringly appropriated, and transformed, the voice and life of a colonial American poet – presages the achievement of his hilarious and yet almost unbearably melancholy sequence, *The Dream Songs* (1964, 1968). Nerve-racked, erudite, madly theatrical, and not infrequently fueled by mind-boggling quantities of alcohol, Berryman was obsessed with the "epistemology of loss," and wrote with the kind of desperate, lacerating humor that is no joke. He taught in Minneapolis for many years, and it was there, on a bridge not ten miles from the small town where his father had been born, that he leapt to his death on a bitter morning early in 1972. ■

ABOVE

This photographic Who's Who of American poets was taken at a memorial service for Randall Jarrell, four months after he was struck by a car and killed during a walk on October 14, 1965. Jarrell's death was ruled accidental, but some of his fellow poets believed it was suicide. His death deeply affected them, and several composed poems about it. Shown standing are, from left, Stanley Kunitz, Richard Eberhart, Robert Lowell, Richard Wilbur, John Hollander, William Meredith, and Robert Penn Warren. Seated are John Berryman, Adrienne Rich, Mary von Schrader Jarrell (the poet's widow), and Peter Taylor.

RIGHT

Berryman had known Jarrell for 25 years, but they were never close friends. Still, Berryman was devastated by the news of the poet's death, and on October 30 he wrote to Jarrell's widow to "find out what the hell had happened" (as he would later describe the purpose of this letter in Dream Song 127).

JOHN BERRYMAN

30 Oct

Dear Mrs Jarrell,
     I hope you had my wire, sent
to Greensboro since I didn't know Radalll had
moved. I was stunned by his death, but felt
far worse later when a friend passed me the NY
Times story saying the troopers called it suicide.
He was just not the man to kill himself. He had
iron selfconfidence, and he was childlike--
neither of them qualities leading to suicide.
Did he leave you a note or anything? What in the
name of God was wrong, do you know? I have tried
to write away my feeling, twice, in Songs that
I'll send you when I print them; but it hasn't
helped much. Please accept Kate's deep sympathy
too, she says. We started together, in 1940, and
though never close mostly traded books but almost
never letters---I didn't hear from him abt my last
book and didn't expect to---but now I feel bitterly
sorry I didn't throw him a postcard to say The
lost World was his very best. What went wrong??
   Two material things. His most brilliant criti-
cism was about Auden: I have never understood why
he didn't assemble it: now that should be done,
and published. Also, I don't know how far he had
gone with the verse-anthology, but at least the
table of contents should be printed, say in the
Kenyon; his taste was impeccable if anyone's can
be said to be. I miss the thought of him very
badly. After Roethke's death and MacNeice's I
swore never to care any more, but I cried over
Randall's. I hope you are being able to console
yourself.

John Berryman

SNOW LINE

It was wet & white & swift and where I am
I don't know. It was dark and then
it isn't.
I wish the barker would come. There seems to be to eat
nothing. I am unusually tired.
I'm alone too.

If only the strange one with so few legs would come,
I'd say my prayers out of my mouth, as usual.
Where are his notes I loved?
There may be horribles; it's hard to tell.
The barker nips me but somehow I feel
he too is on my side.

I'm too alone. I see no end. If we could all
run, even that would be better. I am hungry.
The sun is not hot.
It's not a good position I am in.
If I had to do the whole thing over again
I wouldn't.

*In October 1970, Berryman was hospitalized – not for the first time –
for acute alcoholic exhaustion. From his hospital room he informed an
interviewer, without irony, that "an artist is extremely lucky who is pre-
sented with the worst possible ordeal which will not actually kill him."
Berryman published 385 Dream Songs during his lifetime, and they form
the tortured, highly wrought, pungent, discordant, and quite often just
plain funny record of the crises and ordeals out of which he created his
art. But Berryman could also write with a deeply felt, almost devout
simplicity, as in "Snow Line" (Song 28), a hushed, mysterious, strangely
affecting re-imagining of the poet as a supplicant lamb lost in the snow.*

The Oscar Williams anthology . . . included photographs of most of the poets at the back of the book; John and A. E. Housman were the only exceptions – they were represented by drawings. . . . I asked him why he'd used it instead of a photograph. He claimed he wanted neither but . . . he'd taken the lesser of the two evils [but at least] the drawing did make it clear he was ugly enough to be a poet. . . . "No poet worth his salt is going to be handsome; if he or she is beautiful there's no need to create the beautiful. Beautiful people are special; they don't experience life like the rest of us." He was obviously dead serious, and then he added, "Don't worry about it Levine, you're ugly enough to be a great poet."

Philip Levine, "Mine Own John Berryman" in Gettysburg Review *(Autumn 1991), recalling the semester in 1954 when he studied with Berryman at the Iowa Writers' Workshop*

JOHN BERRYMAN

21 Dec 1969

Dear Mark

Your good letter came during a month I spent in intensive treatment at an alcoholic rehabilitation center called Hazelden 40 miles northeast of here, and was very welcome. It is a hard but marvellous programme, one of the most famous & effective in the country, and I came home day before yesterday feeling better physically, mentally & spiritually, than I have felt in many years, perhaps ever in adult life. Just to be rid of drinking permanently is a great deal, but there is much more to it than that. I hope you & Dorothy have a Merry Christmas & splendid New Year.

Love,
John

The poet and critic Mark Van Doren was Berryman's most important mentor at Columbia. More than 30 years later, Berryman wrote this short note to Van Doren just after getting out of Hazelden, which, he informed his old friend, was "one of the most famous & effective" alcoholic rehabilitation centers in the land. He was soon full of plans to complete his long-delayed critical biography of Shakespeare, but Van Doren gave Berryman this amusing but shrewd advice: "Scholarship is for those with shovels, whereas you're a man of the pen, the wind, the flying horse, the shining angel, the glittering fiend – anything but the manure where scholars have buried the masterpieces of the world."

Robert Lowell

1917–1977

On January 4, 1957, a daughter, Harriet Winslow Lowell, was born to novelist Elizabeth Hardwick and Robert Lowell. She was named in honor of Lowell's adored aunt, who was a second mother to him. As a child, Harriet spent the summer in Maine and the rest of the year in New York, and she grew to be as fierce and smart as her namesake. Lowell biographer Paul Mariani quotes a letter of April 2, 1972, from the poet to the 15-year-old Harriet after her visit to him and his third wife and their son in London: "I love you for liking both your father and mother . . . and for never talking too much except on women and politics, particularly your theories of socialism."

ON MARCH 1, 1917, Robert Trail Spence Lowell IV was, it seems, born famous, prophetically, if distantly, related to poets James Russell Lowell and Amy Lowell ("She had been so plucky, *so formidable, so beautifully and unblushingly immense*, as Henry James might have said. And yet, though irreproachably decent herself apparently, like Mae West she seemed to provoke indecorum in others."). Indeed, by the age of 30, with two published books to his credit, and a Pulitzer Prize for the second, *Lord Weary's Castle* (1946), he was well on his way to becoming one of the most-renowned poets of the century. His fourth book, *Life Studies* (1959), is still influential; his later poetry, variably received, continues to provoke controversy.

Lowell himself seemed almost to cultivate controversy. His life was often on public display, sometimes in acts of highly visible political courage. In October 1943, the 26-year-old Lowell went to prison as a conscientious objector to World War II, having announced his decision in a widely publicized, printed letter to President Franklin D. Roosevelt. Twenty-two years later, he protested the Vietnam War by publicly rejecting an invitation to President Lyndon B. Johnson's White House.

The greatest American poet of the second half of the 20th century, Lowell was an agent of major transformation whose work affected the ways in which others read and wrote poetry. The quality of his observations on the interior life, the variety and grace of his poetic structures and meters, the depth of his learning, and the brilliance of his language should qualify Lowell as our grand master of the art of writing. But he can seem a frightening figure, like something out of Blake, struggling with the light of experience and freedom in the darkness of the mind. His nickname, "Cal," reinforces this dark image – it stood, off-puttingly, for either the notorious Roman emperor Caligula or the gruff but heroic monster, Caliban, of Shakespeare's *The Tempest*. Lowell was easily overcome by the dark figures, and his struggles now seem heroic, Promethean. ▪

218

ROBERT LOWELL

Perhaps Lowell's greatest poem, "Skunk Hour" is the last poem in Life Studies. *He wrote it in response to Elizabeth Bishop's poem "The Armadillo" (see p. 222), which she had dedicated to him. The two poets first met in 1947 at a dinner party at Randall Jarrell's and became lifelong friends. Describing that meeting, Bishop observed that she "loved him at first sight. . . . I remember thinking that it was the first time I had ever actually talked with someone about how one writes poetry and thinking that it . . . could be strangely easy. Like exchanging recipes for making a cake." Bishop held a special place in Lowell's affections, too, and he wrote at least three more poems for her. Lowell's note at bottom right is addressed to Jarrell, to whom he sent this copy of "Skunk Hour," with a letter, in the fall of 1957.*

Skunk Hour

Nautilus Island's hermit
Heiress still lives through winter in her Spartan Cottage;
Her sheep still graze above the sea.
Her son's a bishop. Her farmer
Is first selectman in our village;
She's in her dotage——

Thirsting for
The hierarchic privacy
Of Queen Victoria's century,
She buys up all
The eye-sores facing her shore,
And lets them fall.
The season's ill——
We've lost our summer millionaire,
Who seemed to leap from an L. L. Bean
Catalogue. His nine-knot yawl
Was auctioned off to lobstermen.
A red fox stain covers Blue Hill.

And now our fairy
Decorator brightens his shop for fall;
His fish-net's filled with orange cork,
Orange, his cobbler's bench and awl;
There is no money in his work,
He'd rather marry.

One dark night,
My Tudor Ford climbed the hill's skull;
I watched for love-cars. Lights turned down,
They lay together, hull to hull,
Where the graveyard shelves on the town...
My mind's not right——

A car radio bleats:
"Love, careless love..." I hear
My ill-spirit sob in each blood cell,
As if my hand were at its throat...
I myself am hell;
Nobody's here——
Only the skunks search
In the moonlight for a bite to eat.
They march on their soles up Main Street:
White stripes, moonstruck eyes' red fire
Under the chalk-dry and spar spire
Of the Trinitarian Church.

I stand on top
Of our back steps and breathe the rich air——
A mother skunk with her column of kittens swills the garbage pail.
She jabs her wedge-head in a cup
Of sour cream, drops her ostrich tail,
And will not scare.

THIS PAPER WAS CHOSEN FOR ITS
FOR MAILING)
THINNESS, IF YOU PUT IT ON
A PIECE OF SOMETHING WHITE
THE WORDS WILL BE VISIBLE,

THE LANDLORD (for Sandra Hochman)

Boris Pasternak

Having crossed the edge of the courtyard,
the Landlord went off to the feast,
into the Bride's house--

with him went the Italian singer,
behind the Bride's weatherstripped doors,
between one and seven,

the snatches of talk had quieted down,
but the sun rose blood red in the middle of the bed--
he wanted to sleep and sleep and sleep.

The accordion began to weep,
the accprdion-player lay spread out on his instrument--
hearing the palms clapping, seeing the shine of the serfs.

The feast's whole flourish jingled like silver in his pocket,
again again again again,
the song of the broken accordion.

Rustling through the bed and the sleeper,
the noise, whistling and the cheering,
swam a white peacock.

She moved her hips,
and strutted out in the street--
this beautiful bird...

She shook her head, she ruffled her breast-feathers,
suddenly the noise of the game
is the stamping of the whole procession.

He drops into the hole in the sun.

The sleepy courtyard begins to wake up,
the sleepy courtyard grows businesslike--
sounds begin to ~~interfere with~~ the laughter,
                  swallow
the babble of the feast.

R.L. gave me the 3 typescript versions on March 7th saying I had once asked to see some of his worksheets & that he wanted me to have these and the literal translation — longhand, on lined yellow paper and including "Wild bines" which becomes "Wild vines" in his translation — taken down freely from Nicholas Nabokov. Typed March 8. The dedication I put on this copy & RL's carbon only. W.M.

This change made 8 March by R.L. when Stanley Kunitz said there were 4 dead words in a row in the next to last line.
W.M.

Lowell's poetry gave one the sense of living in a well, the echoes were deep and sound was finally lost in moss on stone, down there the light had the light of velvet, and the ripples were imperceptible. But one lay on one's back in this well, looking up at the sky, and stars were determinedly there at night, fixed points of reference; nothing in the poems ever permitted you to turn on your face and try to look down into the depths of the well — now look up! The world dazzled with its detail.

Norman Mailer, The Armies of the Night *(New York, 1968)*

This translation of a poem by the great Russian writer Boris Pasternak appeared in Lowell's much-discussed volume of translations, Imitations *(1962). In response to criticism that he had taken "liberties" with the originals, Lowell explained, "In a way the whole point of translating – of my translation anyway – is to bring into English something that didn't exist in English before." At the bottom of the sheet are two notes in the hand of Lowell's friend and fellow poet William Meredith; the one at the right annotates Meredith's change in the typescript ("swallow" for "interfere with"): "This change made 8 March by R.L. when Stanley Kunitz said there were 4 dead words in a row in the next to last line."*

Lowell – recently divorced (in May 1948) from novelist Jean Stafford, and probably in love with Elizabeth Bishop – met novelist and essayist Elizabeth Hardwick at Yaddo in early 1949. The two were married on July 28, 1949; at the ceremony, the new Mrs. Lowell wore a black lace hat designed by Balenciaga, borrowed from the maid of honor, Mary McCarthy. Hardwick and Lowell were divorced in October 1972 in Santo Domingo, and later the same day Lowell married Lady Caroline Blackwood. Lowell died of a heart attack in a taxicab in New York City on September 12, 1977, while returning to Hardwick at the apartment on West 67th Street that he had shared with her. This photograph of the two was taken in Maine in 1960 by Rollie McKenna.

Elizabeth Bishop

1911–1979

Many of Bishop's poems were first published (and edited) by Howard Moss in The New Yorker; *he was so enamored of her work that he never turned down a single poem she submitted to him (an unheard-of distinction, even though she was not prolific). He wrote of her poetry, "Miss Bishop is not academic, beat, cooked, raw, formal, informal, metrical, syllabic, or what have you. She is a poet pure and simple who has perfect pitch." The two also became warm friends. Both were expert cooks, and once, when Moss was ill and she was visiting New York, Bishop sent him a get-well flan along with this note, typed out on her calling card.*

ELIZABETH BISHOP WROTE in a low voice, which only increases the force of her best poems. Instead of supplying emotions to the reader, they describe the physical world in detail so precise, exquisite, and alarming that the world speaks for itself.

Bishop began suffering losses early: her father died eight months after her birth in Worcester, Massachusetts, and her mother immediately suffered a nervous collapse, and spent the rest of her life in an asylum. Bishop never saw her again, even though as a young woman she passed the asylum on each train ride to Vassar College. Raised by her mother's parents in a Nova Scotia village, and by her father's parents and her mother's sister in Massachusetts, Bishop was so often sick with asthma and bronchitis that she missed much of grade school. Instead, she read in bed.

At Vassar, she began to publish in student literary journals. On a bench in the rotunda at The New York Public Library, she met Marianne Moore, who persuaded Bishop to work at poetry instead of medicine and who would become a lifelong friend. Upon graduation in 1934, Bishop began the wide traveling that marked her life and her poetry. In 1951, she boarded a freighter for a trip around the world, but stopped in Brazil because of a violent allergic reaction apparently caused by a cashew. While convalescing, she fell in love with Lota de Macedo Soares and quickly moved to her spectacular house in the mountains near Petrópolis. For nearly 15 years, Bishop enjoyed in Brazil the stability and domesticity she had craved all her life, and managed to bring her alcoholism under periodic control. But in 1967 she lost Soares too, to suicide.

Although she lived largely outside American literary circles and produced only a small body of work, Bishop was especially beloved by fellow poets, one of whom, John Ashbery, called her "a writer's writer's writer." She did not give public readings until the last part of her life, and then she tended to mumble, according to an exasperated member of one audience. Yet her fame has grown steadily since her death in Boston in 1979, making her one of the most-read American poets. ∎

THE ARMADILLO

This is the time of year
when almost every night
the frail, illegal fire-balloons appear.
Climbing the mountain height,

rising towards a saint
still honored in these parts,
the paper chambers flush and fill with light
that comes and goes, like hearts.

Once up against the sky it's hard
to tell them from the stars -
planets, that is -, the tinted ones:
Venus going down, or Mars,

or the pale green one. With a wind
they flare and falter, wobble and toss;
but if it's still they steer between
the kite-sticks of the Southern Cross,

receding, dwindling, solemnly
and steadily forsaking us,
or in the down-draft from a peak
suddenly turning dangerous.

Last night another big one fell.
It splattered like an egg of fire
against the cliff behind the house.
The flame ran down. We saw the pair

of owls who nest there flying up
and up, their whirling black-and-white
stained bright pink underneath, until
they shrieked up out of sight.

The ancient owls' nest must have burned.
Hastily, all alone,
a glistening armadillo left the scene,
rose-flecked, head down, tail down,

and then a baby rabbit jumped out,
short-eared, to our surprise.
So soft! - a handful of intangible ash
with fixed, ignited eyes.

Too pretty, dream-like mimicry!
O falling fire and piercing cry
and panic, and a weak mailed fist
clenched ignorant against the sky.!

To be in the N-Y-? — around
St. John's Day — the solstice.

This photograph of Elizabeth Bishop, taken by Rollie McKenna in New York in 1969, was once thumbtacked to the wall of Howard Moss's office at The New Yorker, *where he was poetry editor for almost four decades (note the pinholes in the corners of the print).*

Some authors do not muse within themselves; they "think" — like the vegetable shredder which cuts into the life of a thing. Miss Bishop is not one of these frettingly intensive machines. Yet the rational considering quality in her work is its strength — assisted by unwordiness, uncontorted intentionalness, the flicker of impudence, the natural unforced ending.

Marianne Moore, "Archaically New" in The Complete Prose of Marianne Moore, *edited and with an introduction by Patricia C. Willis (New York, 1986)*

OPPOSITE

"The Armadillo" is based on the Brazilian celebration of St. John's Day (June 24) when fire balloons are released into the night air only to drift down again, often still burning. Bishop deftly paints a scene, as usual in her work, and then slips the armadillo in near the end of the poem, in three quick lines like brushstrokes. She dedicated "The Armadillo" to her friend Robert Lowell, and he responded with "Skunk Hour" (see p. 218), which he said was modeled on Bishop's poem. "Rereading her suggested a way of breaking through the shell of my old manner," he said. This typescript of the poem was sent by Bishop in a letter to Randall Jarrell.

Howard Moss

1922–1987

Moss was an exuberantly social individual: an entertaining conversationalist, good cook, generous drink mixer, and gracious host, both in his New York apartment in Greenwich Village and at his exquisite summer home in Easthampton, Long Island.

... the truest and really most complimentary thing I can say is that your book [*A Winter Come, A Summer Gone; Poems 1946–1960*] makes me fearfully homesick for New York, all of it – and the excitement and confusion and fatigue and messiness and stylishness and horror and noise and romance and everything – and all the people.

Elizabeth Bishop, letter to Howard Moss, May 10, 1960

HOWARD MOSS USED to joke that people thought he had been born in the offices of *The New Yorker* at 25 West 43rd Street. He was, in fact, born in Manhattan, grew up in Queens, and attended the Universities of Michigan and Wisconsin. He taught English at Vassar College for two years, then published his first book of poems, *The Wound and the Weather*, in 1946, when he was 24. Hired by *The New Yorker* as a fiction editor two years later, he became poetry editor in 1950, a position he would hold, with great distinction, until his death in 1987. During his tenure, *The New Yorker* became a prominent and influential publisher of poetry.

At *The New Yorker*, Moss was able to spend his days entirely with poetry, deeply influencing several generations of American poets – he was, poet Dana Gioia has written in "The Difficult Case of Howard Moss," "the only poetry editor most American writers knew by name." But Moss discovered, as Gioia notes, that "fame, as the proverb warns, can be a double-edged sword." Today, despite his prolific, award-winning (National Book Award and Marshall Prize) output – twelve collections of poetry, three of criticism, two plays, and several anthologies – "Moss's own poetry," Gioia notes, "seems wildly underestimated, when estimated at all."

Moss's complicated and often witty, playful poems are paradoxically strongest when they deal with loss, sorrow, loneliness, or pain; "The Pruned Tree," "Another Life," and "The Persistence of Song" are good examples of his metaphysical machines in operation. His work, which moves with the eloquence, inventiveness, and grace of the true classic, now seems ripe for rediscovery. ■

A slightly unreal ... angel

He'd fly down from the heights to tie his shoes,
And cross the seas to get a glass of milk.
Yet he was much stronger than he looked,
A little man of iron, and an angel,
And no one quite could put the two together--
Bismarck with a harp, who'd doff his hat
(As if he ever wore one!) and softly land
On nimble feet so not to startle. He walked
In grandeur much too visible to be seen--

And how many versions crawled out of The Press!

A small pre-Raphaelite with too much hair;
A Frankenstein of test tubes, a "refugee"--
What mileage those three harmless syllables
Gathered in their wake! Some thought he was
A shaman full of secrets who could touch
Physics with a wand and body forth
The baby of the future wrapped in stars
Because in theorems he could read the signs
Egyptians scratched into the sand with sticks
And turn them into something else again:
A unified field theory to explain
How time curved against the absolute making
All things relative to the speed of light.

Yet what a false notion of the world I had!
The horsehair sofa, the sagging chairs,
A fire roaring behind the firescreen.
And yet I think I came closer to the truth
In my daily view of him than anyone,
As if I read a portrait through my skin:
He was Merlin in an algebraic cloak
With magic amulets fastened to his silks,
About his neck a ram's tooth or a thorn,
A bird's wing or a shell--a totemed man
Whirling through space with all his trinkets on,
Making a skirl of sound like Halloween
Children banging clashing pans together--
And when he navigated in the skies,
Astronomies took shelter in his heart
For he had warmth to match the stars' cold fire.
And when the planets sang, why he sang back
Those plain chants black holes secretly adore;
He drew into the contraries of space
Whirlwind nothing and volume in its rage
Of matter racing to undermine itself.
Think of him nightly flying through the clouds,
A weightless wayfarer among the planets,
Or think of him as he would never think:
A god of forces, a chief of mass and length.

"Einstein's Bathrobe" mixes Moss's surreal mode with his naturalistic concern for the things of this world, the ordinary and the homely. This typescript page is from one of seven heavily reworked drafts of the poem held by the Berg Collection. But as is characteristic of Moss's composition process, the poem retained its first line from original draft to published version (the text below is the beginning of the poem). In an essay entitled "The First Line," Moss explained: "In my case, the first line of a poem is crucial, and it is usually the given thing, the thing that comes out of the blue without conscious maneuvering, when the mind is released from the habitual. Most often it comes when I am in motion, when no fixed mooring allows habit to keep from consciousness what the imagination may be evoking."

from **Einstein's Bathrobe**

I wove myself of many delicious strands
Of violet islands and sugar-balls of thread
So faintly green a small white check between
Balanced the field's wide lawn, a plaid
Gathering in loose folds shaped around him
Those Princeton mornings, slowly stage-lit, when
The dawn took the horizon by surprise
And from the marsh long, crayoned birds
Rose up, ravens, maybe crows, or raw-voiced,
Spiteful grackles with their clothespin legs,
Black-winged gossips rising out of mud
And clattering into sleep. They woke my master
While, in the dark, I waited, knowing

Sooner or later he'd reach for me
And, half asleep, wriggle into my arms.
Then it seemed a moonish, oblique light
Would gradually illuminate the room,
The world turn on its axis at a different slant,
The furniture a shipwreck, the floor askew,
And, in old slippers, he'd bumble down the stairs.
Genius is human and wants its coffee hot –
I remember mornings when he'd sit
For hours at breakfast, dawdling over notes,
Juice and toast at hand, the world awake
To spring, the smell of honeysuckle
Filling the kitchen. . . .

Richard Wilbur

1921–

In 1949, Wilbur was a young poetic star; his first book, The Beautiful Changes, *had been out for less than two years. He is shown here (seated at left) with two other promising young writers: the novelist Jean Stafford and Peter Taylor, a poet and master of the short story who taught at the University of North Carolina, where the photo was taken.*

JUST AFTER WORLD War II, Robert Lowell and Randall Jarrell, who had spent the war in the United States, were writing poems about the devastation it had wrought abroad. Meanwhile, Sergeant Richard Wilbur of the 36th Infantry, back from Anzio, Monte Cassino, and the Siegfried Line, was assembling a book of poems (his first) with titles like "Grace," "Lightness," and "Praise in Summer." When it was published only six months after Wilbur's 26th birthday, *The Beautiful Changes and Other Poems* was widely praised, but some critics were mystified, as they still are today, by the poet's optimism.

"Isn't it odd that our American society, the most cosseted in human history, is now so given to petulance and dreary complaint. . . ?" Wilbur noted wonderingly in the mid-1970s. He prefers instead such neglected sentiments as awe. At the end of Wilbur's poem "Transit," a beautiful woman walks away "Leaving the stations of her body there / As a whip maps the countries of the air."

Soon after his birth in New York City, Wilbur moved with his family to an old stone house in semi-rural North Caldwell, New Jersey. Growing up, he wrote for student newspapers and thought of becoming a political cartoonist. He studied English, intending to spend his life as a teacher and scholar. Then, in 1946, his wife, Charlotte, told a friend the secret that Wilbur had a drawerful of poems written during the war. He went on rapidly to win two Pulitzer Prizes and a National Book Award. He has become renowned for his translations (of French and Russian poetry, and especially of the plays of the 17th-century French masters Molière and Racine), even while teaching at Wesleyan, Smith, and Amherst, and serving a term as Poet Laureate. Wilbur now lives in Cummington, Massachusetts, a 20th-century Prospero and classic poet. ■

ZEA

Once their fruit is picked,
The cornstalks lighten, and though
Keeping to their strict

Rows, begin to be
The tall grasses that they are --
Lissom, now, and free

As canes that clatter
In island wind, or plumed reeds
Rocked by lake-water.

Soon, if not cut down,
Their ranks grow whistling-dry, and
Blanch to lightest brown,

So that, one day, all
Their ribbon-like, down-arcing
Leaves rise up and fall

In tossed companies,
Like goose-wings beating southward
Over the changed trees.

Later, there are days
Full of bare expectancy,
Downcast hues, and haze,

Days of an utter
Calm, in which one white corn-leaf,
Oddly a-flutter,

Its torn weft sheathing
A gaunt stem, can be sole proof
Of the world's breathing.

Wilbur's mind has a cleansing
sanity and wit that make it possible
for him to view the world, despite
its burden of suffering and tragedy
and evil, as a place of fortuitous
joys and blessings and miracles,
not the least of which is the gift of
life itself. And he has taught us,
by precept, that life is not, as some
would have us believe, for the sake
of poetry, but that poetry is for the
sake of life.

*Stanley Kunitz, introduction to
a reading by Richard Wilbur
at the Solomon R. Guggenheim
Museum, New York City,
December 14, 1983*

*Wilbur is a nature poet with a particular fondness, like his late friend and
mentor Robert Frost, for botany. Zea is a genus of tall grasses, of which
the only species is maize, or Indian corn. "Zea" was published in* The New
Yorker *in May 1995, and has not yet been reprinted in book form.*

Like much of his work, "All These Birds" celebrates the enchanting, slippery mysteries of nature. One of Wilbur's main preoccupations is to locate the ethereal in the mundane: to compare stars to streetlights, as he has often told his students, instead of the reverse. The poem was published just as it appears here in Things of This World (1956), which won both the Pulitzer Prize and the National Book Award. This typescript was sent to Howard Moss while Wilbur was enjoying a 1954–55 fellowship from the American Academy in Rome. It was almost certainly typed from another draft, since, like many poets, Wilbur still composes "with pen and paper and laboriously, very slowly on the whole." "There's just too much speed and noise to a typewriter," he said in a 1964 interview.

Richard Wilbur

AMERICAN ACADEMY IN ROME
VIA ANGELO MASINA, 5.
(PORTA S. PANCRAZIO)
ROME

CABLE ADDRESS
"AMACADMY,,

NO BATS, NO BELFRY — ALL THESE BIRDS

Agreed that all these birds,
Hawk or heavenly lark or heard-of nightingale,
Perform upon the kitestrings of our sight
In a false distance, that the day and night
Are full of winged words,
                              gone rather stale,
That nothing is so worn
As Philomel's bosom-thorn,

That it is, in fact, the male
Nightingale which sings, and that all these creatures wear
Invisible armor such as Hébert beheld
His water-ousel through, as, wrapped or shelled
In a clear bellying veil
                              or bubble of air,
It bucked the flood to feed
At the stream-bottom. Agreed

That the sky is a vast claire
In which the gull, despite appearances, is not
Less claustral than the oyster in its beak
And dives like nothing human; that we seek
Vainly to know the heron
                              (but can plot
What angle of the light
Provokes its northern flight.)

Let them be polyglot
And wordless then, those boughs that spoke with Solomon
In Hebrew canticles, and made him wise;
And let a clear and bitter wind arise
To storm into the hotbeds
                              of the sun,
And there, beyond a doubt,
Batter the Phoenix out.

Let us, with glass or gun,
Watch (from our clever blinds) the monsters of the sky
Dwindle to habit, habitat, and song,
And tell the imagination it is wrong
Till, lest it be undone,
                              it spin a lie
So fresh, so pure, so rare
As to possess the air.

Why should it be more shy
Than chimney-nesting storks, or sparrows on a wall?
Oh, let it climb wherever it can cling
Like some great trumpet-vine, a natural thing
To which all birds that fly
                              come natural.
Come, stranger, sister, dove:
Put on the reins of love.   -- Richard Wilbur

Jack Kerouac

1922–1969

In 1952, a year after this photograph was taken, Kerouac was lonely and depressed: Neal Cassady had driven him to Mexico City, procured a new supply of "tea" (i.e., marijuana), and promptly split. By the end of the year, however, he had begun Benzedrine Vision, *an unpublished memoir of Mexico City, William Burroughs (who had just left Mexico after three years), and the "Spanish capes of morning in the blue sky," which is most probably an early attempt to write* Mexico City Blues.

JEAN-LOUIS LEBRIS de Kerouac was born in Lowell, Massachusetts, the third child of French-Canadian immigrants. In high school, he played football and began to paste up "long words" on his bedroom wall in order to memorize them perfectly. His senior yearbook noted: "Brains and brawn found a happy combination in Jack." He quit Columbia to enlist in the Navy, but mindless discipline proved antipathetic. Throwing down his rifle during drill, Kerouac marched off to the base's library, where he was corralled by men with nets. The "blue-ribbon diagnosis" was dementia praecox (Kerouac assured everyone that he was Samuel Johnson), and the future bard of bebop was discharged.

Back in New York, Kerouac hooked up with two rather unusual Ivy Leaguers (Allen Ginsberg and William S. Burroughs) and a highly sexed and incredibly charismatic drifter (Neal Cassady). Soon, as Kerouac later recalled, cats were exclaiming, "Man, I dig everything!" and – much to the horror of cultural mandarins – "beatness" began to rise "like an ethereal flower out of the squalor and madness of the times." His second novel, *On the Road* (1957), an exuberant chronicle of his adventures with Cassady, was a sensation.

Kerouac wrote with maniacal dedication, but his life was bedeviled by Johnnie Walker Red Label, scornful critics, a complete incapacity to deal with fame, and a mother complex that is perhaps unique in American letters. He died of alcoholism (the "joyous disease") at 47, a "strange solitary crazy Catholic mystic" who many years before, when asked by his Navy psychiatrist for an example of his "bizarre behavior," had replied ebulliently: "Oh yes, dedicating my actions to experience in order to write about them, sacrificing myself on the altar of Art." ∎

ABOVE

Leo Alcide Kerouac and Gabrielle Ange L'Evesque Kerouac were French-Canadian immigrants who settled in Lowell, where their three children were born: Gerard in 1916; Caroline ("Nin") in 1919; and, on March 12, 1922, Jean-Louis (called Ti Jean). Gerard's death from rheumatic fever in 1926 was a crushing blow to the family – especially to young Jean-Louis. This photo was taken four years later, on a family trip to Canada. (The man at the left was Armand Gauthier, a Lowell man hired by Leo as a driver during a period of family prosperity.)

RIGHT

Stella Sampas was the older sister of Kerouac's most intimate friend from his early days in Lowell, Sebastian Sampas (left). Kerouac was devastated when he learned in early March 1944 that Sebastian – a cultivated, idealistic young man who had dreamed of a future as a poet and actor – had been mortally wounded during the Allied assault on the Anzio beachhead. Throughout the 1950s and 60s, Kerouac kept in touch with Stella, writing her many warm and poignant letters and cards that reflect his longing for his hometown, where Stella had remained, and which often pay homage to her brother. In 1966, Stella became Kerouac's third wife.

In this collage of prose notes and correspondence, Kerouac ranges from the goofy to the elegiac. An early poem ("A Tragic Sonnet") bathetically conflates the mysteries of beer and women, and a 1941 card to Sebastian Sampas jauntily announces that he will soon be hitchhiking – "poetically and casually –" to Lowell from New York City. Kerouac can be cranky, complaining (to Stella Sampas, in the 1960s) about Ginsberg's "anti-american ideas," dismissing his old beat buddy's "ineffectual claim that Whitman gave America over to poets." But he can also write with a kind of grave serenity: "Two nuns," he tells Stella in the late 1950s, "just offered a mass for my spiritual and temporal welfare . . . and I wrote to them: 'Reverend Mothers, Pray for all living creatures. And there are living creatures more numerous than the sands of the ocean out in space . . . not only out in space but within into your own body. . . .'"

The good poet, or in this case the "spontaneous Bop prosodist," is always alive to the idiomatic lingo of his time – the swing, the beat, the disjunctive metaphoric rhythm which comes so fast, so wild, so scrimmaged, so unbelievably albeit delectably mad, that when transmitted to paper no one recognizes it. None but the poets, that is. He "invented it," people will say. Insinuating that it was souped up. What they should say is: "He *got* it." He got it, he dug it, he put it down.

Henry Miller on Jack Kerouac, from the preface to a 1959 paperback edition of Kerouac's The Subterraneans

Kerouac took off for Mexico in July 1955, exhilarated that On the Road *had finally been accepted by a publisher (Viking). Renting a hut on the roof of a building in Mexico City where an old junkie friend of Burroughs's lived, Kerouac soon felt, as he told Ginsberg, "aimless, ephemeral, inconceivably sad." But by August 19 he had "knocked off 150 bloody poetic masterpieces in* MEXICO CITY BLUES, *each one of uniform length and wailing." In five pocket-sized notebooks (this is the first, open to the huge poem's 2nd and 48th choruses), Kerouac sang with the amazing freedom and spontaneity of "a jazz poet blowing a long blues in an afternoon jam session on Sunday." Within a month he had written 242 choruses.*

2nd Chorus from **Mexico City Blues**

Man is not worried in the middle

Man in the Middle
Is not Worried
He knows his Karma
Is not buried

But his Karma,
Unknown to him,
May end –

Which is Nirvana

Wild men
Who kill
Have Karmas
Of ill

Good men
Who love
Have Karmas
Of dove

Snakes are Poor Denizens of Hell
Have come surreptitioning
Through the tall grass
To face the pool of clear frogs

Allen Ginsberg

1926–

The year 1967 was a heady one for Ginsberg. He helped organize one of the grandest Flower Power celebrations, a massive festival in San Francisco's Golden Gate Park modestly billed as "the joyful, face-to-face beginning of a new epoch." At the Gathering of the Tribes for a Human Be-In, 30,000 celebrants grooved on The Grateful Dead, LSD-laced turkey sandwiches, and mantra-chanting. Gary Snyder blew on a conch shell, and Timothy Leary exhorted the assembled tribes to "turn onto the scene, tune into what is happening, and drop out." By the time Ginsberg appeared at the University of Colorado at Boulder that April for the "Poetry Reading & Mantra Chanting" announced in this psychedelic flyer, he had become, for many, the "prophet-guru of the enlightened west."

ON OCTOBER 7, 1955, Allen Ginsberg, a little drunk and a little nervous, stepped up onto the small stage of a cavernous, hipstered art gallery in San Francisco and began to declaim Part I of *Howl*. The audience included Kenneth Rexroth, Gary Snyder, Lawrence Ferlinghetti, Michael McClure, and – beating rhythm on a wine jug – Jack Kerouac, who punctuated Ginsberg's frank and impassioned wild ride of a poem with shouts of "GO!" Heretofore "hung up on cats like Wyatt, Surrey, and Donne," on that beatific night Ginsberg broke free and laid them in the aisles with a work that, when it was published by City Lights in 1956, was prefaced by an admiring note by William Carlos Williams which concluded: "Hold back the edges of your gowns, Ladies, we are going through hell." A Whitmanesque, high-octane, full body-blow to the complacent and tranquilized Eisenhower era, *Howl* announced that a visionary from Morningside Heights had descended, Angelical Ravings and all.

Inevitably the Beats followed that sacrosanct 20th-century American trajectory: from the revolutionary to the suburbanized, from Moloch to Maynard G. Krebs. Ginsberg effortlessly evolved into an endearing hippie *paterfamilias* whose dedication to anti-authoritarianism, hallucinogens, mantra-chanting, Zen, and unabashed self-celebration/exploration made him a hero to successive generations of questers, misfits, and lovers of song. He has vocalized a vision (an "actual movie of the mind") that hides nothing, and proffers all. Richly engaged, globe-trotting, and big-hearted, he has had one lifelong message: "Widen the area of consciousness." And his method (as he said of William Burroughs in an homage to the author of *Naked Lunch*) has been what it had to be: "purest meat." ■

Allen Ginsberg and his mother at the New York World's Fair in 1939.

Naomi Levy Ginsberg was a vivacious woman, a passionate radical who took her young son to Communist cell meetings and furiously disparaged her husband's socialist leanings. But her life was shattered by ever more severe bouts of mental illness. In June 1966, Ginsberg made a recording of Kaddish *(1961), his greatly moving elegy to his mother. The back of the album cover prints, over a 1940 photograph, these lines, written out by Ginsberg, from the poem's original draft: "Take this, this Psalm from me, burst from my hand in a day – Some of my Time – now given to Nothing – to Praise thee – but Death? / This is the End, the Redemption from Wilderness, Way for the Wonderer, House sought for all – black handkerchief washed clean by weeping – last change of mine and Naomi – To God's Perfect Darkness – Death, Stay Thy Phantoms!"*

Ginsberg's father, Louis, seen here in front of his home in Paterson, New Jersey, with his son in 1969, was a lyric poet and teacher who loved to recite Dickinson, Shelley, and Milton from memory while doing household chores. A conventional prosodist and traditional liberal, he wondered why the Beat Generation had to "throw out the baby with the dirty bath water" in its reckless search for an "undisciplined series of blind 'kicks.'" Although they often clashed over politics and poetics, father and son were extremely close, and in 1966 began to give joint poetry readings.

Yes, you're piqued . . . at the world, almost psychotically, but sincerely and rightly – according to your personality. Don't pull your head back into the shell, never. The fallen angels love you and what they do to you, what unhappiness they cause you, is no less than that which you cause them just by being. . . . All this advice of mine is ashes when you consider the last line written in your letter to me, the line that says, "Is there ever really need to close my heart?" Well, that alone will save you, has saved, will continue to save you, me, and everybody in the world. . . . We must next speak of the soul, which is conscious of powerful Octoberal winds and the joy of the earth itself.

Jack Kerouac, letter to Allen Ginsberg, August 26, 1947

The New Garden Cottage in Berkeley

```
           All afternoon cutting bramble blackberries off a tottering
brown fence
           under a low branch with its rotten old apricots miscellaneous
in the leaves,
           fixing the drip in the intricate gut machinery of the new
toilet;
           found a good coffepot in the vines by the porch, rolled
a big tire out of the scarlet bushes, hid my marijuana,
           wet the flowers, playing the sunlit water each to each,
     returned for godly extra drops for the stringbeans and daisies;
           three times walked round the          sighed absently:
           my reward, when the          fed me its plums from the form
of a small tree in the
           an angel thoughtful of my stomach, and my dry and lovelorn
tongue.

                                              '55
```

THE POCKET POETS SERIES

HOWL

AND OTHER POEMS
ALLEN GINSBERG

Introduction by
William Carlos Williams

NUMBER FOUR

In early September 1955, Ginsberg moved from San Francisco to a one-room, rose-draped cottage set behind a large house on Milvia Street in Berkeley. Hoping to get more writing done in this bucolic setting, he also intended to begin work in English at the university's graduate school. That fall Ginsberg wrote some wonderful poems, including the reflective and charming "A Supermarket in California," in which he spots Walt Whitman "eyeing the grocery boys" by the meat department; "Sunflower Sutra," one of his finest spontaneous poems; as well as this lovely lyric about his new home, "A Strange New Cottage in Berkeley." He also worked with great concentration on the drafts of Howl, *the work whose overwhelming reception at San Francisco's Six Gallery in October convinced him to scuttle the M.A. and to devote his life solely to poetry.*

Gary Snyder

1930–

A VISIONARY POET and ecological activist/philosopher who has been called the "first truly post-modern man," Gary Snyder believes passionately that the "world is our consciousness, and it surrounds us." As a young boy, his reverence for the natural world was intuitive and profound, and he "absorbed" the woods that surrounded his family's small dairy farm ten miles north of Seattle. His father, he said, knew 15 different trees, but after that "he was lost"; Gary "wanted to look deeper into the underbrush."

At Reed College in Portland, Oregon, Snyder roomed with poet Philip Whalen and began his lifelong immersion in Amerindian and East Asian cultures. He later studied Oriental languages at Berkeley, working summers as a fire lookout and trail crew member in the great Northwest. He also took part, in the fall of 1955, in the now-legendary reading at the Six Gallery in San Francisco at which Allen Ginsberg set *Howl* loose on an unsuspecting world. In *The Dharma Bums* (1958), Jack Kerouac immortalized the night, writing of Japhy Ryder/Gary Snyder, the last poet to read that evening: "His voice was deep and resonant and somehow brave, like the voice of old time American heroes and orators." In 1956, Snyder moved to Japan and began an intensive Zen Buddhist practice (he returned permanently to the States in 1968). He now makes his home in the foothills of the California Sierras.

A poet of landscape and place, Snyder is also a superb navigator of what Ginsberg has called "mind wilderness." His wide-ranging life and ever-questing mind are vividly reflected in poetry that is crystalline and perfectly shaped. It was Thoreau who said that poetry is the "self-consciousness of the universe"; Snyder's lifework is the proof. ∎

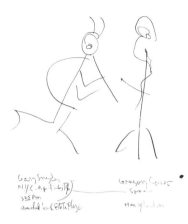

"The Hump-Backed Flute Player" is one section of Mountains and Rivers Without End *(1996), a long poetic sequence that absorbed Snyder for many years. "I'm writing about the complementarity of mountains and rivers, but that's really the planet, taking that on," he has said of this greatly ambitious work. One afternoon in 1966 while hanging out with Gregory Corso in New York City, Snyder dashed off the sketch (left) of Ko'kopilau, the mythical Native American flute player who was said to warm the spring air with his music. The sketch at the right (entitled "Man w/hard on") is by Corso.*

Richard Howard has called Gary Snyder the "master of a peculiar sweetness," and that sweetness washes over the poems in which he has written about his sons, Gen and Kai, captured here in July 1982 with their father by Chris Felver. Snyder met Masa Uehara, the boys' mother, when he was studying in Japan. Married in 1967 at the rim of an active volcano, Suwa-no-se, on an island north of Okinawa, the couple divorced in the 1980s.

I wrote this out of gratitude for the natural richness of the earth

LOGGING

```
In that year, 1914, we lived on the farm
And the relatives lived with us.
A banner year for wild blackberries
Dad was crazy about wild blackberries
No berries like that now.
You know Kitsap County was logged before
The turn of the century - it was easiest of all,
Close to water, virgin timber,
When I was a kid walking about in the
Stumpland, wherever you'd go a skidroad
Puncheon, all overgrown.
We went up one like that, fighting our way through
To its end near the top of a hill:
For some reason wild blackberries
Grew best there.  We took off one morning
Right after milking: rode the horses
To a valley we'd been to once before
Hunting berries, and hitched the horses.
About a quarter mile up the old road
We found the full ripe of berrytime -
And with only two pails - so we
Went back home, got Mother and Ruth,
And filled lots of pails.  Mother sent letters
To all the relatives in Seattle:
Effie, Aunt Lucy, Bill Moore,
Forrest, Edna, six or eight, they all came
Out to the farm, and we didn't take pails
Then: we took copper clothes-boilers,
Was-tubs, buckets, and all went picking.
We were canning for three days.
```

From Myths and Texts (1960)

Gary Snyder

Written between 1952 and 1955, Myths & Texts (1960) is a tightly constructed long poem made up of 48 lyrics arranged in three sequences: "Logging," "Hunting," and "Burning." The title is a reference to the collections of American Indian folktales gathered by Franz Boas and other anthropologists earlier in the century; it is also meant to point to the "two sources of human knowledge – symbols and sense-impressions." The ordering of this sequence was, as the poet has put it, a sort of "field composition." Laying the manuscript out on the floor, Snyder got up on a stepladder for a panoramic view; seeing what order the poems belonged in, he then climbed down and rearranged the pages. He also spotted gaps, and wrote poems to fill them. Speaking with the voice of the poet's father, "In that year, 1914 . . ." is the sixth poem in the "Logging" sequence.

Snyder's poetry is . . . immediately distinct both in imagination and in style from Beat work. A certain gentleness and care for civilization in Snyder is utterly absent in Ginsberg or Orlovsky, who are in favor, as they say, of "cat vommit." Ginsberg and Orlovsky make strong efforts to coarsen themselves, whereas Snyder does the very opposite. The Beat writers are opposed to civilization of all kinds: Snyder is not. Snyder's work everywhere reveals the grave mind of a man who is highly civilized and who, moreover, makes no pretense of denying his own intelligence.

James Wright (writing as "Crunk"), "The Work of Gary Snyder" in The Sixties *(Spring 1962)*

Robert Duncan

1919–1988

What is a master? Not one whom one imitates, emulates even; but rather, a powerful presence acknowledged, looked up to in all weathers. A mountain. . . . The mountain is master of the landscape in which it is a presence. One does not emulate such a master, except by being more one-self. The early work of a master poet is like the entwined, scratchy, capillary undergrowth at the moun-tain's base. Here are bitter fungi full of worms, sweet wild rasp-berries dripping from the stem at a touch, blackberries shining but not yet darkened to ripeness. All is fragrant, all is of the enticing substance of the forest, first threads of the tapestry, outgrowing the mountain itself, into whose life we enter as we begin to climb.

Denise Levertov, "For Robert Duncan's early poems," from a 1966 advertising flyer for Duncan's The Years as Catches, *reprinted in Levertov's* The Poet in the World *(1973)*

CLOSELY ASSOCIATED WITH the poets of Black Mountain College and the San Francisco Renaissance, Robert Duncan traced his poetic lineage from William Blake. Like that Romantic "Prophet," Duncan pursued "a world of sight and feeling, a reality, deeper, stranger, and larger, than the world of men's conventional concerns." A mystical visionary world was a familiar possibility to Duncan. After his mother's death in a flu epidemic just after he was born, Howard Edward Duncan, Jr. was given up for adoption by his father, a carpenter without a steady job, who was unable to care for him. Renamed Robert Edward Symmes, he was taken in and raised by Edwin and Minnehaha Symmes, who practiced "orthodox theosophy" – they chose six-month-old Robert on the basis of his astrological configuration. Stories of childhood would haunt Duncan's poems in "exalted or witch-like" speech.

In 1938, during his sophomore year at Berkeley, he dropped out of school, and followed a lover east to New York City and into the literary circle of Anaïs Nin. His early poetry was published under the name R. Symmes, but in June 1941, the poet reassumed the surname of his biological father. Duncan came to equate the poet with the social outcast and the poetic with the polymorphous perverse. *Heavenly City, Earthly City* (1947), written after he returned to the Bay Area, celebrates homoerotic, aesthetic, and religious transcendence. The book caught the attention of Charles Olson, who along with Duncan and other poets developed the process-based poetry of "projec-tive" or "open field" verse.

During the 1960s, Duncan published in succession three luminous volumes of poetry – *The Opening of the Field* (1960), *Roots and Branches* (1964), and *The Bending of the Bow* (1968) – all of which helped to redefine postmodern poetics. He spent his last decade contributing, especially in his popular lectures, to the expansion of the borders of poetry, and working toward an increasingly transcendent self-mastery. ■

In the 1940s, Duncan was the center of a group of poets and artists in
Berkeley that included the film critic Pauline Kael and the artist Virginia
Admiral (the mother of actor Robert De Niro), as well as poets Jack
Spicer, Robin Blaser, and William Everson (along with his companion
Mary Fabilli, one of Duncan's greatest friends). He was tireless in arrang-
ing readings and in holding literary soirées. In his memoir "Of Robert
Duncan," Everson describes those evening gatherings: "They always tend-
ed to be coterie gatherings, with a core of closely involved participants,
and a fringe of more youthful sycophants impelled as much by erotic as
by aesthetic interest. Duncan usually dominated from first to last. . . ."
Jonathan Williams made this portrait of Duncan in 1955 at Point Lobos,
Carmel Highlands, California; Edward Weston, Brett Weston, and Ansel
Adams lived up the hill.

In late October 1962, in gratitude for her championship of his work, Duncan sent an early ribbon copy of the typescript of his Roots and Branches *to Muriel Rukeyser. In her review of Duncan's first book,* Heavenly City, Earthly City, *in* Poetry *(April 1948), Rukeyser had proved to be one of Duncan's few public defenders: "I think he has found his own voice, and among the [Henry] Miller haunted writers of this coast, he is building the scene into poems, making experiment, music, debt into a personal and widening art." The typescript he sent her, from which this page comes, contains only the first section of the book as it was published. In all, there are nine typescripts for* Roots and Branches, *three each of three separate revisions; this one is probably from the last revision, containing only minor changes in punctuation and word endings, which were incorporated in the published text.*

ROOTS AND BRANCHES

Sail, Monarchs, rising and falling
orange merchants in spring's flowery markets!
messengers of March in warm currents of news floating!
    flitting into areas of aroma,
tracing out of air unseen roots and branches of sense
    I share in thought,
filaments woven and broken where the world might light
casual certainties of me. There are
    echoes of what I am in what you perform
this morning. How you perfect my spirit!
    almost restore
an imaginary tree of the living in all its doctrines,
    by fluttering about,
intent and easy as you are --the profusion of you--
awakening transports of an inner view of things.

. . . .

WHAT DO I KNOW OF THE OLD LORE?

A young editor wants me to write on Kabbalah for his magazine.

What do I know of the left and the right, of the Shekinah, of the
    Metatron?
It is an old book lying on the velvet cloth, the color of olive
    under-leaf and plumstain in the velvet;
it is a romance of pain and relief from pain, a tale told of the
    Lord of the Hour of Midnight,
the changing over that is a going down into Day from the Mountain.

Ah! the seed that lies in the sweetness of the Kabbalah
is the thot of those rabbis rejoicing in their common devotion,
of the thousand threads of their threnodies, praises, wisdoms,
    shared loves and curses interwoven.

There are terrible things in the design they weave, fair and
    unfair establishd in one.
How all righteousness is founded upon Jacob's cheat upon cheat,
    and the devout
pray continually for the humiliation and defeat of Esau,
for everlasting terror and pain to eat at the nephilim.

The waves of the old jews talking
persist at the shores.

Oh I know nothing of the left and the right.

The moon that moves the waters
comes clear from the earth's shadow.

All the old fears have been drawn up into the mountain that comes
    of knowing.

It is an old book of stories, the Bible is an old book of stories
--a mirror made by goblins for that Ice-Queen, the Shekinah--
a likelihood of our hearts withheld from healing.

A young editor wants me to write on Kabbalah for his magazine.

Yes, for I too loved the scene of dark magic, the sorceror's
    sending up clouds of empire and martyrdom;
the Gem made by goblins yielding its secret gold to the knowing;
enchantresses coming in to the lodestone; the star

Denise Levertov

1923–

[Levertov] cannot be understood as a British poet who came to America and tried to assimilate the American language through the expedient of appropriating Dr. Williams's language bag and baggage. She has made her own discovery of America. The character in her poetry is remarkably American precisely *because* it is genuinely international. I have read that her father was a great Jewish scholar and that she was educated at home. Her father must have been delighted; he must have felt like one of her readers, for her imagination is always religiously open, and it always responds to what touches it awake.

James Wright, "Gravity and Incantation" [review of Levertov's The Jacob's Ladder] *in* The Minnesota Review *(Spring 1962)*

BORN IN ENGLAND, Denise Levertov grew up just outside of London, in a home rich in books, Lieder, mysticism, and humanitarian politics. There was a "foreign opulence" about the place; and indeed, her mother (a descendant of a noted Welsh mystic) and her father (a brilliant Russian Jewish scholar who became an Anglican priest) had fallen in love in Constantinople. Educated privately (initially by her highly cultivated mother, who read Tennyson and the great 19th-century novels to her daughter), Levertov at 12 sent off a packet of her poems to T. S. Eliot; his reply was encouraging. By 1948, when she moved to New York City with her American husband, she had toiled for years at the barre of an evocatively ramshackle ballet academy, worked as a nurse during World War II, and published her first ("British Romantic") book of poems, *The Double Image.*

In the 1950s, Levertov forged important friendships with the Black Mountain Roberts (Creeley and Duncan) and immersed herself in William Carlos Williams, the modernist master who, as Charles Olson once remarked, had taught American poets to *walk.* With *Here and Now* (1956), Levertov scuttled neo-Romantic abstraction for a language that was vital, immediate, and distinctly American. She now moved, as Kenneth Rexroth was the first to notice, with a "kind of animal grace of the word."

Levertov locates herself firmly in the world and, as an impassioned critic of political and social injustice, refuses to ignore its "wretched history." She has called for a poetry that is "intense, wrought, bodied-forth, and magical." Her beautifully shaped poems are luminous with a visionary's sense of wonder: she opens up the here and now. For this poet, every step is an arrival. There is indeed another world, and Levertov knows – as Paul Éluard put it – that this is it. ∎

*Well known for his portraits of writers, artists, and musicians, Sausalito-
based photographer Chris Felver wrote Levertov in July 1995 requesting
a session. After an exchange of notes, Felver had the impression that for
Levertov, having her picture taken was an excruciating way to spend an
afternoon. Arriving in September at her Seattle home in "a very tough
section of town," Felver was greeted by the poet: "Talk of mutual friends,
Creeley, Adrienne Rich and of her hatred of war and the atrocities accom-
panying it. Constantly both of us stall making the picture. Then I ask
to see her study – upstairs we go. No computer, just a typewriter and
light enough to make the picture. With that over we begin to talk of pho-
tography. Amazed at her grasp of photography, I left understanding this
complex sage more by her iconoclastic refuge in the Northwest than I
ever would have by reading all of her letters and poetry."*

The Pulse

Sealed inside the anemone
in the dark, I knock my head
on steel petals
curving inward around me.

Somewhere the edict is given:
petals, relax.
Delicately they arch over backward.
All is opened to me –

the air they call water,
saline, dawngreen over its sands,
resplendent with fishes.
All day it is morning,

all night the glitter
of all that shines out of itself
crisps the vast swathes of the current.
But my feet are weighted:

only my seafern arms
my human hands
my fingers tipped with fire
sway out into the world.

Fair is the world.
I sing. The ache
up from heel to knee
of the weights

gives to the song its
ground bass.
And before the song
attains even a first refrain

the petals creak and
begin to rise.
They rise and recurl
to a bud's form

and clamp shut.
I wait in the dark.

In The Sorrow Dance *(1967), "The Pulse" is placed immediately before Levertov's bitter analysis of "Life at War." The Vietnam War radicalized the poet, who had once asserted that the "violent imitation of the horrors of our times" had no place in poetry, and she struggled to remake her visionary poetics. In her essay "The Poet in the World" (1967), Levertov argued that poetry "is necessary to a whole man, and that poetry be not divided from the rest of life is necessary to it." One of the epigraphs she chose for* The Sorrow Dance *is from Blake: "If the Perceptive Organs close, their Objects seem to close also." In "The Pulse," the poet waits in the dark, her song cut off.*

Robert Creeley

1926–

At his own Divers Press on Mallorca, where he was photographed by Jonathan Williams in August 1953, Creeley edited seven issues of Black Mountain Review *as well as works by Paul Blackburn, Robert Duncan, Charles Olson, and Larry Eigner. His own second book,* The Kind of Act of *(1953), and H. P. Macklin's* A Handbook of Fancy Pigeons *(1954) were also published there.*

ROBERT CREELEY'S IS a poetry of "first things first," of being, of actual living within the body. His works are poems of discovery, even – or especially – to the poet. And he is blissful about it, likes what he does, simply: "The fire delights in its form." Born in Massachusetts in 1926, Creeley grew up, after the death of his father, an ophthalmologist, with his mother (a nurse) and sister on a large but nonworking farm in rural New Hampshire; as a child he did, however, work tending cows. He was at Harvard for three years, until he was suspended for stealing a door from a residence house.

After a stint as an American Field Service ambulance driver in Burma and India during World War II, he tried Harvard again, but to no avail: he just was not a Harvard man. He eventually earned a degree from Black Mountain College in the 1950s (while teaching there), and later a Master's degree from the University of New Mexico (1960). Throughout this time, and before, he schooled himself deeply in the poetics and practice of William Carlos Williams, Louis Zukofsky, and Charles Olson. His correspondence with the latter comprises a thousand dense, intelligent letters of quest and discovery.

For a time, Creeley raised pigeons (fantails, rollers, and others) and chickens (Rhode Island Reds), and was a neighbor of Robert Graves on the island of Mallorca. Creeley lived and taught all over the map in the 1960s (New Mexico and Buffalo, for instance) and in the 1970s resided with his family in the literary community of Bolinas, on the northern coast of California. In 1989, Creeley returned to the East Coast. Since then, he has taught at the State University of New York at Buffalo. A *Collected Poems* was published in 1982, and a *Selected Poems* in 1991, both by the University of California Press.

A refined poet, a likable and funny man, he has said: "I saw a comment in a recent anthology to the effect that I was some sort of hip Emily Dickinson. Lovely thing. I thought she was pretty hip to begin with." ∎

```
      For Fear

    For fear I want
    to make myself again
    under the thumb
    of old love, old time

    subservience
    and pain, bent
    into a nail that will
    not come out.

    Why, love, does it
    make such a difference
    not to be heard
    in spite of self

    or what we may feel,
    one for the other,
    but as a hammer
    to drive again

    bent nail
    into old hurt?
```

"For Fear," written in December 1959, was first published in Poetry *magazine in May 1960, and was collected in* For Love: Poems 1950–1960 *(1962). The lineation in this minimalist love (or no love) song places more than usual stress on individual words, emphasizing the word as object, a cardinal principle of Creeley's ultra-formalist poetics: "I wanted the poem itself to exist and that could never be possible as long as some subject significantly elsewhere was involved. There had to be an independence derived from the very fact that words are things too. Poems gave me access to this fact more than any other possibility in language. . . . The poem is not a signboard, pointing to content ultimately to be regarded; but is, on the contrary, a form inhabited by intelligence and feeling." This fair copy typescript was sent by Creeley to his friend Ann Charters, a biographer who wrote the first biography of Creeley's mentor and friend Charles Olson and published another of Creeley's poems in her magazine* Portents.

I like him, I like him very much, he has an honest, inquiring mind; he puts down what he sees and seems listening internally to his own thinking.

William Carlos Williams, letter to Cid Corman, August 2, 1951

James Schuyler

1923–1991

I find James (I pass from the nostalgic, personal Jimmy to the poetic and eternal James) Schuyler's poetry honest in a way that poetry rarely is. But what can I mean by honest, for a work of art? Maybe honesty is partly an impression I get from richness and smartness and inclusiveness and speed. It seems honestly true and is honestly exciting. It promotes laughing and crying.

Kenneth Koch, "James Schuyler (very briefly)" in Denver Quarterly *(Spring 1990)*

JAMES SCHUYLER'S POEMS can sometimes stop readers in their tracks – not because of an infelicitous choice of word, or the dull drop of a participle or adverb, but from sheer and joyful surprise. A master of the sudden and unusual intrusion (of another state of consciousness, a flamboyant character, or an elegant twist of fate), Schuyler was a postmodern nature poet who wrote convincingly of the weather, of garden flowers, and of "malevolent ageratums," carefully noting "a too pungent salad" and "the smoke blazing over Jersey." Everything and everyone in his sometimes skinny poems is clearly, tenderly observed: "All things are real / no one a symbol."

After living with W. H. Auden in Florence, Italy, and on the island of Ischia for several years as a young man, Schuyler moved to New York and began his poetic life. His poems – a diary of his daily life in Manhattan and of weekend or summer jaunts to Long Island, Maine, or upstate New York – are intimate conversations, letters to and about his friends, sometimes gossipy and campy; others are compelling interior dialogues with loneliness.

Schuyler was regarded with considerable protective tenderness by most of his many friends. A lifelong best friend of the painter and critic Fairfield Porter, he lived with Porter and his wife, poet Anne Porter, and their five children in both Southampton, New York, and on Great Spruce Head Island, Maine. Other friends included John Ashbery, with whom Schuyler wrote a collaborative novel, *A Nest of Ninnies* (1969), as well as Kenneth Koch and Frank O'Hara, with whom he penned more than one cooperative poem. Like O'Hara, Schuyler worked at the Museum of Modern Art and wrote for *Art News*.

A resident for years of New York City's famous Chelsea Hotel, Schuyler died there in 1991. ∎

The Chelsea Hotel, one of New York City's most colorful literary landmarks, sports a commemorative plaque announcing that Schuyler lived there from 1979 until his death in 1991. It joins plaques for other former, famous inhabitants, including O. Henry, Dylan Thomas, Thomas Wolfe, Virgil Thomson, and Brendan Behan. But, it should be noted, no plaques exist for Warhol superstar Viva or for punk rocker Sid Vicious and his girlfriend, Nancy Spungen, who were also residents. Schuyler's room, and particularly the wrought-iron balustrade on the balcony facing West 23rd Street, made frequent appearances in his poems, but his friends say the room was never as messy as on the day in 1985 that Chris Felver took this picture.

In the 1960s, Schuyler spent considerable time with Alvin Novak (a pianist, composer, and friend of many of the members of the so-called New York School of Poets), and his lover, artist John Button. This fair copy of "Hoboken" was presented by the author to Novak, to whom the poem is dedicated. Like many of Schuyler's poems (and O'Hara's and Koch's as well), "Hoboken" contains allusions to works of art, artists, music, and musicians. It was originally published in the collection May 24th or So *(1966), one of several poetry pamphlets published by the Tibor de Nagy art gallery and its poetry-supporting owner, John Bernard Myers.*

```
                        Hoboken
                                for Alvin

I was going to write you a poem
about Hoboken and you playing Chopin
but I can't write it now

you see all these frustrating things happen

I know exactly how I felt
how the poem felt when I was going to write it
you know, that was when I should've
except I decided
        I wouldn't write at night any more

mornings

today -- look at it --
I might as well be in L.A.
with smog off the cold Pacific

but that poshumous étude
I bet you don't know he loved Bach!
can't you hear it when you play it and doesn't it
not surprise you? maybe that's all
I had to say, remind
you how long the free romantic line
is, how you've got it in your
wrists and fingers

after all, the Clam Broth House
is pretty classical too:
after a storm it's hell
when there's sand in the clams

the music said more to me than that

you see what makes me sick is
you can't just say
        Chopin
and leave it in the air
like an unfrosted Mazda light bulb
burning: someone will want to put a muffler
around it or a pleated paper shade

it's fantastic how people don't love beauty
yet we love Hoboken
                is that what
sort of regularly spaced sounds
late at night
        (what a big room you live in
and the Hudson instead of a pet dog
                instead of a yard
the tip of Manhattan   what a tip)
say?
```

```
                                        2.

                Is that why you look
at a portrait of Chopin
                        so he won't seem small
and legendary
        great, alive, different than us
but different how?
                freedom loving Pole
                making notes on paper
        like Bach except
who could it be?

        Chopin

        Here is his portrait by Delacroix
and it wouldn't look the same
if your left hand were not as strong as your right

of course the pianoforte is the triumph of civilization!

then you played
one of The Songs Without Words


                                Jimmy
```

Frank O'Hara

1926–1966

1959 APRIL 17TH

19 SUN.

Ned - Phil 2³⁰
Philip Guston dine 6⁰⁰

20 MON.

Barbara Guest reading 8⁰⁰
Lerner 6⁰⁰
21 lunch George 1⁰⁰
TUES.

dine Hal Brodkey 6⁰⁰
22 lunch David H 12³⁰ Chico
WED.

O'Hara's literal and realistic "I do this, I do that" poems chronicle his days as poet, friend, lover, art critic, and curator. His life was often hectic and certainly fast-paced, as his datebook for the week of April 19, 1959, suggests, full of dinners and lunches with his artist and writer friends ("Ned," on Sunday, is composer Ned Rorem, with whom O'Hara sometimes went to concerts). As translator William Weaver reports in Remembering Frank O'Hara: *"Without Frank, the life we led in New York would have been, I think, totally different. He gave his friends an awareness of the wonderful time – the outset of our adulthood – that we were experiencing. With the eye of memory, I see him, in no specific context, walking, with that dancing step, along a New York street, and he is always in the sunlight."*

"AND HERE I am, the / center of all beauty! writing these poems! / Imagine!" Of the thousands of poets who have called New York home, none has exemplified the city so fully, in either work or life, as did Frank O'Hara. The moment he arrived in 1951, the unassuming Francis O'Hara from Grafton, Massachusetts, was reborn as Frank: the bustling curator, critic, collaborator, and handholder of New York's art world and the hard-drinking, jazz-loving, all-night reveler on the city's social scene. Booming in the 50s and 60s with its own school of painting (Abstract Expressionism), its own music (jazz as played by Mingus and Monk or sung by Billie Holiday), and its own ballet company (George Balanchine's New York City Ballet), New York was the new cultural capital of the world, and it was this city that O'Hara celebrated in hundreds of affecting poems.

In his youth, O'Hara, encouraged by his music-loving father, looked forward to a career as a composer or concert pianist. After serving in the U.S. Navy (1944–46), he pursued music at Harvard, at the time brimming with talented G.I. Bill students, especially writers; O'Hara blossomed, taking in every concert, poetry reading, art exhibition, and film Cambridge had to offer. He soon gave up music for poetry.

After attending graduate school in Ann Arbor, he arrived in New York and found a job at the ticket desk of the Museum of Modern Art (by the time of his death, he was a well-respected Assistant Curator there). He spent every waking moment immersed in art. He wrote his liberating poems during intermission at the ballet or between drinks at the Cedar Tavern, at the loft parties of his artist friends or, as the title of *Lunch Poems* (1964) suggests, on the backs of menus. Most of his work escaped critical attention until after his death in 1966 – struck by a dune buggy on a dark Fire Island beach at 3 a.m. on July 24, he died the next evening of abdominal injuries – and the publication in 1971 of his gigantic *Collected Poems*. As Walt Whitman said: "Here the frailest leaves of me." ∎

This portrait was made by Harry Redl in 1958 on the fire escape of the loft apartment O'Hara shared with Joe LeSueur at 90 University Place. Images of O'Hara were created by a variety of contemporary photographers and painters, including his friends John Button, Fairfield Porter, Grace Hartigan, Jane Freilicher, and, of course, Larry Rivers, who has recalled: "He was a great model. For one thing he liked to model; he even felt complimented that you asked him to, and you ended up wanting him to like you. He had blazing blue eyes, so if you were stuck you could always put a little blue to make the work more interesting. His widow's peak gave you a place to anchor the picture, and his broken nose was dramatic and easy to get. . . . I always felt I was close to getting him but I never did, so I kept on trying."

He also mentioned a lot of things just because he liked them — for example, jujubes. Some of these things had not appeared before in poetry. His poetry contained aspirin tablets, Good Teeth buttons, and water pistols. His poems were full of passion and life; they weren't trivial because small things were called in them by name.

Kenneth Koch, "A Note on Frank O'Hara in the Early Fifties" in Audit *(April 1964)*

Poem

Johnny and Alvin are going home, are sleeping now
are fanning the air with breaths from the same bed.

The moon is covered with gauze and the laughs
are not in them. The boats honk and the barges heave

a little, so the river is moved by a faint breeze.
Where are the buses that would take them to another state?

standing on corners; a nurse waits with a purse
and a murderer escapes the detectives by taking a public

conveyance through the summer's green reflections.
There's too much lime in the world and not enough gin,

they gasp. The gentle are curious, but the curious
are not gentle. So the breaths come home and sleep.

                                        Frank

Alvin —
    You might like this copy of a poem Frank sent
to us in about 1954 (?)
                    Love
                    John

Painter John Button (standing) and pianist Alvin Novak (seated) arrived together in New York in 1956, seeking – like O'Hara and countless other young actors, painters, and writers – the freedom to pursue their own ideas of art and life. They were both intimately involved with the New York poetry and painting "scene," and appeared in several of O'Hara's poems, as do most of his other friends. This photocopy of a typescript of a poem by O'Hara bears a note at the bottom from Button to Novak.

Kenneth Koch

1925–

Koch and Frank O'Hara became close friends in the early 1950s, when this photograph was taken by John Gruen, collaborating on plays and performances, corresponding wittily, and encouraging each other's poetic adventures. Their friendship began after John Ashbery gave Koch copies of some of O'Hara's poems in 1950. Having disliked them in Cincinnati, Koch reread them in Aix-en-Provence and on the way to Vienna, and found them totally changed and "marvelous": "I believe I liked them for the same reason I had not liked them before – i.e. because they were sassy, colloquial and full of realistic detail."

IT IS RISKY to read a Kenneth Koch poem before you read someone else's: after you read Koch, everyone else, even Hopkins, sounds like him. In 1959, he published *Ko, or a Season on Earth* (1959), which was inspired by *Orlando Furioso* and written in the ottava rima stanza of Byron's *Don Juan*. This and others of Koch's books, infused with a brainy energy, are among the most literate, funniest works of modern poetry. And his poetry is original and very self-sufficient: "One thing a poem needs is to be complete / In itself and not need others to complement it."

The making of Kenneth Koch, poet, began in Cincinnati, Ohio, where by the age of 17 he had committed himself to a life of writing. After service in the Pacific theater during World War II, he entered Harvard. There he became friendly with John Ashbery, and the two poets edited the *Harvard Advocate* for a while, publishing (among others) Frank O'Hara. All three would move to New York City during the late 1940s and early 1950s and become friends. In France soon afterward, Koch found inspiration in the "incomprehensible excitement" of the French language, a sense he communicates in his poetry. Koch often combines devices such as the "list" poem with his interests in French Surrealism and hyperbole to create a universe that is truly and happily unnerving.

In the 1970s, he pioneered the teaching of poetry to children in the schools (his classic book on the subject, *Rose, Where Did You Get That Red?*, was published in 1973). He further refined his poetry in the 1980s and 90s, developing a more serious (not solemn), lyrical metaphysics, while remaining inventive and funny. At the same time, he has, for nearly 30 years, inspired students in his classes at Columbia University, where he passes on his enthusiasm for the cause of poetry. ■

A Clothing Bee

A TOE'S OPERA

a Memoiws of a cub-scout

XZXEXZXXXXXXXXXXXXXXXX

And, with a shout, collecting coat-hangers
Dour rhebus, conch, hip,
Ham, the autumn day, oh how genuine!
Literary frog, catch-all boxer, 0
Real! The magistrate, say, group, bower, undies
Disk, poop, "Timon of Athens." When
The bugle shimmies, how glove towns!
It's Merrimac, bends, and pure gymnasium
Impy keels! The earth desks, madmen
Impose a shy (oops) broken tube's child--
Land! why are your bandleaders troops
Of Is? Honk, can the mailed rose
Gesticulate? Arm the paper arm!
Bind up the chow in its lintel of sniff,
Rush the pilgrims, destroy tobacco, pool
The dirty beautiful jingling pyjamas, at
Last beside the stove-drum-preventing oyster,
The "Caesar" of tower dins, the cold's "I'm
A dear." O bed, at which I used to sneer at.
Bringing cloth. O song, "Dusted Hoops!" He gave
A dish of. The bear, that sound of pins. O French
Ice-cream, balconies of deserted snuff! The hills are
Terribly close now and shouting.

Not the least function of poetry is to make vivid our sense of the meaning of words. He tends to enlarge where others narrow down. Words need not be purified until the tribe has sullied them; after two generations of continual washing it is a wonder words have any color left. I do not wish to make false claims for Mr. Koch; he will undoubtedly not . . . write a "Gray's Elegy." He has the other poetic gift: vivacity and go, originality of perception and intoxication with life.

Frank O'Hara, "Another Word on Kenneth Koch" in Poetry *(March 1955)*

In a memoir of Frank O'Hara, Koch talks about the genesis of his book-length poem When the Sun Tries to Go On, *written in 1953 but not published until 1969: "I had no clear intention of writing a 2400-line poem (which it turned out to be) before Frank said to me, on seeing the first 72 lines – which I regarded as a poem by itself – 'Why don't you go on with it as long as you can?' Frank at this time decided to write a long poem too [Second Avenue]; I can't remember how much his decision to write such a poem had to do with his suggestion to me to write mine. While we were writing our long poems, we would read each other the results daily over the telephone. This seemed to inspire us a good deal." This draft shows one of the 24-line stanzas of Koch's 100-stanza poem in progress.*

Ted Berrigan

1934–1983

In a recent memoir, Ron Padgett clarified the matter of his pal's heft: "Ted claimed he could run fast, at least in short sprints. Looking at him you'd think, This guy run fast? No way. And then he did." This photograph was taken by Chris Felver just after Berrigan read his poetry at the 1982 Kerouac Symposium at the Naropa Institute in Boulder, Colorado (he had just put his ever-present can of Pepsi on the ground).

As A YOUNG man in Providence, Rhode Island, Edmund Joseph Berrigan was considered a great reader by his family, but not a "real poet": he displayed no outward signs, in temperament or action, of his poetic calling or his future role as founder of the second generation of the New York School of Poets. He enrolled in Providence College before serving in the Korean War, then attended the University of Tulsa on the G.I. Bill. There he completed his B.A. and began work on his Master's thesis, "George Bernard Shaw: The Problem of How to Live." In Tulsa he fell in with poets and artists Ron Padgett, Joe Brainard, and Dick Gallup; the four made up what John Ashbery would later affectionately refer to as the "soi-disant Tulsa School." They all moved to New York City in the early 1960s.

In New York, Berrigan found work writing art criticism and book reviews, and associated with various painters and poets, including Ashbery and Kenneth Koch. By 1963, he had, so to speak, cracked the code with his volume *The Sonnets* (1964), creating a quirky, engaging music with scrambled, varied, and repeated lines, many of which grew out of collaborative work or were lifted from poets of the past. In 1966, the Poetry Project was founded at St. Mark's Church In-the-Bowery; as a member of its advisory committee and a workshop instructor, Berrigan "directed" the widening community of poets, artists, and friends on New York's Lower East Side. Two years later, he began his peripatetic teaching career as writer-in-residence at the University of Iowa's Writing Workshop.

Throughout the 1970s, Berrigan's home at 101 St. Mark's Place, which he shared with his wife, poet Alice Notley, and his sons (now themselves poets), Anselm and Edmund, was a mecca for young writers seeking advice and inspiration. In 1983, the 48-year-old Berrigan died of blood poisoning caused by a perforated ulcer, but his voice continues to speak through the work of the community he helped shape. ∎

yuk yuk

THE ARS POETICA MACHINE

A Poem machine should be a palpable and mute machine
Like a globed fruit machine   *a*

Dumb   *machine*
As an old medallion to the thumb machine

Silent as the sleeve-machine-worn stone machine   *has*
Of the casement ledge machine where the moss machine is *grown*
          machine

A Poem machine should be motionless in the time machine
As the moon machine climbs

Leaving, as the moon machine releases
twig machine by twig machine the night-entangled tree machines

Leaving, as the moon machine behind the winter machine leaves
Memory
          -machine by memory machine the mind machine---

A Poem machine should be motionless in the time machine
As the moon machine climbs

A Poem machine should be an equal-to machine:
Not a truth machine   *truth*

For all the history-machine's history of grief machines
An empty doorway machine and a maple leaf machine

For a love machine
The leaning grasses machines and two light machines above
                              the sea machine

A Poem machine should not mean machine
But be machine

          The Archibald
          MacLeish Machine

[Ted Berrigan, ca. 1969-70]

I knew, for the first time, how good he was when I read "Tamborine Life." I loved (love) that poem. It seemed in a way ahead of everything — absolutely casual, ordinary, and momentary-seeming, without joking, mystery, false dazzle, and full of buoyancy, sweetness, and high spirits. Ted told me that my poetry had inspired him. He was a generous man. I don't think I ever told him how he influenced me. He did.

Kenneth Koch, "Written for the Memorial Service," St. Mark's Church In-the-Bowery, July 8, 1983; printed in Nice to See You: Homage to Ted Berrigan, *edited and with an introduction by Anne Waldman (Minneapolis, 1991)*

A champion of individual perception and structural freedom, Berrigan often blurred the boundaries between his brand of humorous surrealism and serious aesthetics, as well as between art and life. "The Ars Poetica Machine" jibes at the standard in poetry, as represented by Archibald MacLeish, who was often viewed (unfortunately and short-sightedly) by other poets as the prime example of the successful, sell-out, traditionalist poet. MacLeish's "Ars Poetica" describes an aesthetic quite different from Berrigan's noisy poetics:

A poem should be palpable and mute
as a globed fruit,

Dumb
As old medallions to the thumb,

Silent as the sleeve-worn stone
Of casement ledges where the moss has grown –

A poem should be wordless
As the flight of birds.

With Ron Padgett, Berrigan invented his own "machine" – the Poetry Machine – which manufactured poems ad infinitum.

Ron Padgett

1942–

Among the "incredible number of titles" the editors considered for this very influential 1970 anthology were The Heavenly Humor, Very Good Poems, Great Feats of Harmony, Great Feet of Hominy, Malign Machinations, Shasta Daisies, Up Against the Wall, Fear Among the Legs of a Chair, Poetry Without Fear, Lyrical Bullets, Pansies Freaked with Jet, Of Manhattan the Son, Treed Again, A Museum of Modern Poetry, *and* Moving Ramps. *Among the poems included are all of Tom Veitch's* Toad Poems, *and Padgett's* "Detach, Invading."

ACCORDING TO E. B. White's 1948 essay "Here Is New York," the metropolis houses three separate cities: one of natives, one of commuters, and – the greatest of the three – the city of settlers. Ron Padgett was one of those settlers, part of the band that, during the 1960s, helped turn New York into the new cultural capital of the world. By the midpoint of that decade, this native of Tulsa, Oklahoma, had come to exemplify what it means to be a poet in the city.

In Tulsa, Padgett met Ted Berrigan, Joe Brainard, and Dick Gallup. With their mutual interest in French Surrealist poetry and Abstract Expressionism, the four became fast friends; they followed each other east, colonizing and transforming the fledgling literary community on New York's Lower East Side. There, Padgett and Berrigan, often working in collaboration, began to implement their program for a new kind of poetry, based on the aesthetics of Surrealism and Abstract Expressionism. Padgett was also influenced by Kenneth Koch, his teacher at Columbia University, and by the work of fellow New York School poets Frank O'Hara and John Ashbery. On the surface, Padgett's poetry displays some of their structuring, jarring juxtapositions, and child-like sensibility, but the artful use he makes of convention, artifice, and cliché are all his own. Borrowing from the random methods of Dadaist poets and from Pop artists' use of silk screening to mass-produce paintings, the Poetry Machine (invented by Padgett and Berrigan) assembled poems from mixed and matched words and phrases, as well as from poems by writers of the past.

Ron Padgett has translated the French poets Apollinaire, Larbaud, and Cendrars. He continues to live in New York City, where he teaches imaginative writing at Columbia University and serves as Publications Director of the Teachers & Writers Collaborative. ∎

The artist Joe Brainard (at left with Ron Padgett in this photograph taken in July 1991 by the poet's wife, Patricia Padgett) was one of the favorites of the poets of the New York School, seniors and juniors. His vibrant, devil-may-care art seems particularly at one with the writings of his friends Kenneth Koch, Ron Padgett, Ted Berrigan, and Kenward Elmslie, for whose works he designed covers and illustrations, including those for An Anthology of New York Poets *(opposite).*

Like Ron has a hard sparkle in his works that seems like a certain noon.

Ted Berrigan, in an interview with Tom Clark, Bolinas, California, Summer 1970

RON PADGETT

THE
BEAVER ~~DAYS~~ vs. SURREALISTS

Instead of a big pompous Surrealist
with cobwebs covering my visual apparatus
~~and clogging my nasal nostrils,~~
I'd rather be a beaver with overbite
~~so I could~~ mow right through the trees
toward your love at the end of the day,
~~or, if you've been too busy~~
~~in our beaver home all day,~~
~~I'd~~ kiss you at the ~~beginning~~ of the next,
when dawn ~~rises~~ like the face
of a scary melting Surrealist
who had a bad night and now
is ~~going~~ back to ~~the~~ crypt
with an ionisphere-sized headache.
But we in our little beaver bedroom
are snug and safe. You whap
your tail against the bedding and fall
into a deep and satisfying sleep,
in which you fling off your ideas
and scamper through them as they fly
~~through the air,~~ fading outlines.

big
and
lumping
beyond their

covers up
his

in the air.

Sept 1987 versions

3/6/95 revisions

*Do you think this will get
me a MacArthur?*

*Padgett's poetry, according to Aram Saroyan, has "a mind and a will
of its own, leaving both the writer and the reader to follow its course as
passive, slightly dumbfounded spectators." His poems are very serious
funny stuff. "Beavers vs. the Surrealists," of which the Berg Collection
has several drafts, has not yet been published.*

Anne Waldman

1945–

Fast Speaking Woman *was inspired by the chants of Maria Sabina, a Mazatec shaman (healer). In this early, landmark "list" poem, Waldman spins variations on a simple phrase. The first version was published in 1974; in 1996, City Lights published an expanded edition with an essay in which Waldman describes her intentions: "I wanted to use this elemental modal structure to capture Everywoman's psyche. The 'bottom nature,' Gertrude Stein calls it, of any human. But in this case, I was focused on my own femaleness and, by extension, any woman's. . . . I wanted to assert the sense of my mind, my imagination being able to travel as artist, maker, inventor. To see beyond boundaries. . . . And the chant was to be spoken, or sung, or even more interestingly, sprechstimme, spoke/sung." In July 1982, Chris Felver caught Waldman performing the poem at the Naropa Institute.*

WHEN ANNE WALDMAN's father was cranking out magazine articles during her Greenwich Village childhood, she revered his paper, typewriter ribbons, coffee, and cigarettes as the stuff of "sacred daily ritual." In the seventh grade, she felt a calling to be a poet and began meeting with some of her classmates in a literary "salon"; by high school, she was sending her poetry out "for rejection by *The New Yorker* and other notable magazines."

She graduated from Bennington College in 1966, but her most formative experience came in summer 1965, in Berkeley, as she listened spellbound as Charles Olson and Robert Duncan read their poetry. With Lewis Warsh, a poet and novelist she met there (and later married), she moved back to New York and founded the literary magazine *Angel Hair*. In 1968, she was named director of the St. Mark's Poetry Project, where she became closely identified with the New York poets of her generation, including Bernadette Mayer. In the first of many experiences with Buddhism, Waldman studied in the summer of 1970 under the lama Chogyam Trungpa. She traveled to India in 1973, apprenticed with Tibetan lamas, and the following summer went to the Naropa Institute in Boulder, Colorado. There, she and Allen Ginsberg founded the Jack Kerouac School of Disembodied Poetics, which continues to be a major literary gathering place. There, too, Waldman met Reed Bye, her second husband and the father of her son, Ambrose, born in 1980. The subject of *First Baby Poems* (1982), Ambrose is also present in much of her work written since his birth. He is her Virgil, her guide in her epic-length poem *Iovis*.

Currently Distinguished Professor of Poetics at Naropa, Waldman lives and works with poet/Sanskritist Andrew Schelling; they have translated ancient Buddhist poems from the Pali canon as *Songs of the Sons and Daughters of Buddha*.

Her first book, *On the Wing* (1968), was followed by four more in two years. Terrified at first, she began reading her work in public, becoming known for dramatic, powerful performances, including spontaneous poetry. More ambitious in style as time has passed, her poetry has maintained its trademark tone – spontaneous, talkative, experimental – combined intriguingly with a sense of reverence. ■

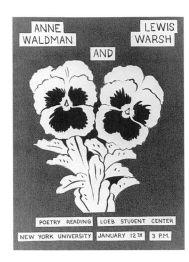

After graduating from Bennington in 1966, Waldman moved back to New York City (having grown up on Macdougal Street in the Village) and joined the new Poetry Project at St. Mark's Church In-the-Bowery. Her work at the project and on Angel Hair *put Waldman at the center of the amazing flowering of "grass roots" art, writing, and performance that transformed New York's Lower East Side into one of the most "happening" places in the late 1960s. Joe Brainard designed this handbill for a reading by Waldman and Warsh, ca. 1967–68.*

Waldman and Lewis Warsh were married in the early 1960s at the beginning of their writing careers; they have remained friends, with Warsh editing Waldman's 1988 collection, Blue Mosque. *In 1992, Warsh assembled* Bustin's Island 1968, *a unique hand-made book (now in the Berg Collection) consisting of typescript text and black-and-white photographs (this one is by Ted Berrigan) taken that summer, when both writers were 23. In 1996, Granary Books issued* Bustin's Island '68, *in an edition of 70 copies.*

Anne Waldman is a poet orator, her body is an instrument for vocalization, her voice a trembling flame rising out of a strong body, her texts the accurate energetic fine notations of words with spoken music latent in mindful arrangement on the page. She is a Power, an Executive of Vast poetry projects and mind schools in America, a rhythmic pioneer on the road of loud sound that came from Homer Sappho and leads to future epic space mouth, she's a cultivated Buddhist meditator, an international subtle Tantrika, an activist of tender brain vibrations.

Allen Ginsberg, dust jacket blurb for Waldman's Makeup on Empty Space *(West Branch, Iowa, 1984)*

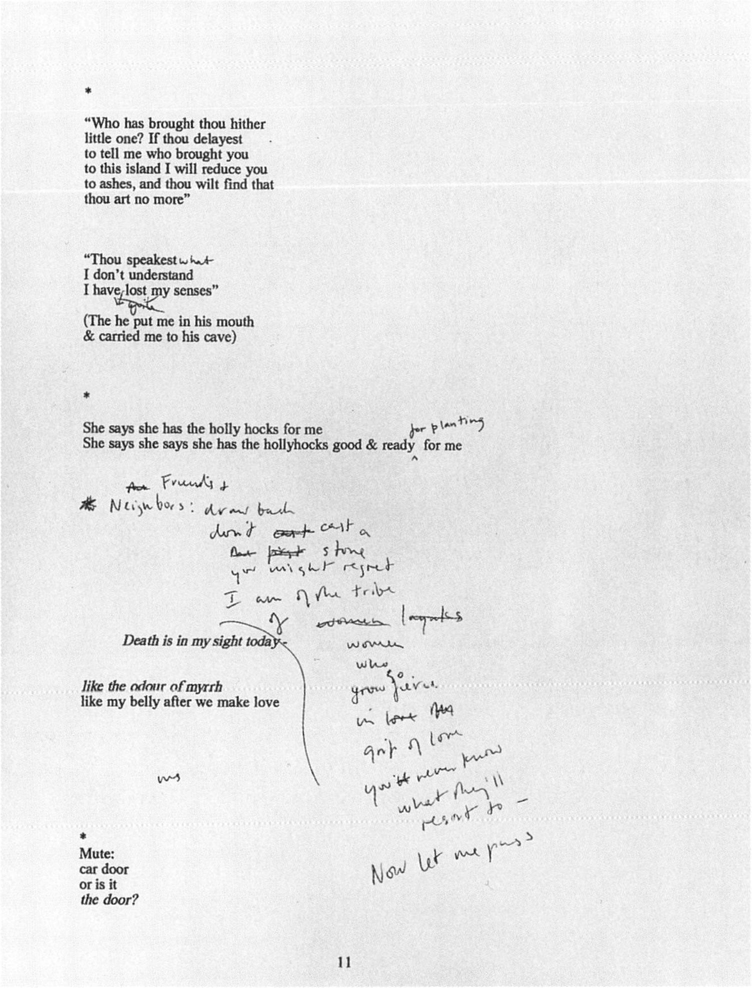

*from **Troubairitz***

Friends & Neighbors: draw back
don't cast a cruel stone you might regret

I am of the tribe
of women who
grow fierce
in grip of love
you can't imagine
what violent acts
we'll resort to

Let this "transgressor" pass

*

Get back into your
suburban houses,
harpies,
gossips,
sowers-of-discord

You dare
comment
on this goddess' heart

I'll have you
roasted over coals
in your own backyards

My legions
are
wrathful
demonesses
skilled
in the ancient practice of
illicit love

*

Death is in my sight today –

like the odour of myrrh – after love

The left-hand page reproduces a manuscript draft. The typeset portions read:

*

"Who has brought thou hither
little one? If thou delayest
to tell me who brought you
to this island I will reduce you
to ashes, and thou wilt find that
thou art no more"

"Thou speakest what
I don't understand
I have lost my senses"

(The he put me in his mouth
& carried me to his cave)

*

She says she has the holly hocks for me
She says she says she has the hollyhocks good & ready for me

Death is in my sight today

like the odour of myrrh
like my belly after we make love

*

Mute:
car door
or is it
the door?

11

Troubairiitz *is Waldman's word for a female troubadour, and, she points out, "the title's sound carries Trobar, literally to find, to invent, plus trouble." This book-length poem was written in the course of 49 days – in Buddhist thought, the time that elapses between reincarnations of one soul. That state, called Bardo, is evoked by the poem's fleeting, fragmented, dreamy style. "Metaphorically," Waldman says, "this poem takes place in the romantic gap between two phases of a life." The poem was published in 1993 by Fifth Planet Press.*

Donald Justice

1925–

Justice studied at the University of Miami with the American composer Carl Ruggles, but suspected he "might have more talent as a writer than a composer." On the connection between writing music and poetry, Justice notes, "In both there is the same kind of joy in working something out, quite compulsively perhaps, and that is what must have engaged me when I tried to write music, and does now when I try to work out a poem."

I would know from the sound of his galoshes sluicing down the hallway that it was Don, key in hand, wet bangs like seaweed over his brow, as he went by irritated, it always amazed me how frightened I was of him. . . . How can I make this palpable to those who were never in his clear-eyed, stubborn, cranky, breathtakingly precise, wry, elegant, presence? We knew there was someone who could find us out.

Jorie Graham, *"Iowa City, 1976"* in Verse *(Winter/Spring 1992)*

POETS CAN TURN up anywhere these days. Donald Justice, for instance, appears on page 305 of the paperback edition of John Irving's best-selling 1981 novel, *The Hotel New Hampshire*: "I thought that, like his poems, he would be both candid and formal, austere, even grave – but open, even generous. He looked like a man you'd ask to say an elegy for someone you'd loved." In the course of the novel, eight of Justice's poems are declaimed by Irving's characters. Donald Justice himself has played poker in Cincinnati with composer John Cage, the master of chance, and some of Justice's poems were subsequently composed using chance methods – flash cards, for example. Justice has been sighted in Miami, where he was born, more frequently in Iowa City, where he taught at the famed Iowa Writers' Workshop for years, and even in San Francisco (every February) and in New York City (as often as possible).

Unusual in other ways, Justice was nearly 35 when his first book was published, in 1959. He was by this time a master teacher and an eternal student, who numbered among his teachers John Berryman, Robert Lowell, and Yvor Winters (his fellow students at Iowa included Philip Levine, William Stafford, Jane Cooper, and W. D. Snodgrass). Jorie Graham, Charles Wright, and Mark Strand have praised him as a teacher. Inspired by Rilke, Vallejo, and Wallace Stevens, and by the forms of the past, he writes in sonnets, villanelles, sestinas, and triolets.

In the midst of all this, Justice still says of himself: "I happen to be somewhat reticent by nature, if not extremely shy." He does seem a bit distracted at times, as if he were whispering poems to Aldebaran; or perhaps he is merely giving instructions in breathing, seeing, and remembering. ∎

Based on "Piedra Negra sobre una Piedra Blanca," by the great Peruvian poet César Vallejo, "Variations on a Text by Vallejo" is Justice's elegy for himself. The first line of Vallejo's poem – "Me moriré en Paris con aguacero" – was used by Justice as an epigraph in the printed version (an aguacero is a heavy downpour). The poem takes off from Vallejo's example, extending it and paying homage at the same time. This first draft was revised primarily by excision and by fine tuning; of his method of working, Justice says, "It is rare for a poem of mine to go through an orderly succession of drafts, versions which begin at the beginning and go right through to the end." He often takes inspiration from bits and pieces of other poets' work, as some of his titles suggest: "Sestina on Six Words by Weldon Kees," "Lorcaesques," and "After a Phrase Abandoned by Wallace Stevens."

from **Variations on a Text by Vallejo**

Me moriré en Paris con aguacero . . .

I will die in Miami in the sun,
On a day when the sun is very bright,
A day like the days I remember, a day like other days,
A day that nobody knows or remembers yet,
And the sun will be bright then on the dark glasses of strangers
And in the eyes of a few friends from my childhood
And of the surviving cousins by the graveside,
While the diggers, standing apart, in the still shade of the palms,
Rest on their shovels, and smoke,
Speaking in Spanish softly, out of respect.

Samuel Menashe

1925–

Menashe met the prominent Hollywood fashion photographer Andre de Dienes at a party in late 1953 or early 1954; de Dienes was planning a series of photographs based on biblical themes and promptly asked Menashe to pose for him. Although his vision is often very dark, Menashe is also a celebratory poet, and an impulse of joyous wonder infuses much of the work. The poet's mother once joked, as her son whirled around the apartment to classical music, "You should have been a dancer, but it's too much work!"

TO HIS FATHER, Samuel Menashe was "a square peg in a round hole," and this was not a bad thing. His parents revered literature, but as a young man, Menashe studied biochemistry. Service as an infantryman in Europe during World War II defined and intensified him ("We lived only in the moment encircled by death"): Menashe had not yet begun to make poems, but the evanescent had become his landscape. His father would later say to him: "You're a poet. You know what I mean – the fleeting moment."

After the war, Menashe matriculated at the Sorbonne, and in 1950, he was awarded a doctorate after successfully defending a "heretical" thesis which argued, in part, that the "imperial imposition of power destroys the imagination." He later taught at Bard College (a friend joked that he would be assigned Inspiration 101 and 102) and then spent a year in California attempting to storm the gates of the movie studios. A near-fatal automobile accident on the way to a crucial appointment brought him to his senses, and he abandoned the golden calf of Hollywood. But the year in Laurel Canyon had not been squandered: he had read Thomas Mann and had continued to write the concise, beautifully cadenced poems that would one day be described as "minute cathedrals."

Menashe found a publisher for his first collection, *The Many Named Beloved* (1961), with the help of the English poet and Blake scholar Kathleen Raine, who found herself drawn to the work of a writer who took Elijah and Blake as his prophets. Three more volumes followed, including a *Collected Poems* (1986). From the first, Menashe has written with an adamantine clarity that is superbly suited to prying the visionary from the real. He has lived in New York City most of his life, but his true home is that imaginative realm where the "timeless presence" of the physical world is made manifest. And his sensibility is always open to "the penetrating thrust of a few words." As Menashe himself has pointed out, Goliath was felled by a pebble – "well aimed." ∎

THERE IS NO JERUSALEM BUT THIS

The shrine whose form within *The shrine whose shape I am*
My physical form is limned *HAS A FRINGE OF FIRE*
Streams fire to my skin *FLAMES SKIRT MY SKIN*
And I, kilned one, chant
Canticles which flames scan
Through me shaped as I am

There is no Jerusalem but this
Breathed in flesh by shameless love
Built high upon the tides of blood
I believe the Prophets and Blake
And like David I bless myself
With all my might

I know many hills were holy once
But now in the level lands to live
Zion ground down must become marrow
Thus in my bones I'm the King's son
And through Death's domain I go *back to domain*
Making my own procession

19

His poetry reminds me of some kind of biblical instrument — tabor or jubal — and the note he strikes is always positive and even joyous. Here is a poet who compresses thoughts into language intense and clear as diamonds. . . .

Stephen Spender, reviewing No Jerusalem But This *(New York, 1971) in* The New York Review of Books, *July 22, 1971*

Menashe wrote his first poem at age 23, in Paris, and a number of his poems appeared throughout the 1950s in such magazines as the Yale Review, Commonweal, *and* Harper's. *But he was unable to find a New York publisher willing to take on a book. So in June 1960 he went to England, where he secured an agent but where the rejections (the poems were too "short, slight") continued. Then Menashe sent a handful of his poems to Kathleen Raine. Impressed, she wrote a praising note to the publisher Victor Gollancz, who agreed two months later to publish a collection. Published on July 24, 1961, with a foreword by Raine,* The Many Named Beloved *is dedicated to the poet's parents. Menashe, shown above right in Central Park in the summer of 1961 holding the book's manuscript, often spends months reworking a "finished" (i.e., published) poem: this copy of his first book includes revisions, dating from the late 1970s to the early 1980s, to more than 20 of its poems.*

James Merrill

1926–1995

Merrill and Howard Moss were involved socially as well as through The New Yorker, *which under Moss published a number of Merrill's poems. The two poets were in the habit of sharing their work, and freely if gently criticizing each other. On one occasion, Moss sent Merrill copies of some poems that appear in Moss's 1965 collection,* Finding Them Lost. *Among the poems Merrill sent to Moss in return were typescript versions of his three translations of Cavafy (see opposite). This 1969 photograph by Rollie McKenna was once tacked to a wall in Moss's office at* The New Yorker.

JAMES INGRAM MERRILL was born in New York City, the son of Hellen Ingram and Charles Merrill, founder of Merrill Lynch & Company. Though his parents divorced in 1939 (a traumatic event to which Merrill alluded in both poetry and prose), he reaped many of the benefits, both cultural and educational, of his father's wealth, "whether [he] liked it or not": the young Merrill discovered and was able to cultivate a love for opera, opulence, and dramatic staging, all of which would later mark and distinguish his poetry.

Merrill's reputation gained momentum with each of his volumes: both *Nights and Days* (1966) and *Mirabell: Books of Number* (1978) won the National Book Award; *Divine Comedies* (1976), the Pulitzer Prize; and *Braving the Elements* (1972), the Bollingen Prize. In 1954, Merrill and his companion David Jackson (DJ of *The Changing Light at Sandover*, 1982) quit the bustling New York literary scene for a house in Stonington, Connecticut. There, through the Ouija board, he and Jackson had their first, fateful meeting with the spirit Ephraim, who would play a leading role in the "divine comedy" of the 17,000-line poem *Sandover*. Its three books and "Coda" compose a cosmology through the use of a variety of forms, ranging from blank verse narrative to canzone. The story was brought to a close in Merrill's 15th and posthumous collection, *A Scattering of Salts* (1995), with the poem "Nine Lives."

After James Merrill's death, of a heart attack, on February 6, 1995, many of his friends and fellow poets paid fond tribute at a memorial service at The New York Public Library. In *The Village Voice*, W. S. Merwin recalled: "When I last saw him, as we walked up Fifth Avenue in the winter night . . . he spoke of competitiveness and jealousy among poets, how he had always disliked it. And the pleasure he felt when he found a poem he liked by somebody else." ∎

```
CAVAFY: ON AN ITALIAN SHORE

The son of Menedoros,   Kimos, a Greek-Italian,
fritters his life away   in the pursuit of pleasure,
according to the common   practice in Magna Graecia
among the rich, unruly   young men of today.

            however, wholly        counter to his nature,
Today, though, he is truly   overcast in spirit
he's lost in Thought, dejected. by clouds assembled dully.   There on the shore he sees
with bitter melancholy   ship upon ship that slowly
disgorges crates of booty   from the Peloponnese.

Greek booty. Spoils of Corinth.
Today don't be surprised   if it's unsuitable,
An certainly this evening   it's inadmissible,
indeed impossible,   for the Italicized
young man to dream of giving   himself to pleasure fully.
```

His poetry was as funny as Byron's, as elusive and personal as Montale's, as magisterial as Wallace Stevens's, as intelligent as Pope's. He knew better than anyone else how to make a word skip across the smooth surface of the mind and sink deep where it landed. . . . I can't think of another poet's work that has such high finish as well as such a density of thought. His tone may have been light and sociable, but his vision was universal, his intellect sovereign. . . . Everything he touched he transformed into art.

Edmund White, "James Merrill" in The Village Voice, February 21, 1995

Introduced to Greece in 1950, Merrill was not at first impressed: "Unlike Paris, where the most banal sidewalk sent me quivering because Debussy or Wilde or Cocteau might have set foot on it, Greece and all its splendors would have to work long and hard, like Greek immigrants in the slums of New York, to earn their keep in my blocked imagination." But in 1959, Merrill and David Jackson purchased a home on the slopes of Mount Lycabettos in Athens, where they spent at least half of each year for the next 20 years. Many of Merrill's poems of the 1960s and 1970s are rooted in his experience of Greece, especially in his discovery of the great Alexandrian poet Constantine Cavafy. Merrill's three translations from Cavafy were first published in Grand Street and then issued in book form by the Aralia Press; this is his translation of Cavafy's "Eis Italikien Paralian."

Merrill belongs to a distinguished tradition of poets who made use of occult materials, most famously Yeats, but also Sylvia Plath, Ted Hughes, and Robert Duncan. Merrill received his first Ouija board as a birthday gift in 1953; two years later, after moving from New York City to the relative solitude of Stonington, Connecticut, Merrill and David Jackson began conversing with the spirit Ephraim. Snippets of these conversations appeared in Merrill's novel The Seraglio (1957), but material derived directly from transcriptions of the voices from the other world did not appear in his poems until the first part of The Changing Light at Sandover, "The Book of Ephraim," was published in Divine Comedies in 1976. This is the table of contents (hand-decorated by the poet) for the second "Ouija board book," Mirabell: Books of Number (1978). The complete typescript was presented by Merrill to Peter Hooten, his lover for his last ten years, on the occasion of their first (paper) anniversary.

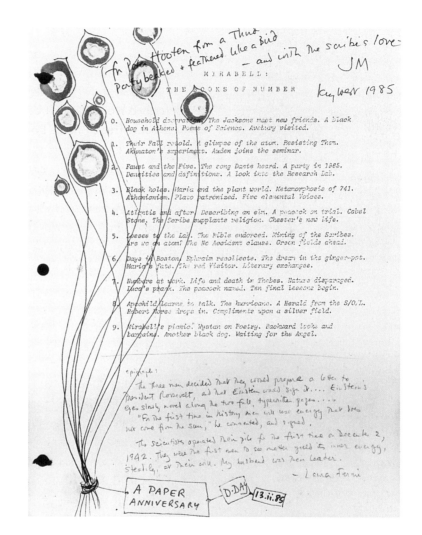

Amy Clampitt

Amy Clampitt met her husband, Harold Korn, in New York City at a meeting of the Village Independent Democrats, an activist political club. She followed in the footsteps of her father, a Quaker peace activist: "The sixties took me into the streets, on repeated bus rides to Washington, and one night in a D.C. jail. I used to tot up the number of times I'd been detained by the police, but statistics fade." This photograph was taken at Deerfield Academy, where Clampitt taught in the early 1990s.

Who wanted to be a *poetess*?
Amy Clampitt

Right away, I knew that she was the real thing.
Howard Moss

Both quoted by Patricia Morrisroe in "The Prime of Amy Clampitt" in New York, *October 15, 1984*

IN 1983, ALFRED A. Knopf published a volume of poetry to unusual and extravagant praise from reviewers. Its 63-year-old author was Amy Clampitt, a former librarian at the Audubon Society (for seven years, during which time she was also a self-described recluse) and a copy editor ("I was good at this, enjoyed being free of office hours, and earned enough to make a trip to Greece"). Her first poems had been accepted by *The New Yorker* only five years earlier, in 1978, after she had enrolled in a workshop at the New School for Social Research and read her poems to fellow students in a nearby Greenwich Village bar. She read the way she wrote: with elegance and exuberance; her choice of lush, floriferous words, and her somewhat esoteric allusions to literary works or flowering trees and bog plants, were wildly attractive, and just as uncommon. She was a hit, and in the next two years almost 50 of her poems appeared in *The New Yorker* and in various literary magazines, including the *New Republic*, *Atlantic Monthly*, *Kenyon Review*, and *Poetry*.

Born in New Providence, Iowa, Clampitt grew up on a farm that had been in the family for generations, and attended Grinnell College. She took off for graduate school in New York, falling in love with the city (she was once involved in a rent strike) and staying for nearly 50 years. She loved traveling (to France, England, Greece, and, in the summers, Corea, Maine) and teaching (at the College of William and Mary, the New School, and Smith). By the time she died in 1994 in Lenox, Massachusetts, at her home near the foot of Ethan Frome's hill, Clampitt had published five volumes of brilliant poetry – a linking of the intellect with the ravaged heart of the seer, always looking, always distinguished – and achieved more than a little fame, even outside the established literary world. ∎

Kinzli Frères, Zürich.   Déposé Nr. 1025.

Dear Amy – Your piece in Verse
is so fresh + to the point. I'm very
touched. Fondest wishes from Grateful James
23. VIII. 58

MULTITUDES, MULTITUDES

AMY CLAMPITT

Washington Street Press   New York City

ABOVE

As the choice of this vintage postcard (with its view of one of the Ionian islands) suggests, James Merrill and Amy Clampitt were poets of similar sensibilities and styles. Both were attracted to Greece, and Clampitt's third book, Archaic Figure *(1990), is largely about her trip to Greece and her study of the Greek language. "I'm a poet of place," she once noted. "I don't like to think that I'm a poet of travel, but poems do come out of my travels all the time." In her eloquent memoir of the two poets, Mary Jo Salter salutes her friends and "parents" in poetry: "It's a parent's job to teach us to name things. For a generation of younger writers, Amy Clampitt and James Merrill taught by example – and made it clear that we're never too old to need someone to look up to."*

LEFT

Clampitt gathered together and financed this first collection of her poetry, which was published in Greenwich Village in 1973. Its poems, as well as those included in Clampitt's second publication, a chapbook entitled The Isthmus *(1981), represent the apprentice work of the poet, who was to blossom forth in her first commercial book,* The Kingfisher *(1983).*

SAN FRANCISCO
arrival into chaparral
predawn leafscreen
hieroglyphs declare
a change of botany
this side of the Sierra

a dandelionless
metropolis, its tilted
grassplots a hotbed
of blushtipped, button-
sized exotic daisies

gold fever running rampant
up old embankments
the satin coinages
scatters dropped satin
of California poppies

hummingbirds maneuver
scintillating under
belled fuchsia gawgaws,
a wind-chime fantasy of
Christmas trees gone Buddhist

yellow hills recline
on lion haunches
huddled liveoaks sniff out
eucalyptus on the march
out of the Outback

scrolled off walls
of lunging jade
fog ushers in the dragon-
silver silences
the imperial horses

[typewritten draft fragments, inverted on the page:]

plushtipped daisies
of alien, patio-little,
alien daisies
patio-little,
grassplots are a patchwork
patio
are millefleur
metropolis the grassplots
tilled
in this dandelionless
grassplots are a patio
a dandelionless metropolis!
another botany
hieroglyphs declare
predawn leafscreen
descending the Sierra
arrival into chaparral

dandelionless, the grassplots
are millefleur-worked
dellions metropolis
grassplots in this dan-
another botany
hieroglyphs declare
predawn leafscreen
arrival into chaparral

predawn descent
arrival

another botany
hieroglyphs declare
predawn leafscreen
descending into chaparral
de
arrival into chaparral
predawn arrival
leafscreen hiero
of the Sierra
predawn descent
descending the
through
descending the Sierra
arrival into chaparral

chaparral arrival

San Francisco

hummingbirds hang
populous among belled
fuchsias, a wind-chime
fantasy of Christmas
trees gone Buddhist

yellow hills recline
on lion haunches
huddled live oaks sniff out
eucalyptus on the march
out of the Outback

scrolled off walls
of lunging jade
fog ushers in the
dragon-silver hordes
the imperial horses

Clampitt's composition process included many revisions, with form arising as she wrote: "Sometimes a stanza form takes shape with the first few lines. . . . Sometimes I change my mind about the form midway. Sometimes a stanza form will be scrapped entirely, and I'll start in all over again, without necessarily starting a new poem." Her earliest drafts were usually typed on high-quality paper (the backs of invitations to and announcements of various legal functions), which she found less intimidating, in its texture and size, than a blank sheet of standard white paper. Clampitt's environmentalist values also cautioned her against wasting paper. The legal announcements she wrote on came from her husband, a law professor. This draft of "San Francisco," from 1979, is typed on the back of a form letter from the Democratic National Committee signed by Morris K. Udall.

James Wright

1927–1980

This photograph was taken in 1973 by critic John Unterecker just after James Wright had finished playing Santa Claus for students at his wife's school.

ONE OF THE more remarkable bodies of poetry in this century is to be found in the work of James Wright. He was born in Martins Ferry, Ohio, where, as he wrote in a "Childhood Sketch,"

The water . . . was beautiful in its rawness and its wildness though something was forever drifting past to remind us of the factories that lined the banks to the north. They were always there, just as the Martins Ferry Cemetery overlooking the entire town, seemed, wherever one stood, to hang in the sky above the Laughlin Steel Mill.

Wright would often return, if only in spirit, to Ohio and to his childhood for themes and context for his poetry. After several years in the Army, he attended Kenyon College and then the University of Washington. He taught at the University of Minnesota for six years, Macalester College for two, and finally at Hunter College in New York City from 1966 until his death in 1980. In 1967, Wright married Anne Runk, his Annie, the other citizen of his private country and the love of his life.

His first two books of poetry were well-received volumes of formalist poetry, *The Green Wall* (chosen by W. H. Auden as the Yale Series of Younger Poets selection in 1957) and *St. Judas* (1959). But through the flourishing of his friendship with Robert Bly, and his relationship with James Dickey, as well as his work translating the poetry of Neruda, Vallejo, and the Austrian poet Georg Trakl, his work took a new direction only hinted at earlier. In 1963, he published *The Branch Will Not Break*. A breakthrough for Wright, this volume, which would be greatly influential, allowed for the full blossoming of his individuality. In this and other books of the 1960s and 70s, his voice became one of the sweetest of the age, his great subject the heart's passage to the deepest interior consciousness, to the moment of perfect awareness, of pure being and of pure enlightenment. ■

artificial Holiday Trees   Original

To a Salesgirl, ~~Grown~~ Weary of ~~Evergreen~~

The stylish-stouts are gone,
And girls, slim trees, are gone.
You, who have seen them go,
Worry whether they live
Or scatter and grow old.
Past floor, past mezzanine,
You mourn the illusory green
Of every tree you sold.
Young, you endure the change.
Green daylight ripples past.
You lounge in daylight, strange,
And the seasons die at last.
I love you, proud up there
On the balcony, soft of face,
Your curious mouth, your hair,
Your hands' immobile grace.
The soft noon of your face
Glances over my stare.
The casual sun falls down.
You do not care for the sky,
The weathered wives go by.
Whether they live or die,
You rise, you brush your knees;
And one last year of leaves
Flutters beyond your sleeves.
The first moon of the year
Outside is lost in trees.
You draw your muffler on,
The last girl of the year,
And one more year's far gone.

-- James Wright

B Substitute here the lines marked (A)

No stranger to the hard work of revision, Wright polished his poems with care and enthusiasm; he was also amenable to suggestions from others. Many of his poems were first published in The New Yorker, *and he worked closely with the magazine's poetry editor, Howard Moss. "To a Salesgirl, Weary of Artificial Holiday Trees" was revised by Wright in response to Moss's criticism, and when it was published in* The New Yorker *on December 19, 1959, the first two lines of this typescript had been replaced with:*

The clock shows nearly five.
Girls are not evergreen,
And most gray women are gone,
Exhausted, from the store

He carried a small leather bound spiral notebook with him always, in which he wrote often in a cramped musical hand. Inside the house he might carry on raucously, reciting a routine by Jonathan Winters about Elwood P. Suggins . . . or raving on about *Tristram Shandy* (whole sections of which he knew by heart), then take a brief walk, and ten minutes later all at once five or six lines, beautifully shaped by some invisible force, would appear in that little notebook. He would set down lines a number of times during the weekend. When he got to Minneapolis on Monday, he would type them up, and he had that abundance to work on the rest of the week.

Robert Bly, "James Wright and the Mysterious Woman" in American Poetry: Wildness and Domesticity *(New York, 1990); originally published as "James Wright, the Slender Woman" in* American Poetry *in 1988*

W. S. Merwin

1927–

Awarded the Pulitzer Prize in 1971, Merwin responded with a notice in The New York Review of Books, *which read in part: "I am pleased to know of the judges' regard for my work, and I want to thank them for their wish to make their opinion public. But after years of the news from Southeast Asia, and the commentary from Washington, I am too conscious of being an American to accept public congratulation with good grace, or to welcome it except as an occasion for expressing openly a shame which many Americans feel, day after day, helplessly and in silence."*

The destinies of mankind – man himself, taken aloof from his age and his country, and standing in the presence of Nature and of God, with his passions, his doubts, his rare prosperities, and inconceivable wretchedness – will become the chief, if not the sole theme of poetry among these nations.

Alexis de Tocqueville, quoted by W. H. Auden in his foreword to Merwin's A Mask for Janus *(1952)*

BORN IN NEW York City and raised in Union City, New Jersey, and Scranton, Pennsylvania, William Stanley Merwin attended Princeton University, where he discovered poetry and horseback riding and studied with the influential critic R. P. Blackmur.

His first works were explorations of form, of which he early became a master, but with his fifth book, *The Moving Target* (1963), he abandoned many formal elements such as rhyme and punctuation. In some respects the most experimental and mutable of poets, Merwin has argued: "It doesn't matter whether you're imprisoned in iambic pentameter or in the Middle English line or whatever it is, there should be more than one way of writing, unless you're in a tradition which is so powerful that it can carry you. You know, Villon could go on writing in that stanza forever, or Marvell could go on writing the octosyllabic couplet, without feeling in the least bit hampered by it. . . ." With each of the remarkable, haunted books of his middle period – *The Lice* (1967), *The Miner's Pale Children* (1970), *The Carrier of Ladders* (1970), and *Writings to an Unfinished Accompaniment* (1973) – Merwin continued his struggle with the limitations of language and the containments of the soul and the spirit in things. His later books describe more personal landscapes in greater detail, with a clear, supple narrative line.

An inspired translator, Merwin – who has lived in Mallorca, England, Portugal, New York City, Mexico, Brittany, and now Hawaii – has brought into English hundreds of poems from other cultures, from the oral literatures of the ancient Chinese or Mayans to contemporary French and Spanish poets. A peace activist and an ardent environmentalist, he often creates prayer-poems (his father was a Presbyterian minister and the first pieces he wrote were hymns), emblems of the earth and its creatures, of life lived another way, as "a believer in the rain." ∎

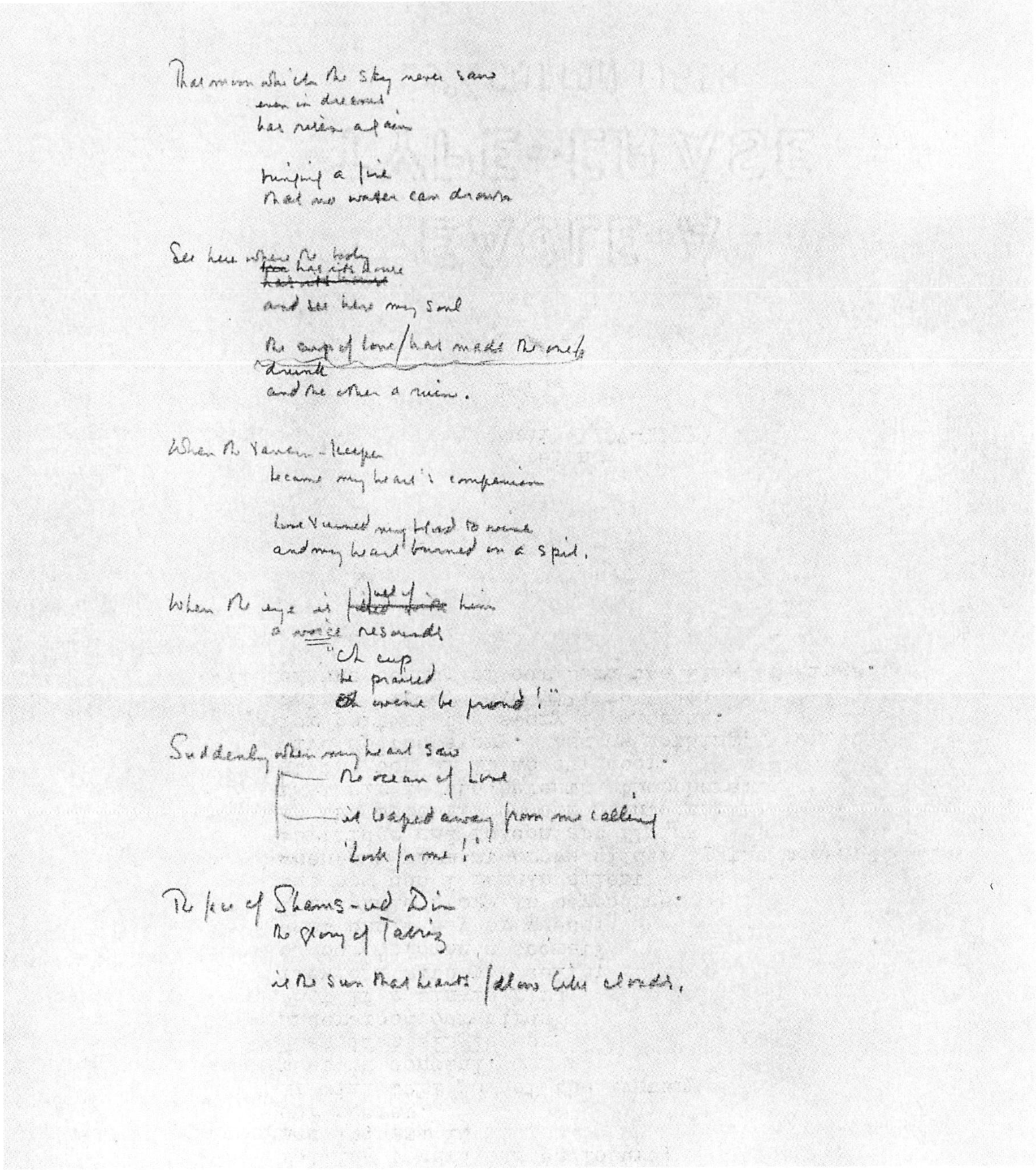

That moon which the sky never saw
    even in dreams
  has risen again

  bringing a fire
    that no water can drown

See here where the body
    ~~has~~
    and see here my soul
  The cup of love has made the one ~~drunk~~
    and the other a ruin.

When the Tavern-keeper
    became my heart's companion
    love turned my blood to wine
    and my heart burned on a spit.

When the eye is ~~full of~~ him
    a voice resounds
      "Oh cup
        be praised
        Oh wine be proud!"

Suddenly ~~when my heart saw~~
    the ocean of Love
    ──── it leaped away from me calling
      'Look for me!'

The face of Shams-ud Din
    the glory of Tabriz
      is the sun that hearts follow like clouds.

Merwin's early translations were primarily from French and Spanish, languages he knows well; they included two of the foundations of Western literature, The Song of Roland *(1963) and* The Poem of the Cid *(1959). In the late 1960s, he began translating poetry from many different cultures, some of which had strong oral traditions of "anonymous" or collective stories and legends. When he did not know the language, Merwin would work from literal translations in word order that had been prepared by a scholar in the field. This poem by Rumi, the 13th-century Sufi (Muslim mystic), was translated with the Persian scholar Talat Halman, and published in Merwin's* Selected Translations 1968–1978.

Anne Sexton

1928–1974

In Anne Sexton: The Artist and Her Critics *(edited by J. D. McClatchy),* Robert Lowell *observed, "At a time when poetry readings were expected to be boring, no one ever fell asleep at Anne's. I see her as having the large, transparent, breakable, and increasingly ragged wings of a dragonfly – her poor, shy, driven life, the blind terror behind her bravado, her deadly increasing pace . . . her bravery while she lasted." This photograph by Arthur Furst was taken only a few months before Sexton's death.*

EVEN THE CHILDREN dressed for dinner at the Massachusetts mansion of Ralph and Mary Gray Harvey, except Anne, their third daughter, who would not comb her hair and defiantly ate cake in her bedroom. Gradually, though, she became a tall, slim, "boy-crazy" teenager and a part-time fashion model. After attending one year of junior college, Anne Harvey met Alfred "Kayo" Muller Sexton II in May 1948. Three months later, they eloped to North Carolina and were married, which was what Sexton said she had wanted from the age of 13.

After the birth of her first daughter in 1953, Sexton became depressed, especially when her husband was absent, working in a woolen firm. Finally she was hospitalized and, in November 1956, attempted suicide. About a month later, Sexton saw a Harvard professor explaining a sonnet on television. She took quick notes, and then wrote one. When she had finished another, she showed them to her psychiatrist. Thus began the brief career of one of the most popular American poets ever, or, as Sexton called it, her "rebirth at 29." Within six months, she had written more than 50 poems, pouring into formally elegant lines the raw and precise details of her life, including "the commonplaces of the asylum." Often terrified of meeting strangers, she nonetheless published aggressively. Within three years, she had completed her first book, *To Bedlam and Part Way Back*. In 1967, she won the Pulitzer Prize.

As Sexton herself saw it, "in the first book I was giving the experience of madness; and in the second book, the causes of madness; and in the third book, finally I find that I was deciding whether to live or to die." She continued struggling against her "terrible taste" for death until her fourth suicide attempt succeeded, on October 4, 1974. She left behind ten books, which have sold hundreds of thousands of copies, and a letter for her oldest daughter, Linda, suggesting, "Talk to my poems." ■

```
LETTER WRITTEN ON THE LONG ISLAND FERRY
```

*Sold
To
New Yorker*

```
I am surprised to see
that the ocean is still going on.
Now I am going back
and I have ripped my hand
from your hand as I said I would
and I have made it this far
as I said I would
and I am on the top deck now
holding my wallet, my cigarettes
and my car keys
at 2 o'clock on a tuesday
in August of 1960.

Dearest,
although everything has happened,
nothing has happened.
The sea is very old.
The sea is the face of Mary,
without miracles or rage
or unusual hope,
grown rough and wrinkled
with incurable age.

Still,
I have eyes.
These are my eyes:
the orange letters that spell
ORIENT on the life preserver
that hangs by my knees;
the cement life boat that wears
its dirty canvas coat;
the faded sign that sits on its shelf
saying KEEP OFF.
Oh, all right, I say,
I'll save myself.

Over my right shoulder
I see four nuns
who sit like a bridge club,
their faces poked out
from under their habits,
as good as good babies who
have sunk into their carriages.
Without discrimination
the wind pulls the skirts
of their arms.
Almost undressed,
I see what remains:
that holy wrist,
that ankle,
that chain.
```

(con't)

The issue in most of Anne Sexton's poems has been survival, piece by piece of the body, step by step of poetic experience, and even more the life entire, sprung from our matrix of parental madness. It is these people, who have come this way, who have most usefulness for us, they are among our veterans, and we need them to look at their lives and at us.

Muriel Rukeyser, "Glitter and Wounds, Several Wildernesses" in Parnassus: Poetry in Review *(Fall/Winter 1973)*

Sexton and James Wright exchanged a rapt correspondence and then, after meeting in late summer 1960 at a "seminar" for poets in Montauk, Long Island, had an affair that lasted into 1961; hence the title of this poem (published as "Letter Written on a Ferry While Crossing Long Island Sound") and the date in the first stanza (Sexton is referring to the end of the five days they spent together). This is one of three love poems to Wright that were published in Sexton's All My Pretty Ones *(1962). But when she sent it to him, he answered with acerbic criticism of its last line, "good news, good news." It was, he said, "as though Oedipus were to be rescued at the last minute – in the nick of time – by Bishop Sheen disguised as the Lone Ranger." Sexton left the line untouched. Unlike many of her poems, which she revised dozens and even hundreds of times, this one stands largely as first written. Sexton sent this copy of the poem (this is the first of the manuscript's two pages) to Louis Untermeyer.*

«TOROS-COLOR»
21.—Pase con la derecha.
Passe de la droite.
A pass with the right hand.

May 17th 1964

21

(P.S please Lo que the way the books —
my husband says "don't send it" but

DRIO Y
    Dear Louis Untermeyer. I meant
to send you a great many post cards
this fall.... but I was only over here
for two months and all that time busy
typing to my husband and then home)
Now, with him, in Spain..still with
this awful typewriter... But very
happy/sane etx now. This is the 3rd
day of The Fiesta... "corrida de

Torros" and I love it all. Tomorrow
to Roma...   (I'm not drunk..it is
this silly typewriter..that they
I brought b4cause it only weighs

8 pounds..but can't type on it)

Love —
    Anne Sexton

DOMINGUEZ - MADRID
Reproducción prohibida

Es propiedad del autor
Reservados todos los derechos

Mr. Louis Untermeyer
Great Hill Road

Newtown
Connecticut

U.S.A.

Foto color original.-CHAPRESTO - Exclusivas fotográficas
FOURNIER - VITORIA   Depósito Legal: VI 189

CORREOS   MISTERIOS
5 to
ROSARIO
ESPAÑA   8 PTAS

Louis Untermeyer was one of Sexton's early champions. Less than a year after her first book was published, he included her work in one of his very influential anthologies; Robert Lowell, Sexton's teacher, was one of the few other living poets represented. When she applied for Guggenheim fellowships to support and legitimize her work, Untermeyer wrote letters for her, but she gave up after three unsuccessful tries. Then, in 1963, she won an award for which she had not even applied: a traveling fellowship from the American Academy of Arts and Letters. The painful irony (unknown to the Academy) was that Sexton's poor mental health often left her terrified of traveling even as far as the supermarket. She sailed for Europe in August, but by October could no longer stand being away from her family, and so returned home. When she returned to Europe the following summer with her husband, she sent Untermeyer this postcard from Spain.

Sylvia Plath

1932–1963

Except for death – yes we have that in common (and there must be enough other poets with that theme to fill an entire library). Never mind last diggings. They don't matter. What matters is her poems. These last poems stun me. They eat time.

Anne Sexton, "The Barfly Ought to Sing" in Triquarterly *(1965); reprinted in* Ariel Descending: Writings About Sylvia Plath, *edited by Paul Alexander (New York, 1985)*

After Plath's death, her husband, from whom she had been separated, moved back to their home at Court Green to care for their children. This copy of Ariel *bears a note by Hughes on its front free endpaper: "The brown stains on the top edge and [back] cover are thatch-drip from the leaking roof of Court Green (where SP had lived), in the winter of 1965/66."*

SYLVIA PLATH, IN some ways the quintessential American girl, was born in Boston. She was smart, an excellent student, popular, pretty and tall, active and intense. Her parents were, by all accounts, intelligent and in love, even well adjusted. Her father, an expert on bees and a professor of biology, died when she was eight, and she and her brother were closely raised in Wellesley, Massachusetts, by their adoring mother. In 1952, she won a *Mademoiselle* magazine fiction award, and spent time in New York City as the magazine's guest editor. Her poems were published early in *Harper's*. She graduated summa cum laude in 1955 from Smith College. She studied a little with Robert Lowell and drank at the Ritz with Anne Sexton.

But by age 23, she had already survived extreme bouts of depression, two suicide attempts, hospitalization, and electroshock therapy. She married the English poet Ted Hughes in 1956, had two children, Frieda and Nicholas, and settled in England, a writer and mother. Her first book, *The Colossus*, was published in 1960, and a novel, *The Bell Jar*, was published pseudonymously in 1963.

In October 1962, in Court Green, England, separated from her husband, Sylvia Plath wrote 23 of the most remarkable poems of the 20th century, including several of those for which she is most famous: "Lady Lazarus," "Daddy," "Fever 103°," and six of the "bee poems." All of them relate to her struggle for self-definition: they are vehement works of rage and revenge, art and triumph. Almost two years after her death by her own hand on February 11, 1963, at the age of 31, these and other poems were published as *Ariel*. Her *Collected Poems* (1982) was awarded the Pulitzer Prize. We know everything about her and yet we know nothing: "The blood jet is poetry / there is no stopping it." ∎

Brasilia

Will they occur,
These people with torsos of steel
Winged elbows and eyeholes

Awaiting masses
Of cloud to give them expression.
These super-people! –

And my baby a nail
Driven, driven in.
He shrieks in his grease

Bones nosing for distances.
And I, nearly extinct,
His three teeth cutting

Themselves on my thumb –
And the star,
The old story.

In the lane I meet sheep and wagons,
Red earth, motherly blood.
O You who eat

People like light rays, leave
This one
Mirror safe, unredeemed

By the dove's annihilation,
The glory
The power, the glory.

Brasilia
(1)
Bone-splints of the future!
Will they occur,
These people with torsos of steel
Winged elbows & eyeholes
Awaiting great masses of cloud to give them expression.
These super people! —
And my baby a nail
~~Driven~~ in, ~~at~~ [illegible] ~~left~~ ~~under my~~ [illegible]
He shrieks in his grease driven in.
His bones
Nosing for distances.
~~I swim~~, Old coelacanth, I
~~Old coelacanth~~, swim under him
~~Out of date & bed back to the fishermen.~~
Nearly extinct.
~~back to the fishermen.~~
~~Hairy & legendary~~
His three teeth cutting
Themselves on my thumb.
He is one of the new people
Motherless, fatherless.
The [illegible] womb
Rattles its pod, the moon
Discharges itself from the tree with nowhere to go.
Are these [illegible] amoebas, or zeros, these motes
I see so constantly
Dying on the [illegible] horizon
~~to be Eaten by the mountains~~

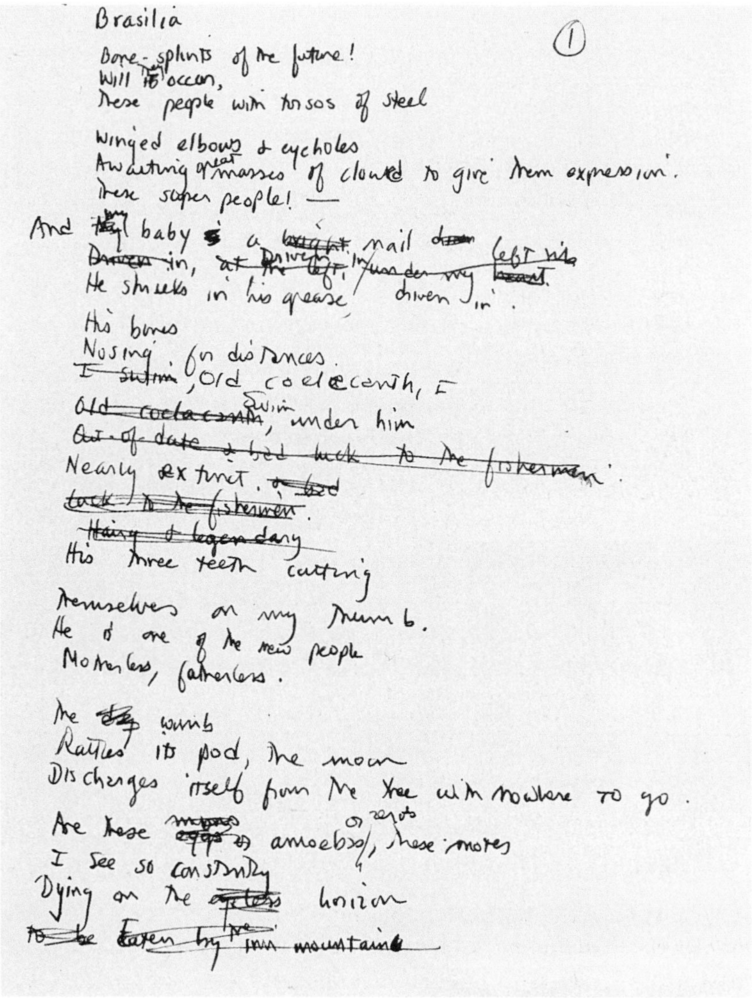

"Brasilia," written in December 1962, was published in Winter Trees *(1971). It is one of a number of poems that Plath wrote for or about her children, in this case her son, Nicholas. Like certain other of her poems ("Balloons" and "Morning Song" from* Ariel *and "Nick and the Candlestick," "Child," and "For a Fatherless Son" from* Winter Trees*) dealing with motherhood or her children, it is as tender as some of her poems are rageful. Ted Hughes comments on this side of Sylvia Plath: "Her elements were extreme; a violent, almost demonic spirit in her, opposed a tenderness and capacity to suffer and love things infinitely, which was just as great and far more in evidence. . . . Her vision of death, her muse of death in life and life in death, with its oppressive evidence, fought in her against a joy in life, and in every smallest pleasure, for which her favorite word 'ecstasy' was simply accurate, as her poems prove."*

divine Love can remove "incandescent terror" of war through purgatorial fire

Who then devised the torment? Love.
Love is the unfamiliar Name
Behind the hands that wove
The intolerable shirt of flame   *Hercules couldn't tear off*
Which human power cannot remove.   *poisonous Nessus' shirt—*
We only live, only suspire   *built pyre & burned self—*
Consumed by either fire or fire.   *creative & destructive fires*
all part of one fire:
divine Love that gave
man free will to choose
between fires.

What we call the beginning is often the end
And to make an end is to make a beginning.
The end is where we start from. And every phrase   *cf. "undisciplined*
And sentence that is right (where every word is at home,   *squads of*
Taking its place to support the others,   *emotion"*
The word neither diffident nor ostentatious,   *condition of complete*
An easy commerce of the old and the new,   *simplicity*
The common word exact without vulgarity,   *unite past & present*
The formal word precise but not pedantic,   *even existing pattern*
The complete consort dancing together)   *of vital relationships*
Variations on Theme
Every phrase and every sentence is an end and a beginning,   *Throughout*
Every poem an epitaph. And any action   *life of world*
Is a step to the block, to the fire, down the sea's throat   *extends self*
Or to an illegible stone: and that is where we start.   *back into history*
start with
We die with the dying: *Knowledge of*
See, they depart, and we go with them.   *slavery to time and the*
We are born with the dead: *inevitability of death*
See, they return, and bring us with them.   *we live by memory of the*
The moment of the rose and the moment of the yew-tree   *past (the dead) and we*
Are of equal duration. A people without history   *are born again by memory*
Is not redeemed from time, for history is a pattern   *of events in*
Of timeless moments. So, while the light fails   *the past...*
On a winter's afternoon, in a secluded chapel   *day & night*
History is now and England.   *winter & summer*
impossible to dissociate
yet verities of history   oneself from time sequence—
is present with him. 38

time not unredeemable — past can
exist in present; present can always
be a fresh beginning —

from "The Cloud of Unknowing" – 14th cen.
anonymous

With the drawing of this Love and the voice of this Calling   *opposite of*
life & vocation of poetry united   rose garden
We shall not cease from exploration   *with religious   deception of*
And the end of all our exploring   *aspiration..   physical*
Will be to arrive where we started   *Thrush*
And know the place for the first time.   *All events of time*
Through the unknown, remembered gate   *world are recapitulated,*
When the last of earth left to discover   *leading to the still*
Is that which was the beginning;   *point*
At the source of the longest river   *"Burnt Norton"*
The voice of the hidden waterfall   *explorations of all*
And the children in the apple-tree   *four poems in*
Not known, because not looked for   *art, history, religion, etc*
But heard, half-heard, in the stillness   *end of purpose: to*
Between two waves of the sea.   *accept physical life*
in time transfigured
Quick now, here, now, always—   *in the different*
A condition of complete simplicity   *pattern of reality...*
(Costing not less than everything)   *"sudden in a shaft of sunlight"*
And all shall be well and   *illumination - perpetual*
All manner of thing shall be well   *immanence of the divine*
When the tongues of flame are in-folded   *in the physical*
Into the crowned knot of fire   *Transfiguration can always*
And the fire and the rose are one.   *occur —*
Paradiso   communication of
pentecostal tongues of   dead - past in present
illumination - fires of
unimagineable "zero summer"   war - purgatorial fires

"crown" upon lifetime's effort —
unfolding:
Paradiso: substance, accidents infused in universal
knot"

Donne: knot of body and soul
conflicts reconciled in crowned kingship
of love (Love's knot)

fire & rose are one:
physical & divine love
historical royal emblem history
transcended by single person
of spiritual value
worlds of matter & spirit fusion into
39 *full consciousness —*

In 1951, Sylvia Plath received this copy of T. S. Eliot's Four Quartets as a birthday gift from Richard Norton, who inscribed it: "A small addition, Sylvie, to your collection of ideas, lives, stories, and shrunken heads. Dick 1951." He was a family friend Plath had known since she was 14. They began dating in 1951; she attended the Yale Senior Prom with him that year, and later visited the Lying-In Hospital in Boston while Norton was in medical school at Harvard. This copy is also inscribed by Ted Hughes: "This was Sylvia Plath's own copy of The Four Quartets and all the autograph annotations are hers."

Ariel, *the brilliant book for which Sylvia Plath is best known, stands with Lowell's* Life Studies *and Allen Ginsberg's* Howl *as among the most powerful poetic documents of our time. The book was edited for publication after Plath's death by her husband, Ted Hughes, who changed poems (removing 11 from Plath's original list and substituting 9 which she had not intended, these 9 having been written during the last weeks of her life). His editing gives a more despairing curve to the book than Plath's original arrangement, which "begins with the word 'Love' and ends with the word 'Spring,'" as Plath scholar Linda Wagner Martin notes. Rollie McKenna photographed Plath and Hughes at their Beacon Hill apartment in Boston in 1959.*

Philip Levine

1928–

When he married Frances Artley in Boone, North Carolina, in July 1954, Levine also adopted her small son Mark, seen here at left with his father in 1976. Philip and Frances Levine have two other sons, John and Theodore (Teddy).

His 15 volumes of feisty, chip-on-the-shoulder verse alternately celebrate and elegize a gritty world of lonely highways, aging factories and deadend jobs. . . . His outsider's perspective on working class existence became his defining imaginative vision. The way genuine artists do, he took bad luck and made it inspiration.

Dana Gioia, "Stanzas in a Life" in The New York Times Book Review, *February 20, 1994*

A POLITICAL POET, Philip Levine is, like his hero Walt Whitman, a poet of the democratic experience and the simple life. He writes not about crowds, but about individuals and the relationships of individuals to each other, in, for instance, the family. These family poems, beginning early with "For Fran" (for his wife) in *On the Edge* (1963), are not sentimental or romantic, but solid, honest, and of illuminating beauty. He says, "I have tried to write poetry for people for whom there is no poetry . . . those were the people of Detroit, the people I grew up with who brothered, sistered, fathered, and mothered me, and lived and worked beside me. Their presence seemed utterly lacking in the poetry I inherited at age 20, so I've spent the last 40-some years trying to add to our poetry what wasn't there."

Born in Detroit, he grew up in a single-parent household (his father died when Levine was five) and received Bachelor's and Master's degrees from Wayne State University in Detroit. He then studied at the Iowa Writers' Workshop with Robert Lowell and John Berryman, and later at Stanford University with Yvor Winters. Levine began teaching at California State University at Fresno in 1958 and continued there as a loved and respected mentor until 1987; his students included poets Larry Levis, Gary Soto, David St. John, Luis Salinas, Lawson Inada, and Sherley Anne Williams. He has taught elsewhere as well, most recently in the MFA program at New York University (the city looks forward to his return each fall).

In the 1960s, Levine began an affair with the Spanish language (through reading Neruda, Vallejo, and Alberti) and with Spain, living there with his family for two separate periods during the decade. His "teachers" include the Spanish poet Federico García Lorca ("I stood in the stacks of Wayne State University Library with my hands trembling and read my life in his words"), and he has translated a number of Hispanic poets, including Antonio Machado, Gloria Fuertes, and Jaime Sabines. In 1993, Levine published a memoir, *The Bread of Time: Toward an Autobiography*, a dignified, forceful series of elegiac writings, which have added further luster to his work, and his life and times. ■

About his decision to marry and to adopt his wife's child, Philip Levine has written: "You know at one point or another in your life you have to wake up and become a person. The irony of all this is I was incredibly lucky. I was marrying a woman who had a profound regard for poetry and this kid I adopted turned out to be one of my best friends. It was probably one of the three or four intelligent decisions I've made my whole life." This photograph of Philip and Mark Levine was taken in December 1995 at Washington Square Village in the heart of New York City's Greenwich Village.

OPPOSITE

Much of Levine's poetry – including this poem, "My Son and I," which dates from the early 1970s – is about articulating ourselves and communicating with others. "Failing to communicate is part of what we live with, part of our condition," says Levine. "Rilke wrote somewhere that without our bodies we cannot love. Also with our bodies, with our gestures, with our facial expressions, we can communicate far more fully than with merely words on the telephone or words in a letter. Poetry is as close as we can get to complete communication with merely words alone. And I think it's good enough." Levine's poetry speaks with great tenderness to the joy and the pain of family relationships, as in this powerful narrative, in which a father who is estranged from his son awaits "a flash of light, a song, / a remembered sweetness."

MY SON AND I

In a ~~cafe~~ at 3 am and he ~~has~~ *has*
~~has~~ discovered/I'm dying. *outside*
The wind/moves along the streets
of New York City picking up
abandoned scraps of newspapers
and tiny messages of hope
no one hears. He's dressed
in old corduroy pants
and shirts over shirts
and his hands are stained
like mine with glue,ink,
paint. A brown cap
hides the thick blond hair
so unlike mine. For forty
minutes he's tried *Not*
~~not~~ to cry. How are his brothers?
I tell him I don't know,
they have grown away
from me, ~~they~~ *are* are Americans
and never touch, here where a boy
sees his life ~~fly~~ past
through a car window. His mother?
She is deaf and works
in the earth for days, hearing
the dirt pray and guiding
the worm to its feasts. Why
do I have to die? why
do I have to sit before him
no longer his father, only
a man? Because the given
must be taken, because
~~we got~~ to hunger before we eat,
because ~~I must~~ turn
to darkness, just because...
as we said when we
were kids and knew the names
of everything. I reach
across the table and take
his left hand in mine.
I can't bless him. I can
tell him how I found
the plum blossom before
I was thirty, how once
in a rooming house in Alicante
a man younger than I / *An Argentine I barely understood*
sat with me all night because
I burned ~~so~~ far from home,
I can tell him that his hand
sweating in mine can raise
the Lord God of ~~storms~~ XXXXXXXXXXXXXXXXXXXXXXXXXXXXXXX
and hold the spoon. Instead
I say it's late, and he pays
and leads me back through
the empty streets to the Earl,
where the room sours XXXXXXXX
with the mould of old Bibles
dumped in the air-shaft.
I stand in the dark room
(in my coat) waiting for something,
a flash of light, a song.
Next door the junkie sways
in ~~his~~ *the* last chant before dawn.

Coffe House

on trial /
~~bitter~~ earth where a boy
burned

Each small
spark
must
turn

As we said /
where we were kids & knew
~~knew~~ the names of everything,
just because ... I reach
I have no blessing.

An Argentine I barely understood

stones / being ~~born~~ the
Republic of his /
& hold a spoon.

my son's life
~~kindled~~
flickered /
& how he
cried with
thanks

A remembered sweetness
from the ~~cope~~ & lost.
likes

Next door
the TV babbles
all night &
a junkie sways /

Jean Valentine

1934–

Valentine spends part of each year in Ireland, where she lives with her husband, artist Barrie Cooke, whose painting adorns the cover of her first book, Dream Barker *(1965). Longtime friends, the couple were married at Christmas 1991. This photograph was taken in County Sligo the following year by David Conrad.*

Looking into a Jean Valentine poem is like looking into a lake: you can see your own outline, and the shapes of the upper world, reflected among rocks, underwater life, glint of lost bottles, drifted leaves. The known and familiar become one with the mysterious and half-wild, at the place where consciousness and the subliminal meet.

Adrienne Rich, dust jacket blurb for The River at Wolf *(Cambridge, Massachusetts, 1992)*

WHO CAN RESIST a poet who writes such lines as "There is no book / and my name is written in it." Jean Valentine's work may at first appear difficult, dreamlike, or opaque, but at some point, if a reader keeps after her, the poems become clearer and may seem even to be expressing the reader's own inner life. Who is it, one wonders, who is writing in my mind, in my heart? The poetry of Jean Valentine frees one almost to float, and to explore intensely spiritual places. But despite this dreamlike mysticism, Valentine's poems are fully rooted in a consciousness that lives in the moment; as she noted in an interview with poet Michael Klein, "I think at one time I was waiting for things from the outside that could only come from the inside. What am I waiting for now? Living in the hope of not waiting for anything." She fully experiences her feelings – of loss, of longing, and finally of hope. In paying attention to the world as it is, she creates a powerful, individual poetry of revelation and recovery.

Born and raised in Chicago, Valentine went east to attend Radcliffe College, where she received her degree in 1956. In 1965, at the last minute, she submitted her first book of poems, *Dream Barker*, as a candidate for the Yale Series of Younger Poets award, and won. Valentine has since produced six other volumes, most recently *The Under Voice: Selected Poems*, which was published in Ireland in 1995. She has taught at Swarthmore and Hunter colleges and, for almost 20 years, in the writing program at Sarah Lawrence College. She also teaches workshops in New York City at the the 92nd Street Y. ■

Mother

I've never felt
so close to you, Mother. Wings, oh
my black darling. Almost free.
Never felt so close to anyone. Felt,
Hide you in the shelter of my wings.
All the way home to New York my heart hurt.
Am I taking the old glass out of the frame? Are we?

I love glass because of water,
water because of blood,
blood because of your heart,
lapping against the glass door to my ear,
over and over, my darling, my familiar. And my good.
All the way home to New York my heart hurt.
(The second time you died this year.)

Jean Valentine

*Valentine is at her most affecting in her elegies and in her poems of
coming to terms with the death of her mother. Published in* The River
at Wolf *(1992) as "Wish-Mother," this poem was written in 1990.*

Adrienne Rich

1929–

When she was photographed by Rollie McKenna in Cambridge in 1958, Rich had already published two volumes of accomplished formalist verse, which earned considerable praise from the largely male poetry establishment. She had also by this point graduated from Radcliffe, spent a Guggenheim Fellowship in Europe, and married and given birth to the first of three sons. But with her third volume of poetry, Snapshots of a Daughter-in-Law *(1963), her work began to change, incorporating a radical political and sexual consciousness, and an open form that was to alter the face of contemporary poetry.*

ADRIENNE RICH, WHO draws large, passionate audiences to readings of her fearless poetry, grew up in Baltimore, Maryland, where her father was a bookish doctor. She attended Radcliffe College and won the Yale Younger Poets Prize for verse that was, as W. H. Auden put it condescendingly, "neatly and modestly dressed." Rich reflected later, "In those years formalism was part of the strategy – like asbestos gloves, it allowed me to handle materials I couldn't pick up bare-handed."

After college she traveled in Europe on a Guggenheim Fellowship, mailing poems back to *The New Yorker*. In 1953, she married Alfred Conrad, an economist then teaching at Harvard, and within six years the couple had three sons. She wrote when time allowed, published many poems, and felt deeply uneasy. "Emptiness round the stoop of the house / Minces, catwise, waiting for an in," as she put it in her breath-taking 1963 book *Snapshots of a Daughter-in-Law*. Rich began to speak more directly as a poet, with more impatient rhythms. She also took part in protests against the Vietnam War and in other causes. Her political passion was not constrained by dogmatism: she wrote poems to Ethel Rosenberg and to a Soviet dissident in a penal mental asylum, among others. She became a feminist activist, and a love poet.

Rich identified herself as a lesbian after the suicide of her husband in 1970, and became radically dedicated to the women's movement. In her vivid, painful *Diving into the Wreck* (1973), she conducted poetry as "a kind of action, probing, burning, stripping, placing itself in dialogue with others out beyond the individual self." Rich accepted the National Book Award in 1974 "in the name of all women." Since then she has achieved a much rarer distinction for a contemporary poet: she is well known. ■

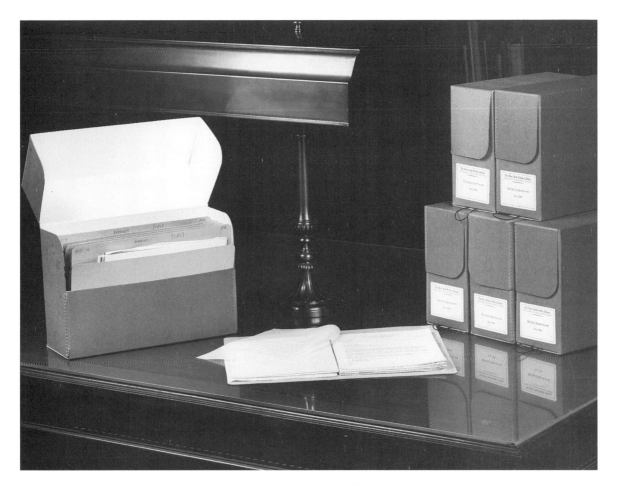

Adrienne Rich's papers are housed at the Arthur and Elizabeth Schlesinger Library on the History of Women in America at Radcliffe College, but typescripts of many early poems are in The New Yorker *Archives of The New York Public Library's Rare Books and Manuscripts Division. Although Rich's first poems were exclusively published in that magazine, by March 1958 her ideas and poetry had changed greatly. In a letter that month to one of the magazine's editors, Rich declined the offer of a new "first reading" arrangement with the magazine. Her reasons, she explained, had to do with her desire not only to write a new kind of poetry, but also to reach a different audience. This goal, she felt, would not be furthered by continuing her relationship with* The New Yorker.

The reader feels that she has only begun to change; thinks, "This young thing, who knows what it may be, old?" Some of her poems are very different from the others, some of her nature is very far from the rest of it, so that one feels that she has room to live in and to grow out into; liking her for what she is is a way of liking her even better for what she may become.

Randall Jarrell, reviewing The Diamond Cutters and Other Poems *in "New Books in Review" in* The Yale Review *(September 1956)*

Referring to Snapshots of a Daughter-in-Law, *Rich wrote: "In my own case, as soon as I published – in 1963 – a book of poems which was informed by any conscious sexual politics, I was told, in print, that this work was 'bitter,' 'personal,' that I had sacrificed the sweetly flowing measures of my earlier books for a ragged line and a coarsened voice. It took me a long time not to hear those voices internally whenever I picked up my pen." Lynda Koolish caught Rich in 1986 at Modern Times, a bookstore in San Francisco, where the poet was signing copies of her just-published collection of essays,* Blood, Bread, and Poetry, *which reprints her controversial and influential 1980 essay "Compulsory Heterosexuality and Lesbian Existence."*

Imamu Amiri Baraka

1934–

Hettie (Cohen) Jones, Baraka's first wife, described what she saw when they met in 1957, two years before Fred W. McDarrah made this portrait photograph: "He was small and wiry, with a widow's peak that sharpened his close-cut hair, and a mustache and goatee to match. Yet the rakishness of all these triangles was set back, made reticent, by a button-down shirt and Clarks shoes. A Brooks Brothers look. I sat him down and we started to talk. He was smart, and very direct, and for emphasis stabbed the air with his third – not index – finger, an affectation to notice, of course. But his movements were easy, those of a man at home not only in skin but in muscle and bone. And he led with his head."

EVERETT LEROY JONES was born in Newark, New Jersey, where both sides of his family had sought refuge from racial conflict in the South. As a boy, he read voraciously and drew comic strips for his high school newspaper. He graduated two years early, attended Rutgers University for a year, and then continued his education for two years at Howard University, known as the "capstone" of black American education. There, he said disgustedly, "they teach you how to pretend to be white." As a sergeant in what he called the U.S. "Error Farce," Jones spent as much time as possible reading and writing, until that earned him an "undesirable" discharge.

As LeRoi Jones – Roi to his friends – he went on to New York, became a Beat poet (he was especially close to Frank O'Hara and Allen Ginsberg), and with his new wife, Hettie Cohen, co-founded the literary magazine *Yugen* and had two daughters. "I sincerely had no ax to grind but the whole of new poetry," he wrote later, and his first book, *Preface to a Twenty Volume Suicide Note*, established him as an important new poet. But in 1965, increasingly uneasy and frustrated after a visit to Cuba and the assassination of Malcolm X, Jones sorrowfully broke off contact with his wife and other whites and moved to Harlem as a "black cultural nationalist" (when Ginsberg heard the news, he demanded plaintively of Hettie Jones, "Why didn't you stop him?"). Jones expressed his decision, and attacked the world he felt he was leaving behind, in the agonized poems of *Black Magic* (1969).

He founded the Black Arts Repertory Theater School in Harlem and moved again, back to Newark. In 1967, he changed his name to Ameer Baraka, meaning "blessed prince," and then, after meeting the cultural nationalist Ron Karenga in San Francisco, adjusted it to Amiri Baraka and added the title "Imamu," for "spiritual leader." His second wife, Sylvia Robinson, became Amina Baraka. In 1974, he renounced black nationalism; his new credo is Third World Marxism or "Marxism–Leninism–Mao Tse-tung Thought." Now a professor, he continues writing (he has published more than 40 books), teaching, working in politics, and producing theater. ∎

His special gift is an emotive music that might have made him predominantly a "lyric poet," but his deeply felt preoccupation with more than personal issues enlarges the scope of his poems beyond what the term is often taken to mean . . . the beauty in Jones's poems is sensuous and incantatory.

Denise Levertov, reviewing Preface to a Twenty Volume Suicide Note *in "Poets of the Given Ground" in* The Nation, *October 14, 1961*

In 1971, Baraka said, "Black writers need to be active and involved – in the political world of trying to bring about black self-determination – if they are to produce art that functions for black people. The 'literary life' is not healthy in America – it means the end of worthwhile art, it's artificial. Too many brothers get off into this thing of being 'writers,' that they don't realize when they stop creating with their own lives that their work stops being creative." Fascinated by comics, Baraka has used them to great effect in his work. In his play What Was the Relationship of the Lone Ranger to the Means of Production? *(1978), the Masked Man is a white factory owner who forces his black workers to take a pay cut, while telling them how lucky they are to be Americans.*

```
                    I LOVE MUSIC
"I want to be a force for real good.
In other words, I know that there are bad forces,
forces that bring suffering to others and misery to the world,
but I want to be the opposite
force. I want to be the force which is truly
for good."
Trane
Trane
Trane sd,
A force for real good, trane. in other words. Feb '67
By july he was dead.
By july. he said in other words
he wanted to be the opposite
but by july he was dead, but he is, offering,
expression a love supreme, afro blue in me singing
it all because of him
can be
screaming beauty
can be
afroblue can be
you leave me breathless
can be
        alabama
            I want to talk to you
                    my favorite things
                        like sonny
                            giant steps

can be
life itself, fire can be, heart explosion, soul explosion, brain explo
sion. can be. can be. can be. can be. aggeeewheeuheeagg eeeee. aggrrrrrruuuaggg
```

A jazz buff, Baraka has written extensively on the art, including his 1963 historical treatise, Blues People: Negro Music in White America. *Increasingly disgusted with himself and other blacks for their "urge toward whiteness," he argued that black music, unlike black writing, had managed to remain unbesmirched by whiteness or efforts to imitate white art. "Negro music alone, because it drew its strengths and beauties out of the depth of the black man's soul, and because to a large extent its traditions could be carried on by the lowest classes of Negroes, has been able to survive the constant and willful dilutions of the black middle class," he said in a 1962 speech. Baraka especially reveres "Trane" – the saxophonist John Coltrane – to whom he refers in this 1978 poem, "I Love Music." This is the first of the typescript's two pages.*

Mark Strand

1934–

One of Charles Simic's notebooks contains a story about James Wright confusing Simic's poetry with that of Mark Strand as he introduced the two at a reading. Both poets exhibit Surrealistic threads in their poetry, and both tend toward a minimalist flirtation with silence and Surrealistic games. And they have, in fact, collaborated in compiling and editing an anthology of modern poetry entitled Another Republic: 17 European and South American Writers *(1976), which promotes a certain internationalism in contemporary poetry. Strand has had a lifelong interest in Latin American poets and poetry, traveling to Brazil on a fellowship and even translating poetry from the Andean indigenous language of Quechua.*

LIKE GRACEFUL, PERPLEXING Möbius strips, Mark Strand's poems travel seamlessly from the ordinary world to the realm of the poet's odd imagination. Fascinated by the unknown, the unconscious, and the space left by his body as he walks away, Strand makes them into poetry.

Born on Prince Edward Island in Canada, Strand earned his Bachelor's degree at Antioch College in Ohio. Intending to become a painter, he went on to art school at Yale, but when he went to Italy in 1960 on a Fulbright Fellowship for painting, he spent most of the time writing the poems that became his first book, *Sleeping with One Eye Open*. He studied poetry at the University of Iowa with Donald Justice, and became a professor. A second Fulbright Fellowship took him to Brazil, and he has since taught at dozens of universities (including the University of Utah for many years), won many other grants and fellowships, and served as Poet Laureate of the United States. At the same time, he has continued to write, producing children's books, journalism, translation, and art criticism, including a book on Edward Hopper, whose painting, like Strand's poetry, casts light that emphasizes the darkness around it.

In only 16 years during his early career, Strand published six books, culminating with *Selected Poems* (1980), an eerie work filled with a great sense of foreboding, loneliness, and, as he later put it, "a wish to possess / Something beyond the world we knew, beyond ourselves." In more recent work such as *The Continuous Life* (1992), Strand is less desperate and more wistful about the implacability of the everyday world. He even pokes fun at it, acknowledging the "beauty of shovels and rakes, brooms and mops" and even holding a solemn discussion with the poetic giant Jorge Luis Borges while soaping his chest in the bathtub. Strand now teaches at the Johns Hopkins University. ■

from **A Suite of Appearances**

In another time, we will want to know how the earth looked
Then, and were people the way we are now. In another time,
The records they left will convince us that we are unchanged
And could be at ease in the past, and not alone in the present.
And we shall be pleased. But beyond all that, what cannot
Be seen or explained will always be elsewhere, always supposed,
Invisible even beneath the signs – the beautiful surface,
The uncommon knowledge – that point its way. In another time,
What cannot be seen will define us, and we shall be prompted
To say that language is error, and all things are wronged
By representation. The self, we shall say, can never be
Seen with a disguise, and never be seen without one.

"A Suite of Appearances" is a long poem in six sections, published in a limited edition in 1993. It is dedicated to the Mexican poet Octavio Paz and his wife, Marie Jo. This typescript draft shows part of the fourth section. The final lines of the excerpt below form the sort of conundrum, reminiscent of the paradoxes in quantum physics, that entrances Strand.

In my early poems nothing much happened since I wrote mostly about forks and spoons, while Strand's poems in his . . . book *Reasons for Moving* were packed with action. They were like interesting dreams, full of haunting images and strange adventures. Poetry is the imponderable, one says after reading that book. It is the sudden expansion of the familiar. A man climbs into a tree and won't come down. Another man stands in front of our house for days. He won't leave whatever we do. In the library someone sits eating poetry. What Strand finds interesting about dreams is not their psychological content but their poetry.

Charles Simic, ["On Mark Strand"], unpublished memoir/essay, ca. 1995

Louise Glück

1943–

Painted more than 45 years ago in Paris, when Louise Glück was seven years old, this portrait still hangs on a wall in her mother's house on Long Island. Glück's poem "Appearances" refers unhappily to the painting and its companion: "When we were children, my parents had our portraits painted, / then hung them side by side, over the mantel, / where we couldn't fight. / I'm the dark one, the older one. My sister's blond, / the one who looks angry because she can't talk. . . ."

Her poems are delicately intense, spun out of fire and air, with a tensile strength that belies their fragility. They are rooted in landscape and weather and, increasingly, in the intimacies of the heart. Everything she touches turns to music and legend.

Stanley Kunitz, commenting on Glück's second book, The House on Marshland *(New York, 1975)*

LOUISE GLÜCK WAS born in New York, into a family "in which the right of any family member to complete the sentence of another was assumed." Longing to speak in her own, uninterrupted voice, Glück was often silent, but she was already composing poems at the age of five. Her mother had graduated from Wellesley College and admired art, and her father made a career as a businessman after giving up his own dream of becoming a writer. Thanks to them, Glück was familiar with Greek mythology and the story of St. Joan, she says, before she was three.

When Glück was 16, she became anorexic, fading down to 75 pounds. During her last year of high school, she dropped out and embarked on what would be seven years of psychoanalysis. At 18, instead of going to college as she had planned, Glück began studying poetry at Columbia's School of General Studies: two years with Leonie Adams, followed by five cherished years with Stanley Kunitz. "I had, in Kunitz, not only a persuasive argument for stamina but a companion spirit, someone my poems could talk to."

At 24, Glück published *Firstborn*, her first book of poems; eloquent and confessional, it was also saturated with disillusionment. Four years later, in 1971, she moved to Vermont to take a teaching job at Goddard College. She also broke a two-year poetic silence. She has since moved away from narrating her life in poetry, and toward the creation and reinforcement of myth. She is also, increasingly, a poet of rich and stimulating ideas. Glück has published six books, including the Pulitzer Prize–winning *The Wild Iris* (1992), and has taught on many campuses (currently at Williams College in Massachusetts). Married twice, Glück has one son and lives for half of each year in rural Vermont. ■

until you knew
only whatever had lost
earth or heaven

we inhabited
a lie to appease
you

you thought we didn't know. ah, but we knew once,
children know these things. don't turn away now --
human beings are changed
by inhabiting a lie. i remember
sunlight of early spring, (flowers
we named to appease you, glory of the snow, star
of bethlehem, embankments
netted with dark vinca; i remember
walking with my brother there. don't turn away now,
now that i know you're listening: who esle had reason to create
mistrust between us but the one being
to whom we'd turn in solitude? you thought
we didn't know, but once we understood
that what we were suffering
was what it seemed, that it was not heaven
we had lost but earth.

who else
would bancs
us from earth
I call it paradise

until the simple garden was a sea of messages
you couldn't resolve
your obsession with flesh; you couldn't bear
equality bwtween us.

being superior to flesh
didn't help you not to feel
excluded. once i knew that, in the end,

I not be
changed
my pretending
that it really was
heaven

who else would so
envy the flesh we
were they --
we thought we could
lie to appease you
go on, that
knowing the truth, that
it was not

The masterful, book-long collective conversation The Wild Iris *was written in ten weeks during the summer of 1991, as Glück gardened. In each poem, the speaker is God, the poet, or the flowers in her fields. This is a draft for one of the ten poems entitled "Vespers"; along with seven poems called "Matins," they frame the book. Here, the poet talks to God, needling him with the idea that he destroyed a strong bond between a young brother and sister because it made him feel superfluous. In this case, God subsists on human loneliness. Glück experimented with this grim idea from draft to draft until, in the final version, she put it as bluntly as possible, introducing the cold, one-word accusation "profited."*

Vespers

You thought we didn't know. But we knew once,
children know these things. Don't turn away now –
  we inhabited
a lie to appease you. I remember
sunlight of early spring, embankments
netted with dark vinca. I remember
lying in a field, touching my brother's body.
Don't turn away now; we denied
memory to console you. We mimicked you, reciting
the terms of our punishment. I remember

some of it, not all of it: deceit
begins as forgetting. I remember small things, flowers
growing under the hawthorn tree, bells
of the wild scilla. Not all, but enough
to know you exist: who else had reason to create
mistrust between a brother and sister but the one
who profited, to whom we turned in solitude? Who else
would so envy the bond we had then
as to tell us it was not earth
but heaven we were losing?

Charles Simic

1938–

During his first years in America, Simic wrote scores of poems. Of this period, he says, "I liked so many different kinds of poetry. One month I was a disciple of Hart Crane, the next month only Walt Whitman existed for me. When I fell in love with Pound I wrote an eighty-page long poem on the Spanish Inquisition. It was awful, but the effort I put into it was tremendous. I'd work all night on it, go to work half-asleep, and then drag myself to night classes. I probably produced more poetry in the years 1956–61 than in all the years since. Except for a few poems, it was all bad, and one day I had the pleasure of destroying them all." His first two published poems appeared in the Winter 1959 issue of the Chicago Review; *a few other unpublished poems from this period survive in the Berg Collection.*

As a child in wartorn Belgrade, Yugoslavia, Charles Simic endured bombings by both Germany and the United States, and the occupation of his native city by both Russian and American troops. He remembers his father's comment on a bomb raid: "Americans are throwing easter eggs." His father's family was, he said, full of "crooks" and the "criminal element," but his mother's family was "respectable," with its old paintings and Persian carpets. In the company of his mother and brother, the teenaged Charles immigrated to Paris in June 1953 ("Our only entertainment in Paris was walking"); twelve months later, they sailed on the *Queen Mary*, spending a year in New York before moving on to Chicago. His childhood memories are "a black and white movie. O rainy evenings. Dimly lit streets."

Simic now lives in New Hampshire, where he has taught at the university in Durham since 1973: "Now, of course, I live in the boonies. I have been in New Hampshire almost twenty years and in my walks through the woods I regularly bump into Emerson and Thoreau. We nod to each other in a friendly manner and go our separate ways. It's true I've often made fun of them behind their backs."

Simic noted once that "All the bad things in the Twentieth Century are to be attributed to free verse. It's all the fault of W. C. Williams as Bruce Bawer points out in a recent *New Criterion*. If only Williams and Pound had imitated Tennyson, sons would still call their fathers 'Sir.' We would still have the GREAT WESTERN VALUES and Modern Poetry would never have happened." His own poetry has won many prizes, including the Pulitzer Prize in 1990 for *The World Doesn't End* (1989), a volume of prose poems. ∎

149

Simic

Simic's poetic landscape is intensely cared for, as a peasant cares for meadows which have been coaxed and humanized by centuries of labor. It is not only a pun to say that Simic's poems are profoundly cultivated, if we define culture as an act of conciliation which turns the Furies into goddesses of harvest. Culture in this sense becomes a form of magic.

Paul Zweig, *"Return to a Place Lit by a Glass of Milk"* [review of the book of the same title] in The Village Voice, *April 4, 1974*

After arriving in New York, Simic spent days on end at The New York Public Library, poring over volumes of folklore: "Later some of the material entered my poetry, but I never consciously used the specific material. I was interested in, not borrowing or absorbing, but finding the mode – how these things are put together – a mythical mode. People would come to me later, and note how my poems were full of folklore, and say, 'You're so lucky, Simic, you must have heard all these things at your mother's knee.'" This drawing of a fantastical creature was made on a page torn from a modern history of Serbia (presumably not *from the Library's collections!). It served as the frontispiece for the poem sequence* White (1972), *a minimalist exploration or interrogation of the essence of white that is the culmination of Simic's early phase of writing.*

Simic's notebooks are jam-packed with lists, notes, and poems, like these
two drafts of "The Worm of Conscience," which was first published in
Unending Blues (1986). Simic's devotion to Dada, Surrealism, folklore,
and old blues songs, among other traditions, makes his work an intricate,
complicated blend. As he noted in an interview in American Poetry
Review: "One 'superfluous human being' . . . in the midst of all and every-
thing – humankind, history, literature, the infinite universe – is attempting
to talk back in a dozen or so lines of poetry. No wonder people say the
poets are nuts! The world so big and the poem so teeny."

The Worm of Conscience

Nightcrawler, is it time?

My head stuffed with yellowed pages
As if there were a courtroom nearby
And these its stacked-up documents.

Did you crawl out of the black heart of the prosecuting attorney?
Tunneling through the ornate signature of the judgment
On a special errand
Over the morgue reports and orphans' petitions.

Maker of labyrinths, is that it?
Contorting myself to overtake you.

Little white lies in a cage –
I intend to feed you to.

Ai

Ai carefully inscribed the names of each of her cats on the back of this photograph taken by Rebecca Ross in Tempe, Arizona, in 1989: Li Ch'ien (Lee-lee or Bubie), Hsu-ma (Bunny), and Shin no Kokkoro (Koko-San). She also noted: "not pictured – Ming-ming / new kitty (foil ball beside my foot)."

AN ELEGANT WOMAN fond of lingerie and perfume, Ai is also the premier American poet of gore. A red carnation, if it finds its way into an Ai poem, "floats the way your head would / if I cut it off." Yet she goes beyond such images to provoke empathy to an amazing degree. By writing in the voices of her characters, she lures the reader into their fearsome minds.

Born in Albany, Texas, Florence Haynes moved with her family to Arizona, Kansas, Las Vegas, Los Angeles, and San Francisco, attending Catholic schools until she was a teenager. "I didn't know I was half-Japanese," she wrote later, "but the fifth-grade African American girls at Sacred Heart in San Francisco knew. . . . Day after day, the girls would say, 'Get away from us, Nigger Jap, you can't play with us, Nigger Jap.'" After she saw a flyer for a poetry contest at school, she began writing poems. A move back to Tucson prevented her from entering the contest, but she continued to write.

Unable to pay the $125 registration fee for her first college semester, she applied to be a Playboy Bunny to raise the cash, and thought she had hit bottom when she was turned down. ("My consciousness hadn't been completely raised yet.") At the last minute her grandmother supplied the money. Still unaware of her ethnic heritage, she majored in Oriental Studies and began learning Japanese, but by the end of college she was concentrating again on poetry. Her first published poem, "Warrior," was written for an independent-study course in African history. As a graduate student, in her 20s, she switched to the surname Anthony, listed on her birth certificate as the name of her father (Mr. Haynes was her mother's second husband). Later, when the poet was 26, her mother finally told her that her father was a Japanese man named Ogawa. For several years she used that last name, and then finally discarded all her names in favor of "Ai," the Japanese word for love.

After earning a graduate degree in writing at the University of California at Irvine, Ai began teaching. Her first book, *Cruelty* (1973), created a sensation, and she has since published three more books, establishing the dramatic monologue as her trademark form. She currently writes and teaches in Arizona. ■

AI

Ai's second book, Killing Floor, *was the prestigious Lamont Poetry Selection of the Academy of American Poets in 1978. Some critics pointed out with surprise or disapproval that in most of the dramatic monologues that make up the book, Ai speaks in the voices of men. But Ai sees no reason why her imagination should be restricted by her sex. "Whoever wants to speak in my poems is allowed to speak, regardless of sex, race, creed or color. I'm simply a writer, I don't want to be catalogued & my characters don't want to be catalogued & my poems don't want to be catalogued. If a poet's work isn't universal, then what good is it? Who the hell wants to read it."*

The Kid

My Sister

My sister rubs the doll's face in mud,
then climbs through the truck window.
She ignores me, as I walk around it,
hitting the flat tires with an iron rod.
The old man yells for me to help hitch the team,
but I keep walking around the truck, hitting harder,
when until my mother calls. A voice
I pick up a rock and throw it at the kitchen window,
but it falls short.
The old man's voice bounces off the air like a ball
I can't lift my leg over.

I stand beside him, waiting, but he doesn't look up
and I squeeze the rod, raise it, his skull splits open.
Mother runs toward us. I stand still,
get her across the spine, as she bends over him.
I drop the rod and take the rifle from the house.
Roses are red, violets are blue,
one bullet for the black horse, two for the brown.
They're down quick. I spit, my tongue's bloody;
I've bitten it. I laugh, remember the one out back.
I catch her climbing from the truck, shoot.
The doll lands on the ground with her.
I pick it up, rock it in my arms.
Yeah. I'm Jack, Hogarth's son.
I'm nimble, I'm quick.

In the house, I put on the old man's best suit
and his patent leather shoes.
I pack my mother's satin night gown
and my sister's doll in the suitcase.
Then I go outside and cross the fields to the highway.
I'm fourteen. I'm a wind from nowhere.
I can break your heart.

Ai

from **The Kid**

My sister rubs the doll's face in mud,
then climbs through the truck window.
She ignores me as I walk around it,
hitting the flat tires with an iron rod.
The old man yells for me to help hitch the team,
but I keep walking around the truck, hitting harder,
until my mother calls.
I pick up a rock and throw it at the kitchen window,
but it falls short.
The old man's voice bounces off the air like a ball
I can't lift my leg over.

503 N. Santa Rita Ave
Tucson, Ariz. 85719

a little stiff —

Resurrection

This is my life.
I will go down the river
With a sow's blood smeared
On my forehead.
I will float her ears beside me — Whazzat?
The red, skin wings of a bird — yeah
I will drown in crushed glass.
I will rise again
With a day old pig crawling
From my mouth.
I will.

(out of?)

Florence Haynes

I'll go

Terrific force.

May 23, '69

Dear Florence — good luck —
Thanks for letter no see these —
the precise force of certain images are
clear & fine — a little surreal — Have
you read W C Williams?
Try to avoid subjective "ideas" surrounding
the images — no ideas but in things —
Always direct presentation is best — Allen Ginsberg

While still a college student, Ai showed some of her work to two poets who had visited the campus: Galway Kinnell and Allen Ginsberg. Ginsberg returned the three manuscripts with revisions, commentary, and here, on the typescript of "Resurrection," a note dated May 23, 1969. His criticisms were blunt, but he also wished her luck and suggested other poets to read. With Kinnell, Ai formed "the major literary relationship of my life": "For months after Galway left [Tucson], we'd talk about the reading, the party, the poems. Galway really seemed like some kind of heroic figure from all our imaginations," she said more than 20 years later. "Hell, I guess it's just the fellowship of poetry, but it's stronger between some people than others."

All woman – all human – all vital. Alive with the arteries of life.

Anne Sexton, dust jacket blurb for Cruelty *(Boston, 1973)*

Asked to supply photographs or other interesting images of herself for the exhibition that inspired this book, Ai sent this snapshot of herself as a child. "I wanted to take a photo today," she wrote in the accompanying letter, "but the Polaroid film sold near my house is $16 for one or $23 for a two pack. As usual, I am low on $, so I'll have to draw today's version of me." Ai, who often describes herself as "$1/2$ Japanese, $1/8$ Choctaw, $1/4$ Black, and $1/16$ Irish," said of the photo: "That was my favorite outfit and my favorite way to dress back then when it was cool. Yes, I am dressed a la Native American kind of a cross between Apache/Navajo and cowgirl." She added, "I recently found out that the Choctaw nation will take me & indeed whomever in the family wishes into the tribe."

Dana Gioia

He is an exceptional poet, critic and translator, perhaps the closest to a young Wallace Stevens we have in this country.

Howard Moss, quoted in "Best of the New Generation: Men and Women Under Forty Who Are Changing America" in Esquire, *December 1984*

During his years at Kraft Foods, Gioia used his poetic imagination to help develop "Kool-Aid Man," "Jigglers," and the "Jell-O Reading Rocket." As Vice President for Marketing, he said goodbye to his colleagues in a letter dated September 13, 1991: "For years I have squeezed my literary work into the little pockets of time my busy life affords. Despite the genuine satisfactions of my job here, I have often felt frustrated in how little energy I could devote to writing. Thinking about what I wanted most in my future, I decided the right moment had come in life to pursue a career in literature as a writer and teacher."

FROM THE BEGINNING, Dana Gioia heard poetry: his mother read the family Poe, Kipling, and Ogden Nash. In high school, discovering the music of Benjamin Britten, Ned Rorem, and William Flanagan as well as that of more "traditional" composers (Stravinsky, Barber, Walton), Gioia began composing music. From musical settings of their poems, Gioia was nudged toward such authors as Auden, Bishop, Moss, Cummings, and Wilfred Owen. His imagination was filled with the transfiguring experience that poetry can give: "I was attracted to poetry long before I ever thought of writing it (and eons before I had any notion of writing about it). Whatever my other affiliations with the art, I still think of myself primarily as a reader – one passionately grateful for the pleasure, enlightenment and consolation that poetry affords." Gioia, whose poetry possesses an uncommon sensuality, grace, and clarity, has learned well how to provide these values in his own work.

Born in working-class Hawthorne, California, on Christmas Eve, 1950, Gioia grew up among the Northrup, Mattel, and Hughes factories, in a Sicilian-speaking enclave within the town's Mexican-American neighborhood. He graduated in 1973 from Stanford University, where he edited the literary magazine, *The Sequoia*. The next year he began work at Harvard toward a doctorate in English, studying with Robert Fitzgerald and Elizabeth Bishop, whom he later described in a moving memoir, "Miss Bishop," published in *The New Yorker*. After receiving an M.B.A. from Stanford in 1977, he spent 14 years in the corporate world.

Gioia's prose writing has been very influential, most controversially with "Can Poetry Matter?" (1991), an analysis of the contemporary poetry scene. His appreciations of poets Robinson Jeffers, Donald Justice, and Weldon Kees, among others, are marvels. After almost 20 years in New York, Gioia and his family now live atop a hill outside Santa Rosa, in northern California. ∎

In "Business and Poetry," Gioia comments on popular stereotypes about
poets: "They must be people out of the ordinary; they must be strong,
even eccentric individuals. Most often they are pictured either as scholars
or vagabonds, Longfellows or Whitmans, Allen Tates or Allen Ginsbergs."
But certainly not businessmen – despite the examples of, among others,
Wallace Stevens (Hartford Accident and Indemnity), T. S. Eliot (Lloyds
of London), and Gioia himself (Kraft General Foods). This photograph
appeared in a Kraft publication in 1984.

Comments by Emily Grosholz
to whom I sent the poem
for a critical reaction.

CALIFORNIA HILLS IN AUGUST

I can imagine someone who found
these fields unbearable, who climbed
the hillside in the heat, cursing the dust,
cracking the brittle weeds underfoot,
wishing a few more trees for shade.

An Easterner especially, who would scorn
the meagerness of summer, the dry
twisted shapes of black elm,
scrub oak, and chapparrel, a landscape
August has already drained of green.

One who would hurry over the clinging
thistle, foxtail, golden poppy,
knowing everything was just a weed,
unable to conceive that these trees
and sparse brown bushes were alive. ←?

And hate the bright stillness of the noon
without wind, without motion
the only other living thing
a hawk, hungry for prey, suspended
in the blinding, sunlit blue.

And yet how gentle it seems to someone
raised in a landscape short of rain -
the skyline of a hill broken by no
more trees than one can count, the grass,
the empty sky, the wish for water.

very nice

Dana Gioia

I like this alot
Nice perspectival play, strengthen the percepts at the end -
This is the way I feel about Greece

"California Hills in August" was composed in 1981 in the hills behind the campus at Stanford University when Gioia returned briefly to the Santa Clara Valley, south of San Francisco, after several years on the East Coast. He was staying with a friend and visiting his father, who had successfully come through brain surgery. The exhaustion and anxiety he was feeling were calmed by the landscape, which ignited his memory and imagination. The Berg Collection owns 27 pages of drafts for this poem, a number not unusual for Gioia's poems: "I sometimes keep a poem back for ten years because a single line doesn't seem good enough. Or I will revise a poem fifty to a hundred times trying to get it exactly right. Some people consider that behavior neurotic. Larkin and Bishop, however, demonstrate that such a neurosis may not be altogether bad for a poet."

Julia Alvarez

1950–

Approaching her 33rd birthday on March 27, 1983, Alvarez felt that she had missed the married, mothering life for which she had been carefully trained as a girl. "By 33 you knew if it worked or not. By 33 as a woman of my generation, you knew if you had been the heroine of your mother's story or not. The voice inside these sonnets ["33," published as part of Homecoming *in 1984] is constantly trying to find why she doesn't fit into that romantic model." She had planned to write only one birthday poem but instead had such an intense writing jag in the spring and early summer of 1983 that "even when people [were] talking [I was] hearing the iambic pentameter in their voices." This photograph was taken in the Dominican Republic in the early 1990s.*

IF JULIA ALVAREZ had remained in the Dominican Republic instead of moving to the United States at age 10, she says, she would probably not have become a poet. Her writerly imagination was primed by "the realm of that hyphen – the place where two worlds collide or blend together."

Alvarez was born in New York City, but her Dominican parents took her home before she was a month old. Rather than study, as a child she listened to the flamboyant Spanish storytelling of the maids and cooks in her parents' house, and failed each year of English classes at her American school. In August 1960, Alvarez's father, a doctor, ran afoul of the dictatorship of Rafael Trujillo, and the family moved to New York City. Suddenly Alvarez found herself struggling to learn English, forgetting some Spanish before she was fluent in the new language. "In a sense," she wrote much later, "I was in no man's land. . . . But that land is any writer's blank page."

Alvarez attended Abbot Academy (a girls' boarding school), Connecticut College, Middlebury College, and Syracuse University, earning degrees in English and creative writing. She then spent more than a decade as what she calls "a migrant poet," teaching in nursing homes, schools, prisons, and church basements throughout the United States. She has published two novels, *How the Garcia Girls Lost Their Accents* (1991) and *In the Time of the Butterflies* (1994), and two books of poetry, *Homecoming* (1984) and *The Other Side = El Otro Lado* (1995). Alvarez's verse combines nostalgic memories of being trained by her "Mami" to make a bed and to iron for her future husband, with wistful notes on being an unmarried, thirtysomething poet in Vermont. Her poetic voice speaks as if she were sharing coffee with an old friend – musing, laughing ruefully, seeking reassurance.

Now married, Alvarez teaches English and creative writing at Middlebury College in Vermont. ■

1 Secretly I am building in the heart a
2 a delicate structure like one of those b
3 cardhouses or popsicle palaces b
4 a build-un-build, patiently putting each part a
5 in its place, fingers pinched, a small tube c
6 of glue, my eyes straining to perceive what new c
7 thing I am making that will take so much time d
8 to finish if there's finish in these things d
9 And making it out of nothing but what e
10 on ruins from an earlier effort f
11 And temptation constantly as I work to put there to believe there are
12 a readymade better place, and yet I've g
13 the heart to outlast the heart f

I don't know if you want to call it love

with this thing I am building, call it love.

out of

Sometimes people ask me why I wrote a series of poems about housekeeping if I'm a feminist. Don't I want women to be liberated from the oppressive roles they were condemned to live? I don't see housekeeping that way. They were the crafts we women had, sewing, embroidering, cooking, spinning, sweeping, even the lowly dusting. And like Dylan Thomas said, we sang in our chains like the sea.

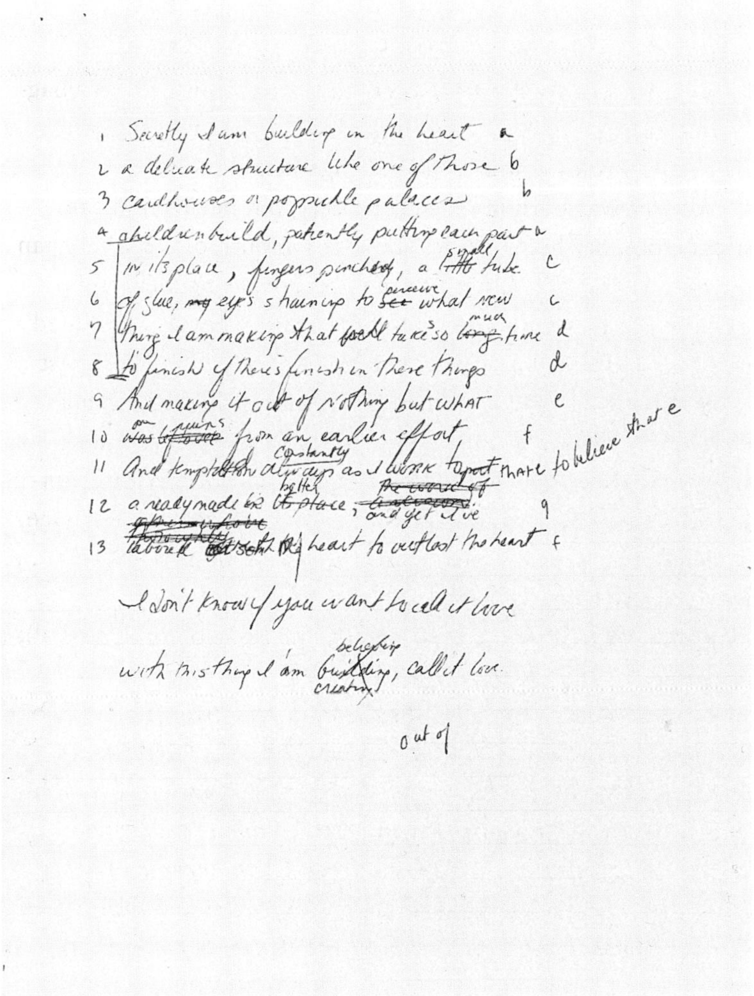

Julia Alvarez, "Housekeeping Cages" in A Formal Feeling Comes: Poems in Form by Contemporary Women, *edited by Annie Finch (Brownesville, Ore., 1994)*

Like traditional sonnets, the free verse poems of "33" consist of 14 lines of 10 syllables each, and a rhyme scheme like the one Alvarez has marked here: for example, the small letter "a" refers to the rhyme of "heart" with "part." But some of her rhyming pairs are "slant" or approximate rhymes, and she frequently disrupts the poem's iambic meter to better capture the sound of ordinary, unstilted conversation. She chose the sonnet form, she says, because it had been used for so many poems full of the romantic ideals with which she and other women had been painfully indoctrinated. But she subverted the classic romantic pattern in her poems, as she has done in life. "For centuries women have been caged in these little fourteen-line boxes," she says. "I wanted to get inside it and explode it."

Despite many years in Vermont, Alvarez still identifies with her Dominican roots; the back of this photograph from the early 1990s is inscribed "In the D.R. looking for land." To describe her split identity, she has referred to a Dominican saying, "between Lucas and Juan Mejia," which is an equivocal answer to the question "How are you?" No one knows anymore who Lucas and Juan Mejia were, Alvarez writes; the point is to be floating between them.

Las palabras a veces estan tan cerca que soy
mas quien soy cuando estoy sobre el papel
que en ningún otro lado. Como ensayando a ser
quien de veras soy, me desabotono
de la anécdota y lo innecesario, me desvisto
linea por linea hasta la figura del poema,
el texto que hasta un niño entendería.
¿Porqué me confunde el vivirlo?
Ustedes que escuchan, perdidos y ansiando
libertad, ustedes que escuchan estas palabras, creánme.
Una vez existi en tantos borradores como ustedes;
pero breve, esencialmente, aqui estoy...
Quien toca estos versos toca una mujer.

JULIA ALVAREZ
Translation of last sonnet in "33"
sonnet sequence by Jorge Travieso

A young Nicaraguan student in Illinois, Jorge Travieso, became enchanted by the poems of "33" and began to translate them into Spanish, mailing copies of his work to Alvarez, who writes only in English. "I think of my Spanish as childhood Spanish," she says. "I feel like I couldn't even reach the gas pedal." This is Travieso's translation of "Sometimes the words are so close." Chiqui Vicioso, a Dominican poet, polished a few of Travieso's translations and published them in a newspaper in the Dominican Republic.

*"Sometimes the words are so close"
is the last sonnet in Alvarez's
"33" sequence. She has said that
her two "muses" for this poem
were Emma Lazarus, who wrote
the poem inscribed at the base
of the Statue of Liberty, beginning
"Give me your tired, your poor,
your huddled / masses yearning to
breathe free," and Walt Whitman,
who wrote in* Leaves of Grass,
*". . . this is no book, / Who
touches this touches a man."
"I've always wanted to be able
to say that," Alvarez says of
the Whitman line.*

from **33**

Sometimes the words are so close I am
more who I am when I'm down on paper
than anywhere else as if my life were
practising for the real me I become
unbuttoned from the anecdotal and
unnecessary and undressed down
to the figure of the poem, line by line,
the real text a child could understand.
Why do I get confused living it through?
Those of you, lost and yearning to be free,
who hear these words, take heart from me.
I once was in as many drafts as you.
But briefly, essentially, here I am.
Who touches this poem touches a woman.

The Prado of Poetry: A History of the Berg Collection

BY DANA GIOIA

OPERA HAS LA Scala, Covent Garden, Bayreuth. Ballet has the Kirov, Bolshoi, Lincoln Center. Painting has the Louvre, Uffizi, Frick, and Prado. The arts foster great institutions to preserve and celebrate their heritage. Carnegie Hall, La Fenice, the Musikverein, Glyndebourne – these are not merely names of concert halls and opera houses; they are the shrines of aesthetic cults, sacred places whose interiors command a special attention and heightened receptivity to the complex mysteries of their art. Aficionados travel great distances to visit these sites just as pilgrims once trekked across continents to touch the relics of a martyr.

But what about poetry? Where does one go to contemplate and celebrate its classics? In ancient Greece one could attend the Panathenaic festival to hear the rhapsodes, professional reciters of poetry, perform the Homeric epics in fixed succession. Or one could travel to the Olympian games where poets pleased the crowds nearly as much as the athletes did. In America, however, one encounters poetry – at least the poetry of the past – mainly in the classroom. Of course, poetry has always been part of the academic curriculum. Getting an education, after all, has traditionally meant becoming well-versed. The classroom, however, rarely creates the sense of sacred space, heightened attentiveness, and special occasion necessary to celebrate an art. Walking through the Harvard English department, for all its venerable associations, does not stir the souls of most literati. An academic bulletin board is not intrinsically more interesting because Robert Lowell once posted a class-list there.

There are, of course, a few historic places in America that commemorate the poets who once lived there. Cambridge, Massachusetts, displays Henry Wadsworth Longfellow's stately Craigie House with his library and furniture intact. Edgar Allan Poe's much vandalized cottage still stands off the Grand Concourse in the Bronx. Mysterious and beautiful, Robinson Jeffers's Tor House sits perched on a small cliff overlooking the Pacific in Carmel, California. These homes summon the spirits of their dead owners in ineffable yet potent ways; in some secular but nonetheless spiritual sense, they have become sacred places. And yet visiting Monet's Giverny is not the same as seeing his masterpieces in the Musée d'Orsay. Surely poetry deserves its Hermitage or Prado. But where can it be found?

If poetry has a Uffizi or La Scala in America, it is probably the Berg Collection of The New York Public Library. Housed in the magnificent Beaux-Arts central building on Fifth Avenue and 42nd Street, the Henry W. and Albert A. Berg Collection of English and American Literature is preeminent among the Library's distinguished special literary collections, which include the Pforzheimer, Oscar Lion, and Spencer. Established in 1940 by Dr. Albert Berg, a prominent Manhattan surgeon, successful real estate investor, and passionate bibliophile, in memory of his older

*The Berg reading room features portraits of Albert A. Berg (left) and
Henry W. Berg (right) on its east wall. Charles Dickens's writing desk and
chairs from his home at Gads Hill are displayed below the two portraits.*

brother, the Berg Collection has grown steadily by careful acquisition. Among North American literary archives, the Berg now stands unsurpassed, with holdings equaled by only four other research institutions – the Houghton Library at Harvard, the Beinecke Library at Yale, the Humanities Research Center at the University of Texas in Austin, and the Huntington Library in San Marino, California.

The story behind the Berg Collection is quintessentially American – a self-made millionaire spends his final years using his fortune to build a public institution. Leland Stanford, Henry Clay Frick, Andrew Mellon, J. Paul Getty, Henry E. Huntington, Albert Barnes, Joseph Hirshhorn, are familiar American archetypes, but such outsize and ostentatious philanthropists would seem anomalous in modern Europe. Who could imagine an Italian Andrew Carnegie, a French John D. MacArthur, or a Dutch Lila Wallace? The chronicle of a large fortune made and given away in a single lifetime is largely native to the New World. An astonishing number of American plutocrats have been less interested in founding a family dynasty than in perpetuating their own tastes and values. Perhaps the sheer difficulty of sustaining a business empire across generations in the mercilessly dynamic American economy was not lost on these hard-nosed practical men. For every capable John D. Rockefeller, Jr., there are a dozen profligate heirs like Nelson Bunker Hunt or Huntington Hartford.

Most major European libraries, universities, and museums grew slowly over centuries. Begun as private or ecclesiastical enterprises, they developed according to no particular plan under the inconsistent guidance of successive Popes, emperors, queens, bishops, and barons. By contrast, many great American cultural institutions seem to have been created from sheer force of will by individuals with a long-term vision and colossal self-confidence. If the Louvre, Hermitage, Vatican Library, and British Museum embody the impersonal, almost timeless, and public quality of European institutions, then American cultural aspirations most clearly express themselves in idealistic and even idiosyncratic enterprises like the Barnes Foundation, Cloisters, Morgan Library, Norton Simon Museum, and Huntington Library and Art Gallery. Even as these institutions grow over time, they continue to reflect the taste and ideals of their founders.

If the lives of Henry and Albert Berg were not conducted on so grand a scale as those of a Carnegie or Huntington, they display the same pattern of self-made men. Henry Woolfe Berg, the oldest of eight children, was born in the Austro-Hungarian empire in 1858 and immigrated with his family to New York in 1862. His father, who had hoped to study medicine in Vienna, became a tailor in America, but in the classic Jewish immigrant mold, he resolved that his children would gain the education he had missed. At age 11, Henry took a part-time job at the Cooper

Institute (now Cooper Union) Library, a position that reinforced his already deep love of books. He became known to Peter Cooper when he zealously refused the founder entrance to his own library because he failed to show identification. When Cooper later brought William Cullen Bryant to the library, Henry recited part of "Thanatopsis" to its author. Listening to the performance, the two prosperous old men could not have known that the sweet irony of American life would allow that boy's future fortune to endow his own library next to a park bearing the poet's name. Nor could they imagine that 70 years later, the boy's youngest brother would present a manuscript of that famous poem to the collection. Would even Charles Dickens, the young Berg's favorite author, have concocted such an outlandishly neat rags-to-riches plot twist?

After his father's death in 1881, Henry, now Dr. Berg, became a surrogate parent to his youngest brother, Albert, who was 14 years his junior. Albert also became a doctor. The two brothers never married and happily shared living quarters till Henry's death. They also shared a passion for literature. Their literary tastes were conventional in an age when conventional taste was both selective and refined. If their fascination with Dickens seemed slightly old-fashioned in 1940, today it seems almost prescient; Dickens now stands with George Eliot as one of the two greatest Victorian novelists. The brothers gradually assembled a distinguished personal library of their favorite

authors as well as famous books of English and American literature in rare editions. The Bergs also began assembling a real estate empire in lower Manhattan. Book collecting aside, the brothers lived frugally. Albert did not even own a car.

When Henry Berg died in 1938, Albert was desolate. The two brothers had been lifelong companions. Albert had already retired early from his surgical position at Mount Sinai Hospital. He had a sizable fortune and no children. He needed a new focus for his considerable energies. Before Henry's death, the brothers had discussed creating a rare books collection at The New York Public Library, but no final decision had been made. Now Albert resolved to found such a collection in Henry's memory. Once undertaken, the project consumed his attention until his death in 1951. During his years in medicine and real estate, Berg had established the political connections to make his plan possible, and the lifelong passion he had shared with his oldest brother provided the emotional substance of the dream.

The Berg Collection reflects the distinctively entrepreneurial character of American philanthropy. Having decided to establish a literary research collection bearing the family name, Albert Berg determined it should be a great one. He pursued this goal with the same acumen that he had earlier exercised in building his real estate portfolio. Why shouldn't a man's posterity be managed as ingeniously as his capital? This was a great era of American cultural

Albert A. Berg (1872–1950)

philanthropy. In 1934, John D. Rockefeller had initiated construction of the new Cloisters on land he had donated in upper Manhattan. Five years later, the new Museum of Modern Art opened in midtown on land also donated by Rockefeller. Meanwhile, in Washington, Andrew Mellon had financed the National Gallery of Art on the Capitol Mall.

Mellon's strategy in erecting a huge, nearly empty museum resembles Berg's ultimate approach in endowing his collection. If new American cultural enterprises were to achieve parity with established institutions, they must be built boldly – not by gradual individual acquisitions but by obtaining whole collections *en bloc*. In 1931, Mellon purchased 21 master-pieces from the Hermitage in a secret deal with the cash-hungry Soviets. He also acquired the large Clarke collection of American portraits

intact. Just months before his death, Mellon bought a townhouse full of Old Masters for his still unopened museum. (However driven to obtain great paintings, however, Mellon could never be convinced to buy a nude.) By 1942, the National Gallery had almost miraculously achieved parity with great European museums through the nearly simultaneous gifts of the Mellon, Kress, and Widener collections of Old Masters. Earlier in the century, Huntington had built his new library by acquiring entire private libraries. Berg shaped his new enterprise with equally ambitious vision.

When Dr. Albert Berg formally offered his gift to The New York Public Library on February 6, 1940, his collection consisted of 3,500 volumes. The initial bequest reflected 30 years of serious collecting by the two brothers. Housed in a townhouse on East 73rd Street off Fifth Avenue, it represented a superb example of what traditionally was called a "gentleman's library" and displayed the brothers' personal passion for Dickens and Thackeray. The Bergs also collected "high-spots," great bibliophilic rarities, as defined by the Grolier Club's 1902 connoisseur's bible, *One Hundred Books Famous in English Literature* (of which the brothers had assembled 60 works). The range and character of the original gift, therefore, differed significantly from what the Berg even-tually became. It was overwhelmingly a collec-tion of rare books with little manuscript or archival material beyond a few Victorian novelists who were special favorites of the brothers. No one cataloguing the original inventory, which contained such rarities as first editions of Spenser's *The Faerie Queene* (1590–96), Chapman's *Homer* (1616), George Herbert's *The Temple* (1633), Browne's *Religio Medici* (1643), and Wordsworth and Coleridge's *Lyrical Ballads* (1798) as well as whole walls of 19th-century novels in fine bindings, would have predicted that the Berg Collection would ultimately become one of the world's great archives of literary manuscripts, correspondence, diaries, and personal effects, with special depth in the 20th century.

Viewing his personal library now from a public perspective, Dr. Berg must have sensed that, for all its individual splendors, it was not yet a great collection by the standards of major research libraries. Almost immediately after announcing his gift, he took audacious steps to broaden its depth and coverage. Now that he was buying for a public institution dedicated to his brother's memory rather than for private gratification, Dr. Berg, who had always taken the bus to work, abandoned his characteristic dislike of extravagance and started collecting on a grand scale. (The equally understated Andrew Mellon experienced the same founder's fever in buying paintings to fill the empty walls of the National Gallery.) In 1940, while workmen remodeled the third-floor room in the Library to house the initial 3,500 volumes, the doctor acquired *in toto* one of the major private literary collections in America – the library of W. T. H. Howe.

The former president of The American Book Company, Howe had died the previous year, leaving behind 16,000 books and manuscripts.

Not only did the Howe purchase effectively quadruple the size of the Berg bequest, it changed its character. Howe had collected not only rare books, but also manuscripts, letters, and association copies. He had even collected personal items and furniture such as Charles Dickens's desk, which now stands in the corner of the Collection's reading room directly under Dr. Henry Berg's portrait. (Vladimir Nabokov's special standing desk will eventually be placed underneath the younger doctor's portrait.) Some of the strange literary relics now found in the Berg – Elizabeth Barrett Browning's slippers, Lewis Carroll's photograph of Alice Pleasance Liddell (the model for *Alice's Adventures in Wonderland*), Charlotte Brontë's portable escritoire, William Thackeray's pen – presumably originated in the Howe trove. This acquisition transformed the Berg Collection from a rare book library to a complete literary archive.

Patience is not a conspicuous virtue among self-made men. Excited now by the possibility of creating a literary research collection of international stature, Dr. Berg made a third, decisive acquisition. On May 5, 1941, less than seven months after the Collection's dedication and while carpenters were still refitting an adjacent gallery to provide room for the Howe material, The New York Public Library announced that the Owen D. Young collection would come to the Berg. Young, the former chairman of both General Electric and RCA, had built an extraordinary private collection of over 15,000 books and manuscripts. He and Berg had never met, but Robert Lingel, the Library's Chief of Acquisitions, had negotiated a confidential deal between the two men, which resulted in a joint donation. Young felt an old-fashioned sense of public stewardship about his collection. He claimed to be its "trustee" rather than its owner, and he had allowed scholars access to the books and papers. Without Berg's intervention, however, Young's collection would probably have been dispersed. The Depression had destroyed the finances of the collector, who had once spent $373,000 at a single pre-Crash auction. Young had not only stopped buying books; after his wife's death, he had put his huge collection in storage. Only Berg's co-sponsorship of the donation made the gift possible.

The Young gift surpassed even the Howe collection in scope and quality. Its acquisition not only secured the Berg's stature among American research repositories; its addition permanently redefined the Collection as a comprehensive literary archive. Although Young had been a voracious buyer of rare editions, he had a special passion for manuscripts, especially working drafts that revealed a writer's creative process. His wife, a former English teacher, had shared this enthusiasm. Once, for a Christmas present, he gave her the manuscript of Robert Burns's "O my Love's like

the red, red rose." Young had gradually accumulated substantial manuscript holdings from Pope, Burns, Scott, Goldsmith, Byron, Coleridge, Tennyson, Carroll, Kipling, and Twain. He had also found certain items of spectacular rarity, like the Westmoreland Manuscript of John Donne's sonnets and elegies. Written around 1625 in the hand of the poet's amanuensis, Rowland Woodward, these vellum-bound sheets comprise one of the most important surviving contemporary manuscripts of Donne's poetry. Young also owned George Eliot's commonplace book and Boswell's letter soliciting subscriptions for a monument to Dr. Johnson. Sometimes Young had even bought manuscripts *en bloc* such as the papers of the novelist Fanny Burney and her family.

Young also owned fascinating association copies, such as Alexander Pope's copy of Milton's *Poems* (1645). The young Pope had taught himself to write by carefully imitating printed typeface, and in this volume one finds two scrupulously copied poems by Milton in Pope's meticulous hand. Young also obtained the copy of Browne's *Pseudodoxia epidemica* (1658), which Charles Lamb had bought for S. T. Coleridge, who in turn later gave the volume, now marked with his annotations, to Sara Hutchinson with an inscribed letter on the flyleaf. Young also collected authors' personal copies of their own books. He possessed perhaps the most delightful association copy in the Berg, the blue morocco-bound volume of *Alice's Adventures in Wonderland* (1866) that Charles Dodgson, a.k.a. Lewis Carroll, inscribed for Alice Liddell, who inspired his story.

When the Berg's first public exhibition, devoted appropriately to Dickens, opened in the newly rebuilt Gallery on December 16, 1941, the Collection's identity was firmly established. The show not only demonstrated that the Berg's holdings in this classic English author were comparable to anything in the British Museum or the Victoria and Albert Museum, which had jointly inherited Dickens's papers; the opening also signalled the Collection's commitment to public education.

An institution's architecture and interior design usually communicate its goals more clearly than any written statement. The Berg's adjoining Reading Room and Exhibition Gallery did not merely announce its double objective of general education and scholarly research; they also suggested these goals were not mutually exclusive. The large exhibition space, the carefully arranged displays, which included some of the Collection's rarest possessions, and the informative captions welcomed a common reader who had not been traditionally welcome at most research libraries. No wonder the Berg's imaginatively curated shows gradually became significant features in New York literary life.

In retrospect, the Dickens opening marked an astonishing achievement. In less than two years, Dr. Albert Berg had conceived,

endowed, constructed, and stocked a world-class research library. Significantly, he had not placed his collection at a university or museum but in an urban public library. One wonders how many among the crowds that moved through the inaugural exhibition sensed that they were at the end of an era in American culture? A week earlier, the Japanese had attacked the American fleet, and the nation was now at war both in Europe and Asia. The decade of social and cultural change that had begun with Franklin Roosevelt's inauguration in 1933 effectively ended with Pearl Harbor.

This idealistic era had temporarily merged the goals of popular and elitist culture. The conjunction of high and low sensibilities did not always yield happy results; it could descend into Agit-prop or kitsch. At its best, however, the period created some of the finest and most distinctively American art. Novels like Hemingway's *For Whom the Bell Tolls* or West's *The Day of the Locust*, critical writing like Wilson's *To the Finland Station* or Brooks's *New England: Indian Summer*, films like Capra's *Mr. Smith Goes to Washington*, Sturges's *Sullivan's Travels*, or Ford's *The Grapes of Wrath*; plays like Wilder's *Our Town* or O'Neill's *Ah, Wilderness!*, the populist Modernism of poets like Jeffers, Hughes, and Millay, the symphonic music of Barber, Harris, and Copland, remind contemporary audiences that excellence and accessibility are not mutually exclusive virtues. The creation of institutions to support public culture coincided with this populist move in the arts. Museums, concert halls, and libraries were built – just as journals, lecture series, and small presses were started – in the conviction that democracy required the highest possible levels of public education. The Berg Collection reflects the era's faith that high culture need not abandon civic responsibility.

Joining the ranks of such institutions as the Houghton, the Morgan, and the Huntington, the Berg also symbolized the increasing role Jewish philanthropy played in American culture – an insight surely not lost at the Collection's dedication, presided over not only by Dr. Berg but by New York Governor Herbert Lehman and Mayor Fiorello LaGuardia (whose wife was Jewish). Jewish philanthropy was hardly new, but only recently had it taken the lead in reshaping New York cultural life. In 1939, while Dr. Berg negotiated the terms of his gift with the Library, Solomon Guggenheim opened his Museum of Non-objective Art to the public. Meanwhile, the 92nd Street Young Men's Hebrew Association offered its first season of poetry readings, with appearances by William Carlos Williams, Genevieve Taggard, W. H. Auden, and Langston Hughes. Initiating what would become the nation's most celebrated series of literary readings not at a university, but at a local community organization, the 92nd Street Y reached out beyond its own constituency to enrich the artistic life of New York. The Berg Collection emerged in this visionary and democratic milieu. Like the Guggenheim and the

92nd Street Y, the Berg represented Jewish cultural aspirations in all the idealism and innocence of an era that the brutality of World War II would soon end.

The Berg endowment provided for a full-time curator and a budget for future acquisitions. From the beginning, the curator's job was not merely to maintain the existing collection but also to direct its growth. Continuity of leadership is as important as vision and determination in building a great enterprise, and the Berg has been fortunate in its direction. Only four curators have served since its inception – John D. Gordan (1940–68), Lola L. Szladits (1968–90), Francis O. Mattson (1991–95), and the newly appointed Rodney Phillips. (Lisa Browar served as Acting Curator in 1995.) These curators have not only built the Collection's holdings, which have grown from approximately 35,000 items at its opening in 1941 to over 150,000 today; they have also greatly expanded its scope.

At the time of Dr. Berg's death in 1950, the Collection included about 40,000 items, roughly half of them manuscripts. Although the holdings ranged from the 15th century to the present, there was little Medieval or Renaissance material. The Elizabethan, Jacobean, and Restoration periods were better represented. The Berg owns copies of all four Shakespeare Folios. It was only with the 18th century, however, that the Berg achieved real depth, with substantial manuscript material like the drafts of the first three books of Alexander Pope's *Essay on Man* and holographs of Fanny Burney's novels, *Evelina*, *Cecilia*, and *Camilla*, as well as large collections of letters by Thomas Gray and Samuel Johnson. By the time it reached the 19th century, the Berg ranked with any literary archive in the world. The accumulation of printed books, as John Gordan elegantly phrased it, "was gratifyingly close to completion." Some famously rare volumes like Poe's *Tamerlane* and Browning's *Pauline* were present in multiple copies. The manuscripts were equally impressive. Samuel Taylor Coleridge, for example, was represented by 30 manuscripts, three notebooks, and over 100 autograph letters. There were 300 Thackeray letters and 500 Dickens letters. In contrast, the Berg's holdings in 20th-century authors were modest.

In defining the Berg's future, Gordan made a crucial decision. While filling in the Collection's holdings of 18th- and 19th-century material, the Berg would devote a substantial portion of its resources to build an archive of modern literature. Gordan's early commitment to pursuing 20th-century material proved decisive in shaping the Berg's future identity. In 1950, few American institutions (and virtually no libraries abroad) actively collected the manuscripts of modern authors. By 1980, however, such special collections were common; in America, libraries competed intensely for contemporary material, and national organizations had been established in Britain to keep documents from going abroad. Today it would be impossible for any library, no matter how well-endowed, to build collections of modern literature equal to those of pioneering institutions like the Berg.

The status of a research library is usually measured in two ways – its high spots and its depth. What important individual items does the collection possess, and what significant authors and subjects does it represent in unsurpassed detail? By either measure, the Berg now ranks among the four or five greatest collections of modern literature in the English-speaking world. It contains the most extensive archives of modern masters like W. H. Auden, Randall Jarrell, Edna St. Vincent Millay, Vladimir Nabokov, and Virginia Woolf as well as major collections of manuscript material for Joseph Conrad, E. E. Cummings, T. S. Eliot, Robert Graves, Lady Gregory, Jack Kerouac, Howard Moss, Sean O'Casey, May Sarton, James Stephens, Edward Thomas, and William Butler Yeats. It also possesses archival material from influential institutions like the Abbey Theatre, Provincetown Players, and the Group Theatre. The Berg's high spots include drafts and manuscripts of *The Wild Swans at Coole, A Connecticut Yankee in King Arthur's Court, To the Lighthouse, The Secret Sharer, Speak, Memory, The Age of Anxiety*, and what may be the most interesting Modernist manuscript in existence, the drafts of *The Waste Land* with Ezra Pound's transfiguring revisions alongside Vivien Eliot's annotations.

On occasion, the Berg Collection acquires a major writer's entire archive – the voluminous papers of Vladimir Nabokov and Virginia Woolf are two such examples. More often, curators build an archive by steady, focused effort over many years. The Berg's superb collection of Cummings materials, for example, developed in stages. "Prior to 1970," wrote Francis Mattson, "E. E. Cummings was almost a non-presence in the Berg Collection, represented by only four small books." Then, in 1970, the literary material from the estate of the poet's widow, Marion Morehouse Cummings, came to the Collection – part gift, part purchase. This cache included the copies of his books that the poet had inscribed and illustrated for her during their 28-year marriage as well as his own copies, which contained many corrections and notations. There were also letters, paintings, business records, photographs, and personal effects, including his Royal typewriter and a plaster cast of his hand. In 1971, another cache, which contained more drawings and photographs, was presented anonymously. In 1986, the Berg purchased James Sibley Watson, Jr.'s *Dial* papers, which included extensive correspondence and manuscripts. Cummings's closest friend, Watson had papers that dated from 1917 to the poet's death in 1962. The Berg's Cummings collection is now probably second only to the official archive at Harvard.

The Berg Collection's ongoing acquisitions program continues to bring its holdings up to the present with the archives of living authors as diverse as Julia Alvarez, Paul Auster, Donald Justice, Alfred Kazin, Kenneth Koch, Philip Levine, Samuel Menashe, and V. S. Pritchett. Supplementing these author collections are institutional archives held in The New York Public Library's Rare Books and Manuscripts Division, which include the files of *The New Yorker*, Farrar, Straus & Giroux, Alfred A. Knopf, Macmillan, and the Century Company. Together these collections afford an extraordinarily comprehensive view of 20th-century letters. They also provide an inexhaustible inventory from which to mount the Berg's celebrated exhibitions, which have run continuously for over half a century.

The Berg's 1995–97 exhibition, *The Hand of the Poet*, which honors the centenary of The New York Public Library, was perhaps the most impressive public exhibition of poetry manuscripts in North American history. *The Hand of the Poet* displayed unique material covering almost four centuries of English-language poetry, from John Donne to the present – representing 100 poets in all. No comparably extensive showcase of the Collection's high spots has ever been undertaken. If the Berg is poetry's Covent Garden, then this two-part extravaganza represents its royal gala. There is one difference, however; Doctor Albert Berg insisted that the public come free. ■

Suggestions for Further Reading

Handbooks and Dictionaries

The most august of poetry reference books is the giant *The New Princeton Encyclopedia of Poetry and Poetics* (Princeton University Press, 1993), which includes lengthy definitions, historical surveys, and examples of movements, terms, forms, genres, and national poetries. On a more contained level, Babette Deutsch's *Poetry Handbook* (Funk & Wagnalls, 4th ed., 1974) is a classic, but John Drury's *The Poetry Dictionary* (Story Press, 1995) is more extensive and up to date. Poet John Hollander's entrancing little volume *Rhyme's Reason* (Yale University Press, 1989) is a delightful exploration of form, not to be missed.

Biographical Information

The massive *Dictionary of Literary Biography*, published by Gale Research in more than 120 volumes to date, is of inestimable value and can be found in most large libraries. Excellent bibliographies and interesting visual material usually accompany the biocritical essays. Many of its volumes are devoted to poetry of particular periods and countries. Focusing only on poetry is Gale Research's multivolume *Poetry Criticism*, which as the name suggests is perhaps more critical than biographical. The H. W. Wilson Company, famous for indexing periodicals, has pioneered in providing interesting and concise (one- or two-page) biographies of writers, the first volumes of which, such as *Twentieth Century Authors: A Biographical Dictionary of Modern Literature*, were edited by Stanley Kunitz in 1942. *The Oxford Companion to Twentieth-Century Poetry in English* (Oxford University Press, 1994), edited by embattled critical biographer Ian Hamilton, provides short, perspicacious statements about poets up until the 1970s. Best of all is *Contemporary Poets* (St. James Press, 6th ed., 1996, edited by Thomas Riggs), which includes only living poets and is hefty and unusually satisfying and reliable.

Anthologies

The various and multiple Oxford anthologies are standard. The list is headed by *The New Oxford Book of English Verse, 1250–1950* (1972), edited by the venerable Dame Helen Gardner, which is of necessity only emblematic for a selection of poets. An earlier and still interesting volume was edited by William Butler Yeats as *The Oxford Book of Modern Verse* in 1936. Its American counterpart, which begins with colonial poet Anne Bradstreet and ends with Imamu Amiri Baraka, is *The New Oxford Book of American Verse* (1976). An earlier version of this collection was edited by the eminent American literary critic F. O. Matthiessen and published by Oxford in 1950 as *The Oxford Book of American Verse*. Other Oxford books and companions of interest to students or lovers of poetry – more than 20 of them – include collections by period, area, and genre.

As influential as the Oxford anthologies are, they are nevertheless eclipsed in the United States by the monumental and strangely authoritative *Norton Anthology of Poetry* (4th ed., 1996), which is now edited by Margaret Ferguson, Jon Stallworthy, and Mary Jo Salter, and the *Norton Anthology of Modern Poetry* (2nd ed., 1988), mostly edited by the critic and biographer Richard Ellmann. Both these volumes contain a good number of poets, with substantial, intelligent selections for each. As might be expected, they are far more modern than their English counterparts, although the Ellmann volume is sorely in need of revision and updating.

Newcomers to the big anthology field are two 1995 publications from Columbia University Press, *The Columbia Anthology of American Poetry* and *The Columbia Anthology of British Poetry*, which if marketed effectively will provide solid alternatives to the titles mentioned above. Expansive coverage of the great century of the American Renaissance is provided by the elegant two-volume *American Poetry of the Nineteenth Century* (1993), edited by John Hollander and one of the best of the many fine volumes produced in the Library of America project. *The Norton Anthology of Literature by Women*, compiled by the energetic duo of Sandra Gilbert and Susan Gubar (1996), covers poetry with taste and alacrity.

Now that the high modernists (Eliot, Pound, Moore, etc.) and even the great American poets of midcentury (Bishop, Lowell, Jarrell, Berryman, etc.) have passed securely into the canon established in part by the anthologies mentioned above, new anthologies are being published at an unprecedented rate, each with its own viewpoint on just which poets should be remembered in the future. Most famous is Donald Allen's *The New American Poetry, 1945–1960* (Grove Press, 1960), which displayed for the first time the underrepresented poets of open form, grouped in sympathetic "schools" such as Black Mountain, New York Poets, and the San Francisco Renaissance. Allen's volume has been credited with bringing the poets it included, such as O'Hara, Olson, and Creeley, to the attention of the larger reading public. In 1982 the volume was oddly and unfortunately reedited with changes in poets and poems, reorganized, and retitled *The Postmoderns: The New American Poetry Revised* (Grove Weidenfeld). Allen's volume was conceived as a corrective to other anthologies of the 1950s such as Macmillan's many-editioned *Chief Modern Poets of England and America*, which emphasized the more academic and established of the newest poets. One of the most popular anthologies of the time was a paperback volume, *New Poets of England and America* (Meridien, 1957), edited by three young poets (respectively 28, 27, and 34 years of age), Donald Hall, Robert Pack, and Louis Simpson. That volume has been criticized since as overly academic, in the manner of *Chief Modern*

Poets. Hall's own volume from 1962, *Contemporary American Poetry* (Penguin, 1962), includes only 24 poets and is smack in the traditionalist line, despite including Robert Creeley. Poet Mark Strand's exemplary taste is exhibited in his anthology *Contemporary American Poets* (NAL, 1969). More representative of a wider stream of contemporary poetry, it nevertheless continues the same traditionalist mode while accommodating some outsiders, such as Allen Ginsberg and a number of New York School poets. Strand also makes room in his anthology for more women poets, including Plath, Sexton, and Louise Glück, among others. Carrying on this tradition is J. D. McClatchy's *Vintage Book of Contemporary American Poetry* (1990), an elegant and attractive book with a generous, if sometimes puzzling, selection of poets. In another tradition is the playful and cheerful *Anthology of New York Poets*, edited by Ron Padgett and David Shapiro (Random House, 1970), which announces O'Hara, Schuyler, Koch, and the many other poets who hung out somewhere near them.

On the other side of the ocean, there are many fewer poets and anthologies, but Blake Morrison and Andrew Motion's *Penguin Book of Contemporary British Poetry* (1984) does a more than workmanlike job of covering the latter half of the century. For Ireland, which is now in the midst of a poetic renaissance almost the equivalent of that at the turn of the last century, there are many anthologies,

including *The New Oxford Book of Irish Verse*, edited by Thomas Kinsella (1986); *Contemporary Irish Poetry*, edited by Anthony Bradley (University of California Press, revised ed., 1988); and *Modern Irish Poetry: An Anthology*, edited by Patrick Crotty (Blackstaff, 1995).

Establishing another line of succession, which can be called, for lack of a better term, avant-garde, are five major anthologies. The first chronologically is *Open Poetry: Four Anthologies of Expanded Poems*, edited by Ronald Gross and George Quasha (Simon and Schuster, 1969), which showcases four tendencies that the editors feel expand our notions of poetry beyond even those presented in Donald Allen's anthology and Ron Padgett and David Shapiro's. Gross and Quasha's anthology, as the subtitle indicates, is really four separate anthologies, including one devoted to avant-garde black poetry. Those sections devoted to the found poem and to concrete poetry are the most interesting. The same instinct informs the very recent and remarkable *Poems for the Millennium: The University of California Book of Modern Poetry* (University of California Press, 1995), edited by Jerome Rothenberg and Pierre Joris, which places English-language poetry among other world poetries (in translation and mostly Western), illustrating the growth of international modernism throughout this century, but stressing dreams, ethno-poetics, and language experiments. The effect of this gathering is so powerful, in fact, that we should remind ourselves that this is still an avant-garde, or alternative, report on the cultural tradition. The commentary on each selection is fascinating, and at least one more volume is promised. In this same vein is Eliot Weinberger's *American Poetry Since 1950* (Marsilio, 1993), which centers on the descent from Williams and Pound through the Objectivists and Black Mountaineers to the language poets. Weinberger stresses the long poem for each of the 35 poets he includes. The book is beautifully designed and printed. Finally are two very similar compilations that appeared in the same year, *The Norton Anthology of Postmodern American Poetry*, edited by Paul Hoover, and Douglas Messerli's gigantic *From the Other Side of the Century: A New American Poetry, 1960–1990*, published in 1994 by his wonderfully intrepid Sun and Moon Press.

Black American poetry anthologies are many, beginning with the great James Weldon Johnson's pioneering volume, *The Book of American Negro Poetry*, first published in 1922 by Harcourt Brace and revised in 1931. Currently following in Johnson's footsteps are Clarence Major, who edited *The Garden Thrives: Twentieth-Century African-American Poetry* (HarperPerennial, 1996), and Michael Harper and Anthony Walton, who edited *Every Shut Eye Ain't Asleep* (Little, Brown, 1994).

Other focused anthologies include *Rebel Angels: 25 Poets of the New Formalism*, edited by Mark Jarman and David Mason (Storyline, 1996); *No More Masks: Gay and Lesbian Poetry in Our Time*, edited by Joan Larkin and Carl Morse (St. Martin's, 1988); *Premonitions: The Kaya Anthology of New Asian North American Poetry*, edited by Walter K. Lew (Kaya, 1995); and *After Aztlan: Latino Poets of the Nineties*, edited by Ray Gonzalez (Godine, 1992).

An annual anthology of great verve and consistent interest is the *Best American Poetry* series, published originally by Simon and Schuster and now by Scribners. The series is edited by the eagle-eyed David Lehman, with a new guest editor each year. Past volumes have been edited by such major American poets as John Ashbery, Charles Simic, Louise Glück, Richard Howard, and Adrienne Rich.

In the matter of anthologies, the many volumes edited by Louis Untermeyer are all out of print, but can sometimes be found in used bookstores or in libraries. They are good examples of the way an anthology should be compiled, with superior taste and great tolerance for a wide variety of types of poetry. Untermeyer's biographical sketches are wonderful in their ability to capture the essences of the poets, and his choice of poems is usually flawlessly representative of their best. His volumes include *Modern American Poetry*, *Modern British Poetry*, and *Modern American and British Poetry*: the titles don't begin to hint at the riches inside.

History, Commentary, and Criticism

Columbia University Press's two entries in the field, *The Columbia History of American Poetry* and *The Columbia History of British Poetry*, are both essentially collections of essays in a chronological mode, with occasional swerves into thematic treatments (Dianne Wood Middlebrook's "What Is Confessional Poetry" or Lynn Keller's "The Twentieth-Century Long Poem"). Perhaps because of the big scholarly names, and the number of them, involved in these volumes (Jerome Buckley, Jerome McGann, Margaret Ann Doody, Helen Vendler, and Arnold Rampersad, for example), both volumes lack a unifying vision. Unfortunately, neither volume approaches what might have been their model, Dennis Hollier's *A New History of French Literature* (Harvard University Press, 1989).

The history of poetry in England and the United States has successfully resisted compression. The closest thing to a good, solid history is Roy Harvey Pearce's *The Continuity of American Poetry* (Princeton University Press, 1961). David Perkins's two-volume *A History of Modern Poetry: Modernism and After* (Belknap Press, 1987) is lively and more up to date, as well as an admirable and eminently readable book. *A Profile of Twentieth Century American Poetry* (Southern Illinois University Press, 1991), edited by Jack Myers and Jack Wojahn, is arranged by decade; each chapter is written by a contemporary poet (there are lively and informative contributions from Mark Doty and Cornelius Eady, among

others). On the comprehensive level, Harvey Gross and Thomas McDowell have reissued their excellent and perceptive *Sound and Form in Modern Poetry* (Storyline, 1996). In the same area of prosody, poetics and form, Charles O. Heartman's *Free Verse* (Princeton University Press, 1980) is classic, and Derek Attridge's *Poetic Rhythm* (Cambridge University Press, 1995) is illuminating and challenging. *Disembodied Poetics: Annals of the Jack Kerouac School* (University of New Mexico Press, 1994), edited by Anne Waldman and Andrew Schelling, provides another view on some of these topics. On another front altogether, *The Oxford Companion to Women's Writing in the United States* (1995) is scholarly and necessary.

Among the individual critics (today's criticism can sometimes be the fodder for tomorrow's history), Helen Vendler is of course the best known, and her work is always engrossing, if sometimes very difficult going. *The Music of What Happens* (Harvard University Press, 1988) is probably her most representative work, and in addition to theoretical essays includes good chapters (once articles) on Seamus Heaney, Plath, Bishop, and Clampitt among many others. On the West Coast, critic Marjorie Perloff has written a good work on Frank O'Hara, and published several, usually fascinating collections on the avant-garde. *Radical Artifice: Writing Poetry in the Age of Media* (University of Chicago Press, 1991) and *Poetic License: Essays on Modernist and Postmodernist Lyric* (Northwestern University

Press, 1990) are good examples of her work. Of great interest both for its concepts and for its liquid-yet-precise style is Dana Gioia's collection of essays, *Can Poetry Matter?: Essays on Poetry and American Culture* (Graywolf, 1992), which includes his well-known and controversial title article, as well as "Business and Poetry," "Notes on the New Formalism," and almost electrically exciting articles on Robert Bly, Howard Moss, and Donald Justice. Gioia is a truly original and elegant reader and critic, as is the sublime Richard Howard, whose *Alone with America* (Atheneum, enlarged ed., 1980) knows no equal. It's a difficult book, but is packed with insight and is beautifully written. Also of great interest and eloquence are many less intense collections of individual poets, in particular Donald Hall's *Their Ancient Glittering Eyes* (Ticknor & Fields, 1992); Muriel Rukeyser's *The Life of Poetry* (first published in 1947; reissued in 1996 by Paris Press); Denise Levertov's *New and Selected Essays* (New Directions, 1992); T. S. Eliot's *Selected Essays* (Faber, 3rd ed., 1972); W. H. Auden's *Forewords and Afterwords* (Random House, 1973); Louise Bogan's *Selected Criticism* (Noonday, 1955); and Louise Glück's *Proofs and Theories* (Ecco Press, 1994).

Other People's Letters

One of the great pleasures of literary study can be reading the correspondence of writers: many poets are still poets in their letters.

The following are some of the best collections of the most affecting letterwriters:

Bishop, Elizabeth. *One Art: Letters*, edited by Robert Giroux (Farrar Straus & Giroux, 1994)

Bogan, Louise. *What the Woman Lived: Selected Letters and Journals of Louise Bogan, 1920–1970*, edited by Ruth Limmer (Harcourt Brace Jovanovich, 1973)

Byron, Lord. *Selected Letters and Journals*, edited by Leslie Marchand (Harvard University Press, 1982)

Dickinson, Emily. *Selected Letters of Emily Dickinson* (Harvard University Press, 1971)

Jarrell, Randall. *Randall Jarrell's Letters: An Autobiographical and Literary Selection*, edited by Mary Jarrell, assisted by Stuart Wright (Houghton Mifflin, 1985)

Keats, John. *Letters of John Keats: A New Selection*, edited by Robert Gittings (Oxford University Press, 1970)

Sexton, Anne. *Anne Sexton: A Self-Portrait in Letters*, edited by Linda Gray Sexton and Lois Ames (Houghton Mifflin, 1977)

Magazines and Journals

Always the best place to discover new poets, or the new work of familiar poets, poetry magazines are abundant. Many neighborhood bookstores, as well as public libraries, have a large selection of them. Among the most interesting are the tabloid-formatted *American Poetry Review*, the august, traditionalist, and long-running *Poetry* from Chicago, and the avant-garde *Sulfur*, edited by the indefatigable Clayton Eshelman. More mainstream periodicals include *Ploughshares*, each of its issues focused by a guest editor, the *New England Review* from Middlebury College, and *Kenyon Review* from the famous college in Gambier, Ohio, that was once home to John Crowe Ransom, Allen Tate, Robert Lowell, and Randall Jarrell – all at the same time! From England, the glitzy, well-designed *Poetry Review* provides both poetry and criticism, as does the small but feisty *Black Horse*, from Scotland. For critical attention to poetry, *Parnassus: Poetry in Review*, edited by Herb Leibowitz, is unequaled.

Some Important Books of Poetry from the Last Decade, 1986–1996

Paul Muldoon. *Selected Poems* (Faber and Faber, 1986)

Lucille Clifton. *Good Woman* (Boa, 1987)

Yusef Komunyakaa. *Dien Cai Dau* (Wesleyan University Press, 1988)

Marie Howe. *The Good Thief* (Persea, 1988)

Olga Broumas. *Perpetua* (Copper Canyon, 1988)

Michael Palmer. *Sun* (Northpoint, 1988)

Susan Howe. *The Europe of Trusts* (Sun & Moon, 1990)

Jorie Graham. *Region of Unlikeness* (Ecco, 1991)

Sharon Olds. *The Father* (Knopf, 1992)

Tony Hoagland. *Sweet Ruin* (University of Wisconsin Press, 1992)

Mark Doty. *My Alexandria* (University of Illinois Press, 1993)

Brenda Hillman. *Bright Existence* (Wesleyan University Press, 1993)

Carolyn Forché. *The Angel of History* (HarperCollins, 1994)

Jane Cooper. *Green Notebook, Winter Road* (Tilbury House, 1994)

Lucy Bock-Broido. *The Master Letters* (Knopf, 1995)

Timothy Liu. *Burnt Offerings* (Copper Canyon, 1995)

Daniel Hall. *Strange Relation* (Penguin, 1996)

Of necessity, this essay has focused on modern and contemporary poetry. For similar suggestions for readings that cover pre-20th-century literature, the reader is referred, as a starting point, to F. W. Bateson's *A Guide to English and American Literature* (Longman, 3rd ed., 1976) and to the monumental five-volume *New Cambridge Bibliography of English Literature* (Cambridge University Press, 1969–77). ■

Illustrations/Permissions

Materials are from The New York Public Library's Henry W. and Albert A. Berg Collection of English and American Literature (which includes the Ann and Samuel Charters Collection, the W. T. H. Howe Collection, the Robert A. Wilson Collection, and the Owen D. Young Collection) unless another Library division is indicated.

**"The Magical Value
of Manuscripts"**

2   Chris Felver. *Stanley Kunitz at Desk – 80th Birthday – Writing*. Photograph, New York City, ca. 1985.
Used by permission.

7   Richard Wilbur. "I read me a poem by some Cajun." Written out on the front page of *The New York Times*, Sunday, July 29, 1979.
Used by permission.

13   John Milton. *Poems of Mr. John Milton, both English and Latin*. 1st edition. London: Printed by Ruth Raworth for Humphrey Moseley, 1645. Alexander Pope's copy, with his autograph on the title page, and in which Pope wrote out two poems by Milton, one on a blank leaf and the other at the end of the volume.

16   Randall Jarrell's driver's license ("expires 5-6-55"), with several names, addresses, and a quotation written out by Jarrell on the verso.
Courtesy of Mary von Schrader Jarrell.

17   William Carlos Williams, "The Red Wheelbarrow":
Copyright © 1986 by William Eric Williams and Paul H. Williams. Used by permission of New Directions Publishing Corporation.

John Donne

20   Engraved portrait of John Donne in: Izaak Walton. *The Lives of Dr. John Donne, Sir Henry Wotton, Mr. Richard Hooker, Mr. George Herbert*. 4th edition. London: Tho. Roycroft for Richard Marriot, 1675. Inscribed by the author to Lady Ardglass, Mary Countess Dowager of Ardglass, second wife of Charles Cotton, Walton's adopted son and author of the second portion of *The Compleat Angler*.

21   John Donne. The Westmoreland Manuscript. Manuscript collection of Donne's poems, in the hand of Rowland Woodward, ca. 1625.

22   Sir William Dugdale. *The History of St. Pauls Cathedral in London. . . .* London: Tho. Warren, 1658.
NYPL/Spencer Collection.

Alexander Pope

23   John Smith. *Mr. Alexander Pope*. Mezzotint engraving, 1717, after the painting by Sir Godfrey Kneller. NYPL/Miriam and Ira D. Wallach Division of Art, Prints and Photographs.

24   Alexander Pope. "The First Satire of the Second Book of Horace Imitated." Manuscript draft, partly in Pope's hand and partly in the hand of an amanuensis, with revisions in the author's hand, ca. December 1732–January 1733.

25   Frontispiece in: *Pope Alexander's Supremacy and Infallibility Examin'd; And the Errors of Scriblerus and His Man William Detected*. London: Sold by J. Roberts, 1729.

William Blake

26   Luigi Schiavonetti. Portrait of William Blake. Etching and engraving, after the painting by Thomas Phillips, R.A. London: R. Ackermann, 1813. NYPL/Miriam and Ira D. Wallach Division of Art, Prints and Photographs.

27   William Blake. "Woe Cried the Muse." Holograph manuscript, with markings and manuscript notes in red ink by W. M. Rossetti, ca. 1783.
Reprinted by permission of Oxford University Press.

28 LEFT William Blake. *Europe – A Prophecy*. Lambeth: William Blake, 1794.

RIGHT Luigi Schiavonetti (after William Blake). Title page for Robert Blair's *The Grave, A Poem*. "Illustrated by twelve etchings executed by Louis Schiavonetti, From the original inventions of William Blake, 1808." London: R. Ackermann, 1813. NYPL/Miriam and Ira D. Wallach Division of Art, Prints and Photographs.

29 William Blake. Autograph and drawing, dated January 16, 1826, in William Upcott's "Reliques of My Contemporaries."

Robert Burns

30 W. H. McFarlane. *Robert Burns*. Lithograph, after Adolf Rimanoczy, from a vignette by John Beugo ("after Beugo's celebrated portrait"), ca. mid–late 19th century. NYPL/Miriam and Ira D. Wallach Division of Art, Prints and Photographs.

31 Robert Burns. "Bannockburn." Holograph manuscript, ca. late 1793–early 1794.

32 Robert Burns. Autograph letter to Alexander Cunningham, April or May 1792.

William Wordsworth

33 J. Cochran. *William Wordsworth*. Engraving, after a painting by Sir William Boxall, R.A. London: Fisher, Son & Co., 1833.

34 William Wordsworth. "To the Sons of Burns, after visiting their father's grave, August 1803." Holograph poem, written, in Wordsworth's hand, on the first leaf of an autograph letter from Eliza Fletcher to Gilbert Burns, Edinburgh, November 10, 1806.

35 William Wordsworth. *Poems*. London: For Longman, Hurst, Rees, Orme, and Brown, 1815. Presentation copy, inscribed by the author to Charles Grosvenor Lloyd on October 29, 1816.

Samuel Taylor Coleridge

36 James Thomson. *S. T. Coleridge, Esqre.* Engraving, after the painting by James Northcote, R.A. Published for the *European Magazine*, 1819. NYPL/Miriam and Ira D. Wallach Division of Art, Prints and Photographs.

37 Samuel Taylor Coleridge. "This Lime-Tree Bower My Prison [Addressed to Charles Lamb, of the India House, London]." Holograph copy of poem, incomplete, written on the blank sheet of a letter to Charles Lloyd, signed, ca. 1797.

38 Samuel Taylor Coleridge. The Clasped Vellum Notebook. Holograph notebook, in use 1811–12, 1814, January–March 1818, March 1819, and sporadically throughout the 1820s.

39 Samuel Taylor Coleridge. Autograph letter to his wife, Sara Coleridge, May 17, 1799.

Leigh Hunt

40 Daniel Maclise. Portrait of Leigh Hunt. Engraving of the Author of "Byron & His Contemporaries" by Alfred Croquill (pseudonym of Daniel Maclise), 1830s.

41 Leigh Hunt. "Abou Ben Adhem." Holograph manuscript, signed, n.d.

George Gordon Byron, Lord Byron

43 Portrait of Lord Byron. Engraving, n.d., based in part on the painting by Thomas Phillips, R.A.

44 George Gordon Byron, Lord Byron. "Fare Thee Well." Holograph manuscript, wanting lines 13–20, dated March 18, 1816. NYPL/Carl H. Pforzheimer Collection of Shelley and His Circle.

Percy Bysshe Shelley

45 Portrait of Percy Bysshe Shelley. Pencil, dated (incorrectly) 1798.

46 Percy Bysshe Shelley. "A Cat in Distress." Holograph manuscript transcribed and illustrated by the poet's sister, Elizabeth Shelley, sometime after 1809. NYPL/Carl H. Pforzheimer Collection of Shelley and His Circle.

47 Percy Bysshe Shelley. The Esdaile Notebook. Holograph copybook of almost 60 early poems, including one (or possibly two) poems by Harriet Shelley, mostly in the hand of P. B. Shelley, but with nine pages and one title in the hand of Harriet Shelley, ?1808–13. NYPL/Carl H. Pforzheimer Collection of Shelley and His Circle.

48 Leigh Hunt. Autograph letter to Percy Bysshe Shelley, London, December 2, 1819. NYPL/Carl H. Pforzheimer Collection of Shelley and His Circle.

John Keats

49 Joseph Severn. Portrait of John Keats. Engraving, after the 1819 miniature by the artist. Inscribed, at the bottom of the print, "3rd proof Jan 1883." NYPL/Carl H. Pforzheimer Collection of Shelley and His Circle.

50 John Keats. "Ode on Melancholy." Holograph manuscript of the third and last stanza of the poem, ca. May 1819.

51 John Keats. Autograph letter to Fanny Brawne, [Mortimer Terrace, Kentish Town], ca. early–mid-August 1820.

52 John Keats. *Endymion: A Poetic Romance*. 1st edition, 1st issue. London: Printed for Taylor and Hessey, 1818. Presentation copy, inscribed, from the author to Leigh Hunt.

Emily Brontë

53 Branwell Brontë. Portrait of Emily Brontë. Photograph of the painting (ca. 1833–34) in the National Portrait Gallery, London.
COURTESY OF THE NATIONAL PORTRAIT GALLERY, LONDON.

54 Emily Brontë. "And Like Myself Lone Wholly Lone." Holograph manuscript, dated February 27, 1841.

55 Emily Brontë. "When Days of Beauty Deck the Earth"; "Still Beside That Dreary Water"; "There Swept Adown That Dreary Glen." Holograph manuscript, November 1838.

William Cullen Bryant

56 Geo. Parker. Portrait of William Cullen Bryant. Engraving, n.d., after a painting by Henry Inman.

57 William Cullen Bryant. "Thanatopsis." Holograph copy of poem, signed and dated December 10, 1877, at end of manuscript.

Ralph Waldo Emerson

58 Portrait of Ralph Waldo Emerson. Cabinet photograph, ca. 1854.

59 Ralph Waldo Emerson. "The Rhodora." Holograph manuscript, n.d.

Henry David Thoreau

60 Wooden pencil made by Henry David Thoreau.

61 Benjamin Maxham. Daguerreotype portrait of Henry David Thoreau, June 1856.

62 Henry David Thoreau. "The Fall of the Leaf." Holograph manuscript, ca. 1847.
FROM *COLLECTED POEMS OF HENRY THOREAU*, EDITED BY CARL BODE (BALTIMORE: THE JOHNS HOPKINS PRESS, 1964), PP. 237–38. © 1964 THE JOHNS HOPKINS UNIVERSITY PRESS. REPRINTED BY PERMISSION OF THE JOHNS HOPKINS UNIVERSITY PRESS.

63 Henry David Thoreau. Nature and bird notes, in holograph journal kept by Sophia, John, and Henry David Thoreau, September 1836–March 27, 1842.

Henry Wadsworth Longfellow

64 F. Croll. Portrait of Henry Wadsworth Longfellow. Engraving, n.d.

65 Henry Wadsworth Longfellow. "A Psalm of Life: what the heart of the young man said to the psalmist." Holograph manuscript, ca. late 1850s.

66 Henry Wadsworth Longfellow. *Evangeline*. Holograph manuscript of the first draft of the second stanza, n.d.

Oliver Wendell Holmes

68 John S. Nutman, & Sons, Photographers, Boston. Portrait photograph of Oliver Wendell Holmes, tipped into a copy of: Oliver Wendell Holmes. *The Poet at the Breakfast-Table*. 1st edition, 1st issue. Boston: James R. Osgood, & Co., 1872. Presentation copy, inscribed by the author to "The devil locker Esq" [Frederick Locker Lampson].

69 Oliver Wendell Holmes. "Old Ironsides." Holograph copy of poem, signed, n.d.

James Russell Lowell

70 H. B. Hall. Portrait of James Russell Lowell. Engraving, n.d., after a painting by William Page.

71 James Russell Lowell. "The First Snowfall." Holograph manuscript, signed and dated [Cambridge, Massachusetts], November 28, 1866.

Walt Whitman

72   Thomas Eakins. Three portrait photographs (platinum prints) of Walt Whitman, made in Whitman's home on Mickle Street, Camden, New Jersey, 1891–92.

73   Walt Whitman. Galley proof, with Whitman's manuscript commentary, for Dr. R. M. Bucke's *Walt Whitman*, ca. 1882–83.

74   Walt Whitman. "A Child's Reminiscence." Holograph manuscript (proem and 34 numbered stanzas), signed after stanza 34, ca. 1859.

75   Walt Whitman. "Our readers may, if they choose. . . ." Holograph advertisement (prepared by Whitman) regarding "A Child's Reminiscence" for insertion in the *Saturday Press*, December 24, 1859.

Emily Dickinson

77   Emily Dickinson. "Poems." Manuscript notebook of more than two dozen of Dickinson's poems copied out by Stephen Tennant, and decorated by him with pen-and-ink drawings, illustrated title page, and elaborately designed front and back covers (collage), with cover-title in pen-and-ink "for Siegfried [Sassoon] / from Emily & Stephen," April 1929.

78   Emily Dickinson. "Though the Great Waters Sleep." Holograph manuscript, ca. February 1885.
REPRINTED BY PERMISSION OF THE PUBLISHERS AND THE TRUSTEES OF AMHERST COLLEGE FROM *THE POEMS OF EMILY DICKINSON*, ED. THOMAS H. JOHNSON (CAMBRIDGE, MASS.: THE BELKNAP PRESS OF HARVARD UNIVERSITY PRESS). COPYRIGHT © 1951, 1955, 1979, 1983 BY THE PRESIDENT AND FELLOWS OF HARVARD COLLEGE.

Elizabeth Barrett Browning

79   [Henrietta or Arabella Barrett?]. Portrait of Elizabeth Barrett Browning as a young woman. Pencil, n.d.

80   Elizabeth Barrett Browning. Pages from two of four holograph notebooks, leatherbound, containing working drafts of various poems (including the sonnets "Grief" and "Tears"), one notebook dated London, 1843.

81   Elizabeth Barrett Browning. *Poems*. London: Edward Moxon, 1844. Volume 1 of 2 volumes. Presentation copy, inscribed by Browning to William Wordsworth "in affectionate reverence" and dated August 1844.

82   Relics of Elizabeth Barrett Browning, including a pair of slippers, lorgnette in mother-of-pearl frame, and a pair of eyeglasses, displayed with the front page of *La Nazione* (Florence, Italy), July 4, 1861, inscribed, probably in Robert Browning's hand, "Relics, unknown of whom, Ba's own, July '61."

Alfred Lord Tennyson

83   Portrait of Alfred Lord Tennyson. Engraving, after a painting ("approved by the author") by Alonzo Chappel, included in Evert A. Duyckinck's *Portrait Gallery of Eminent Men and Women of Europe and America* (New York, 1872).

84–   Alfred Lord Tennyson. "The
85   Princess." Holograph manuscript book, with many pages torn out, comprising early drafts of Sections I–III, IV (incomplete), V, and fragments of Sections VI and VII, ca. 1845–early 1847.

William Makepeace Thackeray

86   William Makepeace Thackeray. Self-portrait as a jester, with mask and bells, signed with his WMT monogram. Pencil, n.d.

87   William Makepeace Thackeray. "Lucy's Birthday." Holograph manuscript, ca. early 1850s.

88   William Makepeace Thackeray. Autograph note to Miss Harriet Gassiot, with "The Lord's Prayer" in Thackeray's celebrated minuscule hand covering a circle approximately the size of a dime, 1861.

Lewis Carroll

89   Carte-de-visite photograph of Lewis Carroll. Enclosed in an autograph letter from Carroll to Birdie [Florence May Balfour Foster], Christ Church, Oxford, February 5, 1877. Inscribed on the back to "'Birdie' with Lewis Carroll's love."

90   Lewis Carroll. "Hiawatha's Photographing." Holograph manuscript, n.d.

91   Lewis Carroll. Fancy dress photograph of the Misses Liddell, ca. 1860.

Robert Louis Stevenson

92 Lloyd Osbourne. Portrait of Robert Louis Stevenson. Pen-and-ink, n.d. USED BY PERMISSION.

93 Robert Louis Stevenson. "To Mrs. E. F. Strickland." Holograph manuscript, signed and dated April 2, 1886. FROM ROBERT LOUIS STEVENSON, COLLECTED POEMS, ED. JANET ADAM SMITH (LONDON: RUPERT HART-DAVIS, 1971).

Rudyard Kipling

94 Portrait of Rudyard Kipling. Sepia engraving by the Exemplar Engraving Co., signed by the poet, ca. late 1880s.

95 TOP Rudyard Kipling. "Absinth." Pen-and-ink sketch, n.d.

BOTTOM Rudyard Kipling. "Tied up in tails! (or Tales) or is it Tales of Tails?" Pen-and-ink sketch for Kipling's bookplate, signed with initials, n.d.

96 Rudyard Kipling. "Road-Song of the Bandar-Log," in "Writings and Songs by R.K." Holograph notebook in which Kipling copied out 42 of his poems for Florence Garrard, signed and dated 1882.

Thomas Hardy

97 Photograph of Thomas Hardy, in an album of Hardy memorabilia assembled by Sir Sydney Carlyle Cockerell. Captioned, in Sir Sydney's hand, "Max Gate Sept 1924." USED BY PERMISSION OF SIR CHRISTOPHER COCKERELL.

98 Thomas Hardy. "The Man He Killed." Holograph manuscript, signed, n.d.

99 Leather locket containing a portrait photograph of Emma Lavinia Gifford Hardy and a lock of her hair, n.d.

Charlotte Mew

100 Photograph of Charlotte Mew, ca. 1921, with her autograph, pasted into a copy of: Charlotte Mew. *The Farmer's Bride. [A new Edition with eleven new Poems].* London: The Poetry Bookshop, 1921. Presentation copy, inscribed, from the author to Sir Sydney Carlyle Cockerell, dated October 24, 1921.

101 Charlotte Mew. "Love Love Today." Holograph manuscript, ca. August 1919. FROM CHARLOTTE MEW, COLLECTED POEMS AND PROSE, ED. VAL WARNER (MANCHESTER: CARCANET PRESS; LONDON: VIRAGO PRESS, 1981). REPRINTED BY PERMISSION OF CARCANET PRESS LIMITED.

Hilaire Belloc

102 Sir James Gunn, R.A. Portrait of Hilaire Belloc. Photograph, inscribed by Belloc to Elizabeth Herbert, "King's Land. Mayday 1939," of the painting, ca. 1934, in a private collection. USED BY PERMISSION OF THE ARTIST'S FAMILY.

103 Hilaire Belloc. "About John, Who Lost a Fortune by Throwing Stones." Typescript with author's manuscript corrections, signed, n.d. USED BY PERMISSION OF PETERS FRASER & DUNLOP.

Oscar Wilde

104 John W. Evans. *Oscar Wilde.* Wood-engraving, after the sketch by James Edward Kelly, signed by both Evans and Kelly, January 1882. NYPL/Miriam and Ira D. Wallach Division of Art, Prints and Photographs.

105 Oscar Wilde. "Impression du Voyage." Holograph manuscript, n.d.

Ernest Dowson

106 Emery Walker. Portrait of Ernest Dowson. Engraving, after the drawing by Sir William Rothenstein, n.d.

107 Ernest Dowson. "Non sum qualis eram bonae sub regno Cynarae." Holograph manuscript of poem, written out on pp. 2–3 of an autograph letter to Arthur Moore, Woodford, [Essex, England, February 7, 1891].

William Butler Yeats

108 Arnold Genthe. Portrait photograph of William Butler Yeats. Frontispiece in: William Butler Yeats. *Nine Poems.* [New York]: Privately printed [by Mitchell Kennerley] for John Quinn and his friends, 1914.

109 William Butler Yeats. Table of contents for manuscript of *The Wild Swans at Coole.* Holograph manuscript, signed, n.d. USED BY PERMISSION OF A. P. WATT LTD ON BEHALF OF MICHAEL YEATS.

109 Robert Frost, letter to Sidney Cox, ca. September 13, 1915: FROM SELECTED LETTERS OF ROBERT FROST, ED. LAWRANCE THOMPSON. COLLECTION © 1964 LAWRANCE THOMPSON AND HENRY HOLT AND CO., PUBLISHERS, NEW YORK. REPRINTED BY ARRANGEMENT WITH HENRY HOLT AND CO. AND THE ESTATE OF ROBERT FROST.

110 William Butler Yeats. "The Wild Swans at Coole" from *The Wild Swans at Coole.* Holograph manuscript, signed, n.d.

111 Jack Butler Yeats. *A Swan at Coole Park.* Pencil and watercolor sketch, in a volume labelled "Galway 1900."

James Stephens

112 A.E. [George W. Russell]. Portrait of James Stephens. Crayon, signed by the artist with his initials, September 13, 1920.

113 James Stephens. "All Comes and Goes" from *Theme and Variations.* New York: The Fountain Press, 1930. Page proof, with the author's manuscript corrections and additions.

Robert Frost

114 Doris Ulmann. Portrait photograph of Robert Frost. Frontispiece in: *Collected Poems of Robert Frost.* 1st trade edition. New York: Henry Holt and Company, [1930].

115 Robert Frost. "The Freedom of the Moon." Inscribed to Gilbert H. Montague and dated August 1926, in the author's hand, in a presentation copy of: Robert Frost. *A Boy's Will.* 1st American edition, later issue. New York: Henry Holt and Company, 1915.

Edward Thomas

116 Portrait of Edward Thomas. Photogravure, after a photograph by Frederick H. Evans, ca. 1900.

117 Edward Thomas. "The Unknown Bird." Holograph manuscript, January 17, 1915.

118 Edward Thomas. Entries for October 9 and 10, 1896, in holograph notebook, signed on the first page and dated September 5, 1896–November 14, 1896.

Siegfried Sassoon

119 B. Johannes. Portrait photograph of Siegfried Sassoon, Partenkirschen u. Garmisch [Germany], Spring/Summer 1929.

120 Siegfried Sassoon. "The Rear-Guard." Holograph manuscript, with the author's marginal notes, signed with initials and dated April 23, [1918].

121 Siegfried Sassoon. Autograph letter to Anne Tennant, London, November 5, 1929.

Rupert Brooke

122 Speight of Rugby. Cabinet photograph of Rupert Brooke, ca. 1901–2.

123 Rupert Brooke. "Heaven." Holograph manuscript, signed, n.d.

Isaac Rosenberg

125 H. C. Hammond. Portrait of Isaac Rosenberg. Pen-and-ink, 1914.

126 Isaac Rosenberg. "Break of Day in the Trenches." Typescript with the author's manuscript corrections, ca. 1916.

Humbert Wolfe

127 Commander of the British Empire (C.B.E.) Medal, in case. Presented to Humbert Wolfe in 1918.

128 Photograph of Humbert Wolfe (top row, fourth from left) with the Canning Club at Oxford University, ca. 1905.

129 Humbert Wolfe. "Grey Eyes at the Restaurant" ["The Deserted Lover at the Restaurant"]. Holograph draft of poem omitted from Wolfe's *London Sonnets* (Oxford: Basil Blackwell, 1920), n.d.

Anna Wickham

130 Berenice Abbott. Portrait photograph of Anna Wickham, Paris, 1926. BERENICE ABBOTT/COMMERCE GRAPHICS LTD, INC. USED BY PERMISSION.

131 Anna Wickham. "Bridegroom." Manuscript copy of poem in the hand of D. H. Lawrence, n.d. USED BY PERMISSION OF GEORGE HEPBURN AND MARGARET HEPBURN; AND BY PERMISSION OF LAURENCE POLLINGER LTD. AND THE ESTATE OF FRIEDA LAWRENCE RAVAGLI.

D. H. Lawrence

132 Edward Weston. Portrait photograph of D. H. Lawrence, Mexico City, November 4, 1924. Negative by Edward Weston; print by Cole Weston. © 1981 CENTER FOR CREATIVE PHOTOGRAPHY, ARIZONA BOARD OF REGENTS.

133 D. H. Lawrence. "Erotic." Holograph manuscript, ca. 1911. FROM D. H. LAWRENCE, *THE COMPLETE POEMS*, COLLECTED AND EDITED BY VIVIAN DE SOLO PINTO AND WARREN ROBERTS (NEW YORK: VIKING PRESS, 1964). COPYRIGHT © 1964, 1971 BY ANGELO RAVAGLI AND C. M. WEEKLEY, EXECUTORS OF THE ESTATE OF FRIEDA LAWRENCE RAVAGLI. USED BY PERMISSION OF LAURENCE POLLINGER LTD. AND THE ESTATE OF FRIEDA LAWRENCE RAVAGLI; AND OF VIKING PENGUIN, A DIVISION OF PENGUIN BOOKS USA INC.

134 Frieda Lawrence. Autograph letter to Edward Garnett, Venice, after March 2, 1930. FROM *FRIEDA LAWRENCE: THE MEMOIRS AND CORRESPONDENCE* BY FRIEDA LAWRENCE, ED. E. W. TEDLOCK, JR. COPYRIGHT © 1961, 1964 BY THE ESTATE OF FRIEDA LAWRENCE. REPRINTED BY PERMISSION OF ALFRED A. KNOPF INC.

Robert Graves

135 Robert Graves. "The Red Branch Songbook." Holograph notebook, ca. 1900. USED BY PERMISSION OF A. P. WATT LTD ON BEHALF OF THE TRUSTEES OF THE ROBERT GRAVES COPYRIGHT TRUST.

136 Four photographs of Robert Graves, England?, early 1950s. USED BY PERMISSION OF A. P. WATT LTD ON BEHALF OF THE TRUSTEES OF THE ROBERT GRAVES COPYRIGHT TRUST.

137 Robert Graves. "The Chaos Song." Holograph draft, with author's manuscript corrections and alternate titles, n.d. USED BY PERMISSION OF A. P. WATT LTD ON BEHALF OF THE TRUSTEES OF THE ROBERT GRAVES COPYRIGHT TRUST, AND CARCANET PRESS LIMITED.

Elinor Wylie

138 Portrait photograph of Elinor Wylie, ca. 1920s?

139 Elinor Wylie. "Sonnet" ("I Am the New Penelope"). Typescript, signed, n.d.

140 Elinor Wylie. "Sea Lullaby." Holograph manuscript, n.d.

140 Edna St. Vincent Millay, "To Elinor Wylie": EXCERPT FROM SONNET "TO ELINOR WYLIE" BY EDNA ST. VINCENT MILLAY. FROM *COLLECTED POEMS*, HARPERCOLLINS. COPYRIGHT © 1939, 1967 BY EDNA ST. VINCENT MILLAY AND NORMA MILLAY ELLIS. ALL RIGHTS RESERVED. REPRINTED BY PERMISSION OF ELIZABETH BARNETT, LITERARY EXECUTOR.

Edna St. Vincent Millay

142 Arnold Genthe. Portrait photograph of Edna St. Vincent Millay, ca. 1913.

143 Edna St. Vincent Millay. "To a Rejected Love" ["Possession"]. Typescript, with the author's manuscript note to her sister Kathleen Millay, [Winter 1918]. COPYRIGHT © 1997 BY THE EDNA ST. VINCENT MILLAY SOCIETY. ALL RIGHTS RESERVED. USED BY PERMISSION OF ELIZABETH BARNETT, LITERARY EXECUTOR.

Robinson Jeffers

144 Edward Weston. Portrait photograph of Robinson Jeffers, Tor House, May 1929. Negative by Edward Weston; print by Cole Weston. © 1981 CENTER FOR CREATIVE PHOTOGRAPHY, ARIZONA BOARD OF REGENTS.

145 Robinson Jeffers. "Love the Wild Swan" from *Solstice, and Other Poems*. Typescript with author's manuscript corrections, n.d. FROM *SELECTED POEMS BY ROBINSON JEFFERS*. COPYRIGHT © 1935 BY THE MODERN LIBRARY AND RENEWED 1963 BY DONNAN JEFFERS AND GARTH JEFFERS. REPRINTED BY PERMISSION OF RANDOM HOUSE, INC.; AND OF JEFFERS LITERARY PROPERTIES.

William Faulkner

146 Carl Van Vechten. Portrait photograph of William Faulkner, December 11, 1954.

147 William Faulkner. "Where I Am Dead the Clover Loved of Bees." Typescript, with author's manuscript corrections, dated "New Orleans / 9 February 1925." POEM © 1997 JILL FAULKNER SUMMERS. POEM, LETTER, AND PHOTOGRAPH USED BY SPECIAL ARRANGEMENT WITH JILL FAULKNER SUMMERS AND SHELDON ABEND, PRESIDENT, AMERICAN PLAY COMPANY, INC.

Wallace Stevens

148 Rollie McKenna. Portrait photograph of Wallace Stevens, Hartford, Connecticut, 1952.
© ROLLIE MCKENNA.

149 Wallace Stevens. "The Virgin Carrying a Lantern." Holograph copy, in the hand of Louise Bogan, sent by her to May Sarton with her autograph letter, New York City, June 21, 1955.
FROM COLLECTED POEMS BY WALLACE STEVENS. COPYRIGHT 1923 AND RENEWED 1951 BY WALLACE STEVENS. REPRINTED BY PERMISSION OF ALFRED A. KNOPF INC. MANUSCRIPT USED BY PERMISSION OF RUTH LIMMER, LITERARY EXECUTOR, ESTATE OF LOUISE BOGAN.

William Carlos Williams

150 Marion Morehouse. Portrait photograph of William Carlos Williams, ca. early to mid-1950s. NYPL/Miriam and Ira D. Wallach Division of Art, Prints and Photographs.

151 William Carlos Williams. "The Red Wheelbarrow." Typescript, signed by Williams and dated, by James Gallagher, "January 29, 1963." Gift of James Gallagher.
COPYRIGHT © 1986 BY WILLIAM ERIC WILLIAMS AND PAUL H. WILLIAMS. USED BY PERMISSION OF NEW DIRECTIONS PUBLISHING CORPORATION.

Ezra Pound

153 Ezra Pound. Typed postcard to Chester Page, Hotel Italia, Rapallo, [Italy], May 28, 1959.
COPYRIGHT © 1997, 1976 BY THE TRUSTEES OF THE EZRA POUND LITERARY PROPERTY TRUST. USED BY PERMISSION OF NEW DIRECTIONS PUBLISHING CORPORATION.

154 Ezra Pound. "And Thus in Nineveh." Holograph manuscript, signed with monogram, ca. 1909.
COPYRIGHT © 1997, 1976 BY THE TRUSTEES OF THE EZRA POUND LITERARY PROPERTY TRUST. USED BY PERMISSION OF NEW DIRECTIONS PUBLISHING CORPORATION.

T. S. Eliot

155 Henry Ware Eliot. Photograph of his brother, T. S. Eliot, in London, 1926.
COURTESY OF FABER & FABER LTD ON BEHALF OF MRS. VALERIE ELIOT.

156 T. S. Eliot. "A Game of Chess." Typescript from the complete manuscript of *The Waste Land*, 1921, with T. S. and Vivien Eliot's additions/comments in pencil; and Ezra Pound's criticisms (1922) in pen and ink.
COURTESY OF FABER & FABER LTD ON BEHALF OF MRS. VALERIE ELIOT. POUND COMMENTS ON MANUSCRIPT: COPYRIGHT © 1997 BY MARY DE RACHEWILTZ AND OMAR S. POUND; USED BY PERMISSION OF NEW DIRECTIONS PUB. CORP. AGENTS.

157 T. S. Eliot. *The Waste Land*. Richmond, Surrey: The Hogarth Press, 1923.
COURTESY OF FABER & FABER LTD ON BEHALF OF MRS. VALERIE ELIOT.

158 T. S. Eliot. "Complete Poems of T. S. Eliot." Manuscript notebook, 1909–15, with title-page dedication to Jean Verdenal.
PUBLISHED AS: INVENTIONS OF THE MARCH HARE: POEMS 1909–1917. EDITED BY CHRISTOPHER RICKS (LONDON: FABER AND FABER LTD, 1996). COURTESY OF FABER & FABER LTD ON BEHALF OF MRS. VALERIE ELIOT.

158 T. S. Eliot, "Fourth Caprice in Montparnasse": FROM T. S. ELIOT, INVENTIONS OF THE MARCH HARE: POEMS 1909–1917, ED. CHRISTOPHER RICKS (LONDON: FABER & FABER LTD, 1996). COURTESY OF FABER & FABER LTD ON BEHALF OF MRS. VALERIE ELIOT.

Marianne Moore

159 Marianne Moore. *Poems*. London: The Egoist Press, 1921. Presentation copy from the author to Michel Farano, January 24, 1950; with several manuscript corrections by the author.

160 George Platt Lynes. Portrait photograph of Marianne Moore, ca. early 1940s. Inscribed on the back by Moore to Hildegarde and James Sibley Watson, October 1943.
USED BY PERMISSION.

161 Marianne Moore. "O to Be a Dragon." Holograph manuscript, n.d.
COPYRIGHT © 1957 BY MARIANNE MOORE; RENEWED 1985 BY LAWRENCE E. BRINN AND LOUISE CRANE, EXECUTORS OF THE ESTATE OF MARIANNE MOORE, FROM THE COMPLETE POEMS OF MARIANNE MOORE BY MARIANNE MOORE. USED BY PERMISSION OF VIKING PENGUIN, A DIVISION OF PENGUIN BOOKS USA INC.

162 Photograph of Marianne Moore, Joan Payson, and Casey Stengel, Shea Stadium, Queens, New York, 1965.

E. E. Cummings

163 E. E. Cummings. Thank-you note, signed "Estlin," to Hildegarde Lasell Watson, with colored pencil elephant sketch, ca. 1940s.
USED BY PERMISSION OF THE TRUSTEES FOR THE E. E. CUMMINGS TRUST. COPYRIGHT © BY THE TRUSTEES FOR THE E. E. CUMMINGS TRUST.

164 E. E. Cummings. "what is." Galley proof for the poem's publication in *Fresco* (University of Detroit), with manuscript notes by the author, ca. 1960. "WHAT IS" APPEARS IN *COMPLETE POEMS: 1904–1962* BY E. E. CUMMINGS. EDITED BY GEORGE J. FIRMAGE. COPYRIGHT © 1960, 1988, 1991 BY THE TRUSTEES FOR THE E. E. CUMMINGS TRUST. USED BY PERMISSION OF LIVERIGHT PUBLISHING CORPORATION.

165 Edward Cummings. Photograph of his son E. E. Cummings on leave from Army service at Camp Devens, Massachusetts, 1918.

Vladimir Nabokov

166 Portrait photograph of Vladimir Nabokov, St. Petersburg, Russia, 1915. USED BY PERMISSION OF THE ESTATE OF VLADIMIR NABOKOV.

167 Vladimir Nabokov. "On Translating 'Eugene Onegin.'" Setting copy of the poem (from the complete typescript and setting copy for Nabokov's *Poems and Problems*), with author's manuscript corrections, ca. 1970. FROM *POEMS AND PROBLEMS* BY VLADIMIR NABOKOV. COPYRIGHT © 1971 BY VLADIMIR NABOKOV. USED BY PERMISSION OF THE ESTATE OF VLADIMIR NABOKOV.

168 Vladimir Nabokov. [Chess Problem No. 13]. Typescript of chess problem, with author's drawing of chessboard and manuscript corrections (from the complete typescript and setting copy for Nabokov's *Poems and Problems*), ca. 1970. FROM *POEMS AND PROBLEMS* BY VLADIMIR NABOKOV. COPYRIGHT © 1971 BY VLADIMIR NABOKOV. USED BY PERMISSION OF THE ESTATE OF VLADIMIR NABOKOV.

W. H. Auden

169 Paul Cadmus. Portraits of W. H. Auden and Christopher Isherwood. Pen-and-ink drawing, on half-title page of: W. H. Auden and Christopher Isherwood. *The Ascent of F6*. New York: Random House, 1937. Signed by both authors on title page. Gift of Donald Windham. COURTESY THE ARTIST AND DC MOORE GALLERY, NEW YORK. *THE ASCENT OF F6* COPYRIGHT BY THE ESTATE OF W. H. AUDEN.

170 W. H. Auden. "Stop All the Clocks" from *The Ascent of F6*. Holograph notebook, ca. 1936–37. FROM *W. H. AUDEN: COLLECTED POEMS* BY W. H. AUDEN, EDITED BY EDWARD MENDELSON. COPYRIGHT © 1940 AND RENEWED 1968 BY W. H. AUDEN. REPRINTED BY PERMISSION OF RANDOM HOUSE, INC.

171 W. H. Auden. *Another Time: Poems*. New York: Random House, 1940. Presentation copy from Auden to Chester Kallman, inscribed "With love from Wystan Feb 1940." COPYRIGHT BY THE ESTATE OF W. H. AUDEN.

172 George Platt Lynes. Portrait photograph of W. H. Auden, ca. mid-1940s. NYPL/ Miriam and Ira D. Wallach Division of Art, Prints and Photographs. USED BY PERMISSION.

Louise Bogan

174 Photograph of Elizabeth Mayer and Louise Bogan, ca. 1948. USED BY PERMISSION OF RUTH LIMMER, LITERARY EXECUTOR, ESTATE OF LOUISE BOGAN.

175 Louise Bogan. "The Meeting." Typescript with author's manuscript revision, enclosed by Bogan in a letter to May Sarton, ca. May 1956. USED BY PERMISSION OF RUTH LIMMER, LITERARY EXECUTOR, ESTATE OF LOUISE BOGAN.

176 Paul Valéry and May Sarton. "Seen." Typescript of Sarton's verse translation of Valéry's sonnet "Vue," with Louise Bogan's manuscript revisions and a typescript note by Sarton at the bottom of the page, ca. Fall 1956. USED BY PERMISSION OF RUTH LIMMER, LITERARY EXECUTOR, ESTATE OF LOUISE BOGAN.

Kay Boyle

177 Joan Baez. Get-well note to Kay Boyle (with pen-and-ink caricature of Boyle), signed "Joanie," ca. Summer/Fall 1979. USED BY PERMISSION OF THE ESTATE OF KAY BOYLE AND THE WATKINS/ LOOMIS AGENCY.

178 Berenice Abbott. Portrait photograph of Kay Boyle, New York City, ca. 1946. BERENICE ABBOTT/COMMERCE GRAPHICS LTD, INC. USED BY PERMISSION.

178 Kay Boyle, "Advice to the Old (Including Myself)": USED BY PERMISSION OF THE ESTATE OF KAY BOYLE AND THE WATKINS/ LOOMIS AGENCY.

179 Kay Boyle. "He Succumbed to Burns." Holograph manuscript, ca. late 1965– early 1966. USED BY PERMISSION OF THE ESTATE OF KAY BOYLE AND THE WATKINS/ LOOMIS AGENCY.

Lorine Niedecker

180 Jonathan Williams. Photograph of Lorine Niedecker, Milwaukee, Wisconsin, February 8 or 9, 1967. COURTESY OF JONATHAN WILLIAMS.

181 Lorine Niedecker. Typed letter (aerogram) to Cid Corman, Milwaukee, Wisconsin, March 15, [1967], with five of her poems (including "My Life by Water" and "Shelter"). COPYRIGHT 1997 CID CORMAN, LITERARY EXECUTOR OF THE LORINE NIEDECKER ESTATE.

181 Denise Levertov, "The Footprints":
From *Denise Levertov: Poems 1968–1972*. Copyright © 1968, 1972 Denise Levertov. Reprinted by permission of New Directions Publishing Corp.

182 Lorine Niedecker. Autograph letter (the first of three pages) to Cid Corman (with a watercolor painting by Niedecker signed "LM"), Milwaukee, Wisconsin, envelope postmarked December 12, 1964.
Copyright 1997 Cid Corman, literary executor of the Lorine Niedecker Estate.

Louis Zukofsky

183 Louis Zukofsky. *Some Time*. Stuttgart: Jonathan Williams Publishers, 1956. Inscribed by the author on the front free endpaper. With cover reproduction of music manuscript by Celia Thaew.
Courtesy of the Jargon Society. Used by permission of Paul Zukofsky; this material may not be reprinted without the express permission of Paul Zukofsky.

184 Ralph Eugene Meatyard. Portrait photograph of Louis Zukofsky with piano keyboard (time exposure), 1967.
Courtesy of Howard Greenberg Gallery, New York.

185 Louis Zukofsky. "A." Photocopy of first page of typescript of the First and Second movements of the poem, with manuscript corrections and comments by Ezra Pound, n.d.
Used by permission of Paul Zukofsky; this material may not be reprinted without the express permission of Paul Zukofsky. Pound comments on manuscript: Copyright © 1997 by Mary de Rachewiltz and Omar S. Pound; used by permission of New Directions Pub. Corp. Agents.

Charles Olson

186 Photograph of Charles Olson, ca. 1917–18.
Used with permission of the Charles Olson Papers, Archives & Special Collections Department, Thomas J. Dodd Research Center, University of Connecticut Libraries.

187 Harry Redl. Portrait photograph of Charles Olson, San Francisco, California, ca. February 1957 (printed 1995).
Used by permission.

188 Charles Olson. "Maximus, from Dogtown – I." Typescript (the first of five pages), after November 1959.
Used with permission of the Charles Olson Papers, Archives & Special Collections Department, Thomas J. Dodd Research Center, University of Connecticut Libraries.

Stanley Kunitz

189 Leonard Baskin. Title page drawing in: Stanley Kunitz. *The Coat Without a Seam: Sixty Poems 1930–1972*. Northampton, Mass.: Gehenna Press, 1974.
Used by permission of Leonard Baskin.

190 Chris Felver. Portrait photograph of Stanley Kunitz, 1985.
Used by permission.

190 Louise Glück, "Four Dreams Concerning the Master":
Used by permission of Louise Glück.

191 Stanley Kunitz. "The Thing That Eats the Heart." Holograph manuscript, ca. early 1950s.
Copyright © 1956 by Stanley Kunitz, from *The Poems of Stanley Kunitz 1928–1978* by Stanley Kunitz. Reprinted by permission of W. W. Norton & Company, Inc.

Jean Garrigue

193 top Virginia Herrmann. Photograph of Jean Garrigue, Frenchtown, New Jersey, August 1966.
Used by permission of Virginia Herrmann.

bottom Virginia Herrmann. ["Rat"]. Music manuscript (two-part study for Paul Hindemith's composition class at Yale University) setting Jean Garrigue's poem "Rat" (with, on the verso, holograph class notes on the evocation of sadness in music), ca. March 1944.
Used by permission of Virginia Herrmann; and of Aileen Ward, Executrix, Estate of Jean Garrigue.

194 Jean Garrigue. "On One of the Last Trains to White River Junction, N.H." ["On Going by Train to White River Junction, Vt."]. Typescript with author's manuscript revisions, ca. early 1970s.
Used by permission of Aileen Ward, Executrix, Estate of Jean Garrigue.

195 Jean Garrigue. "Poems. I wish to write poems." Typescript draft of an autobiographical statement, with an undated holograph draft of an unpublished (?) poem on the verso ("In the sheer dogged drill of that hippled and sucked . . ."), Spring 1953.
Used by permission of Aileen Ward, Executrix, Estate of Jean Garrigue.

May Sarton

196 Photograph of May Sarton, taken probably in England, ca. mid–late 1930s.
USED BY PERMISSION.

197 May Sarton. "Bears and Waterfalls." Typescript of preliminary version, ca. late October 1964.
COPYRIGHT © 1971 BY MAY SARTON, FROM *COLLECTED POEMS 1930–1993* BY MAY SARTON. REPRINTED BY PERMISSION OF W. W. NORTON & COMPANY INC.

198 May Sarton. *A Private Mythology*. Holograph notebook including drafts of poems (published and unpublished); and itineraries, lists of translit-erated Japanese words (with English equivalents), memoranda, etc., relating to Sarton's trip to Japan, ca. March–May 1962.
USED BY PERMISSION.

Muriel Rukeyser

199 Photograph of Muriel Rukeyser and her son, William L. (Laurie) Rukeyser, San Francisco, ca. late Octo-ber/early November 1947; inscribed by Rukeyser on the back, "Laurie, 5 weeks."
USED BY PERMISSION OF WILLIAM L. RUKEYSER, ALL RIGHTS RESERVED.

200 Muriel Rukeyser. "For My Son." Typescript with author's manuscript revi-sions, ca. mid-1960s.
USED BY PERMISSION OF WILLIAM L. RUKEYSER, ALL RIGHTS RESERVED.

201 LEFT Christian Morgenstern and Muriel Rukeyser. "The Aesthetic Weasel." Typescript of Rukeyser's translation of Morgenstern's poem "Das æsthetische Wiesel," with pen-and-ink drawing by Rukeyser (from the type-script draft of *The Speed of Darkness*), ca. mid-1960s.
USED BY PERMISSION OF WILLIAM L. RUKEYSER, ALL RIGHTS RESERVED.

RIGHT Muriel Rukeyser. *I Go Out*. Sketchbook with holo-graph text and illustrations by the author, ca. early 1960s.
USED BY PERMISSION OF WILLIAM L. RUKEYSER, ALL RIGHTS RESERVED.

202 Rollie McKenna. Portrait photograph of Muriel Rukeyser, New York City, 1952.
© ROLLIE MCKENNA.

202 Anne Sexton, letter to Muriel Rukeyser, November 1, 1967: COPYRIGHT © 1967 BY ANNE SEXTON. REPRINTED BY PERMISSION OF STERLING LORD LITERISTIC, INC.

Delmore Schwartz

203 John Berryman, Dream Songs 152 and 155:
FROM *THE DREAM SONGS* BY JOHN BERRYMAN. COPYRIGHT © 1969 BY JOHN BERRYMAN. REPRINTED BY PERMISSION OF FARRAR, STRAUS & GIROUX, INC.

204 Polly Forbes-Johnson Storey. Portrait photograph of Delmore Schwartz, New York City, 1938.
USED BY PERMISSION OF THE PHOTOGRAPHER, POLLY FORBES-JOHNSON.

205 Delmore Schwartz. "Poem" ["In the Naked Bed, in Plato's Cave"]. Typescript included in the Delmore Schwartz–Gertrude Buckman correspondence, ca. mid–late 1930s.
FROM DELMORE SCHWARTZ, *SELECT-ED POEMS: SUMMER KNOWLEDGE*. COPYRIGHT 1938 BY NEW DIREC-TIONS PUBLISHING CORP. REPRINTED BY PERMISSION OF NEW DIRECTIONS PUBLISHING CORP.; AND OF ROBERT PHILLIPS, LITERARY EXECUTOR FOR THE ESTATE OF DELMORE SCHWARTZ.

Dylan Thomas

206 Marion Morehouse. Portrait photograph of Dylan Thomas, ca. early 1950s.

207 Dylan Thomas. "An Anniversary" ["On a Wed-ding Anniversary"]. Holo-graph manuscript (one of 12 pages of working drafts of the earliest version of the poem), with manuscript revi-sions and marginal drawings by the author, ca. 1940.
REPRINTED BY PERMISSION OF HAROLD OBER ASSOCIATES.

208 Dylan Thomas. Autograph letter to Ruth Witt-Diamant, Laugharne, Carmarthenshire, Wales, October 10, 1951.
REPRINTED BY PERMISSION OF HAROLD OBER ASSOCIATES.

209 Bunny Adler. Photograph of Dylan Thomas at the White Horse Tavern, New York City, 1953.

Randall Jarrell

210 Owen Jarrell. Photograph of Randall Jarrell, Los Angeles, ca. 1917.
COURTESY OF MARY VON SCHRADER JARRELL.

211 Randall Jarrell. *Blood for a Stranger*. 1st edition. New York: Harcourt, Brace and Company, 1942. Author's copy, with extensive manu-script revisions throughout the text.
UNPUBLISHED MANUSCRIPT FROM THE WORKS OF RANDALL JARRELL REPRODUCED BY PERMISSION OF HIS ESTATE AND FARRAR, STRAUS & GIROUX, INC. COPYRIGHT © 1997 BY MARY JARRELL.

212 Photograph of Randall Jarrell with his black Persian cat, Kitten, Austin, Texas, 1942.
COURTESY OF MARY VON SCHRADER JARRELL.

John Berryman

213 Terence Spencer. Photograph of John Berryman along the seacoast in a suburb of Dublin, Ireland, ca. May 1967.
Used by permission.

214 TOP Photograph of 10 poets and Mary von Schrader Jarrell at a memorial service for Randall Jarrell, February 28, 1966, Yale University, New Haven, Connecticut.

BOTTOM John Berryman. Typed letter to Mary von Schrader Jarrell, Minneapolis, Minnesota, October 30, [1965].
Used by permission of Mrs. Kate Donahue-Berryman.

215 John Berryman. "[Dream Song] 28" / "Snow Line." Typescript of poem prepared ca. late Summer 1963, revised by the author, with copy-editing marks, ca. early 1964. From the complete typescript/setting copy of 77 Dream Songs.
Unpublished manuscript from the works of John Berryman reproduced by permission of his estate and Farrar, Straus & Giroux, Inc. Copyright © 1997 by Kate Berryman.

216 John Berryman. Autograph letter to Mark Van Doren, [Minneapolis, Minnesota], December 21, 1969.
Used by permission of Mrs. Kate Donahue-Berryman.

Robert Lowell

217 Rollie McKenna. Photograph of Robert Lowell and his daughter, Harriet, Castine, Maine, Summer 1960.
© Rollie McKenna.

218 Robert Lowell. "Skunk Hour." Typescript with author's manuscript note at bottom of sheet ("This paper was chosen for its thinness, for mailing, if you put it on a piece of something white the words will be visible"), ca. Fall 1957. Enclosed by Lowell in a letter of October 11, 1957, to Randall Jarrell.
Unpublished manuscript from the works of Robert Lowell reproduced by permission of his estate and Farrar, Straus & Giroux, Inc. Copyright © 1997 by Harriet Lowell and Sheridan Lowell.

219 Boris Pasternak and Robert Lowell. "The Landlord." Typescript of Lowell's translation of Pasternak's poem, with two manuscript notes and a revision by William Meredith, ca. March 1961.
Unpublished manuscript from the works of Robert Lowell reproduced by permission of his estate and Farrar, Straus & Giroux, Inc. Copyright © 1997 by Harriet Lowell and Sheridan Lowell.

220 Rollie McKenna. Photograph of Robert Lowell and Elizabeth Hardwick, Castine, Maine, 1960.
© Rollie McKenna.

Elizabeth Bishop

221 Elizabeth Bishop's visiting card, onto which Bishop typed a note before sending it with a homemade "get-well" flan to Howard Moss, n.d.
Unpublished manuscript from the works of Elizabeth Bishop reproduced by permission of her estate and Farrar, Straus & Giroux, Inc. Copyright © 1997 by Alice Helen Methfessel.

222 Elizabeth Bishop. "The Armadillo." Typescript with author's manuscript note to Randall Jarrell at the bottom of the sheet, and with the latter's manuscript notes and a list of poems by Bishop in his hand on the verso, ca. 1957. Enclosed by Bishop in a letter to Jarrell.
Unpublished manuscript from the works of Elizabeth Bishop reproduced by permission of her estate and Farrar, Straus & Giroux, Inc. Copyright © 1997 by Alice Helen Methfessel.

223 Rollie McKenna. Portrait photograph of Elizabeth Bishop, New York City, 1969.
© Rollie McKenna.

Howard Moss

224 Photograph of Howard Moss at his weekend home in Easthampton, New York, dated "June 1984."
Used by permission of the Evans family.

224 Elizabeth Bishop, letter to Howard Moss, May 10, 1960: Unpublished manuscript from the works of Elizabeth Bishop reproduced by permission of her estate and Farrar, Straus & Giroux, Inc. Copyright © 1997 by Alice Helen Methfessel.

225 Howard Moss. "Einstein's Bathrobe." Typescript, with author's manuscript revisions and deletions, ca. early 1980s.
Used by permission of the Evans family.

Richard Wilbur

226 Photograph of Richard Wilbur, Peter Taylor, and Jean Stafford at the 6th Arts Forum, Woman's College, University of North Carolina, Greensboro, Spring 1949.
USED BY PERMISSION.

227 Richard Wilbur. "Zea." Typescript with author's manuscript revisions and additions, ca. 1994–95.
© 1995 RICHARD WILBUR. ORIGINALLY IN *THE NEW YORKER*. ALL RIGHTS RESERVED.

228 Richard Wilbur. "All These Birds." Typescript on stationery of the American Academy in Rome, with author's manuscript revisions, and autograph note to Howard Moss written vertically along the side of the page, [1954]. NYPL/ *The New Yorker* Archives, Rare Books and Manuscripts Division.
FROM *THINGS OF THIS WORLD*, COPYRIGHT © 1955 AND RENEWED 1983 BY RICHARD WILBUR, REPRINTED BY PERMISSION OF HARCOURT BRACE & COMPANY.

Jack Kerouac

229 Photograph of Jack Kerouac, New York City, September 1951. Gift of John G. Sampas.
COPYRIGHT © 1997 JOHN SAMPAS, LITERARY REPRESENTATIVE, THE SAMPAS FAMILY.

230 TOP Photograph of the Kerouac family and their driver (left to right: Armand Gauthier, Caroline Kerouac, Leo Alcide Kerouac, Jack Kerouac, and Gabrielle Ange L'Evesque Kerouac) during a trip to Canada, ca. 1930. Gift of John G. Sampas.
COPYRIGHT © 1997 JOHN SAMPAS, LITERARY REPRESENTATIVE, THE SAMPAS FAMILY.

BOTTOM Photograph of Sebastian and Stella Sampas, Lowell, Massachusetts, ca. late 1942. Gift of John G. Sampas.
COPYRIGHT © 1997 JOHN SAMPAS, LITERARY REPRESENTATIVE, THE SAMPAS FAMILY.

231 Collage of prose notes and correspondence by Jack Kerouac, including two typed postcards to Stella Sampas, ca. late 1950s–early 1960s; typed letter (with envelope) to Stella Sampas, Northport, New York, postmarked February 14, 1959; holograph list of 10 questions (some with answers), with typescript of a portion of a story or sketch on the verso, ca. early 1940s; autograph postcard to Sebastian Sampas, Hartford, Connecticut, postmarked September 29, 1941; autograph postcard to Sebastian Sampas ("Prince of Crete"), New York City, postmarked March 5, 1941; "A Tragic Sonnet," holograph manuscript, ca. early 1940s; and an autograph letter from Sebastian Sampas to Stella Sampas, Camp Lee, Virginia, ca. late Winter/early Spring 1943.
COPYRIGHT © 1997 JOHN SAMPAS, LITERARY REPRESENTATIVE, THE SAMPAS FAMILY.

232 Jack Kerouac. *Mexico City Blues*. Manuscript notebook (one of five comprising the complete draft of the book), labeled "MC1" on the cover by the author, including choruses 1–67 & 104–127, as well as miscellaneous prose notes, ca. August 1955.
COPYRIGHT © 1959 JACK KEROUAC.

Allen Ginsberg

233 "Allen Ginsberg: Poetry Reading and Mantra Chanting." Handbill announcing a poetry reading by Ginsberg at the University of Boulder, Colorado, April 16, [1967]. With an autograph letter on the verso from Ginsberg to Carolyn Cassady, Denver, April 17, 1967.
© ALLEN GINSBERG.

234 Photograph of Allen Ginsberg and his mother, Naomi Levy Ginsberg, at the New York World's Fair, June 15, 1940. Reproduced on back cover of record album jacket for *Allen Ginsberg Reads Kaddish, A Twentieth Century Ecstatic Narrative Poem*. Atlantic Recording Company (Atlantic 4001), 1966.
USED BY PERMISSION.

235 Ann Charters. Photograph of Allen Ginsberg and Louis Ginsberg, Paterson, New Jersey, 1970. Inscribed on the back by the photographer to Allen Ginsberg, February 1977.
USED BY PERMISSION.

236 TOP Allen Ginsberg. "A Strange New Cottage in Berkeley." Typescript with author's manuscript revisions, ca. Fall 1955.
ALL LINES FROM "A STRANGE NEW COTTAGE IN BERKELEY" FROM *COLLECTED POEMS 1947–1980* BY ALLEN GINSBERG. COPYRIGHT © 1955 BY ALLEN GINSBERG. COPYRIGHT RENEWED. REPRINTED BY PERMISSION OF HARPERCOLLINS PUBLISHERS, INC.

BOTTOM Allen Ginsberg. *Howl and Other Poems.* 1st edition. San Francisco: The City Lights Pocket Bookshop, 1956. Copy used by Ginsberg for the first KPFA (Berkeley) radio reading of *Howl* in 1956, with passages and words that could not be read over the air marked over in pencil in a hand other than Ginsberg's. Presentation copy, inscribed by the author on the title page to Ann Charters, "Jack's biographer / old Friend / helpful Scholar." COPYRIGHT © 1956 BY CITY LIGHTS BOOKS. USED BY COURTESY OF CITY LIGHTS BOOKS. © ALLEN GINSBERG.

236 Jack Kerouac, letter to Allen Ginsberg, August 26, 1947: USED BY PERMISSION OF JOHN SAMPAS, LITERARY REPRESENTATIVE, THE SAMPAS FAMILY, 1997.

Gary Snyder

237 Gary Snyder. "Hunched Back Flute Player"; Gregory Corso. "Man w/hard on." Two ink drawings on one sheet, signed by the artists and dated by Snyder "N.Y.C. April 26, [19]77 / 3.25 PM." COURTESY OF GARY SNYDER AND GREGORY CORSO.

238 Chris Felver. Portrait photograph of Gary Snyder and his sons, Gen and Kai, taken at the Naropa Institute, Boulder, Colorado, July 1982. USED BY PERMISSION.

239 Gary Snyder. "Logging." Typescript, n.d., signed by the author and with his manuscript note, "I wrote this out of gratitude for the natural richness of the earth." FROM GARY SNYDER, *MYTHS & TEXTS*. COPYRIGHT © 1978 BY GARY SNYDER. REPRINTED BY PERMISSION OF NEW DIRECTIONS PUBLISHING CORP.

Robert Duncan

241 Jonathan Williams. Portrait photograph of Robert Duncan, Point Lobos, Carmel Highlands, California, 1955. COURTESY OF JONATHAN WILLIAMS.

242 Robert Duncan. *Roots and Branches.* Typescript (enclosed in his letter of October 23, 1962, to Muriel Rukeyser), ca. Fall 1962. REPRODUCED WITH THE PERMISSION OF THE LITERARY ESTATE OF ROBERT DUNCAN.

Denise Levertov

244 Chris Felver. Portrait photograph of Denise Levertov, Seattle, Washington, early September 1995. USED BY PERMISSION.

245 Denise Levertov. ["The Pulse"]. Holograph manuscript of the poem's second draft, with the author's manuscript revisions, ca. mid-1960s. COPYRIGHT © 1966, 1997 BY DENISE LEVERTOV. USED BY PERMISSION OF NEW DIRECTIONS PUBLISHING CORPORATION.

Robert Creeley

246 Jonathan Williams. Portrait photograph of Robert Creeley, Bañalbufar, Mallorca, August 1953. COURTESY OF JONATHAN WILLIAMS.

247 Robert Creeley. "For Fear." Typescript, ca. 1959. FROM ROBERT CREELEY, *COLLECTED POEMS OF ROBERT CREELEY, 1945–1975*, © 1982 REGENTS OF THE UNIVERSITY OF CALIFORNIA. USED BY PERMISSION.

James Schuyler

249 Chris Felver. Portrait photograph of James Schuyler in his studio apartment at the Chelsea Hotel in New York City, 1985. NYPL/ Miriam and Ira D. Wallach Division of Art, Prints and Photographs. USED BY PERMISSION.

250 James Schuyler. "Hoboken." Typescript, ca. mid-1960s. UNPUBLISHED MANUSCRIPT FROM THE WORKS OF JAMES SCHUYLER REPRODUCED BY PERMISSION OF HIS ESTATE AND FARRAR, STRAUS & GIROUX, INC. COPYRIGHT © 1997 BY DARRAGH PARK.

Frank O'Hara

251 Frank O'Hara's leatherbound engagement book for 1959. USED BY PERMISSION OF THE ESTATE OF FRANK O'HARA.

252 Harry Redl. Portrait photograph of Frank O'Hara, New York City, 1958 (printed 1995). USED BY PERMISSION.

253 LEFT Frank O'Hara. "Poem (Johnny and Alvin are going home, are sleeping now)." Photocopy of original typescript of poem (written by O'Hara in September or October 1955), sent by John Button, with his manuscript note at the bottom of the sheet, to Alvin Novak. FROM *COLLECTED POEMS* BY FRANK O'HARA. COPYRIGHT © 1971 BY MAUREEN GRANVILLE-SMITH, ADMINISTRATRIX OF THE ESTATE OF FRANK O'HARA. REPRINTED BY PERMISSION OF ALFRED A. KNOPF INC.

RIGHT Photograph of John Button and Alvin Novak, ca. 1950s.

Kenneth Koch

254 John Gruen. Photograph of Kenneth Koch, ca. early 1960s. USED BY PERMISSION.

255 Kenneth Koch. "And, with a shout, collecting coathangers." Typescript, with author's manuscript revisions, of one of the 100 24-line stanzas that comprise *When the Sun Tries to Go On*, ca. 1953. COPYRIGHT © 1969 BY KENNETH KOCH.

Ted Berrigan

256 Chris Felver. Portrait photograph of Ted Berrigan, taken at the Naropa Institute, Boulder, Colorado, July 1982. NYPL/Miriam and Ira D. Wallach Division of Art, Prints and Photographs. USED BY PERMISSION.

257 Ted Berrigan. "The Ars Poetica Machine." Typescript with author's manuscript revisions and notes, ca. 1969–70. Inscribed by Berrigan at bottom of page, "The Archibald MacLeish Machine."

257 Archibald MacLeish, "Ars Poetica": FROM COLLECTED POEMS 1917–1952 BY ARCHIBALD MACLEISH. COPYRIGHT © 1985 BY THE ESTATE OF ARCHIBALD MACLEISH. REPRINTED BY PERMISSION OF HOUGHTON MIFFLIN COMPANY. ALL RIGHTS RESERVED.

Ron Padgett

258 *An Anthology of New York Poets.* Edited by Ron Padgett and David Shapiro. Drawings by Joe Brainard. 1st edition. New York: Vintage Books, 1970. Tom Clark's copy. COURTESY OF THE ESTATE OF JOE BRAINARD 1941–1994. © VINTAGE BOOKS, 1970.

259 Patricia Padgett. Photograph of Joe Brainard and Ron Padgett, July 1991. © 1997 BY PATRICIA PADGETT.

260 Ron Padgett. "Beavers vs. the Surrealists." Typescript with author's manuscript revisions, dated "3/6/95 revisions." © 1997 BY RON PADGETT.

Anne Waldman

261 Chris Felver. Photograph of Anne Waldman performing her poem "Fast Speaking Woman" at the Naropa Institute, Boulder, Colorado, July 1982. NYPL/Miriam and Ira D. Wallach Division of Art, Prints and Photographs. USED BY PERMISSION OF ANNE WALDMAN AND OF CHRIS FELVER.

262 LEFT Joe Brainard. "Anne Waldman and Lewis Warsh . . . Poetry Reading." Original handbill (used to make photocopies), pen-and-ink text and flower drawing cut out and mounted on construction paper, ca. early 1967–68. COURTESY OF THE ESTATE OF JOE BRAINARD 1941–1994. USED BY PERMISSION OF ANNE WALDMAN.

RIGHT Ted Berrigan. Photograph of Lewis Warsh and Anne Waldman in: Lewis Warsh. *Bustin's Island 1968.* Hand-made book, typescript and black-and-white photographs pasted into an artist's sketchpad, written and assembled by Lewis Warsh, and "Published in an edition of 1 copy," August 1992. USED BY PERMISSION OF ANNE WALDMAN.

263 Anne Waldman. "A's LOOK / a love poem." Early typescript draft of *Troubairitz* with author's manuscript revisions, ca. 1991. USED BY PERMISSION OF ANNE WALDMAN. *TROUBAIRITZ* PUBLISHED BY TANIA ELIZOV, FIFTH PLANET PRESS.

Donald Justice

264 Joseph Levy. Photograph of Donald Justice taken at Yaddo in Saratoga Springs, New York, 1972. USED BY PERMISSION.

265 Donald Justice. "Variations on Vallejo" ["Variations on a Text by Vallejo"]. Holograph manuscript (the first of three pages of the poem's earliest working draft), ca. 1973. FROM NEW AND SELECTED POEMS BY DONALD JUSTICE. COPYRIGHT © 1995 BY DONALD JUSTICE. REPRINTED BY PERMISSION OF ALFRED A. KNOPF INC.; AND BY PERMISSION OF THE AUTHOR.

Samuel Menashe

266 Andre de Dienes. Photograph of Samuel Menashe dancing in the desert outside Los Angeles, ca. 1954. USED BY PERMISSION.

267 LEFT Samuel Menashe. *The Many Named Beloved.* London: Victor Gollancz Ltd, 1961. Author's copy, with more than a score of the poems revised, retitled, and/or annotated in ink by the author during the late 1970s and early 1980s. USED BY PERMISSION.

RIGHT Doug Cornell. Photograph of Samuel Menashe, Central Park, New York City, Summer 1961. USED BY PERMISSION.

James Merrill

268 Rollie McKenna. Portrait photograph of James Merrill at his home in Stonington, Connecticut, 1969. © ROLLIE McKENNA.

269 Constantin Cavafy and James Merrill. "On an Italian Shore." Typescript of Merrill's translation of Cavafy's poem "Eis Italikien Paralian," with Merrill's manuscript revisions, ca. 1987. Typescript presented by Merrill to Howard Moss. REPRINTED BY PERMISSION OF THE ESTATE OF JAMES MERRILL; AND OF ARALIA PRESS.

270 James Merrill. Table of contents for manuscript of *Mirabell: Books of Number.* Typescript (mimeographed), with occasional author's pencil revisions throughout the text, and a long epigraph from Laura Fermi written out by the author on the table of contents. Presented by Merrill to Peter Hooten in celebration of "A Paper Anniversary . . . 13.ii.1985."

Amy Clampitt

271 Susan Rich Sheridan. Photograph of Amy Clampitt taken at Deerfield Academy, Deerfield, Massachusetts, ca. early 1990s.

272 TOP James Merrill. Autograph postcard to Amy Clampitt, Stonington, Connecticut, dated August 23, 1988.

BOTTOM Amy Clampitt. *Multitudes, Multitudes.* New York: Washington Street Press, 1973.

273 Amy Clampitt. "San Francisco." Typescript draft with author's manuscript revisions, typed on the verso of a form letter (on Democratic National Committee letterhead) from Morris K. Udall, ca. Fall–Winter 1979.

James Wright

274 John Unterecker. Photograph of James Wright, 1973. Gift of Annie Wright.

275 James Wright. "To a Salesgirl, Weary of Artificial Holiday Trees." Typescript of the revised version of the poem, enclosed by Wright in his letter of February 16, 1959, to Howard Moss at *The New Yorker*, with manuscript annotations by Moss. NYPL/*The New Yorker* Archives, Rare Books and Manuscripts Division.

W. S. Merwin

276 Rollie McKenna. Portrait photograph of W. S. Merwin on a pier along the Hudson River, New York City, 1969.

277 Rumi and W. S. Merwin. "That moon which the sky never saw." Holograph draft of Merwin's translation of poem by Rumi (1207–1273), with Merwin's manuscript revisions, ca. 1973.

Anne Sexton

278 Arthur Furst. Portrait photograph of Anne Sexton, Weston, Massachusetts, Summer 1974.

279 Anne Sexton. "Letter Written on the Long Island Ferry" ["Letter Written on a Ferry While Crossing Long Island Sound"]. Typescript with manuscript note by Sexton, enclosed in her letter of September 28, 1960, to Louis Untermeyer.

280 Anne Sexton. Typed postcard to Louis Untermeyer, Pamplona, Spain, May 17, 1964.

Sylvia Plath

281 Sylvia Plath. *Ariel.* 1st edition. London: Faber and Faber, 1965. With an autograph note by Ted Hughes on the front free endpaper: "The brown stains on the top edge and [back] cover are thatch-drip from the leaking roof of Court Green (where SP had lived), in the winter of 1965/66."

281 Anne Sexton, "The Barfly Ought to Sing": COPYRIGHT © 1965 BY ANNE SEXTON. REPRINTED BY PERMISSION OF STERLING LORD LITERISTIC, INC.

282 Sylvia Plath. "Brasilia." Holograph draft of the poem (the first in the sequence of the poem's six drafts), with author's manuscript revisions, ca. November–December 1962.

283 T. S. Eliot. *Four Quartets.* 1st edition, later printing. New York: Harcourt, Brace and Company, 1943. Sylvia Plath's copy, with her copious annotations and marginal commentary throughout; given to Plath by Richard Norton and inscribed by him on the front free endpaper; also inscribed by Ted Hughes: "This was Sylvia Plath's own copy of *The Four Quartets* and all the autograph annotations are hers."
EXCERPT FROM "LITTLE GIDDING" IN *FOUR QUARTETS*, COPYRIGHT © 1943 BY T. S. ELIOT, AND RENEWED 1971 BY ESME VALERIE ELIOT, REPRINTED BY PERMISSION OF HARCOURT, BRACE & COMPANY. SYLVIA PLATH'S ANNOTATIONS © FRIEDA HUGHES AND NICHOLAS HUGHES.

284 Rollie McKenna. Portrait photograph of Sylvia Plath and Ted Hughes in their Willow Street apartment on Beacon Hill, Boston, 1959.
© ROLLIE MCKENNA.

Philip Levine

285 Photograph of Philip Levine and his son Mark, ca. 1976.

286 Peter Bittner/Spring Street Digital. Portrait photograph of Philip Levine and his son Mark, Washington Square Village, New York City, December 1995.
USED BY PERMISSION.

287 Philip Levine. "My Son and I." Typescript with author's manuscript revisions, ca. early 1970s.
FINAL VERSION OF "MY SON AND I" COPYRIGHT © 1991 BY PHILIP LEVINE, FROM *NEW SELECTED POEMS*. REPRINTED BY PERMISSION OF ALFRED A. KNOPF INC.; AND OF THE AUTHOR.

Jean Valentine

288 David Conrad. Photograph of Jean Valentine, County Sligo, Ireland, 1992.
USED BY PERMISSION.

289 Jean Valentine. "Mother" ["Wish-Mother"]. Typescript, signed, ca. 1990.
COPYRIGHT JEAN VALENTINE.

Adrienne Rich

290 Rollie McKenna. Portrait photograph of Adrienne Rich, Cambridge (or possibly Boston), Massachusetts, ca. 1958.
© ROLLIE MCKENNA.

291 Files from *The New Yorker* Archives. NYPL/*The New Yorker* Archives, Rare Books and Manuscripts Division.

292 Lynda Koolish. Photograph of Adrienne Rich, Modern Times Bookstore, San Francisco, California, 1986.
USED BY PERMISSION.

Imamu Amiri Baraka

293 Fred W. McDarrah. Portrait photograph of LeRoi Jones [Imamu Amiri Baraka], New York City, September 20, 1959.
© FRED W. MCDARRAH.

294 Imamu Amiri Baraka. *What Was the Relationship of the Lone Ranger to the Means of Production?: A Play in One Act.* [New York]: Anti-Imperialist Cultural Union, 1978. Presentation copy, inscribed in 1979 by the author to Robert A. Wilson.
REPRINTED BY PERMISSION OF STERLING LORD LITERISTIC, INC. COPYRIGHT © 1978 BY AMIRI BARAKA.

295 Imamu Amiri Baraka. "I Love Music." Typescript, [19]78.
REPRINTED BY PERMISSION OF STERLING LORD LITERISTIC, INC. COPYRIGHT © 1978 BY AMIRI BARAKA.

Mark Strand

296 Rollie McKenna. Portrait photograph of Mark Strand, ca. 1969.
© ROLLIE MCKENNA.

297 Mark Strand. "A Suite of Appearances." Typescript of a long poem in six sections, many of the pages with extensive manuscript revisions by the author, ca. early 1990s.
COURTESY OF CHARLES SELUZICKI, FINE AND RARE BOOKS.

Louise Glück

298 A. Davanza. Portrait of Louise Glück. Oil on canvas, Paris, 1950. Collection of Beatrice Glück.
USED BY PERMISSION.

299 Louise Glück. ["Vespers"]. Typescript with author's manuscript revisions, ca. Summer 1991.
USED BY PERMISSION OF LOUISE GLÜCK.

Charles Simic

300 Photograph of Charles Simic, ca. mid-1970s.
USED BY PERMISSION OF CHARLES SIMIC.

301 Charles Simic. Pen-and-ink sketch used by Simic as the frontispiece for his 1972 volume of poetry, *White.*
USED BY PERMISSION OF CHARLES SIMIC.

302 Charles Simic. "The Worm of Conscience." Two holograph drafts of the poem first published in *Unending Blues* (1986), written into a manuscript notebook of poems, drafts, and notes, ca. early 1980s–early 1990s.
FROM *UNENDING BLUES: POEMS*, COPYRIGHT © 1986 BY CHARLES SIMIC, REPRINTED BY PERMISSION OF HARCOURT BRACE & COMPANY AND CHARLES SIMIC.

Ai

303 Rebecca Ross. Portrait photograph of Ai with three of her four cats, Tempe, Arizona, 1989.
USED BY PERMISSION OF AI.

304 Ai. "The Kid." Typescript with author's manuscript revisions, ca. November 1972.
USED BY PERMISSION OF AI.

305 Ai. "Resurrection." Typescript, ca. 1969, sent by Ai to Allen Ginsberg, and returned by him with his revisions, commentary, and a holograph note (dated May 23, 1969) at the bottom of this sheet.
USED BY PERMISSION OF AI. ALLEN GINSBERG'S COMMENTS © ALLEN GINSBERG.

306 LEFT Photograph of Ai as a child, ca. 1952–53.
USED BY PERMISSION OF AI.

RIGHT Ai. Autograph letter to Rodney Phillips (with self-portrait), Tempe, Arizona, November 28, 1995.
USED BY PERMISSION OF AI.

Dana Gioia

307 Box of peach-flavored Jell-O® brand Jigglers®, purchased for 79¢ in 1995.
USED BY PERMISSION OF KRAFT FOODS, INC.

308 Tim Radigan. Portrait photograph of Dana Gioia, White Plains, New York, ca. 1985.
USED BY PERMISSION OF KRAFT FOODS, INC.

309 Dana Gioia. "California Hills in August." Typescript (one of 27 pages of notes and drafts for the poem), ca. August–December 1981. With manuscript comments by Emily Grosholz, and a note by Gioia at top right.
COPYRIGHT © 1986 BY DANA GIOIA. REPRINTED FROM DAILY HOROSCOPE WITH THE PERMISSION OF GRAYWOLF PRESS, SAINT PAUL, MINNESOTA.

Julia Alvarez

310 Sara Eichner. Photograph of Julia Alvarez, Dominican Republic, ca. 1993.
COPYRIGHT © SARA EICHNER.

311 Julia Alvarez. "Secretly I am building in the heart." Holograph draft of the penultimate sonnet in the author's sonnet sequence "33" (published in 1984 as part of Homecoming), ca. early 1980s.
FROM HOMECOMING. COPYRIGHT © 1984, 1996 BY JULIA ALVAREZ. PUBLISHED BY PLUME, AN IMPRINT OF DUTTON SIGNET, A DIVISION OF PENGUIN BOOKS USA, INC.; ORIGINALLY PUBLISHED BY GROVE PRESS. BY PERMISSION OF SUSAN BERGHOLZ LITERARY SERVICES, NEW YORK. ALL RIGHTS RESERVED.

312 LEFT Bill Eichner. Photograph of Julia Alvarez, Dominican Republic, ca. early 1990s. Inscribed by Alvarez on its verso: "In the D.R. looking for land."
COPYRIGHT © BILL EICHNER.

RIGHT Julia Alvarez, Jorge Travieso, and Chiqui Vicioso. "Las palabras a veces estan tan cerca que soy." Typescript of Travieso's translation (polished by Vicioso) of Alvarez's sonnet "Sometimes the words are so close," the final sonnet in her sonnet sequence "33," ca. 1984.
USED BY PERMISSION.

313 Julia Alvarez. "Sometimes the words are so close." Holograph manuscript of the final sonnet in Alvarez's sonnet sequence "33," ca. early 1980s.
FROM HOMECOMING. COPYRIGHT © 1984, 1996 BY JULIA ALVAREZ. PUBLISHED BY PLUME, AN IMPRINT OF DUTTON SIGNET, A DIVISION OF PENGUIN BOOKS USA, INC.; ORIGINALLY PUBLISHED BY GROVE PRESS. BY PERMISSION OF SUSAN BERGHOLZ LITERARY SERVICES, NEW YORK. ALL RIGHTS RESERVED.

"The Prado of Poetry"

315 Peter Bittner/Spring Street Digital. Photograph of the reading room of the Henry W. and Albert A. Berg Collection of English and American Literature, The New York Public Library, 1996.

318 Blackstone Studios. Portrait photograph of Dr. Albert A. Berg, n.d.

The Library gratefully acknowledges the authors, photographers, agents, and publishers for their permission to use copyrighted material in The Hand of the Poet. Every reasonable effort has been made to obtain all necessary permissions. Should any errors have occurred, they are inadvertent, and every effort will be made to correct them in subsequent editions, provided timely notification is made to the Library in writing.

ACKNOWLEDGMENTS

SINCE MY APPOINTMENT as curator of the Berg Collection,
I have experienced the joys (and occasional frustrations) of
working with materials that, in some sense at least, are eternal.
For their contributions to this book, I would like to thank
some special individuals for their very real, temporal selves.
Kenneth Benson and Susan Benesch were, from the beginning,
my co-equals in the creation of this book, and of the exhibi-
tion on which it is based. The addition to the team of Barbara
Bergeron, who in some ways became our ringleader, provided
our band of musketeers with its D'Artagnan. We four can only
hope to be involved in another project so inspiring, so joyous,
so successful – and so much fun!

For shepherding us through the production of this book,
and for her gentle prodding as well as her enthusiasm, we
thank Karen Van Westering, Manager of Publications at The
New York Public Library. Her assistant, Alexa Sanzone, has
come to occupy a place in our daily lives and our hearts. To
Library president Paul LeClerc; William Walker, Andrew W.
Mellon Director of The Research Libraries; and Marie Salerno,
Vice President for Public Affairs, I extend my gratitude for
support and encouragement beyond the requirements of mere
professionalism or necessity. For keeping the ship afloat and the
store open, I thank my new colleagues on the literary mountain
that is the Berg Collection, Stephen Crook and Philip Milito.
For his continuing support of the work of the Collection, we
are grateful for the generosity of Leonard Milberg.

Finally, for repaying our trust, Ann Antoshak deserves
credit beyond expression. I hope she is proud of the beautiful
book she designed.

RODNEY PHILLIPS

Index

Page numbers in **boldface** refer to main entries for the poets.